Martha Graham

MARTHA GRAHAM

A Biography

Don McDonagh

DAVID & CHARLES
Newton Abbot London

PICTURE CREDITS

Dance Collection, New York Public Library, rephotographed by Raymond Johnson: Insert I, (pp.) 1, 3, 5, 6, 7, 8; Insert II, 2*b*, 3, 4, 5, 6; Insert III, 1, 4*l*. Collection Marguerite Andros Fuller: Insert I, 2. Collection Rouben Mamoulian: Insert I, 4*a*. Collection Thelma Biracree Schnepel: 4*b*. Cris Alexander: Insert III, 4*b*, 5, 6, 7, 8; Insert IV, 1, 2, 3. Collection Stuart Hodes: Insert IV, 4, 7*a*. Arnold Eagle: Photograph on front of jacket; Insert IV, 5, 6. Collection Richard Buckle: 7*l*. Anthony Crickmay: Insert IV, 8.

0 7153 6716 1

First published by David & Charles (Holdings) Ltd 1974

Printed in Great Britain
by Redwood Burn Limited, Trowbridge, Wiltshire
for David & Charles (Holdings) Ltd
South Devon House Newton Abbot Devon

For Edwin Denby

Contents

Acknowledgments

I would like to express my gratitude to all those who shared their recollections of Martha Graham and her work with me, and to my wife, Jenny, whose patient good sense survived my monomania during the two years it took to complete the manuscript. A Ford Foundation travel and study grant enabled me to gather information from locales that otherwise would have been unavailable to me.

At a difficult moment when I was inundated with unprocessed tape recordings, Shields Remine generously offered to transcribe them and conducted two interviews himself, for which I am especially grateful. He also functioned as a friendly but conscientious prod at many stages throughout the project.

I thank my research assistants Dianne McIntyre, Laura Brittain, and Leighton Kerner for their help. Independent voluntary research by John Mueller established key information about the Rochester years, and in Santa Barbara Finis Haskins and Alice Diebler helped substantially to establish the facts of the Graham family's life there.

First among the institutions to which I am grateful is the Dance Collection of the New York Public Library and its helpful, dedicated staff headed by Genevieve Oswald. At one time or another I benefited from its rich store of films, tape-recorded interviews, periodical clipping files, periodicals, iconography files, notebooks, manuscript collections, and books. The information gleaned was invaluable in shaping the text.

I am also grateful to the *New York Times*, the *Chicago Daily News*, the *Chicago Tribune*, the *Los Angeles Times*, the *St. Louis Globe-Democrat*, and the *St. Louis Post-Dispatch* for my use of their reference files. The New York Public Library's Newspaper Division was also helpful, as was its Central Reference Library at Fifth

Avenue and Forty-second Street. Finally I appreciated the intelligent queries and suggestions of my editor, Harris Dienstfrey, with whom I first discussed the project.

D. McD.

New York, N.Y.
November 1973

Martha Graham

Prologue

A black limousine halted before the main entrance of the Brooklyn Academy of Music, and a small, sumptuously dressed, slightly unsteady woman in her mid-seventies stepped onto the curb. The Academy press representative, Thomas Kerrigan, was enormously relieved. The performance of the Martha Graham Dance Company had started, and there were only a few minutes before the end of the first dance, "Diversion of Angels," after which New York City was to award Martha Graham its highest cultural honor, the Handel Medallion.

Assisting Graham up the stairs, Kerrigan explained that they would enter the backstage area of the Academy Opera House through the adjoining Music Hall. Graham had played both houses during her long career, which had begun a half-century before and for which now, on October 2, 1970, she was to be honored. Yet another event had already robbed her of some of the satisfaction. That morning, to her surprise, Graham had read in a front-page article in the *New York Times* what had seemed clear to others for some time: that at seventy-six she no longer was in adequate command of her once marvelous dancing body, which had withstood not just the passage of time, but the rigors of sickness and a certain amount of dissipation. After passing through the darkened orchestra of the Music Hall, Graham found herself in the connecting backstage area in which she waited for her cue to walk onstage.

In the wings, friends (few of them from the early days), members of the company, and the curious were waiting to assure themselves that she had arrived in time. A chair was brought for her while "Diversion of Angels" finished. Dore Schary, the Commissioner for Cultural Affairs, was to present the award with a brief speech. There had been some discussion as to whether, after his presentation, he should assist Graham onstage, since she had been sick off and on over the past several years. It proved to be an unnecessary discussion. Schary never had a chance to move.

During intermission, in front of the gold curtain of the Opera House, which was filled with a combined audience of friends and strangers, Schary delivered a speech in which the word "genius" was prominently featured. Backstage the tiny, frail lady began to feel the electricity of the stage, that state of tension that performers call "being up." She was drawing together all of the strength and performing presence she had for what the audience thought was to be her final appearance. The septuagenarian who had to be helped into the house was remembering herself as the great lady of the theater whose compulsion to dance had resulted in a whole new style of movement. When Schary finished his speech, she was out of the chair, on her feet, and passing through the gold curtain before anyone could move.

She entered in a black and gold gown with matching turban and looked inquiringly at her audience, which was now standing and applauding without reservation. When she was finally allowed to speak, she began with a denunciation of the newspaper reporter who had announced her retirement. She wanted, she said, to appear with her company in the spring. The audience howled with laughter as she announced that she would retire in her own time and that, when the time came, no one would know about it. She suggested that she would go to one of the Greek islands. She certainly would not read about her retirement in the newspaper. So much for the hapless press, with which Graham had had a bittersweet relationship since the start of her career in 1920.

Graham's enjoyment at being in the spotlight again, commanding an audience, was obvious. She began a long, discursive reminiscence on her career, touching on her interest in collecting seashells and on current fashions. She regretted that she was too old for miniskirts and wished that they had been available when she was younger. She criticized the look achieved by combining long boots and dresses, saying that they reminded her of Germany before World War II, a period of her own ascendancy and one in which she had snubbed the Nazi government.

She mentioned fondly the musician-composer Louis Horst, who had encouraged her to try her creative skills when no one else believed in her talent. Horst had died six years before, and she obviously still felt the loss. She touched on the subject of diet and complimented modern medicine on its discovery of vitamins, knowing that their use had extended her own career and life.

The talk was completely extemporaneous. She refused to speak from notes because she was still vain enough not to wear in public the glasses she would need in order to read. Her face was not the chalk-white visage that she presented to her audience during the difficult years of her emergence. She was less extreme in her use of makeup, favoring now a more natural look instead of the highly contrasting color on eyes and mouth that she once had worn.

The face, however, was unmistakable. Her eyes, large globes that looked directly at the person she addressed, were surrounded by dark recesses, with a crescent of eyebrow for accent. The nose retained its simple, rounded bluntness, and the firm mouth a combination of primness and sensuality. The long jaw line arched down from either side of the face to meet in a strong thrusted chin. It was a face that radiated powerful intensity, a face not easily forgotten.

Yet, once offstage, a performer has a way of being forgotten. It was oblivion that Graham dreaded. Time would make its claim even on her. She was reluctant to finish speaking, but finally, with applause in her ears, she disappeared behind the gold curtain. She would dance no longer despite her fierce desire to do so. The audience knew it and she knew it, and neither wished to believe it.

1

Early Years, East and West

"My people were strict religionists who
felt that dancing was a sin. . . . but luckily
we moved to Santa Barbara, California."
Martha Graham

Raw, muscular, but stable Allegheny was the beginning. This burgeoning urban center, which attracted iron and coal magnate Andrew Carnegie as a self-proclaimed son, produced three of the most talented women in America's cultural history. Two of them—Mary Cassatt, the only American included in the circle of the French Impressionists, and the innovative prose stylist Gertrude Stein—pursued their careers at arm's length from the culture that nurtured them. But the third, Martha Graham, remained at home to forge a new art form, "modern dance," and she did so with the same iron will that Carnegie applied to extruding rails.

Allegheny was a town where everything had its fixed, accepted, "natural" place. Located at the joining of three rivers, the Monongahela, the Allegheny, and the Ohio, the site was a perfect one for an urban center. The town developed on the north bank of the rivers in a natural bowl surrounded by hills. It had clear boundaries—the crescent of hills on the north and the rivers on the south shielded the houses, which were aligned in quiet order, not scattered haphazardly about on irregular little plots. Allegheny was first laid out in a spacious, symmetrical design for quiet residential living, but settlers by the scores were attracted to the riverfront location so marvelously served by both rail and river transportation. By the end of the Civil War, the population had expanded to 50,000 and Allegheny Town jealously guarded its independence from the bustling city of Pittsburgh across the river. The U.S. Government built an arsenal as well as a penitentiary in Allegheny. On Hog Back Hill, renamed Seminary Hill, the Presbyterians built Western Theological Seminary. An observatory was constructed, and Observatory Hill later became the campus of Western University of Pennsylvania. The town prospered and grew, moving steadily outward to the north, while Pittsburgh watched its prosperous political wards with acquisitive envy.

In the '90's, labor attempted to organize local industry, and little girls could be frightened by the idea that there might be a "striker" lurking under their beds. The year before Martha Graham was born, the Panic of 1893 briefly upset business, cost many their jobs, and forced some into house-to-house begging for food. Allegheny handled the problem by organizing bread lines to cut down the unsightly begging.

Despite these hardships, the essential optimism and prosperity of the town were unimpaired, and in 1896 it contributed to an advertising booklet extolling the benefits of the area. By then the population had grown to about 150,000. The booklet proudly proclaimed that Allegheny County was "unsurpassed in location, unlimited in resources, unrivaled in the activity, intelligence, and patriotism of her people." The county's boasts indicated values that make it seem very much of the past: "Nowhere are clubs, secret societies, and social organizations of every kind in higher favor." Indeed, a chapter of the Daughters of the American Revolution had been established early in 1891. The town offered an electric trolley service that connected the downtown shopping section to the residential areas, and on Federal Street the four-story department store, Boggs and Buhl, had its own generator and incandescent arc lights.

Allegheny had the energy, moral fervor, and good transportation necessary to produce a classic nineteenth-century success story. The town's social order was stable, and, solidly encased in an attitude of moral rectitude, it did not question the basic assumptions of the age. It was in all a social order that valued responsible and conservative thinking. The many clubs provided an opportunity for the like-minded to gather together socially, and scores of churches enabled them to worship together without any variant opinions disturbing the atmosphere of comfortable concord. Some of the stores had separate entrances for ladies and gentlemen—at Monongahela House, a dry goods emporium, ladies rang a bell for admittance—and restaurants, if asked, would put ladies in private rooms, sheltering them from cigar smoke and possible untoward conversation. Work was the rule of the day, and for children it started early, for most just after their elementary education had been completed. High school was for the economically better off, and college for the rich. The system had placed everything within itself and assigned each part a particular niche. Allegheny and its universe made up a settled world where the channels to advancement were clearly laid out.

Martha Graham was to come from parents with roots deep in the Allegheny world. George Greenfield Graham, her father, was born south of Allegheny in the town of Washington in 1856, a few years prior to the start of the Civil War. Martha's mother, Jane Beers Graham, sometimes called Jennie, was born in 1871 and raised in the town of Mars in Butler County, just north of Allegheny.

George Graham spent part of his childhood in Missouri, where his father had made money in real estate. When it came to deciding upon his own future, he elected to become a physician. He received his degree from the College of Physicians and Surgeons in Baltimore, where he specialized in mental disorders. In the language of his time, he was called an alienist. At the age of twenty-seven he returned to the area of his birthplace to join the Western Pennsylvania Hospital-Insane Department, located at Dixmont just a few miles outside of Allegheny. To a great extent, his was a custodial job. At the time it was a triumph just to be able to diagnose a mental disorder. To treat it was largely beyond the competence of the medical profession. Dr. Graham joined the staff in 1883 as one of two assistant physicians, and two years later was appointed Senior Assistant Physician, a post that he retained for eight years, until May 1893, when he resigned to enter private practice. That year he married Jane Beers, who was fifteen years his junior. Mrs. Beers, Jennie's mother, soon left Mars to live with the Grahams in their spacious home in Allegheny's prosperous Second Ward.

On May 11, 1894, Martha, the Grahams' first daughter, was born.

There followed two years later, on May 15, 1896, a second daughter, Mary, and six years later, March 1, 1900, a third daughter, Georgia, familiarly called Geordie. Martha, like her mother, was the eldest and the smallest of three daughters. Unlike her mother, she was not the prettiest. As she grew up, she chose to copy her mother's hair style, parted in the middle and drawn back severely to a clump at the back of the head. This style was favored as well by her maternal grandmother McNeil, whom Martha occasionally visited in the tiny town of Callery, a little to the north of Mars.

Family ties were close, and there was a fair amount of traveling back and forth between Mars, Callery, and Allegheny. Dr. Graham delivered his wife's sister of twins, a boy and a girl. The arrival of the little boy, Martha's first male cousin, was a real family event, for the three Beers sisters between them had had ten girls before his arrival.

When Dr. Graham left Dixmont, he established his practice on the ground floor of his home. Upstairs were a comfortable sitting room, a nursery, and the bedrooms. To do the household chores and the cooking, Elizabeth Prendergast, a young Irish girl, was engaged. Her good spirits and excellent cooking were a feature of the Graham family until she died. Lizzie, as she was called, was not much older than Martha, and she was more of a confidante to her than a distant member of the older generation. In her later years, Graham, speaking of Lizzie, likened her to the Nurse in *Romeo and Juliet*. A short, heavy person who obviously liked to eat as much as she liked preparing food, Lizzie, jolly and always full of fun, was considered "typically" Irish by the family. Always included in the family outings, she enjoyed the intimacy of the family circle. The girls played spirited theatrical games with her in the kitchen; while upstairs they usually confined themselves to the routine play of "house" and "store."

Sometimes the upstairs games could turn into more than anyone expected. In the nursery one afternoon Martha put an extra touch of realism into a play that she, Mary, and Georgia were creating with a pasteboard miniature theater. Martha, deciding they needed real theatrical illumination, introduced a candle into the set and started a small fire almost immediately. They attempted to smother it with a small rug, and the resultant smoke brought their mother running upstairs to take care of the trouble.

The theater interested Martha as it did most girls at that time.

One of her first attempts at costume design involved pushing her struggling pet terrier into a set of doll's clothes. She was fascinated by animals and observed carefully how they moved.

The children led a relatively restricted life in Allegheny—school during the week and church on Sunday. School rules were strict, as were those of the society that created them. Teachers were "particularly enjoined to regard the moral, social, and physical culture of the pupils as not less important than their mental discipline. They must not allow disorder in their rooms, no falsehood, profanity, cruelty, or any other form of vice, but by precept and example endeavor to form correct, obliging, virtuous habits in the pupils entrusted in their care." The three girls rarely went out alone on the street. They were reared protectively as little ladies. Dr. Graham, envisioning a higher education for all his daughters, made his library available to them. Martha, encouraged by her parents, was a particularly voracious reader.

Because of the relatively late age at which he started his family, Dr. Graham was perhaps a bit remote from his children—and perhaps a bit Olympian. Seemingly omniscient, he once told Martha that he could tell whether she was lying by the way she held herself. But despite his remoteness he and Mrs. Graham maintained a happy home and one that relatives found a pleasure to visit.

From the relatively restrained and proper life in the city, the girls particularly enjoyed visiting their cousins in Mars. There they could race around in the woods beyond their aunt's yard or play near the creek town at the foot of the hill nearby. For all their exuberance, the older generation in Mars still wondered if their own children would ever grow up to be as ladylike as the Graham girls.

Despite its pleasures, life in Mars was as securely rooted as in Allegheny, and Sunday was the Lord's day on which no running or playing was allowed. In the morning the children went to the United Presbyterian Sunday School. When it rained or snowed they were sometimes permitted to go to a Sunday school that was a little closer, at a church that belonged to the Free Methodists. But those were rare occasions, for the family did not approve of the high spirits of the Free Methodists. After Sunday school a large midday dinner was served, after which the children customarily went for a walk or a buggy ride with their parents. In good weather they settled on the front porch, and sometimes took the opportunity to slip off to run and play. On one occasion, Martha's oldest cousin sneaked out the back way to clap and march with the Free Methodists—until retrieved by her father. In Allegheny, Sunday life was a little stricter; for, in addition to morning Sunday school, the Graham girls were required to attend the meeting of the Christian Endeavor Society in the evening.

In all, clearly, it was a well-ordered life. It seems charming now to see in the book of regulations governing behavior in the schoolroom the worries that parents had about their children in those days. "Chewing tobacco or using it in any form in and about the school premises *as well as eating fruit or food of any kind during school hours* [author's italics] shall be strictly prohibited. It shall be the duties of the Principals, Teachers, and Truant Officers of all the wards to gather all the facts with regard to school boys smoking cigarettes [apparently there was no need to worry about girls smoking] . . . and . . . to . . . prosecute under the law when the case can be clearly proved." Between the rigors of the Presbyterian Church and the probity of their home life, it did not seem likely that the Graham girls would ever need such disciplining.

A serious danger of the times was illness. In realistic terms medicine was a catch-as-catch-can art with about a fifty-fifty chance of helping anyone who was sick. It was as scientifically based as, say, alchemy: a mixture of theological hope and a scattered observation of phenomena. Frequently a change in climate was prescribed as the answer to problems that were beyond the doctor's competence to handle.

Physical illness took its toll of the Mars branch of the family. Typhoid had entered through a spigot that delivered unpurified river water, and after a serious illness one brother died and three other children were stricken. Dr. Graham did the best he could to protect his own family. He once showed Martha a drop of water under the microscope in his office. Pointing out the organisms in it, he warned her not to be deceived by the safe appearance of unmagnified water. Still, there was illness in the family. Martha's sister Mary was in delicate health because of asthma attacks, and Mrs. Graham herself had sporadic illnesses after the birth of Georgia.

By 1908, when Mary's chronic asthma was no better and actually getting worse, Dr. and Mrs. Graham vacationed in California with an eye to finding a community in which to settle. The West Coast weather was assumed to be healthier for Mary, and medically speaking, a change of locale was the most helpful thing that Dr. Graham could offer her. The Grahams visited several places in Southern California. The location that suited them best was Santa Barbara, a sheltered, settled community encircled by wooded mountains and the sea.

In an odd way, Santa Barbara was a subtropical version of the topography of Allegheny with its surrounding crescent of hills and water frontage. In addition to the marvelous climate of Southern California, the town had its country club and quota of lodge halls: the Masons, Odd Fellows, and Grand Army of the Republic. Altogether, it seemed a congenial place.

After the Grahams returned to Allegheny they began preparations to move. Dr. Graham purchased a house in Santa Barbara, and later in the year Mrs. Graham, the three daughters, and Lizzie traveled to their new home. Martha was fourteen and ready for high school. Mary and Georgia were twelve and eight, respectively. Dr. Graham remained in Allegheny to attend to his practice. As it turned out, although he visited his family regularly, he did not take up permanent residence in Santa Barbara until 1912.

In later years Martha Graham rhapsodized about life in Southern California as the place where she came upon the "power of the Indian and knew the freedom of the Negro." It was undoubtedly a lyrical exaggeration, inspired by the seductively warm climate, the mild winters, the lavish profusion of exotic plants, and the encounters with cultural traces of the Chinese and Spanish. Some such feeling of release and freedom was quite likely in a young girl who had been brought up in the rigorous Presbyterian climate of Western Pennsylvania, with its closed and established society. Winthrop Sargeant, later the husband of Georgia and a native of California, wrote in an autobiographical memoir that growing up in California makes one believe that anything is possible. That was the milieu to which Graham came in her impressionable adolescent years. And the hedonistic openness of Southern California encouraged her to strive for a new type of life, one out of keeping with her background. In later years, California remained for Graham an oasis, a place of refreshment in which to recover from her labors.

With their move to the West Coast, the Grahams found themselves living in an interesting mixture of cultures. Until the middle of the nineteenth century, the tone of Santa Barbara had been completely Spanish. However, with the influx of Anglo-Saxons from the East the atmosphere changed considerably. English replaced Spanish as the language of the schools, and Victorian gingerbread houses made of wood began to replace houses of Spanish adobe and tile. The town was a jumble of Spanish and Eastern architecture and of ethnic groups. In addition to Yankee and Spanish influences, Santa Barbara was also the home of a small Chinese population consisting of people who settled in hospitable California towns after their initial employment as builders of railroads. In Santa Barbara well-to-do families hired Chinese as servants. Each year the Chinese New Year was celebrated with fireworks and a paper dragon dancing through the streets, and Chinese servants gave presents to the children of their households. In this way many a child was introduced to the delights of candied ginger and other unfamiliar tastes.

In an early interview in *Dance Magazine*, Graham commented on the background sources of her career: "My people were strict religionists who felt that dancing was a sin. They frowned on all worldly pleasures. . . . My upbringing led me to fear it myself. But luckily we moved to Santa Barbara, California, when I was about ten [actually fourteen] years old. No child can develop as a real Puritan in a semitropical climate. California swung me in the direction of paganism, though years were to pass before I was fully emancipated." Graham tended to codify her California experience as representing the opposite pole to her earlier life: freedom as opposed to duty. The East and the West—in effect, her childhood and her adolescence—identified a polarity for Graham. Again and again she would return in her work to the theme of ancestors, forebears of stern rectitude, and their influence on a younger generation growing up in their shadow. Much of the emotional tension that she drew on onstage was derived from her own efforts to push against the strong and unyielding background of her parents and the society in which they were rooted.

The Grahams first settled in a house downtown near the high school that Martha and, later, the others were to attend, a school close enough for Martha to come home for lunch. Sandstone and brick, Santa Barbara High School had one of the most impractical forms of construction imaginable for earthquake-prone country (the residents claimed to fear forest fires more than tremors), and its style provided yet another element of eclecticism in that it owed most to mammoth Romanesque. The school had been built six years before the Grahams arrived. Small by today's standards, it was large enough for the town's needs. Martha's freshman class of forty was one of the largest the school had ever had.

When Graham started high school, she was small physically (she eventually grew to 5′ 2″ in height), but she possessed a strong athletic body. She was noticeable for her quiet determination rather than for physical beauty. Her deportment was prim and her mouth had an assured firmness beneath her large, inquiring eyes. Since most athletic teams and other school activities were closed to freshmen, Graham continued her habit of early childhood and spent a good deal of time reading in the library, which she remembered being flooded with sunlight. She also remembered from this period being greeted in the street by a Roman Catholic priest, Father Villa, who would give her a friendly blessing in passing. Nothing like that had ever happened in Presbyterian Allegheny.

In her sophomore year Graham entered school activities and participated vigorously. She became sophomore editor of the school magazine, *Olive and Gold*, and captain of the girls' basketball team. Her avid reading had naturally pushed her toward the magazine, and her restless energy and naturally athletic body found an equally happy outlet in basketball. Classmates still remark on the energy and drive she displayed as she ran about in her middy blouse, bloomers, and knee socks on the basketball court. As in everything else that was a serious part of her life, Graham strove for perfection. Combining her literary and athletic interests, she wrote a short, two-scene play for the school magazine about the confusion and horseplay of the girls' locker room. She also led a reasonably active social life and was the chairman of the refreshment committee for the sophomore dance.

Graham was encouraged to write by her English teacher, Jane Byrd, who years later commented to a Santa Barbara newspaperman that when she first saw Graham dance she felt that a writer had been lost. It was in a story published in *Olive and Gold* that Graham gave the first public sign that she had any longings for a career. In "Music and Maid," which won third prize in the magazine's short story contest, Ruth Ellis is being sent to a private girls' school in the East. On the train, when she holds the baby of a woman traveler, the other girls comment unkindly about her being a lowly nursemaid. At school, Ruth overhears further cruel remarks and, when she trips while running upstairs, another girl laughs at her. An awkward girl socially, she also makes the mistake of striking a match to light a gas jet in her room, forgetting that the school has electric lighting. Graham describes her heroine through the words of another character: " 'Her hair—her dress is impossible,' one bepuffed young miss had scoffed. 'The mouth was large but possessed of a firmness seldom seen in girlish faces; and the clear skin was like a boy's. Hardly a girl's face, and certainly not pretty!' "

Ruth has been taking singing lessons, even though she had been so strongly encouraged by her father to pursue her education that there was hardly time for the lessons. One day it is announced that the famous singer Madame Schumann-Heink will visit the school. An entertainment is planned in her honor, but Ruth is not invited to participate in the performance. Schumann-Heink finds out about this oversight and, after the other students have presented their offerings, invites Ruth to sing while she herself plays the accompaniment. Of course Ruth sings better than the scornful rich girl, who now comments, "Pretty good for a nursemaid."

It would be a mistake to give the story too close a reading. Yet it does offer some interesting parallels to Graham's own life. It was true, for example, that Graham was not considered the pretty one among her sisters. She herself recalled, "Mary was blond and gorgeous. Geordie had curly auburn hair and big beautiful eyes. And then there was little old slit-eyed me. [Again one must allow for exaggeration.] I was not the pretty one." Further, like the father in the story, Dr. Graham was strongly in favor of higher education and did want to send his oldest daughter east to attend Vassar. The future would show that Graham, like her heroine, had other ideas about her life, though perhaps they were no more definite than an inchoate desire to perform.

Whatever the case, not long after the story appeared Graham had an experience that eventually gave her personal desires definite shape. In 1911, during one of her father's annual visits, he took Martha to Los Angeles to see a concert by Ruth St. Denis, then the most famous of the exotic concert dancers. It was the first dance performance of any kind that Graham had ever seen. As she observed later in life, "Nothing ever came to Santa Barbara!" Nothing had prepared her for the experience of seeing Ruth St. Denis.

St. Denis had a remarkable stage appearance. With her long, sinuous arms and a delicate grace, she created wreaths of mysterious and alluring movement. Her costuming consisted of richly embroidered cloth and airy silks. She wore clusters of jewels. Her music had the pulse of the Orient. Among her dances on the occasion that Graham first saw her were solos from St. Denis's first full-length dance drama, *Egypta.*

St. Denis had begun her career casually enough as a chorus girl in musical shows, in which she provided a decorative background for actors or singers during musical numbers. While on tour in Buffalo she saw a cigarette poster featuring a seated Egyptian goddess, and as she later recalled, the composure and mystery of the figure filled her with an enormous longing to emulate the character she saw portrayed. It was this poster and the feeling it generated that channeled St. Denis's energies toward an independent dancing career outside of the musical stage.

The Oriental music and the exquisite beauty of St. Denis came as a similar revelation to Graham. In the flowing femininity and glamorous appearance of the dancer Graham found an ideal to strive toward. She was thinking what for her upbringing ought to have been unthinkable thoughts, but then in the warmth of California one was tempted to consider anything possible. For another adolescent girl of seventeen, such a trip with her father, the corsage of violets he gave her, and spring itself might all have combined to create similar thoughts—which then would have vanished as quickly as the mood passed. But for Graham it was different. She immediately recognized something toward which she could aspire, although she could in no way have known the difficulty involved in starting a dancing career so late in life. Without anyone in her family realizing it, Graham, perhaps half unconsciously herself, began to prepare to be a dancer. The rest of her life was to be spent trying to realize in her own person the vision that she saw in Ruth St. Denis.*

That August, just before returning to school, Graham made her first amateur dance appearance at a local theater as one of thirty-seven "geisha girls" in a tableau version of *The Mikado.* Returning

* Coincidentally, Ted Shawn, who was to be Graham's teacher at Denishawn and who would guide her early career, had seen St. Denis for the first time only a month previously, when she played a week in Denver. Shawn was also strongly attracted to St. Denis and her dancing —there can be little doubt that her presence exerted a powerful impact— and three years later he became her partner and her husband.

to school, she gave up the girls' basketball team and took dramatics. She played Dido, the queen of Carthage, in the class production of Virgil's *Dido, the Phoenician Queen.*

She also became the secretary of the Quorum, a literary and dramatic debating society. Many of her other interests were still like those of most of her classmates. She found time to be on the reception committee for an informal "at home" given by the girls' tennis and basketball teams; she headed the reception committee of the junior dance and served on the reception committee of the boys' track team dance. Still, however, she had taken a definite turn away from athletic and toward literary and dramatic activities. The diffused longing for a place of special importance that motivated Ruth Ellis in Graham's short story also drove Graham. She had a modestly active social life, but since she was, by her own admission, not the pretty one in the family she strove to make her position, through energy and will, in theatrical and scholastic pursuits.

Senior year was as active as the others: dramatics, *Olive and Gold* (she was now editor-in-chief and also wrote poems for the magazine), and class activities. As vice-president of the student council, she had her picture taken in a mannish-cut jacket, looking very grim and purposeful. Her hair was unfashionably long and parted severely in the center. The look emphasized her natural gravity and also set her apart a little from her sisters. At home, being the eldest child, more responsibility was naturally hers, and Martha, who easily assumed a leading role in the household of women, in many ways also served as a model for her sisters. During Martha's junior year Mary entered Santa Barbara High School, and, like Martha, she tried out for basketball. Later, also like Martha, she joined the Quorum.

In 1912, after a four-year separation from his family, broken only by visits, Dr. Graham retired from practice in the East and settled in Santa Barbara. Rather than set up another practice, he began to speculate in real estate as an investment, buying a half-share in a ranch in the farming area of the Goleta Valley. All together once more, the family made a fine appearance on the street: Dr. Graham with his fashionably trimmed mustache and goatee, the small and delicate Mrs. Graham, the three girls properly and smartly dressed. Warm breezes blew up from the south, and social life for adolescents centered on beach "teas." The most pressing matter was embarrassment if the stocking of a bathing costume became lost in the water.

Meanwhile, the world outside Santa Barbara was changing. Western Europe was preparing to break the longest uninterrupted period of peace in its history, and the pieties of the Victorian age, which were bent but not broken in the Edwardian footnote to Victoria's reign, were to be shredded on the steppes of Russia and the fields of France and Belgium. In New York in 1913, the Armory art show, with its daring exploration of new forms, upset the conventions of native American artists. The vilification of its advanced pictorial art prefigured the vilification that would later lash out at Graham.

Toward the end of her senior year, Martha concentrated upon perfecting her dramatic interpretation of Privacy, the timid yet loving aunt of Prunella, in a play presented by the graduating class in the same theater where two years earlier she had been a geisha girl. A local review, her first newspaper notice, commented that her interpretation was a "fine bit of acting." She was graduated from the school in June 1913, and read the following about herself in her high school yearbook: "Capable, generous, willing to do—To the noblest standard is faithful and true."

Martha Graham now had a critical decision to make: whether to go to an academic school as her parents, particularly her father, had in mind, or to go elsewhere, to attempt something that she herself had in mind, however unclearly. Despite her father's intention that she go to college, neither he nor her mother had entertained the notion of an actual career for their daughter. With the instinct of someone who knows what is not good for her, she drew back from the academic type of school that her parents wished her to attend. For her part, she said, she wanted to go to a school where she would have more opportunity for self-expression. As she would throughout her subsequent life, Graham inevitably chose creative work or expression rather than social comfort or conformity. In the end, Martha proved strong enough to have her way. In the fall of 1913 she entered a school that emphasized "expression," the Cumnock School in Los Angeles. It was not an inexpensive compromise. The fees, high for the time, ran about $1,000 for tuition and board.

2

Learning to Dance

"So far the only value of my work is absolute sincerity."
Martha Graham

The Cumnock School, in the Wilshire district of Los Angeles, had a four-acre campus with buildings constructed in the Old English style of architecture. The school had been founded in 1894 and was divided into three sections: a lower school, a high school, and a junior college. A brochure of the time explained that the school "accommodates boys and girls from 10–20 years of age in their pursuits of learning and self-expression." The brochure continued in a reassuring fashion to describe the school's living accommodations: "Under the supervision of an experienced housemother and resident faculty members, the dormitory is characterized by its friendly homelike atmosphere."

In the fall of 1913 Graham and another girl from Santa Barbara, Marguerite Andrus, went to Los Angeles to enter Cumnock's junior college. The special emphasis of the school was "self-expression"; students, in the higher grades mostly young ladies, were instructed not only in academic subjects but also in the expressive subjects of dance and drama. The idol of many of the students was Ruth St. Denis.

Studies were fairly advanced. Students learned about the theater of Gordon Craig, and they thoroughly explored the mechanics of stage lighting so that they could set a stage without props, using only lights and dark drapes, a radical innovation for the time. Their work also involved motion pictures at a time far ahead of the rest of the academic world. Without a doubt Cumnock was much more satisfactory for Graham than Vassar ever would have been.

At the end of Graham's first year she received an unexpected shock: Her father died. If Dr. Graham had been remote, he had also been a strong and comforting presence. Whatever their disagreements, he had been an anchor around which Martha had moved, and his loss made her anxious about her future.

Dr. Graham had always provided a comfortable living for his family, but his estate was modest, considering the size of the family and the educational aspirations he had had for his children. The total estate was $21,736.40, of which $3,785.65 was in ready cash. The rest was the valuation of household effects, including a Reo automobile, plus the bulk of it, $13,000, representing a half-interest in thirty-five acres of farming land in nearby Goleta. The court allowed $175.00 a month living expenses for the family while the estate was being settled, and it permitted the sale of farm produce, primarily walnuts, to provide additional revenue. Dr. Graham left one-third of the estate to his wife, Jane, and two-ninths to each of his three daughters. This came to about $6,000 apiece. Since the girls were minors, their mother managed their shares.

Although the family was shaken both emotionally and financially, Mrs. Graham decided to continue the education of her children as it had begun. Consequently, in the autumn Martha returned to Cumnock, paying for her schooling with the money left by her father.

Graham's life and thoughts during her years at Cumnock were both intense and indecisive. Though she was edging away from her past, she was unsure of the direction she wished to take. At school, though, whatever she did, she did with her now usual seriousness and unwavering intensity. Some of Graham's classmates sympathetically reacted to her intensity with a rhyme from a play they were studying:

> Miss Lofty has a carriage,
> None have I—

She has jewels upon her bosom,
Inside, I . . .

Some of the students would incline their heads toward Graham indicating that it was she who had "jewels" inside.

Graham stayed at Cumnock for three full years, appearing in plays like *Trelawney of the Wells* and attending dancing classes three times a week. During her last semester, she fell afoul of one of the instructors, Nina Moise (who later became a motion picture director). Graham was reading her graduation recital number, and the entire student body and faculty filled the auditorium. Miss Moise, at the back, began to whisper loudly and caused a slight disturbance. Graham stopped reading, looked at her, snapped her book shut and said, "I will continue reading at another time," and walked off the stage. The daring of it caused a stir. Even then Graham onstage was not a figure to trifle with. As her career progressed, so would her expression of temperament. The stage "intensified life" and expanded her own reactions so that shyness was superseded by artistic assertiveness.

In 1915, at the end of Graham's second year at Cumnock, a new dancing school opened its doors in Los Angeles. This was Denishawn, the creation of Graham's idol, Ruth St. Denis, and Ted Shawn, also a dancer and now St. Denis's husband. The school had been Shawn's idea. In the early spring of that year the company, whose style was a mixture of gossamer, Orientalism, and pageantry, had finished a series of concerts in San Francisco. Shawn persuaded St. Denis, who was not especially interested in business and administrative matters, that it would be wise to establish a permanent home for the company. The establishment of a school would give St. Denis and himself an opportunity to work when they were not touring, and it also would provide a place to store costumes and prepare new dances. Accordingly, the Denishawn Company created the Denishawn School in two large houses in Westlake Park, a district of Los Angeles. Opening for business in the summer of 1915, it offered a wide range of dance styes—ballet, dramatic, and ethnic (it was not Shawn's practice to miss any opportunities for a financial return)—and some academic subjects as well. The school had a modest enrollment at first, but it grew as the Denishawn companies toured and attracted more and more publicity.

In the summer of 1916, having been graduated from Cumnock,

Graham plucked up her courage, took a firm step toward the world of dance, and enrolled in Denishawn's summer session. It was something of a shock to her. To Shawn and St. Denis, Graham's determination was much more evident than her talent. At twenty-two years of age, Graham's only previous dance training had been at Cumnock, and she was inclined to be a little overweight. Moreover, she had spent most of her life in one academic situation or another, and she found the free atmosphere of Denishawn a little overwhelming. Other students there had more feminine grace than she, and she was older than many. Everything combined to make her retiring in class, where she did not speak much but watched intently. The proud girl who had refused to perform before the whispering Miss Moise now quieted herself.

In the normal course of events, Graham could not have anticipated any kind of career as a serious dancer. Traditional ballet training, then and now, starts between the ages of eight and twelve. Even the Denishawn School, which was blazing its own path outside the classic ballet tradition and making demands of dancers that did not depend on childhood dance training, did not seem to offer a possible route to the concert dance stage. Graham, however, persisted. Since first seeing her, she had adored St. Denis as a goddess, and here she was able to study with her. At least that much was to be said in favor of attending Denishawn, and perhaps it was enough.

It was not enough for St. Denis. St. Denis, whose delicacy of gesture inspired writers and sculptors (among them Hugo von Hoffmannsthal and Rodin) to seek her company, had never liked the mundane idea of a school in the first place. She did not like teaching, correcting, and doing all the necessary things that it takes to produce dancers. She was a concert artist and throve on performances. She loved the adulation of the public above all else. She had reached so high a degree of success and popularity that, after appearing in Germany, she had received an offer to have a theater built there to her own specifications. As far as she was concerned, the school, while it might have had sound economic reasons for its existence, was never more than an interlude between appearances. As for Graham, all that the lovely St. Denis saw in her was a short, unmalleable lump. She told Shawn that she couldn't do anything with Graham and didn't want her in her class.

So Shawn took over the teaching of Graham. As the business head of the organization, he did not like to lose a paying pupil. At the same time Shawn was a teacher as much as a performer, and he responded to the challenge of the presumably unteachable young woman from Santa Barbara. The summer proceeded, and one day in class Graham performed a Spanish dance with genuine ferocity. The hidden "jewels" glittered for strangers for the first time in a display of the dance temperament that was to drive her throughout her career. Shawn was pleased, and Graham, working hard, improved so quickly under his guidance that St. Denis subsequently began to use her as a demonstrator in her own classes. Graham, understandably, was pleased, but her relationship with St. Denis never lost its initial uncertainty.

That summer of 1916 Shawn and St. Denis created "A Dance Pageant of Egypt, Greece, and Italy," which gave Graham, who had a small role in it, her first public appearance in a professional dance company. The pageant was presented at the University of California at Berkeley and was in San Diego a few weeks later, after which a shortened version was prepared for a vaudeville concert tour, on which Graham did not go. The transformation of a modestly reared young lady from a strongly conservative background into an active stage performer was not easily achieved. Appearing in the Greek Theater at Berkeley was one thing, but vaudeville was quite another, and Graham went home.

Her next opportunity came as a teacher when Denishawn returned to Los Angeles. American involvement in World War I soon became a declared reality. Shawn volunteered for the Ambulance Corps, Graham had been rolling bandages, and St. Denis started across the country on a Liberty Bond tour. Shawn invited Graham, among others, to live at the studio and teach classes while he was in the army. Thus the flourishing business was maintained. Shawn received his training nearby at Camp Kearny and so was able to supervise the school on weekends.

Graham's new position not only was a step closer to the dance world but actually earned her some money, which was increasingly needed at home. Her father's estate was dwindling. In February, Mrs. Graham had sold off two-thirds of the ranch purchased by her husband, and in July she sold off the rest, making a small profit—the last substantial sum that would derive from the estate. Soon not only Martha but the other two sisters as well were working. Georgia and Mary moved to Los Angeles and Mrs. Graham stayed in Santa Barbara with Lizzie. Georgia joined Martha at Denishawn, Mary got an office job, and all sent money home.

The war ended before Shawn was sent overseas, and he was released from service in December 1918. St. Denis had undertaken yet a second Liberty Bond tour in the fall of 1918 and was occupied until the spring of 1919. Shawn had not performed for a year and a half, and, though he had ballooned to over 190 pounds in the service, he was eager to join St. Denis onstage. Since he would no longer be able to direct the school at a full level of activity, he closed the Westlake facility and kept a small house on Sixth Street, where Graham was put in charge of teaching night classes to adult beginners. Shawn saw this as a holding action until Denishawn could return to its own course.

The position advanced Graham further in her chosen career. Though she was more teacher than performer, she had entered the professional world of dance. Her opportunities as a dancer were still few and far between and limited to a vaudeville appearance or two with other young dancers at the local Capitol Theater (operated by one S. L. "Roxy" Rothafel, who would later hire Graham for the opening of his extravagant Radio City Music Hall in New York City). However, she had begun her career. What had begun one day in the audience of a Ruth St. Denis concert now became a reality. No longer was she a dabbling student; she was now a professional.

Shawn's idea of a qualified dancer was a person with the ability to do what was required at any given moment. He was not a stickler for long periods of training and would often take relative newcomers and place them in positions of responsibility simply because they were available. Thus it was with Graham. In later years she would constantly lecture students about the decades it took her to become a dancer and then an artist, and in a sense that was true. But at the start of her career she was pushed onstage after a relatively short period of training. She was teaching others what she had barely learned herself, and she was performing with hardly any stage experience behind her. It was all part of the trouper's approach used by Shawn, an approach with which Graham finally broke when she launched her own career.

While Shawn was off with St. Denis, Graham remained at the school. When Shawn returned, it was with the realization that, although he still wanted a school, St. Denis did not. The relationship between them was sufficiently flexible so that each often went his or her separate way without breaking up their marriage.

While the school was still located in the house on Sixth Street, Shawn scouted Los Angeles for a suitable property in which to establish the new studio. He discovered a "white elephant" which the owners either had to tear down or rent for whatever they could. The previous tenant had run a ballroom dance school, and the Mississippi Gulf–style building was unsuitable for most other purposes. Shawn struck a bargan for the building and gloated over his new home base. It had a large ballroom with a small stage at one end and a balcony at the other. Shawn put the workshops and small studios on the ground floor. Following the Orientalist style for which the Denishawn Company was famous, he had an Egyptian mural painted in the central hall and the two drawing rooms painted with black lacquer and carpeted in black. The furniture was upholstered in jade, orange, and peacock blue. On the second floor there was a complete kitchen, dining room, and bedroom where Shawn lived. The third floor had space for a few live-in students or staff. There, as a full member of the staff, Graham lived.

Shawn dashed into activity of all kinds. He was in his element. Denishawn was well known from its extensive touring, and students began to enroll and fill the scheduled classes quickly. In addition to running the school, Shawn began to write a book about St. Denis, and, impresario-like, developed acts for individuals and small Denishawn companies to travel the vaudeville circuit. The most successful of the company works was "Julnar of the Sea," which played continuously from the fall of 1919 to the spring of 1921 and was originally sent out in the charge of the school's musical director, Louis Horst. After it was successfully launched, Shawn in 1920 turned to a new task. creating a vehicle for Graham, whose desire to be a featured soloist and whose devotion to dance were obvious.

Among both staff and students, Graham's emotional drive was exceptional. Everyone saw that she drove herself unsparingly and that she worked alone far into the night. It became known that she expected the same commitment from everyone with whom she worked. This intensity could sometimes be expressed in a violent temper, and it was not pleasant to be on the receiving end of one of her rages. Graham did not heat up slowly; she exploded. Her words fed the anger, the anger her outburst, in a spiral of increasing intensity, until sometimes it seemed that nothing could survive her scorn. Yet she could also be extraordinarily kind. Her devotion to dance, her intensity onstage and off were accepted as parts of the same deep forcefulness and commitment.

Shawn considered the various options open to him in creating a role for Graham; the area of Greek dance and myth had been effectively explored by Isadora Duncan, and St. Denis had established her claim to the dances of the East. So for Graham he turned to the legends of the Americas, and subsequently, in her own work, Graham mined these same sources. Shawn thought of Graham as a "beautiful but untamed little black panther." She was not "the Northern European, peaches-and-cream blonde," and her high cheekbones made her exotic. The story he settled on, "Xochitl," was one that he had learned from a Mexican artist, Francisco Cornajo, whose passionate interest in pre-Columbian history and legend had aroused Shawn's enthusiasm. Cornajo did the sets, and Shawn commissioned a score by Homer Grunn. It was a most unlikely beginning for a dancer whose angularity would become so extreme that she one day would be the antithesis of Denishawn.

As the piece opened, a group of native girls were seated in front of a large ziggurat and stylized maguey plants. Xochitl's father staggered in, reeling drunk. He had discovered how to make pulque, an intoxicant drink, and the group decided to take a sample to the Emperor.

In the next scene, the Emperor (Shawn) was surrounded by dancing girls, his guard, and a flute player. After accepting the bowl of pulque from the peasants, he motioned to the girl Xochitl (Graham) to dance. Wearing a long batik scarf, Graham did a "plastique" solo, a typical Denishawn device, full of melting statuary poses; and while she danced, the Emperor sipped the pulque. His passions, already aroused by Xochitl's dance, were now running out of control. He motioned to his dancing girls, and, one by one, they did a little variation to his throne, where they were told to lure Xochitl's father out of the room. The girls fluttered around the old man and took him away. The Emperor stood, flung off his feather cape, and, striding down to Xochitl, began his assault on her.

The duet which Shawn choreographed for himself and Graham made full use of Graham's fury and power, and in later years he complained of the bruised and bleeding lips he received trying to ward off her stage blows. The Emperor returned to his senses after the father threatened him with a dagger. He then married Xochitl, and pulque became known throughout the kingdom as a powerful drink.

"Xochitl" was first performed in June 1920 and was scheduled to go on tour on the Pantages vaudeville circuit. Before that Graham had danced only minor roles in a performance at Long Beach. It wasn't glamorous, but it was professional work, and Graham's stature was not such that it was too lowly for her. Then came the tour, which changed Graham's status as a performer. Since she also served as the company's paymaster, the tour gave her the experience, in miniature, of running a company.

When "Xochitl" went on the circuit, the Emperor was Robert Gorham, Graham's sister Georgia was one of the dancing girls, and the pianist was Pauline Lawrence, who later became the wife of the dancer José Limon. It soon became clear that it was dancing that would offer Graham the chance to express herself. In Tacoma, early in the fall, a newspaper reviewer called her "a brilliant young dancer."

But Tacoma also brought its problems. Gorham broke his toe there, and, because Shawn did not have any other experienced male pupils at the time, he was forced to replace Gorham with a relative newcomer who had come from Lincoln, Nebraska, to join the school only that year. And so the dance drama "Xochitl" became the first major performing vehicle not only for Graham but also for another central figure of modern dance, Charles Weidman.

Why Weidman? One of Shawn's chief requirements for any replacement was that he or she be the right size to fit the existing costume, since the company could not afford to create new costumes for every new interpreter of a role. Gorham was tall and so was Weidman, so he got the nod. In addition, Shawn later commented, "He at least knew his right foot from his left." The difficulties for Weidman were enormous. Shawn had sent him out with only a few hours' rehearsal; he was tall and thin, whereas Gorham was tall and muscular; and the part called for primitive, assertive dancing, while Weidman specialized in lyrical, airborne movement. But at Denishawn the show business tradition of the-show-must-go-on was strong.

When Weidman arrived in Tacoma, Graham was in a state of despair: She had lost the payroll. And when she saw the ill-suited replacement for Gorham, it seemed the last straw. In a short time the wealthy Gorham family solved the payroll problem by replacing the money. But the problem presented by Weidman was more difficult. He could not do his primitive solo realistically enough to satisfy Graham. That, joined with the fact that he had not rehearsed the whole work, led Graham to have him stand by his throne majestically. Only as they had time to rehearse did she slowly work him into the culminating duet.

Graham tore into the role of Xochitl with ferocity. As she did not spare herself, so she did not spare Weidman. This is how she operated throughout her career, with her co-workers often unable or unwilling to respond to what she asked of them. One of her means of showing expression at the time was to bare her teeth. "Teeth, teeth, teeth like a shark," recalled Weidman. She began to modulate the tooth exposure, but not until Louis Horst, who later toured with the group, spoke to her about it did she begin to control the ferocity. At one performance she and Weidman tangled so furiously during the rape scene, falling to the floor in a paroxysm of realistic tumbling, that they became locked together. As the Emperor he wore a large collar with outsized jewels whose claw-like settings became caught on her costume. When Graham hissed, "Get up! Get up!" Weidman replied, "I can't! I can't!" and they rolled helplessly for several moments until they could tear free of each other. Graham was in the habit of beating Weidman so vigorously with her fists during this scene that he began to feel he had to do something to ward her off. His father at one point suggested that, to soften the force of the blow, he expand his chest when he thought he was going to be hit.

Eventually the performance smoothed out, and by the time the tour had progressed down the coast into Los Angeles, where "Xochitl" was to appear in Grauman's Million Dollar Theater, Weidman was fully integrated into the production.

The need to save money and send it home led Graham, Weidman, and Graham's sister Georgia to move in with Mary and a girl friend, who were living in a Hollywood bungalow. Mary and her roommate had the bedroom; Georgia slept on the porch, with the heater; and Weidman and Graham shared a bed, innocently though not without humor. Weidman characterized his role as that of a long hot water bottle for Graham when she was having her period (which she referred to, in coy terminology that perhaps reflected her straitlaced upbringing, as the "zizzlums").

The tour provided Graham with several opportunities to give vent both to her dramatic temperament and to her temper. In a seedy diner she once flashed a grand manner for an uncomprehending waitress by demanding a "serviette." She was greeted with: "A what?" Graham's response in this instance was not anger but a meek change of course. She asked for a napkin. Her first request was an example of a Graham characteristic: assuming a pose to see what would happen, testing the limits to see who she was, where she was, and how far she could go. It was something that she would do throughout her life, at times creating emotional turbulence and often exasperating those closest to her. At another diner, Weidman said something that displeased her—an inconsequential remark so far as he knew—and she swung at him with a grapefruit spoon. Typically, such displays of temper could pass as quickly as they arose. She and Weidman generally worked together harmoniously. Indeed, for the first three years of her career he was her regular partner and even something of a confidant.

On one occasion at Grauman's Theater, Graham displayed a more explosive show of temper. Everyone in the production wore black wigs, and one night an Irish girl, who drank and was in a slightly muzzy state, put the wig on backward. Graham was outraged. In her fury she ripped a telephone from the wall and threw it at the girl who thought of "Xochitl" only as a performance. To Graham it was her life.

At the conclusion of the Grauman dates the tour of "Xochitl" was over, and with it Graham's initial taste of being a "star." Shortly after, on tour with Shawn and playing in her home town of Santa Barbara, she gave her first newspaper interview, explaining her attitude toward performing. The interview was dramatic and intense, as Graham always was, and perhaps somewhat self-inflated. But essentially it was accurate. "So far the only value of my work, if it has any artistic value, is absolute sincerity." Graham's comment was a slighting oblique reference to the show business aspect of Denishawn, which in its priorities usually put artistic expression second. "I could not do anything that I could not feel," Graham said. "A dance must dominate me completely, until I lose sense of anything else. Later what I do may be called art, but not yet." Her roles might have been froth, but she danced them as if they were the most substantial work ever created. For the time being, she was substituting her dancer's energy for the deficiencies of the choreography.

Shawn, while his various companies were out on the road, taught at the school along with Doris Humphrey, who served as the main teacher. Humphrey, who with Graham and Weidman formed the trio that comprised the heroic generation of "modern dance," had come to the school in 1915, when it first opened. She had had extensive ballet training and had been refused a dancing job in Chicago because she was too balletic. She had operated her own school with her mother in Oak Park, Illinois, but had an enormous desire to perform. When one of her early teachers suggested that she go to Los Angeles for the summer course offered by Denishawn, she agreed and thus attracted Ruth St. Denis's attention. Invited by St. Denis to join a concert company she was forming, Humphrey eventually danced with the various Denishawn companies for the next ten years. She was a favorite of St. Denis, just as Graham was not.

In 1920, Shawn and St. Denis had another of the many partings that marked their long professional and personal association. They differed not only on the importance of running a school but on the directions that their careers should take. Shawn's interest had turned to vaudeville as a way to make money, while St. Denis longed for serious concert dancing. Dividing up the available dancers—Humphrey joined St. Denis, Graham joined Shawn—they went their separate ways.

St. Denis began to work on "music visualization" with an all-girl company, for which Humphrey did some of the choreography. It was a form of dancing that told no particular story but created waves of movement corresponding to the mood of the music. The dancers expressed the music in various poses, just as an orator underlines his speech with hand and arm gestures.

Deciding to try a "solo" cross-country tour, Shawn assembled a small group of dancers, Graham and Weidman and two others, Betty May and Dorothea Bowen, with Louis Horst as musical director. Weidman functioned as a combination dresser and dancer, and the women danced the transitions between Shawn's solos. The tour was hastily arranged and erratically scheduled, causing long gaps between dates. Starting in the Los Angeles area, it included a date in

Santa Barbara (the occasion of Graham's first interview), and this appearance was the last time she was seen in her adopted home town in someone else's work.

In Santa Barbara the group appeared at the Potter Theater, where Graham had performed in her high school variety program ten years earlier. On this occasion the local reviewer praised her as an "artist of rare ability." Graham was featured in several typical Denishawn numbers, both ethnic and romantic, including a solo, "Serenata Morisca," and a duet with Shawn, "Malagueña." Fifteen years later, in 1936, Graham would return to Santa Barbara with the reputation of a radical innovator.

On this, her second tour in one of Shawn's companies, a crucial event took place for Graham. She became romantically attached to Louis Horst, a married man ten years her senior, whose wife Betty ran a dance school in San Francisco. St. Denis and Shawn had found Horst in San Francisco after they fired their regular conductor during an appearance there. Horst, a free-lance musician, played vaudeville in addition to working in a saloon, where he would sit and read Pater from a book propped on the music stand. It was Horst who played the piano for Graham's first class at Denishawn, which he joined only slightly before Graham became one of its pupils. To Graham, Horst was a man of the world who had traveled extensively and who enjoyed a wide knowledge of art and music, areas in which she was seriously deficient. Their relationship, which began professionally, ripened into a romance during the tour. It apparently was a relationship of little physical ardor, for Horst was not a passionate man despite his mildly ribald conversational asides. For Graham he perhaps filled a double void both as a source of knowledge that could be of practical use to her and as a stable older man, in some ways like her father. The relationship between them struck deep roots and eventually developed into an affectionate companionship for twenty years. In the end, Horst was to have a singular effect on the whole history of modern dance.

Given the tour's haphazard scheduling, it was in danger of collapse almost constantly, and in Norman, Texas, shortly after it began, it came to an abrupt halt. By luck Shawn was able to borrow enough money from an aunt to travel to New York, where the group, in December 1921, played a successful Broadway matinee at the Apollo Theater on Forty-second Street, at the time a legitimate house, now a generally run-down movie theater. The Apollo was definitely the end of the tour, but Shawn decided to stay in New York to arrange future tours. There was enough money to send the two youngest members of the company, May and Bowen, back to California and to rent a studio at the top of an apartment house on Riverside Drive, where the reduced group made its makeshift living quarters. Thus the Chatsworth apartments became Denishawn-East.

The situation was not altogether bleak. The group's appearance at the Apollo had caught the attention of a leading theatrical agent, Daniel Mayer, who offered to arrange a fall tour. Such a tour would have a stronger chance of succeeding if Shawn would get St. Denis to appear with him, but St. Denis needed persuading. She was very tired of touring with her company—it, too, had been stranded—and she wanted to return to solo engagements, which she felt were the most congenial form of performing for her. But Shawn persuaded her to join the company, and a date was therefore arranged for a joint appearance in Greensburg, Pennsylvania, in February.

Liking this combination, Meyer signed a contract with Shawn and St. Denis and their company for three and a half years. It was a significant jump for both of them. With the Mayer contract, the company graduated from vaudeville and became a fully managed touring group. The Mayer seasons became highly successful, but for the moment there was still a severe money problem. Mayer obligingly arranged a few dates in April and, to help promote the company, scheduled appearances in England beginning in May and an American tour beginning in October. The aim was to garner some foreign reviews, which would provide validation beyond American praise. All this seemed to bode well for Graham, who had her solos and her lead in "Xochitl."

Meanwhile there were several months to get through in New York. Shawn offered lessons in his rented studio and suggested that Graham teach classes to department store girls, an activity comparable, so far as he was concerned, to the evening classes she had taught to working girls in Los Angeles shortly after she first joined the company. Shawn's idea was to get the department stores to pay for the lessons and offer them as a bonus to their salesgirls. But he did not quite understand how the experience of the past several years had changed Graham.

Shawn met Graham and Horst at a neighborhood restaurant called the C & L (among themselves it was referred to as the "Cheap and Lousy"), where he explained his plan to Graham over lunch.

She was not at all receptive. She objected on the grounds of artistic dignity—it was simply something she could not do. For Shawn it was a matter of company survival. Each stated opposed positions strongly, becoming more and more assertive. Finally, Graham stood up dramatically, refusing under any circumstances to go along with Shawn's scheme, and to underscore her point she jerked the tablecloth off the table. Glasses, plates, and silverware hit the floor as she strode to the door, with Horst hurrying after her. Shawn settled with the owner for $20.00 and stormed after Graham and Horst, who were entering a cab. Grabbing its door, Shawn shouted that Graham would never dance with Denishawn again; slamming the door, he smashed the window and left Horst to deal with the driver.

The following day Graham returned to the studio and apologized. Shawn, whose temper matched hers, laughed at her meekness, and together they sat down to try to find an alternate way to earn additional money. Horst was earning a little by playing the piano, and Shawn had a few pupils, so though things were thin they were not impossible.

Graham did give a few lessons to shop girls, but then Shawn had the idea that she should take a job dancing in a show. He had previously placed dancers with John Murray Anderson, who was producing the Greenwich Village Follies series, and he thought he could do the same with Graham. Anderson, a dancer and designer, relied on a mixture of glamour, the exotic, and intelligent wit rather than just show girls to attract his audience, and in general he tried to appeal to the more sophisticated revue public. Shawn therefore arranged an audition for Graham. Unfortunately, Anderson arrived at the theater early, before Graham had a chance to get into costume or make-up. Nothing is quite so tawdry as a theater without its magic, and, with a naked work-light bulb illuminating the stage, Graham in street clothes looked far from what Anderson wanted for the Follies. No matter what she did on the stage thereafter, Anderson was unable to forget the drab appearance Graham presented at this audition. He later told Shawn: "Ted, you've given me wonderful people . . . how could you possibly think I could use this?" It was a disappointment for both of them.

Shawn, irrepressible, had another idea. He had met an experimental filmmaker, Jacob Frank Leventhal, who had developed a motion-picture color stock, trademarked as Prizma Process, and who needed subjects. Since there could be nothing better than dancers to demonstrate the ability of the film to record motion, Leventhal signed a contract with Shawn to make a series of shorts called "Music Films." Graham, Weidman, and others were to be the dancers. Since the movies of the time were silent, each theater had its own small orchestra to play along with the films, and Leventhal placed his camera so that he photographed, along with the dancers, the head and shoulders of Horst, who conducted during the filming. The idea was that the music could be sent along with the films, and the moviehouse orchestra could follow Horst's beat and be in perfect synchronization with the dancers.

In theory it was an excellent idea, but in practice the individual orchestra leaders were leery of turning over command of their players to a film image. A dampening review reported the disconcerting and distracting sight of a film conductor and pit conductor, each flailing away completely out of synchronization with the other. The films themselves were praised for the quality of the color, which was clear and bright without being harsh. Graham did her own "Spanish Dance," "Arabian Duet" with Charles Weidman, and "Bubble" and "Egyptian" with Lillian Powell. It was the sort of dancing mix that had proved popular on the vaudeville circuit and was expected to be successful with the movie public. But somehow Shawn did not receive any royalties. "Never got five cents," he remarked angrily fifty years after the event.

Despite everything, the company survived in various ways. Weidman, who was nimble with his hands, secured one job weaving cloth and another as an extra in a few crowd scenes for D. W. Griffith's *Orphans of the Storm*. Finally, in May, with St. Denis and several additional dancers, the company sailed from Boston for England, where it was to play six weeks at the London Coliseum and a week each in Manchester and Bristol. The trip fulfilled Mayer's hopes, but it was the start of a crisis for Graham.

During the stay in New York, Horst's wife, Betty, remained in San Francisco, running the dance school. Prior to the European trip, Horst suddenly asked Shawn if he would take Betty along as a member of the company. Whatever Horst's reasons for making the request, they were sufficient to convince Shawn, and Betty Horst became a member of the European tour. For Graham what was to have been a foreign lark became, even before it began, a galling experience.

There was worse to come. St. Denis, never impressed with Graham, demanded and got certain of her roles, including, most importantly, the lead in "Xochitl," and this despite the fact that the role had been created especially for Graham and that St. Denis was not suited for the part. But, as the star of the company, St. Denis took the role and redesigned the hairdo, the costume, and the choreography. Where Graham had been a cornered panther, St. Denis was a wilting maiden. The contrast with Graham was so great that Shawn, approaching the rape scene and anticipating Graham's fierce resistance, startled St. Denis into saying on stage, "Darling, there's no sense in being so rough!" Graham thus found herself shoved out of her own roles and out of Louis Horst's life in a single trip. Professionally, the glamorous St. Denis eclipsed her.

Shawn was having difficulties of his own with St. Denis. Not only had he had to persuade her to return to the company, but now she complained that her career had taken the wrong direction when she allowed Shawn to create a company and a school. Complaining also that Shawn was inattentive to her, she told him about a young poet with whom she was in love and who could make her truly happy. St. Denis was fond of Weidman, and so in London when the company decided to revive "Soaring," a dance created by Doris Humphrey for St. Denis's prior tour, Weidman instead of Shawn got the part.

The net effect of their disappointments drove Shawn and Graham together in shared misery, and they wandered around London consoling or, more accurately, not consoling each other. In the Strand one day, as they stood looking at each other, Shawn remarked, "It could just as well be Coffeyville, Kansas, as London, the way we feel." It was no consolation that Betty Horst, even though she was a member of the company, seldom danced. The tour proceeded successfully, but for Graham the hurt remained. The experience was to mark the beginning of her end with Denishawn.

After England there were still several months before the American tour in October. Betty Horst returned to San Francisco, and Graham, with at least a certain rhetorical vigor, resumed her relationship with Horst. Over the summer, in her classes at the New York school Shawn had established, she made offhand remarks about free love and living in sin. Shawn objected, for his usual practical reasons. The theater at that time was not a highly esteemed profession, and dancing was even less so. As a married couple, Shawn and St. Denis had brought a measure of respectability to the field, and in Denishawn schools Shawn tried to maintain a respectable amosphere so that parents would not feel anxious about their children. Shawn lectured Graham and infuriated her. Shawn recalled saying, "Martha, this is a school and what you do behind locked doors is your affair. But what you preach and scream out loud in front of students is our affair, and this hurts Denishawn, hurts us, and you musn't do it." Graham stormed, but Shawn was firm—and the remarks stopped. They were, in any case, perhaps a reflection of her own uncertainty.

The U.S. tour, lasting from October to April, went on as scheduled. Graham regained the lead in "Xochitl," but the star of the company was still clearly St. Denis. For each of Graham's little solos, like "Serenata Morisca," St. Denis had six placed more advantageously toward the climax of the evening. The affair with Horst began to torment Graham, since he would not ask his wife for a divorce. The memory of Betty on the English trip, demonstrating her claim to Horst, only suggested that it might happen again. Being near Horst was becoming intolerable for Graham.

Graham's solos, though, "Moon of Love," "Serenata Morisca," "Lantern Dance," and, most importantly, the large-scale "Xochitl," gave her a chance to be seen. One person who saw her and remembered her was the ambitious young director Rouben Mamoulian, who was then, with some dissatisfaction, staging operas at the Eastman School of Music. His dissatisfaction at Eastman would ultimately provide Graham with an opportunity to take an important step in her own career.

The high point of the tour was the return to New York for twelve performances at Town Hall, where a forestage was built to accommodate the productions. In one of the audiences sat John Murray Anderson of the Greenwich Village Follies, who noticed Graham and went backstage to ask Shawn about her. Anderson was astounded to find out that she was the same apparently hopeless case he had turned down the previous year. Now he wanted to hire her as soon as the tour was over. The offer was opportune. Graham was emotionally frustrated with Horst, who still showed no inclination to divorce his wife, and frustrated professionally, for she was in a company that had its own leading dancer. She accepted Anderson's offer. It was a major decision. She was now on her own.

Graham became the second girl from Denishawn to graduate

into the Greenwich Village Follies. (The first had been Ada Foreman.) As he had done in the past, Shawn let Graham have and use the solos that he had choreographed for her. For some of the dancers who left for other jobs he even prepared new material. It was a farewell present that he always provided.

Though Shawn was not a great choreographer, he had a sense of the theatrical world and what was required to succeed in it, and it always was a source of irritation to him that he received as little recognition from his pupils as he did. "I did it for Martha, I did it for Ada—to help them get booked. And I never expected anything from them. Others always paid a tribute and said, 'This I owe—Papa did this for me. He created these dances and designed my costumes.' [But some others] were altogether too big for their britches and pretended that they were born full-panoplied from the brow of Jove and never owed anything."

This gift, which was real enough, also passed along to the departing dancer a style that had to be overcome before each dancer could achieve his or her individual "voice." The conventions that had determined the direction of Denishawn were those of the second half of the nineteenth century, when exoticism, in the form of Art Nouveau, exerted itself against the machine brutality of the Industrial Revolution. A reaction to the mechanical and the modern, the Denishawn style expressed a yearning for the pieties of a less disturbing time. It was also a luxury that only a secure and affluent society could afford. Enveloped by an exoticism that derived from the use of the legends and myths of the Near and Far East, ancient India, and the Americas, the Denishawn style had a dazzling glamour that floated on the surface of the time like an iridescent film on water. It was the wave of a peacock fan caressing a gold throne on which a god or goddess contemplated the mysteries of life. Sumptuously costumed, bedecked, and bejeweled, it drew on the "lore of the ancients" and wrapped itself in clouds of sexy secrets. It behaved according to the rules of a passing age and did not have any relevance to the immediate here and now—nor did it wish to.

Art Nouveau, with its sinuosities—bending inorganic materials into organic living forms, forcing metal to become like roots or leaves, or glass to take on the shapes and colorations of flowers—was mildly perverse in its attempt to thwart the steady development of the machine and blunt its thrust. It was an attempt to effect a finesse through glamorous skill rather than brute intellectual strength. In literature, decadent aristocrats played unholy games with the dark powers, and musicians like Scriabin created lofty but vague mystical music inspired by one or another of the then current philosophies of feeling.

Denishawn emerged clothed in the conventions of this mode of expression and did not change significantly during the course of its history. To the end of her days, Ruth St. Denis would perform solos like the "White Nautch," and Shawn would spin mystically in "The Mevlevi Dervish." This was the cocoon out of which modern dance emerged. It was able to do so because Denishawn and its founders were seriously concerned with developing dance as an expressive art form. They saw that the natural process had been obstructed by the cast of tradition that ballet had thrown over dance. They felt that new dance forms could be established that would frame serious concerns better than could classical ballet. Though strongly influenced by folk dances of the world (that is, by the past), Denishawn was the first systematic and sustained attempt to provide in Western theater dance a substantial alternative to ballet. It was also the first to find a means of passing the discipline to others.

In its concept, Denishawn was a form of protest. All of the major talents who entered the modern dance field have continued its pattern of protest and reformation. Thus when Graham, and later Doris Humphrey and Charles Weidman, decided that they could no longer subscribe to the conventions of Denishawn, they left with the idea of going beyond them and creating an entirely new language and form of dancing in order to express the ideas that were of the utmost concern to them.

For all its now unreal romanticism, it was in Denishawn that Graham, Weidman, and Humphrey learned the rudiments of their craft. They also gained from it a grounding in theatricality and a sense of professionalism about meeting commitments and preparing themselves for the public. In the developing course of American dance, it is significant that other dance soloists like Isadora Duncan, Loie Fuller, and Maud Allen, who enjoyed successes similar to those of St. Denis, were unable to provide a similar line of succession. The credit for this continuity belongs mostly to Shawn. Though the line of creative development owes more to St. Denis than to Shawn, it was Shawn's ability to organize and teach that gave the substance form. Without Shawn it is likely that little of a lasting nature would have come from St. Denis's efforts, any more than from the efforts of the other dance soloists of her generation.

In Graham's case, of course, it was St. Denis who made the greatest impression. Graham spent much of her early career imitating St. Denis's Orientalisms. Later in life she often patterned her teaching methodology on St. Denis's languid delegation of authority to assistants. She also demonstrated a similar sympathy for the handling of stage properties. St. Denis repeatedly attempted to push Graham aside artistically; Shawn helped Graham to advance her career significantly. Yet, curiously, it was St. Denis whom Graham adored and Shawn whom she dismissed.

3

Becoming Martha Graham

"I worshipped her. She was all tension—lightning. . . .
Miss Graham was the modern."
Bette Davis

Graham was hired for the fifth annual edition of the Greenwich Village Follies. It opened on September 20, 1923, and featured a curtain painted by Reginald Marsh and a sketch, "Three Girls and a Fellow," starring the comedian Joe E. Brown. Like the previous revues in the series, this one was assembled with Anderson's usual relentless pacing, and it ran successfully.

Graham's work did not go beyond what she already had done: The romanticism of Denishawn was good preparation for Broadway. The work was not especially taxing, and it had the further advantages of extricating her from a deep frustration and, no small matter, bringing in a comfortable income. Her position in the Follies made her self-sufficient, and it gave her at least the possibility of a future. It would take a full two years in the Follies for her to realize that she didn't really want the life she was enjoying. What seemed to be a sweet temporary expedient eventually began to have a bitter taste. The girl who had stalked out of her own graduation recitation at Cumnock School sooner or later would leave the Follies.

Graham appeared in two numbers. In "Spanish Fiesta," a loosely strung-together series of four pieces, the show-dancing team Elisa and Eduardo Casino (parents of Rita Hayworth) did three of the pieces and Graham did the fourth—her Denishawn solo, "Serenata Morisca." In "The Garden of Kama," the second number and a more elaborate affair with five dancers, two storytellers, and a singer, she was one of the dancers. The dances, in the terminology of the day, were "arranged" rather than "choreographed" by Michio Ito, and the lead song, which set the Oriental flimflam style, was "Pale Hands I Loved Beside the Shalimar." Ironically, "The Garden" dealt with the same subject as the first joint work ever produced by Shawn and St. Denis. Also called "The Garden of Kama," it had its premiere eight years previously in San Francisco, a year before Graham began studying at Denishawn. The incorporation of such a number in a Broadway variety show, though it filled what was then known as the "art spot," is a sign of just how close to "show business" much of Denishawn was. It helps explain, too, the ease with which some Denishawn dancers could move to Broadway.

The reviewers of this production were kind. In one review, Graham was featured in a flattering cartoon. Another splendidly compared her to Ruth St. Denis. No one seemed to realize that the sexy little Oriental-style dancer was really twenty-nine, and not a dewy twenty. It was part of her force.

Graham rented a studio apartment in Greenwich Village, then in its bohemian heyday. Once established in New York, she began to explore the city and naturally visited a bookstore located near the theater district. Its owner, Frances Steloff, had worked in the drama section of Brentano's for a dozen years and was sympathetic to theater people. She liked their warmth and had acquired a large following of them. When she decided to open her own bookstore, the Gotham Book Mart, she moved as close to the theater district as possible. In the early years of the store, she would remain open until 11 P.M. to accommodate customers from the various shows who could visit her only at that time.

In addition to an extensive stock of costume and design books, the Book Mart had sections on Eastern speculative philosophy and theology. Graham was attracted to this general subject; it was one of the interests that had drawn her to St. Denis. While browsing at the store, she struck up an acquaintance with Steloff and found that the bookstore owner shared her interest. From this beginning, their acquaintance ripened into friendship.

The next season's Follies was much the same, with Graham still dancing roles that were little different from those she had done with Denishawn. It was clear that her step forward into independence also carried the possibility of leading to a cul-de-sac. Stark Young, who was to write most appreciatively of Graham's artistry at a later date, did not notice her in the new edition of the Follies. He thought, though, that the music of Cole Porter and the unity of the production as a whole promised well for its success, even though he personally found the sheer volume of acting, singing, and dancing hard to encompass.

Shortly before Graham entered the Follies, two men who would ultimately provide her with the opportunity to take perhaps the most decisive step in her career were at work quite independently of each other, one in upstate New York and the other in London. George Eastman of the Kodak Company in Rochester was an energetic industrialist who built a good idea into a personal fortune. He was in many respects quite an ordinary man. In recalling him years later, contemporaries found it difficult to describe him physically. He seems to have struck everyone as average in size, manner, and dress. But he had a passion for music, and his wealth and native organizing abilities had led him to establish the Eastman School of Music.

While Eastman's chief interest was chamber and orchestral music, he also had a fondness for opera. After the Eastman School of Music was already in operation, he decided to establish a department that would include training in the staging of operatic productions. On the advice of Vladimir Rosing, a teacher on the school faculty, and George Todd, the chairman of the board of trustees, Eastman asked the theater director Rouben Mamoulian, then unknown in the United States, to head the opera production department. Eastman had never seen any of Mamoulian's work.

Mamoulian, an Armenian Russian, had entered the theater world in London in 1919, when, at the age of twenty, he worked on a musical revue there. Originally from Tiflis, he was visiting his sister in England when the Russian Revolution of 1917 broke out.

Deciding not to return home, he started his career in England. With mammoth confidence and enough skill to back it up, he prospered and soon was directing dramas. By 1921, he found himself with a success, *The Beating on the Door,* which was followed by an attractive invitation from Jacques Ebertot, a major French producer, to visit Paris.

Ebertot took one look at the young Mamoulian and asked where his father was. Only after Mamoulian established that he indeed was the director of the London production Ebertot had admired did the French producer explain his grand scheme to establish a repertory company with three directors, Louis Jouvet, Fyodor Komissarjevski, and a third yet to be determined. For this third position he was considering Mamoulian.

While Ebertot pondered, Mamoulian enjoyed the sights of Paris. In his mail one day was a dramatically long telegram from George Eastman outlining his plans for a department of opera production and inviting Mamoulian to participate. The job would pay reasonably well, the offer was firm, and would include two months' vacation in New York each year with full pay. Being accustomed to the short, almost codelike transmissions common in Europe, Mamoulian found the foot-long message—not so common in the United States either—overwhelming. It concluded: "You must answer yes or no right away and if yes you must sail within two weeks. George Eastman."

In Paris, if offered the job with Ebertot, Mamoulian would obviously be the junior member of the triumvirate; in America he would be an equal partner with Vladimir Rosing. It was an offer that could not be declined. Mamoulian's experience with opera was nonexistent, but his confidence was boundless, and so he set sail for New York.

During his crossing on the S.S. *Homeric,* he met his "first cowboy." The man twirled a lariat while talking, chewing gum, and doing tricks. "He was so witty and so wise, so intelligent, that my heart fell. I thought, 'Where am I going if a cowboy is like this?' One thing he said was, 'I always wondered why the British drink so much tea. Now I know because I've tasted their coffee.' It took me seven or eight months to find out that the cowboy's name was Will Rogers and to learn who Will Rogers was!"

Mamoulian was hired only to stage opera, but he quickly wearied of the restrictions that this job imposed on him and sought ways to expand his activities. He wanted a type of production that would combine all of the theater arts of singing, acting, and dancing. Accordingly, he asked to meet with Eastman for the purpose of proposing the establishment of yet another department.

The meeting was a confrontation between two bold entrepreneurs. Eastman agreed to see Mamoulian in the latter's tiny office on the fourth floor of the music building. As usual, Eastman arrived promptly, announcing, "You have fifteen minutes, Mamoulian." Mamoulian protested. Eastman, squinting at the watch he carried in his vest pocket, observed, "You have thirteen minutes left." At this point Mamoulian announced that the situation was impossible and that, since Eastman was going on a six-month safari, it looked as if the whole project was finished before it could get off the ground. Eastman slammed his hand on the table, "Are you arguing with me, Mamoulian?" To this the showman-entrepreneur Mamoulian responded, "Yes!" The gamble worked. Eastman gave Mamoulian his time, and the result was the founding of the Eastman School of Dance and Dramatic Action. After Eastman's climb up the four flights to Mamoulian's office, the music building also got an elevator.

To run the Department of the Dance, Mamoulian hired Esther Gustafson and Martha Graham. Mamoulian had first seen Graham on her last tour with Denishawn, the same tour that brought her to the attention of John Murray Anderson and the one during which she herself had been so unhappy. When the company played at the Eastman Theater in Rochester, Mamoulian had been impressed with the quality of Graham's dancing. She was by no means the lead dancer, but she had a quality that he believed he could make use of in the scheme he then was beginning to form about theatrical production. He made a note of her name and saw her again in New York when Graham appeared in her second year with the Follies.

By selecting Graham and Gustafson, Mamoulian was hedging his bets somewhat. In Graham he had a performer of dramatic intensity, and in Gustafson a dancer who utilized the Greek veils and flowing movements that Isadora Duncan had developed. Between the two he could pretty well cover the field of contemporary dancing. Because the established ballet vocabulary did not accommodate itself to his developing ideas about stage movement, Mamoulian did not want a highly trained ballet dancer.

The offer appeared to be precisely what Graham thought she now needed. For some time she had felt that unless she left the Follies she would compromise her own artistic convictions. She did not want to be simply an interpretive dancer, whether in the Follies or elsewhere. Her desire was to express *herself* and her own life. This was to be the model of her art. She needed to create, shape, and control the dances she performed, and to perform these dances she needed to invent a way to move her body so that, through gesture and dance-design, she could objectify the gravity and enthusiasms of her sensibility.

Graham, much like St. Denis, was not fond of teaching, but Mamoulian's offer apparently presented her with the opportunity to have a studio and pupils, and the time to work on her own emerging sense of what dramatic dance movement should be. To extricate herself from the Follies, she had already agreed to be on the faculty of a school that John Murray Anderson and Robert Milton were opening in New York in November. (On its glamorous opening night Noël Coward played and sang, and Graham and Ito performed.) The Anderson-Milton School would offer a curriculum of stagecraft, diction, acting, and dance movement, and the position would give her a secure income. The Eastman position seemed to provide just those additional options that she wanted. Now she could begin to create a dance style that was exclusively her own. She agreed to teach full time at the Eastman School in September and October. After that, because of her position at the Anderson-Milton School, she would commute from New York City for only three days every two weeks.

The decision to leave the Follies and Broadway with the aim of creating her own dance works broke the trajectory of Graham's Denishawn-influenced career. She was no longer an entertainer; she was now something else—a dedicated artist. From this point forward, her whole life was to be dominated by her commitment to dance. Everything else—personal comfort, relations with other people—was to take second place. Whenever a conflict occurred between her personal life and her artistic life, the matter would always be resolved in favor of her career. Relentless choreographic accomplishment became her life and sustained her life.

Graham's immediate objective now was to find dancers with whom she could form a company.

The classes that Graham taught at Eastman included students of widely mixed levels of competence, since it was Mamoulian's idea that everyone in the school, whether actor, singer, or dancer, must learn everything. In addition to teaching, Graham also choreographed dances for daily live entertainment that included music, films, and dance. A typical program started with an overture played by a ninety-member orchestra, followed by a newsreel and a soloist, who would sing or play an instrument. After this there would be a feature-length Hollywood film, and then a live production number presented by the students. Since Graham's schedule was full, and since Mamoulian himself chose the thematic line of the shows, Graham found herself choreographing pieces on order and very much in the style of Denishawn. When she began splitting her time between New York and Rochester, she was so pressed that she gave her old Denishawn solo, "Serenata Morisca," to Thelma Biracree, one of the dancers, though the program omitted any choreographer credit.

In Graham's classes, although the demands on her time were such that she did not really have the opportunity to do just as she would have liked, it was clear nonetheless that she was beginning to explore dancing with an eye to forming her own vocabulary of movement. Because of the pressures of time, her enthusiasm for the Eastman teaching position slowly eroded during the year. The pieces that she was doing—"Danse Arabesque," and dances for Mamoulian productions such as "A Corner in Spain," "The Flute of Krishna," and "Dance of the French Dolls"—were revue dances and dances that other people wanted her to do. She had come to Rochester precisely to escape from the artistic dictates of others. So, despite her initial expectations, the Eastman School essentially perpetuated her previous situation. The other staff members did not seem to understand that she wanted to create dances that would stand alone, on their own merit, and not be included in a mixed program of entertainment.

Some members of her class, however, responded to Graham's driving intensity and ambition and to the near-magic aura of inspiration that she was beginning to create around her. These young women, Thelma Biracree, Evelyn Sabin, and Betty MacDonald, became thoroughly enmeshed with Graham's emerging aesthetic. They understood that their previous balletic-based dance training did not prepare them to understand what she was doing. Graham explained patiently and corrected endlessly. In order to be able to create dances designed to express her own personal vision, she had to work with dancers committed to her own aesthetic and able to endure the demands she would make upon them. Thus it was that when she formed her own company it was with Biracree, Sabin, and MacDonald.

The drive that consumed Graham had also seized Louis Horst. By 1925, two years after Graham had left Denishawn, the three extensive Mayer tours covering the entire country and parts of Canada had made the company enormously successful. But Horst had decided to explore his own musical talent, which he could not do on a heavy concert touring schedule. So, at the end of the third tour, he left the Denishawn Company and, in the summer of 1925, went to Vienna to study composition. It was a logical place for Horst, with his German parentage, his knowledge of German, and his sympathy for Germanic culture, which extended to a fondness for beer, cigars, and dachshunds.

Graham had resumed contact with Horst and had seen him before he left. When Frances Steloff and David Moss, her partner and husband, decided to visit Vienna on a buying trip for the bookstore, Graham gave them Horst's address and a cloth cap that he had left behind. By the time Steloff and Moss arrived, Horst had located all the bookstores in Vienna that carried the scenic and costume books they wanted to examine, and thus made the trip a relatively easy and relaxed affair. Horst's efforts were a typical example of his willingness and his generosity in helping others.

St. Denis and Shawn had been very reluctant to let Horst go, and St. Denis wrote to him warmly during his nine-month stay in Vienna about the difficulty they had in replacing him and how much the company missed him. It was a move, though, that Horst had had to make. He had encouraged dancers in the company to strike out on their own, and now he was doing the same.

But Vienna was disappointing. Though the food and atmosphere of the city were congenial and he gained a great deal of weight, the instruction in the school Horst attended was far too conservative for his taste and hardly extended beyond the work of Brahms. More critically, composition did not seem to be the avenue for which his talents best suited him. He soon realized that his most adventurous work had been with dancers.

Graham had been corresponding with Horst in the meantime. Each now had come to a crossroads: Graham had to free herself of Rochester to do her work, and Horst had to face the fact that he was not going to compose works sturdy enough for independent concert performance. It seemed clear that a great deal could be gained by each of them if they were to join forces. Horst was instinctively sympathetic to dance movement and knew that he had done some of his best work as a musical director. Graham, for her part, had much to learn about musical structure and form, and as she proceeded on her own career she would need a musical adviser and accompanist. Horse believed that she had great talent. Beyond all this, there also was the emotional bond between them. In the end, Horst abandoned his musical studies in Vienna and returned to the United States to join Graham in New York. He was still married, and his wife was living in San Francisco.

Horst was fond of saying that an artist, like a plant, needs a wall to grow against; he became Graham's wall. He believed in her talent and encouraged her to develop it. He provided her with sound information about music and art; he introduced her to young composers and induced them to work with her under her conditions. He eventually even rehearsed her Group when she was unable to. He was loyal. And, in addition to being her intellectual sounding board, he was her emotional shelter.

Graham's and Horst's decision to form a working partnership helped to determine the course of dance history. Shortly thereafter, on April 18, 1926, Graham gave her first independent dance recital, with Horst accompanying her. She was thirty-two years old. He was forty-three.

There was very little money available for their first concert, though Horst had taken a job at the Anderson-Milton School as a class accompanist, and Graham had her combined salaries from Rochester and Anderson-Milton. There was no money, however, with which to rent the theater or pay the dancers, even though Graham was getting the theater at cost from the producers of the Follies, A. L. Jones and Morris Green (who saw little chance that this modest dance recital could ever make its expenses and, in effect, told Graham to return to the Follies after her fling), and even though the dancers—Biracree, Sabin, and MacDonald—none over twenty-one, were so dedicated to Graham that they were delighted to work for expenses only. Indeed, their devotion was sometimes adoration. MacDonald and Sabin would gather and save the ravelings from Graham's teaching costume. As St. Denis was to Graham a figure of near reverence, so she appeared to many in her own company. And to others. Something "burned" within Graham, and many already had recognized it in different ways: Shawn, Anderson, Mamoulian, Horst, her three young dancers. Unexpectedly, the money to pay the theater rental and the other expenses came from Frances Steloff, who borrowed $1,000 at a high rate of interest and gave it to Graham. It was an act of faith, for she had never seen Graham dance.

When Graham brought her dancers to New York from Rochester, she worked them even harder than before. For the young women it was an adventure. A week before the day of the concert, Biracree, Sabin, and MacDonald took a late Saturday night train from Rochester after the last of the shows at Eastman Auditorium and arrived in New York on Sunday morning, expecting to be met at Grand Central Station by Graham and Horst. Neither was there. After waiting in the station for a while, they decided to go down to Graham's apartment-studio at Tenth Street and Fifth Avenue. Excited and feeling frivolous, they took a taxi, and finding no one at home, they walked up Fifth Avenue to Child's restaurant where they had breakfast. Returning to the apartment once more, they still found no one at home.

Graham and Horst had in the meantime arrived at the station, and, not finding the young women, started checking to see whether they might have caught a later train or, if not, to find out what had happened to them. Graham was tremendously agitated. Her first concert was a week off and she had *lost* her company. The humor of the situation escaped her. She and Horst took a bus back to Tenth Street, where they found the three women waiting. To one of them, Graham resembled a volcano in her fury. The girls didn't blame her—they had been slightly naughty.

Graham took them to the Marleton Hotel on Eighth Street, just off Fifth Avenue, where they stayed, and then for the rest of the week worked them relentlessly at the studio. The work was almost continuous. Biracree, Sabin, and MacDonald responded to the aura that Graham generated about herself. Never had they encountered such a total dedication which subsumed everything else. They worked hard in an attempt to match Graham's own restless energy, pausing from time to time only for a snack, rarely a solid meal. At the time Graham existed on brioches and coffee, and the three dancers received the same; but during one rehearsal for a piece called "Danse Languide," in which they lay on the floor and worked, their stomachs ached so for food that Graham broke the rehearsal to take them out, finally, to eat a full meal in a nearby restaurant.

Horst played for the rehearsals and the concert, and Graham designed everything, including the lighting, putting into practice what she had learned at the Cumnock School. As she was to do for years, she not only designed the costumes but sewed them. In fitting each of the dancers, she created a "fleshing" undergarment, like a leotard, which they could wear through the various costume changes. Graham made this garment from a tube of Italian silk. After pinning it at the shoulder, she cut out the arm holes and then pinned the tube very tightly along the dancer's body, nipping it in at the crotch.

By the end of the first week the dancers were ready. Wanting to give Graham a memento as an expression of their feeling for her, they bought her a carnelian necklace, spending much more than they could afford. They had the date of the concert engraved on the back, along with the inscription, "To Miss Martha with Love." Graham was so pleased and touched that she wore the necklace as part of her costume in one of the dances.

Mamoulian came down from Rochester for the concert, as did a group of students from Eastman; Anderson, along with members of his and Milton's school, also attended. In the audience, too, were some who would soon thereafter become her pupils and one, Martha Hill, who would become her advocate and champion and who would get modern dance accepted in schools all over the country. In later years Graham was to refer to all the dances she had created for this and other early concerts as "childish things, dreadful." The concert might have been "dreadful," but it changed the course of dance in the twentieth century.

The program, consisting of eighteen pieces, was in the shadow of Denishawn. One of Graham's solos, for example, "Tanagra," despite music by Erik Satie (the influence of Horst, who had included Satie even in Denishawn programs at a time when the composer's name, let alone his music, was unknown in the United States), was in the Denishawn style of Oriental lyricism. The costuming and appointments were elaborate throughout: a chiffon shift, a gold kimono, poppies in Graham's hair, an orange-and-black-striped robe, tapestry fabric, a décor of brilliant lacquer. Graham deliberately emphasized the exotic look that she had used successfully in Denishawn. In "Maid with Flaxen Hair," with music by Debussy, she wore a blond wig with pigtails—extraordinary for a woman who soon would be described as severe enough to give birth to a cube. Graham designed a dance for MacDonald, Sabin, and Biracree that set them melting from one pose into another in silhouette as Horst played Debussy's "Arabesque No. 1" on the piano. What was new and distinctly Graham's was the intensity of the "Gypsy Portrait," and, more than anything else, what was new was the general seriousness of intent. There were indications of new movements that Graham would eventually devise in the quick little tripping steps of "Three Gopi Maidens." It was impressionism but with muscles.

To some onlookers Graham was "modern." An anonymous *New York Times* critic, who reviewed the concert in a notice of scarcely more than a hundred words (the paper did not yet have an assigned dance critic, and the naming of one in the following year, 1927, would signal an important change in the status of contemporary dance), dispassionately commented that "Martha Graham gave an evening of interpretive dance to . . . modern music." Among these moderns, along with Satie, Manuel de Falla, Marcel Bernheim, Cyril Scott, and Eugene Goossens, were Brahms, Schumann, Franck, Schubert, Debussy, Scriabin, Ravel, and Rachmaninoff. The reviewer praised Graham for her ability to create beautiful images and pictures and for her lyrical talent, and mildly chastised her for her lack of power.

But an audience had turned out. Graham had a following, and the concert surprisingly paid its own way. At the very least, Graham was saved from having to hear someone say, "I told you so."

A second concert was given in Rochester the following month, on May 27. Graham derived considerable satisfaction from presenting and appearing in a concert of her own work at a place where previously she had been strictly a teacher. On this occasion she included some of her male pupils in the concert, choreographing a suite from Gluck's "Alceste" to include four couples in addition to herself. Sabin, Biracree, and MacDonald danced the roles they had in New York, and Jean Hurvitz, Robert Ross, Harold Kolb,

Harold Conkling, and Henry Riebeselle were added to fill out the company. Not until ten years later did Graham again work with male dancers.

With these two concerts, Graham began to achieve what, on her departure from the Follies, she had been determined to accomplish. Her task now was to establish the conditions that would enable her to continue. Her school year in Rochester was almost over. In June she created some dances for Mamoulian's production *A Corner in Spain,* the last of her work in Rochester. Mamoulian, whose ambition and restless temperament had brought him from Tiflis to London and Paris, now left Rochester for New York to direct *Porgy* for the Theatre Guild. Graham left as well. Dance diversions for variety shows in Eastman Auditorium were not her idea of dance.

Having left Rochester, Graham might have returned to the theatrical world that supported Denishawn and the Follies. She obviously could succeed there, and the financial return was substantial. At the time that Graham barely broke even with her first concert, Denishawn was receiving $3,500 a week for concert appearances and had definitely graduated into a major theatrical event from the two- to four-a-day shows of vaudeville. But it was not the direction for Graham. She was on a path of her own, in effect inventing the road she was traveling on as she proceeded. At an age when most careers had set their course, Martha Graham was just starting hers. She wanted to create dances out of a new dance vocabulary, to articulate what dance had not yet articulated. Her first concerts were over; she had a small group of student dancers to work with; Horst was at her side.

Graham returned to New York to continue private teaching and choreographing and to teach at the Anderson-Milton School. Money would be a problem for years to come. Graham did not even have the $500 that Shawn demanded if a teacher wanted to become established as a Denishawn instructor. Impoverishment was simply one of the conditions that Graham accepted as part of her private and working life.

Although the instruction in its various disciplines was sound, the atmosphere of the Anderson-Milton School, as one might expect, was unorthodox. In the administrative offices on the top floor someone painted footprints across the ceiling, and one of the staff kept a pet duck in the bathroom. Horst, who was fond of clowning, once puffed his bulky way up to the fourth-floor offices to buss Virginia Lee on the cheek. Laughingly told to get out, he reversed direction, and, pretending seriousness, descended immediately to the ground floor.

The school had classes in acting and ballet as well as in Graham's style of modern dance. Though he played for both the modern and ballet classes, Horst hated ballet. Virginia Lee, who earlier had taken lessons from Graham during Denishawn's brief stay in New York in 1922, recalled Horst eating peanuts at the piano when he played for the ballet classes. She also noticed at this time a change in Graham's bearing and style of teaching. Earlier Graham taught graceful Denishawn movement, with its modified ballet barre and center floor work. Now she demonstrated harder and more forceful movement and was definitely moving away from any suggestion of balletic grace.

Now, as always, Graham exerted the luminous force that drew so many to her. One of Graham's early pupils was actress Bette Davis, who recalled:

> I worshipped her. She was all tension—lightning. Her burning dedication gave her spare body the power of ten men. If Roshanara [an Indian dancer who appeared in New York in the 1920's] was a mystic curve, Miss Graham was a straight line—a divining rod. Both were great, and both were aware of the universal. But Miss Graham was the modern.
>
> I had already learned that the body via the dance could send a message. Now I was taught a syntax with which to articulate the subtleties fully. She would, with a single thrust of her weight, convey anguish. Then, in an anchored lift that made her ten feet tall, she became all joy. One after the other. Hatred, ecstasy, age, compassion! There was no end once the body was disciplined. What at first seemed "grotesque to the eye" developed into a beautiful release for both dancer and beholder.

What was readily communicated in the classroom, however, was not so readily understood on the stage, as Graham was to find out when she attempted to educate the eyes of concert audiences in that form of "grotesque" dancing which she felt was proper for the third decade of the twentieth century. Bette Davis once secured a role in a Broadway play because she had learned from Graham's classes how to fall down a flight of steps without injury. But Graham herself endured one-night stands in her own and others' productions for years.

There were two major influences on Graham at this transitional period. The first was Central European expressionist dance as Graham understood it from books and pictures that Horst had brought back from Germany. Among the most forceful of the expressionist dancers to emerge after World War I was the German Mary Wigman, with her somber dark costumes and percussion-accompanied dances. She and other choreographers had made a break with the exotic dancing of the past, as well as with ballet, and were attempting to establish a style of dance that would speak directly and forcefully to the time, to its disillusionment and privation. This was exactly what Graham wanted to do in her own art, and with her pupils she studied the pictures of Wigman's work.

The second influence was the dancer Ronny Johansson. The dancers in New York kept close watch on one another, and Shawn invited Graham to a demonstration that Johansson was giving at the Denishawn studio. This recital was also an audition, for Johansson wanted Shawn to include her on a company tour of the Orient. Shawn did not care much for Johansson's dancing and remarked to Weidman that he thought her movements were heavy. Weidman suggested that perhaps that was exactly the effect that she was striving for. Shawn did not invite Johansson to join the company at this time, but did later when Denishawn lost Humphrey and Weidman. Meanwhile, another aspect of Johansson's demonstration caught Graham's eye—her use of the floor. She was not the first person to sit on the floor to teach a dance class—Ruth St. Denis had also done that—but Johansson opened Graham's eyes to the possibility of mastering the control of the torso while seated and continuing the class in a standing position only after this was done. As Graham ultimately evolved the technique, her students would settle into the floor with legs spread at a wide angle and begin to work with their arms and torsos, carving out an area of space around them that they could control. It was Graham's eventual belief that once this mastery of the torso came to the student, then there would be no problem of balance. The back and the pelvis therefore became the source of strength for the Graham dancer.

Graham thought nothing of holding rehearsals for nine months in order to put on a single weekend of concerts or, at times, a single

Ruth St. Denis.

The Cumnock School, c. 1914–15.

Top: Martha at right, posing with school friends. *Left and above:* Martha in costume for "Trelawney of the Wells."

Martha Graham as Xochitl.

Above: Dance class (1925) at Eastman School of Dance and Dramatic Action, Rochester, New York. Martha Graham in dress, right front.

Below: Martha Graham and the Trio at time of first New York concert (1926).

Above left: "Three Poems of the East" (1926)
Above right: "Serenata Morisca" (1921).
Left: "Lucrezia" (1927).

Early Graham roles.
New York, 1920's.

Introducing the Group: "Heretic." New York, 1929.

"Heretic" (cont'd).

performance. If she was interested in jumping movements, then jumping became the center of her creative work, and at her next concert the audience witnessed a great deal of jumping. She developed her vocabulary in company rehearsals and tested it in dances. This way of working obviously was for the dedicated and not for those who had a taste only for performance.

The three dancers who were part of Graham's early trio decided that they wanted much more performance work and therefore drifted away to accept more public engagements. "Pretty little things and smart as traps," Graham later described them. Other dancers, however, came to fill their places—others who were willing to subsist on whatever they could earn as waitresses, secretaries, or teachers, and then to drop everything when Graham needed them. Rehearsals were held mostly in the evenings so as not to conflict with daytime jobs. The dancers would dutifully trudge to the studio to rehearse after a day's work, and occasionally they would even forgo their jobs if, for some reason, a rehearsal was called during the day. Rehearsals would sometimes last until midnight and were almost never called off on the Christmas and New Year's holidays.

Each dancer was paid a token $10.00 for performances, which were few and far between. What was obviously driving them all was dedication to an ideal. It wasn't dance in the theatrical sense, it was a crusade, with Graham its extraordinary, divinely touched leader; and like true believers, the more Graham's dancers were scoffed at, the more fervent was their dedication to the cause. Being without money had its drawbacks, but zeal made up for most of them.

Graham at the time worked only with women dancers. Whatever else might be said about this, technically speaking, women were all her creative objectives needed. Her concern at this period was formal: to develop a dance vocabulary appropriate to her ends. For this she did not need either the tension that exists in male-female dancing or the dramatic possibilities of duets and other conventional dance forms. She was out to create a new language of dance, and the task of exploring its full range of expressive possibilities could come later. Not until the late 1930's, ten years later, would Graham feel ready to confront the drama inherent in a male-female encounter. This early approach had an important consequence for Graham's personal life. Except for Horst, she lived very much in an Amazonian world of vestals, most of whom regarded her with awe.

She continued presenting concerts, giving two in 1926. The

first, at Mariarden in Peterborough, New Hampshire, a summer dance-and-drama festival that Ted Shawn had helped establish, brought her some new private students. At the second, in November, she introduced "Three Poems of the East," which was danced to Horst's first score for Graham. Under Horst's tutelage, she was feeling her way to a time when she would work only to new music and when she would not choreograph to repertory standards. She was feeling her way out of Denishawn.

The work and its emerging technique consumed more and more of her time and energy, and she finally left the Anderson-Milton School altogether and concentrated on her pupils in the evening classes she taught at a newly rented studio residence in Carnegie Hall. Financially her situation was precarious. Every cent was put into her concerts. Her own living was secondary; after a day of teaching she and Horst would walk over to a Horn & Hardart Automat at Fifty-eighth Street and Broadway for as inexpensive a meal as possible. Literally everything she had, her money and her eneregy, was being poured into her work.

It was an extraordinarily vulnerable time in Graham's life. Her one real support was Horst, and she hated to lose track of him even for a short time. He was living at the Hotel des Artistes on West Sixty-seventh Street, north of Carnegie Hall, but he did a great deal of accompaniment work for other dancers and spent many nights out. Sympathetic and charging affordable prices, he played for almost all the new dancers. On one occasion, when he had been playing for Michio Ito and Virginia Lee and was not at home when Graham called, she became frantic. She eventually called Lee's parents at 2 A.M. to find out if they knew where Horst was. Graham's control and balance were precarious, and Horst was the anchor that steadied her life. Doris Humphrey wrote to her parents that before a particular student recital, Graham went through her usual "emotional pyrotechnics, being afraid to invite us [Weidman and Humphrey] and fighting with Louis about it, telling us we couldn't come —and changing her mind, ending by calling at the studio twice and telephoning three times to be sure we were coming."

The path Graham had chosen helped set the direction for others. At Denishawn, when Humphrey and Weidman persisted in doing their own work and not making their own interests subservient to the building of Denishawn, Shawn had made no secret of his displeasure. Humphrey and Weidman had hoped to work within the framework of an enlarged Denishawn umbrella but found they could not. They were asked to leave.

While Shawn was away on the company's long tour of the Orient and, later, when Denishawn appeared in the traveling company of the Ziegfeld Follies tour of 1927–28, the slippage of students from his school increased. Gertrude Shurr, one of the teachers who stayed behind, was taking class from Graham on the sly and even encouraging her own pupils to do the same. Humphrey, who had worked with Shurr when at Denishawn, used her in some of her first independent concerts. A year later, when Shurr told her that she wanted to work with Graham, Humphrey was stunned and did not speak to Shurr for years afterward. The feeling among those who were embarking on their own voyages of creative discovery were intense. Though Graham, Weidman, and Humphrey might all have been part of the same flotilla making war on tradition, they were defiantly independent ships. And Shawn disliked them all for not giving Denishawn the credit he felt it deserved.

Early in 1927, Humphrey, who was in the process of making her break, was taking a two-week vacation in Westport when Graham and Horst came to visit. Though she had never been close to Graham, who had toured with Shawn while she toured with St. Denis, Humphrey was eager to talk with her about the trials and tribulations of being on one's own, away from Denishawn. She found Horst much the same jovial, sentimental person she remembered. Graham, however, had changed. She had given another concert in February and was still developing the persona that she was to present to the world. In the privacy of her lonely nights, she sometimes might be near panic. But in the world she had a far different demeanor. "She's extremely artificial," Humphrey wrote in a letter, "not silly, I mean, but like a hothouse flower that grows best in a hot, moist climate, intensely feminine, not a flaming obvious flower—but a night-blooming thing with a faint exotic perfume." It was a quality that Graham had always had. Now, however, she was systematically projecting a mysterious, faintly lofty aura resembling that of Ruth St. Denis.

Gradually Graham began to evolve the movement language that would be suitable for her work, and two concerts in 1927 and one in 1928 showed the change that was taking place. Along with pieces like "Madonna" and "Fragilité," still derivative of her Denishawn days, she performed "Revolt," "Immigrant," and "Poems of 1917."

The very titles suggest the style that was emerging. In these dances she was beginning to shift her creative attention from the past to the present, to find contemporary subject matter for dance.

The magazine *Dance* still thought of her as an expressionist flower, printing a picture of her in a sari, holding up two feathered fans. The caption under the photograph, which had been taken at the time of her first concert, read: "Martha Graham has developed an intimate comprehension of the characteristic significance of Oriental dance philosophy." Others viewed her differently, and as her work changed Graham became the symbol for the new type of dance that was beginning to catch the public's eye.

The symbol had a large group of detractors. "Revolt" attracted the attention of Fanny Brice, who spoofed both the piece and Graham in a sketch for the Ziegfeld Follies entitled "Rewolt." This was the harbinger of the greater bafflement and abuse that were to come. Graham remarked of these years that she went on stage with a "whip" in her hand. She did not want to please or entertain in the standard fashion but to arouse, alert, and stimulate with serious dance pieces that owed nothing to other forms of traditional dance. What she and the other new dancers often stimulated and aroused, however, was ridicule.

The term "modern dance" came into popular usage around this time. A signal event marking its appearance was perhaps the appointment in 1927 of the first dance critic for a New York newspaper —John Martin, hired by the *New York Times*. It was a step that had been taken not for Denishawn but for the generation of unknowns who emerged from Denishawn. To be accorded the stature of an art form that needed its own specialist reviewer was a major breakthrough. It was a recognition, though, that was confined to New York for the bulk of the next decade, during which Graham was to endure the know-nothing responses and abuse of newspapermen who ordinarily covered music or theater or—God help us!—sports, and who unwillingly took on the assignment of assisting at the birth of an art form. Among the ignorant, Graham preferred the sports writers: "At least they are familiar with movement!"

Once there was a term for the kind of dance Graham and others were doing, it immediately began to stand for the exact opposite of all that "ballet" meant. Where ballet was airborne, defying gravity, modern dance hugged the earth and luxuriated, if the word can be allowed in so spare a mode, in percussive motion. Where ballet was pretty in a decorative sense, modern was stark and aggressively unpretty. Where ballet elegantly pointed its feet to lengthen the line of the leg gracefully, modern kept its feet belligerently at right angles to the leg. Where ballet exalted the possibilities of the pas de deux, modern eschewed lifts and concentrated on keeping both feet firmly on the ground. Where ballet rotated the legs to achieve a position of "turnout" in which the legs are seen in profile even though the dancer is facing forward, modern held the feet parallel with doctrinaire tenacity. Where ballet would dance about kings and princes, modern would celebrate the common man—"Revolt," "Immigrant," "Poems of 1917." For modern dancers themselves, ballet was frivolous and, harshest of words, European. It was not relevant to the twentieth century. Modern was serious, relevant, and American.

Unfortunately, the public of the time did not much like American, and it cared equally little for modern. Any foreign artist or art was considered superior to any American artist or art. This feeling dominated both the art world and the musical world of the symphony orchestra and the opera. Similarly, anyone with European training was given preference by the theatergoing public over anyone with American training. As a result, many American painters, instrumentalists, and singers went to Europe in order to further their careers back home. But this option simply was not open to modern dancers; the art in which they were working did not exist in Europe. Denishawn had been able to go to Europe to collect favorable notices before embarking on an American tour, but it was working within a format familiar to European audiences, which had been extensively exposed to exotic dancers from the Middle and Far East.

The situation was galling for modern dancers. It was irritating enough to find Denishawn playing to large houses, but then to have imported artists from Europe more favorably considered than themselves was even worse. Against Europe and ballet, and such European expressionist dancers as Harald Kreutzberg and Mary Wigman, modern dancers could offer little box-office competition. The new generation was creating an art form out of its native experience, and it was doing so without any public support. Idealistic, it was headed for the poorhouse, and Graham was in the forefront.

Poor from the start, modern dance learned to live without

money. In the matter of renting theaters, dancers, out of necessity, were groundbreakers, as they were with almost everything they did. Far from being able to rent a theater for a week, they usually had enough money for one performance, so they used a theater on the day that its regular tenants were not playing. For the legitimate Broadway houses the dark days were Sunday, but, because of restrictive blue laws, all theatrical activity on the Sabbath was officially frowned on. Modern dancers eventually changed this attitude out of sheer necessity.

Because they rented a theater for only one night, they often found themselves dancing in the course of a play's run, so that the stagehands had to strike the play's set and hang black curtains for the dancers. Though many theater stagehands were not interested in doing this, which presented an extra difficulty, the Guild Theater, later renamed the ANTA, was basically sympathetic and therefore received a great deal of the dancers' business. Unlike Denishawn, which had elaborate scenery, modern dancers relied on costuming and lighting effects to do the work of scenery and decor. With a handful of colored gels they would create an atmosphere of intense drama, romance, or turmoil that was modest in cost. Not until 1935 and her dance "Frontier," almost a decade after her first concert, did Graham use a set in one of her works.

For most dance concerts the musical accompaniment was a single piano, often played by Horst. Sometimes there were three-piece ensembles. Even though many houses used for dance concerts had accommodations for a pit orchestra, the custom was to place the musicians in the wings where they could easily see the dance movement on the stage, rather than put them in the pit with a poor view.

In one way, the removal of modern dance from the possibility of economic viability enabled it to travel farther and faster than would have been possible had it been concerned with commercial stability and attracting large audiences. Heedless of material rewards, modern dancers did not have to make any concessions to the taste of a general audience. They could work to please only themselves and the small, sympathetic coterie that formed around them.

Graham was gradually working toward a new stage in her development, the attainment of a permanent company. As she strove for this goal, she would also dance, when asked, in various projects that, for different reasons—either the money or the opportunity they offered—she found attractive. One such project was the elaborate dance and orchestral pageants produced by Irene and Alice Lewisohn, who had founded the Neighborhood Playhouse, the outgrowth of a social settlement house on New York's Lower East Side. The Playhouse, among other things, gave drama classes to local girls as a means of helping them to develop sufficient poise to get secretarial jobs. Both Graham and Horst taught there.

The Playhouse soon expanded its modern horizons when the Lewisohn sisters decided to put on a series of concerts in the mode of "music visualizations," using the Cleveland Orchestra and recruiting local dancers. This program lasted for three years, from 1928 to 1931. The organization of the concerts was the responsibility of Irene Lewisohn, who engaged the orchestra and the dancers and also was the director of the pageant. She was more of a coordinator than a choreographer. The orchestra, out of sight in the pit, was the responsibility of the conductor. As for the movement on stage, Irene Lewisohn left it up to the dancers to invent their own variations. After these were shown to her, she selected the ones that she considered most suitable. It was choreography by committee.

The idea of music visualization did not originate with the Lewisohn sisters. Ruth St. Denis had created her "Synchoric Orchestra" using dancers, spoken poetry, and Schubert's symphony No. 8 ("The Unfinished") nearly a decade before. But the idea seemed to have more relevance to audiences in the late 1920's and the 1930's, when the form was even taken up by ballet choreographer Leonid Massine in his choreo-symphonies.

The Lewisohns' first program, presented at the Manhattan Opera House, included Bloch's "Israel" (with a sculptured "Wailing Wall" set designed by Jo Davidson), Borodin's "On the Steppes of Central Asia" and "Dances from Prince Igor," and Debussy's "Nuages" and "Fêtes." Charles Weidman was used extensively throughout the program, appearing in nearly every work. Graham was A Passing Cloud Form in "Nuages," in which her earthy stride made Weidman think less of a cloud than a solid woman walking. Despite his response, Graham, who danced with Michio Ito, was received well by the audience.

In the program presented the following year, Graham and Weidman danced the leads in Strauss's "Ein Heldenleben." The Lewisohns again brought the Cleveland Orchestra to New York, and the dancers again put the production together, with Irene Lewisohn directing and selecting the various dancers she wanted. Graham, unhappy with the lead male dancer selected by the Lewisohns, asked for Weidman, her partner from Denishawn days. Graham prevailed, and the two of them set about shaping their roles. Although the production as a whole was not received very well, both she and Weidman drew praise for their work.

But 1929 was far more important for Graham for another reason. She gave three concerts, in January, March, and April, during which she introduced several important pieces—"Adolescence," "Vision of the Apocalypse," and "Four Insincerities"—and in the third concert she introduced her first great dance, "Heretic." At this concert she also introduced an expanded permanent company, which she called "The Dance Group." This was an ensemble with which she could work the year round rather than be constrained by the limitations of working with dancers assembled simply for the occasion of a given concert. Her sister Geordie, who had danced with Denishawn for five years, left St. Denis and Shawn to join Martha in the new Group.

By this time Graham had gone through so many styles of movement that she seemed in danger of having no fixed mode of expression. The bulk of the works she had created were solos, and she changed styles from concert to concert. To the infrequent viewer, it therefore came as a surprise that the Graham of autumn 1928, say, was not the Graham of the spring of 1929. A central impulse, however, controlled all these changes. Basically, the process was the gradual elimination of all that she was most familiar with so that she could work in a new way. Each succeeding concert stripped away a little more of what she had learned at Denishawn. She moved closer and closer to stark simplicity. She purged her own movements of the languid look that was favored in Orientalia. Under the influence of Horst, she discarded the music of older composers in favor of music by her contemporaries. She even experimented with creating dances before the music was composed. She firmly abandoned the fluid costuming of the Denishawn days. The thought of wearing a blond wig with pigtails, as she had in 1926 for "Maid with Flaxen Hair" at the first of her concerts, became unthinkable.

Graham blunted gestures and took away romantic ornaments and the embellishments of fluttering fingers or arms drifting out and up. She taught her girls to place themselves in a secure position with ears, shoulders, and pelvis in line so that the slight tilt of the head would give an anticipatory look to the body. Every movement was designed to grow organically out of the one that preceded it, and always Graham gave the dancers verbal images to intensify the weight of the movements. They were told at times that they should walk as if chained, or that they should place their feet on a spot to press it flat. The rehearsal was a mini-performance. Graham demanded performance intensity of her dancers in order to achieve the look she was striving for. It was not combinations of steps that she was assembling; it was a world of movement that was being created. For example, she examined the basic breathing rhythm of the body and the changes that take place when a person inhales and exhales. When the breath is out of the body, certain anatomical changes take place; when the breath is in the body, other changes occur. Graham's observations led to the development of the idea of contraction and release, a basic tenet of her emerging system of movement. When the dancer contracts, the front part of the body shortens and the muscles in the back lengthen. When the dancer releases, the muscles in the front lengthen, giving an emotional lift to the body.

In her March 1929 concert, "Adolescence" celebrated these *rites de passage* and firmly indicated that the expressionist-influenced style was all in the past. "Danza," choreographed for the same program, announced the new direction that her work was to take. It was simple, spare, and percussive. Increasingly, she would indicate the force and direction of a movement and not carry it all the way through. By her third concert, in April, when she introduced her Group and premiered "Heretic," the gaunt, tense, and forceful look had permanently succeeded the flowing, opulent one. Ironically, the dance that the audiences responded to most favorably was the older piece, "Tanagra," a solo from her first concert still heavily influenced by the Oriental lyricism of her Denishawn training.

4

A Serious American Dance

"Mellowness is no part of her. The
freshness that is newness
consumes her."
Ben Washer

Unlike Graham's students at Rochester, the members of the Group were not adolescents; they were young women in their twenties who did not, for the most part, have the sleek borzoi look of today's dancer. They were assorted sizes and shapes, but they had in common a quality of sturdiness that tended to make them look more alike than they really were. Graham selected them for the force that they could bring to her work. In the public's mind dancers were light, ethereal creatures. Graham, however, deployed a squad of strong, powerful women who pounded the earth, rebounded from it, and strode rather than glided across it. She created dances that launched these women like battering rams against the stage conventions of her day. Glamour was definitely out. No one dieted. No one wore make-up to heighten the color of the flesh. Instead, the dancers put on dead-white and made a mask out of the face. To emphasize the look, they layered dark shadow under the eyes. The mouth was a gash of red, the hair drawn straight back and held firmly in a net.

During the early days of the Group, costuming was a tubular jersey dress that extended from the neck nearly to the floor. The costumes made little concession to the individual shapes of the dancers, and nothing was done in the way of alterations to flatter the figure. Graham herself fitted and designed the costumes, and the members of the Group were turned out as replicas of herself.

The look of the Group was that of gaunt, iron-willed Puritans. And as the Puritans had hewn living space out of a wilderness, so Graham and her Group would clear artistic space for succeeding generations. The effect on the public and the critics, for the most part, was to startle, irritate, and annoy. Writing in *The New Republic*, Lincoln Kirstein, whose own absorption with creating a contemporary American dance would often put him in opposition to Graham, gave literate expression to the howls that less gifted writers sent up:

> Her jumps are jolts; her walk, limps and staggers; her runs, heavy blind impulsive gallops; her bends, sways. Her idiom of motion has little of the aerial in it, but there's a lot of rolling on the floor. In her group dances there is achieved a rudimentary polyphony, a seesaw of asymmetrical counterpoint. . . . Miss Graham scorns make-up. One is never for a second allowed to forget this is Martha Graham. Those girls are Martha Graham's group. Her long pale mask, her deep eyes, her expression half between pain and foetal blindness has the ambiguous, frightened humor of an idiot's games. This ambiguity is chronic.

In "Heretic," her first work of special genius, Graham cast herself as a solitary figure outside a wall of disapproving others, danced by the Group. The wall of others stood close to the footlights shoulder to shoulder. At the outset Graham stood away from them, alone in a shaft of bright white light. Then she circled them, and several times attempted to break through the wall they formed. The Group, with minimal movement, tightly resisted her efforts. The music for the piece was a short Breton folk tune repeated eight times. The lilting tune was Graham's leitmotiv as again and again she tried to pass through the wall of women. They denied her entrance to their world with an ominous thump of their heels.

The dance had three sections. In each the wall of women defeated the effort of Graham, the outsider, to make a permanent breakthrough. At the start of a section, as Graham approached, the wall swayed as if in recoil from a poisonous infection. In the first two sections, Graham succeeded in breaking through temporarily, but each time the disapproving women regrouped to oppose any further passage. During the silence between each of the movements, the two forces, the human wall and Graham, returned to their starting places. The third and final time the stubborn thump of the heels was the determining force. The final movement of the dance was the outsider's noiseless fall after failing to penetrate the resistance: the heretic condemned.

"Heretic" was the strong opening fanfare for the decade that would produce the Graham style of dance—that asymmetrical and tension-lined vocabulary of movements that became, in the popular mind, synonymous with all that was implied when speaking of modern dance. Everything in the dance was simple, elemental, and done with a blunt, percussive thrust. Transitions between movements were eliminated, and the dance contained only major dynamic bursts of activity. The pauses between the clusters of gesture isolated the events into discrete units that were aspects of the same situation, clumps of movements that had a relational affinity to one another but no bridges to tie them together. For a theatergoing public habituated to dances of sinuous charm, the demanding no-nonsense approach of "Heretic" was an affront—as much an affront, perhaps, as was the outsider in the dance to its wall of women.

In Graham's creative emotions the theme of the outsider and the rebel was to be a source of many dances. "Heretic" was only the first of them. Created with a group of dancers larger than any she had ever worked with, even at Rochester in the School of Dance and Dramatic Action, it was a simple confrontation told in simple terms: stark, disapproving figures, who did not dissemble their opposition with elaborate gesture, slammed their feet into the ground to deny the outsider passage. The very simplicity of the dance was a stumbling block for most of the public in the same way as were the diagrammatic simplicities and the spareness of much contemporary music of the time. The latter was an irritant to the audience's ears, and Graham was an irritant to their eyes.

To anyone who had ever seen Denishawn, Graham's construction of a dance was not only ugly, it was wrong-headed. Denishawn had bowers of gossamer movement for its dancers to perform. It was an impressionistic adaptation of traditional dance structure.

Thus it contained variations for the soloists and a solo for the principal dancer or, more than likely, a duet for two of the principal dancers. Graham rejected the idea of "individualized" dance and concentrated on creating movement for her group *as a group* and not a collection of separate dancers each ready to spin off at a moment's notice to do individual variations. Most of the work that Graham gave the Group was unison dancing that ignored an individual dancer's special qualities. The Group moved like an army, not like feather-footed acrobats hurtling from one balance to another. In the process of developing the Group, Graham created a company of soloist-level dancers, but for a good many years she paradoxically kept her performers tightly bound in formations. Such dancing was a structural crusade, just as the development of cubist space in painting was. And like cubist painting in its early period, this dancing simply did not have time to be pretty. The framework had to be established first before anything else could be done.

The fact that Graham worked only with females was part of the difficulty. The establishment of the all-girl Group removed any possibility of sexual dramatic tension. There could be no dance in which a swooning girl would be caught in strong male arms. If a girl swooned, she fell. This was not a device to elicit response from a waiting lover, it was a simple direct action. But this is what Graham wanted: straightforward movement forcefully expressed. So the wall of dancers expressed their disapproval by the simple finality of slamming their heels on the ground.

In her dances Graham did not attempt to hide effort in the traditional way by having dancers smile after enormous physical exertions, as if to imply that it was all very easy. Graham showed the energetic vitality of her dancers in the most direct way she possibly could.

In each audience there were some who saw dance clearly and with a fresh appreciation of what Graham was attempting to do. Although these people did not appear in numbers large enough to guarantee her a sufficiently large audience to perform more than a few times each year in New York and elsewhere, their numbers slowly grew. One of Graham's early supporters was John Martin of the *New York Times*, who admired the "stark elemental tragedy" in "Heretic," with its "economy of means" and "essences of movement."

Graham's early audiences saw the themes, in embryo, that she was to explore throughout the decade of the 1930's. They were exposed to the mythical side of her work and also to the strain of morality that distinguished harshly between those who conformed to group mores and those who chose a life outside the group. The Puritan energy and vigor of America drove and shaped all of Graham's work, but did not blunt her sense of inquiry.

That same energy drove Graham herself and shaped her day. It started with private creative exploration alone in her studio. She held her first morning class at the Neighborhood Playhouse. Afterward she returned to the studio to teach beginners or intermediate students. These classes usually finished at 7 P.M., and then she worked with her company, often until midnight. Breaks for snacks were taken during the day, but little other time was reserved for a private life. When her own energy flagged, Horst, a methodical disciplinarian, drove her to continue. Graham's public and private lives became almost indistinguishable.

Graham's choice of 1929 as the year in which to assume the responsibilities of a dance company can only be considered bad luck. There were no performances in the summer, although she had done solo work in the spring, and in October the stock market crashed. There was no immediate impact upon her, but soon she and the entire nation began to feel the pinch of privation. Until the country recovered its economic equilibrium, Graham was to lead, even more than ordinarily, a perilous financial life.

The entire field of modern dance was in a fragmented and highly competitive state. Every dancer felt compelled to do a concert of his or her own work. The solo recital had been the starting point for all of the major figures in the field, beginning with Isadora Duncan, Loie Fuller, and Ruth St. Denis. Both Fuller and St. Denis had formed companies around themselves, but the generation that succeeded them went back to the beginning, to start with the solo concert again. Modern dance, it seemed, was condemned to start over in every generation and could not build on the structure of what had preceded it. This thought disturbed some dancers sufficiently to plan a cooperative effort among themselves, and it was these efforts, the motivating force behind which was Helen Tamiris (the stage name of Helen Becker), that led to the formation of the Dance Repertory Theater.

This was not a repertory company in the usual sense—that is, a single group of dancers performing the work of several different choreographers. Given company jealousies, that would have been impossible. Graham, like the others, regarded her choreographic approach as the only valid one, which was the reason that even taking class with another teacher was considered traitorous in the dance world. The repertory group was, instead, a loose but incorporated amalgamation of individual companies that would each perform its own works on a given program, all the companies to share the expense of renting a theater and the cost of publicity and musicians. But this logical step aroused the suspicion of Doris Humphrey, who wrote to her parents expressing doubts about the legal technicalities involved with the season, adding, "besides, I haven't much faith in Martha Graham; she is a snake if there ever was one."

The first week of the Repertory Theater's performances was scheduled for the second week of January 1930, during which Graham was to perform in another of the Lewisohn pageants. The Graham, Humphrey-Weidman, and Tamiris companies formed the original confederation. The Humphrey-Weidman company performed Monday and Thursday evenings; Tamiris took Tuesday and Friday; and Graham appeared Wednesday and Saturday. Intended as a concentrated presentation of the newest trends in dance, the series was offered on a subscription basis, and each company seemed determined to outdo the others in being adventurous.

Graham herself offered two dramatic experiments. The first was a dance without music, "Project in Movement for a Divine Comedy." Her first such effort, it was destined to be her last. Music, she was to say later, is indispensable for bringing "the emotional content of the movement into focus for the spectator."

The second experiment had far more impact and arose from her central concern with the vocabulary of movement. "Lamentation" (music by Zoltan Kodaly) was a startling solo for herself; it was performed entirely while sitting down. The costuming was no less startling: a sheath of stretch jersey cloth, which in the next several years was to become almost a uniform for Graham and her Group. It was cheap and the fabric had great sculptural possibilities that Graham and others later would explore. She was entering what she later laughingly referred to as her "long woolens" period.

In "Lamentation" Graham sat on a low platform and stretched the material of her costume into long diagonal folds, first on one side and then on the other, while she assumed leaning positions that seemed to defy the stability of a seated figure. All that was visible of her body was her two bare feet, her hands, and a narrow expanse of face, such as would be revealed by a traditional nun's habit. "Lamentation" was a dance of anguish, expressed through stress lines on the fabric, much as the passage of emotional waves leave their traces on the lines of the face. In a sense "Lamentation" is another of Graham's "outsider" works: a portrait of an isolated, solitary sufferer. Perhaps more importantly, it is an expression—in its basic concept no less than its realization—of her drive for compression and conciseness. The approach of this dance was a far cry from the frenzied twirling of fine cloth that had signified agitation in the earlier solos.

First reaction to "Lamentation" was mixed, with even strong supporters of previous years considering it distinguished more for costuming than for creativity. It was, however, a piece that Graham wisely kept in her repertory long after other dances had been allowed to drop away.

As usual, Graham maintained a full schedule of activity and her usual full temper. Almost as soon as she had finished introducing her Group, which ended the repertory program, Graham slipped away to the Mecca Auditorium on Fifty-fifth Street to appear with Charles Weidman in the third of the productions organized by Irene Lewisohn, with the Cleveland Orchestra again in the pit. Graham and Weidman's number was Loeffler's "A Pagan Poem." Its rehearsals had not been without incident. In the midst of one, Graham abruptly burst into a fit of anger and left the stage. No one knew why. Irene Lewisohn, to whose habitually slow speech everyone had become accustomed, announced, "Martha . . . is . . . not . . . in . . . her . . . dressing room. . . . And her . . . coat's . . . gone. . . ."

Weidman was left without a partner, and Lewisohn asked him to take over work on the number. Since he had been bothered by the movement of the dance, to be done on a series of upward-leading steps, he welcomed the chance to do the choreography in a way that would be more easy and natural for himself. At the time he was also happy to work with someone other than Graham, someone not as demanding. Years later, all that Weidman could offer as a possible explanation for the walkout was Graham's irritation that day over a poster outside the stage entrance: "Harald Kreutzberg–

World's Greatest Dancer." But as mysteriously as Graham departed, she returned and received favorable notices for her performance.

A new project arose, and Graham was in great conflict about whether to become involved in a production over which she would not have control. After a period of indecision, she accepted. The ballet choreographer Leonide Massine, then choreographing at the Roxy Theater in New York, doing several shows a day and changing productions each month, had agreed to choreograph his second version of "The Rite of Spring" (Stravinsky's "Le Sacre du Printemps") for the Philadelphia Orchestra. Ten years earlier he had done a version in Europe. The conductor of the orchestra, Leopold Stokowski, at the time the *enfant terrible* of music and a promoter of contemporary works, was in the process of creating the reputation of the orchestra over the outraged protests of most of its board members. "The Rite of Spring" had not yet been played in the United States. For the purposes of the ambitious young Stokowski (who previously had conducted American premieres of two earlier Stravinsky works, "L'Histoire du Soldat" in 1928 and "Les Noces" in 1929), a possible Massine-Graham "Rite" was a godsend. It was to be presented on a program that also would include Schoenberg's "Glückliche Hand," which Rouben Mamoulian, Graham's former employer, was brought in to direct. Interestingly, Doris Humphrey was selected to choreograph the movement and dance the part of The Woman in the Mamoulian production of the Schoenberg, and Graham was selected solely to dance the role of The Chosen in Massine's "Rite."

The choice of the two modern dancers makes sense only in the light of Stokowski's passion for the contemporary. Had the decision been, say, Massine's alone, it is unlikely that two such anti-traditional performers as Humphrey and Graham would have been given the central roles. That Graham had been asked to work with established figures such as Stokowski and Massine meant a new kind of recognition for her. Beyond this, the theater as such very much interested her. This was an interest that would grow.

Rehearsals were punctuated with flare-ups between the two powerful personalities of Massine and Graham. She found herself being asked to become more airborne in her dancing. She had spent the last several years getting down on the floor and using it in a new fashion, and now a ballet choreographer was asking her to change.

In her previous dancing with Denishawn and in the Follies, she had not been particularly noted for the height or the balon of her jump. Weidman had never considered her a "leaper or anything like that. She used to do a peculiar sort of hop, a one-legged thing, when she could get off the floor at all." Massine, however, was not going to be satisfied with a hop. If he was to work with Graham, then she would get off the floor. It was not capriciousness but simply the demands of the choreography, which was using ballet vocabulary. Graham worked on it with the fury that she could bring to any problem she wanted to solve. The whole of the production built to the climactic solo that The Chosen—Graham—had at the end of the dance. When Weidman saw the performance he was astounded. "The effect was sensational. She ran and did splits in the air; they were leaps, genuine leaps." By will, innate physical prowess, and the single-minded intensity of her effort, Graham had mastered what was necessary.

Reaction to the production was mixed. Olin Downes, the music critic of the *New York Times*, stated that although he liked some of the movement of the corps of dancers, and even some of the decor (particularly the twilight of the second section), he really would have preferred the music without the dance. He had nothing to say about Graham's performance and, even worse, credited Doris Humphrey with having done Graham's role of The Chosen as well as that of The Woman in the "Glückliche Hand." It seems inconceivable that any observer would have mistaken the two dancers, but the confusion is perhaps explained by the fact that the reputations of Humphrey and Graham had not yet achieved any large public dimensions. Because the appearance of the Philadelphia Orchestra made the event primarily a musical occasion, the *Times* had sent its music critic, whose duties did not require familiarity with the emerging world of modern dance.

The event, however, meant recognition for Graham. Her reputation for innovation had brought her to the attention of Stokowski, and her association with both him and the world-famous choreographer Massine, the lineal descendant of the great Russian ballet companies of Serge Diaghilev, had confirmed her status among the forward-looking. She had proved that her personal skill was not so idiosyncratic that it could not be put to the service of an important cultural event in collaboration with other major talents. In terms of her career, she had taken another step away from her earlier status as an obscure concert dancer.

It was now four years since Graham had started her concert career with a single concert in the 48th Street Theater. In the course of the four years, she had transformed herself into a scourge of the traditional concert dance. She still looked exotic but clearly was not the sort of girl who could float delicately through cherry blossoms. She had the severity of the vestals who guarded a sacred flame. She had worshiped St. Denis as a "goddess" and was beginning herself to encourage a cult. In time she would become the "high priestess" of modern dance, holding out the promise of artistic satisfaction to those who would abandon a personal life and follow her lead. The effect was potent, it was revolutionary; it would also claim its victims, those whose lives became, in effect, extensions of Graham's own powerful will.

Graham, in her work with the Group and in the development and refining of costumes and movement, was a curious mixture of perfection and insouciance. With costumes, for example, she approached the compulsive. Before the opening of any season, the Group dancers would find themselves gathered together to remake completed costumes that supposedly had been perfect. "It was a general rule that if the costumes were finished they weren't right," Sophie Maslow explained. "We were always sitting up most of the night before [a premiere] with Martha, sewing." When working on a costume, Graham preferred to use as a manikin the dancer who would be wearing it. Quite often the final pinning would have to be redone, since much of it would turn out crooked because everyone was so weary. Seeking the perfect costume Graham would continually rearrange its pieces on the stoic dancer, using safety pins to fit everything together. Even the trio of young women from Eastman remember carrying chains of safety pins—"always safety pins, we called them our daisy chain"—and remaking costumes up to the last minute. Graham insisted that each garment look good not only in repose but also in motion. To achieve the right fit, she would have the dancer wear the unfinished costume while performing the movements of the dance for which it was designed. With the later Group, as costuming sessions crept into the small hours of the morning, some of the dancers, like Gertrude Shurr, for example, to ease the tension of the safety pins and needles whipping in and out, would flit around whatever space was serving as the sewing room, doing pseudo-balletic or Duncan-style dancing and replacing tension with laughter.

Yet, perfectionist as Graham was with the costuming, rather like Ruth St. Denis, she oddly had little or no patience for rehearsing dances. With Horst as her accompanist, however, it made little difference, for Horst became her stern surrogate who ensured that the dancers' group movements were done on the count and together. Graham, in effect, expended her dance energy in creating the movement. To a great extent, she expected Horst and her dancers to achieve the finished look for performance. With a work in which unison action was all-important, after the movement had been created Horst would rehearse until each person was at precisely the right place at exactly the same moment. If a replacement dancer joined the Group, then it was up to the other dancers to teach her the part she was responsible for. At that point Horst became the drill master who shaped the whole piece into its proper form. Often Graham, like St. Denis, would recline on a couch just watching.

She sometimes reclined even when creating a dance. She would issue instructions for everyone to follow, and suddenly, in a complete turnabout, would arise and launch into a most complicated series of movements, do them once, and then expect the Group to repeat them. Ironically, she was, of course, repeating another of the experiences that she had encountered with St. Denis.

As for the basic technique itself, Graham was heedless of anything but what she was immediately interested in. When she was in the process of working with one type of movement, she left the dancers to do whatever else they needed to take care of themselves technically. If Graham was concentrating on percussive movement, rehearsals stressed percussive movement all year and the dancers had sore thigh muscles all year. Not until much later did the classes become more rounded and include elevation, turns, the floor, and center-floor combinations.

Graham sought to create an appreciation of organic movement logic. The carbon copy placement of the body so as to approximate mental images was not her concern. Graham demanded that her dancers think. It was never a question of moving from one pose to another to achieve a finished "picture." Each movement was to evolve out of the movement that came before. The torso was the source of the motor energy, and the spine was the supple spring that was the core of the torso. A movement had to come out of the depths of a dancer and not be imposed from the outside, and the body was launched as if into a resistant medium that had to be thrust aside to allow the movement to have its amplitude and force. Graham's dances were designed to grow out from the inside, like an organic force seeking its proper shape. To achieve the proper degree of understanding, Graham would ask her dancers to think of the "sensation" of the movement—"What went on, what the feel of it was inside the body. When we rehearsed," Jane Dudley has recalled, "Martha was absolutely merciless. I never 'walked' anything." No one "walked" through Graham rehearsals, or if they did they did not last in the Group. Graham was unsparing of herself and equally so of her dancers, who for their part responded with an enormous output of energy, as if driven by some terrific pressure. The energy was apparent at performances in the particular vibrancy of attack that characterized the Group, and it had its origin in the studio where the choreographer and her dancers forged a new language of dance based on dramatic flow.

In 1930 Graham began to take her message to other parts of the country in short concert tours. In January she and Horst had played three dates in the Deep South—at Columbus, Georgia; Tuskegee, Alabama; and Gulfport, Mississippi. The programs that she took with her were a mixture of the old and the new. It was the same in February and March when she had three concerts in upstate New York, at Watertown, Amsterdam, and Millbrook. In February the *Herald Examiner* Arts Club sponsored Chicago's first look at Graham. In March she and the Group appeared in a modestly priced and forward-looking concert series at Manhattan's Washington Irving High School, which annually made an effort to offer significant cultural events to a wider audience than might ordinarily attend. She did not appear with the Group again until December, when a concert was given at the Jewish Community Center in Jersey City.

In total it added up to very few appearances in the course of a year, but it was a distinct shift from the early days (a concert at Eastman or at the summer festival at Mariarden) to performances for a larger public. There was a change in the public, too. Formerly made up mostly of friends, it now comprised curious and sometimes hostile strangers.

During the summer, in June, Graham and Horst played two dates in Seattle, a convenient location, for thus she had her way paid out to the West Coast and could then go down to Santa Barbara to visit her mother, now remarried, and the still faithful Lizzie. Santa Barbara had changed considerably since Graham had grown up there. The changes were not the simple ones brought by progress of years; rather, there had been a major shift in the style of the city. In 1925 Santa Barbara suffered extensive damage in a severe earthquake that flattened sections of town and seriously damaged buildings throughout. Mrs. Graham and a visiting niece, Mrs. Frances Pierce, living in a large house with seven chimneys, during the quake fled outside through the kitchen door—luckily, since the front and side exits were cascaded with falling bricks as five of the chimneys collapsed. Santa Barbara afterward decided not to be the jumble of Victorian, adobe, and stucco houses of previous years but to rebuild in pseudo-Hispanic style.

Two years after the earthquake, Mrs. Graham, who had been a widow for thirteen years, remarried. Her new husband, Homer N. Duffy, was a successful businessman in the Beakins Moving firm. The second marriage lifted an increasingly insupportable financial burden from the Graham sisters. For all practical purposes, only Mary had been able to send help regularly from her salary as a stenographer. Assistance from the others was sporadic.

Graham's visit to Santa Barbara in the summer of 1930 was for relaxation. But there was an important aftermath. Graham and Horst began the return east by way of the Southwest, traveling through New Mexico and the quasi-Christian Penitente region. In general, the Spanish cultural penetration of the United States was not strange to Graham. It had been part of her background in Santa Barbara. But the specific form it took in the desert and mountain country, where it collided with native Indian culture, was new to her. The lushness of Southern California might have induced in a person a form of "pagan" enjoyment of the sun and sea, as Graham often suggested; but in Indian country near Santa Fe, New Mexico, where she and Horst had been offered a cottage, the rock and sand and relentless sunshine of the high desert produced another feeling, a refletive mood conducive to creative work.

Horst and Graham had a field of corn outside the house's little plaza where they breakfasted. In the morning Indian children and burros with bells on their harnesses would climb the hill past the house, and in the evening the jingling of the animals, now loaded with firewood, would be heard again. Graham and Horst were both enormously impressed by the Indian culture, by its rapport with nature, and by the feeling of the landscape itself.

The Spanish named the Rockies and their foothills in California after the saints (thus Santa Barbara), but they called the jagged hills of New Mexico the Blood of Christ Mountains. The land was dry and harsh, and the mixture of Spanish Christianity and Indian nature cults produced curious offshoots, one of which was the sect of the Penitents.

The idea of the penitential society, involving as it does the public processional with the confession of faults and self-scourging, is almost as old as Catholicism, but it had died out in many Catholic cultures by the time the Spanish penetrated the New World. Spain brought the idea to the North American Southwest, where it easily fitted in with Indian customs. The sight in the hills of penitential processions with the surrounding ritual is not unusual to a child growing up in the Colorado–New Mexico–Arizona triangle, but for Graham the whole exotic mixture—from the building style of the meeting houses (constructed with stone or, more commonly, adobe), to the statuary in the houses, to the crosses in the countryside (sometimes on the crests of hills, sometimes in the open or hidden in gorges)—came as special revelation.

For the second Repertory series, in February 1931, Graham took the ritual elements of the region, theatricalized them, and created "Primitive Mysteries" and "Two Primitive Canticles." She had by that time choreographed nearly eighty dances, including her early solos, but "Mysteries" announced to the world that a talent of major proportions was working in dance. "Mysteries" was broader in its reach than anything she had yet attempted. Previously, Graham first had done decorative mood pieces and then dances of protest ("Poems of 1917") or satiric commentary ("Four Insincerities"), working her way toward more abstract dances like "Heretic" or "Lamentation." Now she was tackling the area of myth and of universal ideas, a basic change in subject matter to which she would devote the rest of her career.

In some sense, Graham, through the power of her imagination, realized during the midst of the age of the flapper that certain contentions and demands were shredding the tissue of comfortable beliefs that had made the post–World War I binge possible. Fundamental social shifts were occurring. People found it necessary to submerge themselves into one or another movement in order to survive. The man alone was the man defeated. There no longer was room for dalliance with the romanticism of exotic places and their customs. There was a positive need for intellectual and emotional cleanliness, which in dance meant a commitment to strong unornamented movement. The sinuous flow that had been characteristic of the Denishawn dancer was not the movement with which to meet a moral crisis. The world from which that style of dance had grown was one in which the general terms of living were agreed upon by the majority of society. The benevolence and positive aura of a world united by broad common assumptions had been replaced by doctrinaire narrowness. Open borders became closed checkpoints; casual travelers had to learn to deal with the newly required passport; the man who went into a bar expecting to pour his own whiskey now had it carefully measured out for him. The innocent casualness of another age was replaced by the hard realities of mistrust. Everything was in doubt, and each artistic discipline had begun to set its own house in order. After Graham had been working five years, she produced the mammoth simplicity of "Primitive Mysteries," a work that translated religious myth into stark movement.

This dance had three sections: "Hymn to the Virgin," "Crucifixus," and "Hosannah." The first section begins in silence with twelve girls, all dressed in long, dark blue dresses walking unhurriedly onto the stage in three lines. The line farthest from the audience extends horizontally, and the two others stretch vertically down toward the audience. When the dancers are in place they form a three-sided box. As they proceed, a figure walks into the center of the "box." She is in white, an initiation dress. The dancers step forward on one leg, draw the other leg up to it, then pause before stepping off on the first leg again. The walk thus achieved is deliberate and has a processional pace. Until this point there has been no music. When all the dancers have appeared on stage and the initiate, Graham, stands in the middle, a melody for flute begins, and Graham moves first to one of the side groups and then to the other. With each she stops, and they form a halo of arms around behind her head.

Sharp chords on the piano indicate the force and thrust of the group movements. Graham is the only person who moves alone; all others move in groups. She is the subject of their attention, and at one point she leads the horizontal group around the stage in a dance that files between the two other groups, who face one another in parallel lines. As Graham passes each of the pairs of facing girls, they greet her. One crooks an arm and holds it up, while the girl opposite crooks hers in similar fashion but rests the forearm on the floor and stretches her body out to the side. Thus, one of the girls salutes the sky and the other the ground, and together they form the parameters within which the initiate moves. To conclude the section, the dancers form a circle around the initiate, stepping first to the right and then to the left; then in silence they resume the opening formation and slowly step off the stage.

In the second movement, "Crucifixus," trios predominate, with the initiate in the center of the trio farthest upstage from the audience. Two of the four formations are angled diagonally, the other two are horizontal. The two girls flanking Graham form their arms into an arch over her head. Again, all this is done in silence. At the first note of the music she bursts out from the formation and holds her arms straight out. The group of twelve has formed a large square off to one side, and one of the dancers in the first row raises her leg up higher and higher and then suddenly turns the motion into a giant step by shifting her weight forward onto the leg. The other dancers follow suit one by one until they are all taking long strides in a circle around Graham. As they move they clasp hands behind backs and bend forward, giving an animalistic configuration to the body. They are all impelled forward by some force that is beyond their questioning. As they circle, the music increases in tempo and the steps take on a quality of driven frenzy. It is the climax of their ceremonial, and at the end of the section Graham has become one of the group, no longer a solitary figure. They move off in a silent formation similar to the three-sided open square of the first movement.

For a third time they return in silence. Their pace is the same slow, serious one that began the first two sections. Graham is in the center with an attendant. Two lines of five dancers each stretch out horizontally. One group dashes toward the audience, while the other moves away. The groups fraction into clusters of twos and threes. Graham sinks to the ground and is assisted by her attendant.

Graham sits, and the attendant places her hands behind Graham's head in a blessing. The entire group sits with her and then rolls over onto its knees, the head of each dancer bent to the floor. It is the concluding obeisance. They stand. Graham, in the center with her attendant, walks in a small square, and all walk off in silence, Graham's position as a sacred ritual figure, like the Virgin, confirmed.

The audience at the concert, confronted with the simple mastery of "Primitive Mysteries," cheered. It had never seen the essence of religion presented with such dramatic simplicity. It knew that it was in the presence of choreographic greatness.

"Primitive Mysteries" came from Graham's depths, and she was not sure that it would measure up. Indeed, she was far from confident that it would. She had the feeling that she had "missed it," that she had not been able to do it the way she wanted. Horst tried to assure her that it was the best work she had done. But the restless, driven person inside Graham didn't believe him. The night before the biggest triumph of her early career she had slept in her dressing room, alone, miserable, and unwilling to leave the theater. Now, in the applause, her reward had come.

In all, the dance had an utter economy of means—in its costumes, which Graham created, and in its movement and accompanying music. It had the chaste simplicity that Graham had been striving for. Graham's turn of mind—literary, philosophical, mystical, but above all serious—had produced a genuine masterpiece. The music for "Primitive Mysteries" was composed by Horst while Graham worked on the movement. It consisted of a simple score for flute, oboe, and piano. Despite its limited number of instruments, the music had a closeness in mood and a sympathy for the movement characteristic of most of the scores Horst would compose for Graham. The music probably did not aspire to independent concert status, nor have concert performances materialized, but with Horst's enormous sympathy for and insight into Graham's creative temperament, he created a small unflawed gem.

In drawing the piece out of her innermost being, as she would her most successful works, and in explaining it to the dancers, most of whom were Jewish, Graham confirmed for many their own feelings about religion. "Primitive Mysteries" was not a piece about Catholicism exclusively, although she had spoken of Mary the Virgin when working on it with her dancers; rather, it was a piece about religious feelings in general, feelings that would be recognizable to people of any religion. She had been able to abstract her conceptions to the point where the dance ceased to be the expression of a single event or a single person at a single time but included a great variety of valid experiences that had transpired or would transpire at other times. She had reached a level of meaning that had exceptionally broad implications, extending to the areas that great art reaches. Read purely as a personal statement, the central figure, the initiate, might even have been the choreographer herself, as an innovative force bringing creative life to a group or a society. In any case, "Primitive Mysteries" opened for Graham an area of creative exploration that she would continue to examine throughout the rest of her career, an area where epic mystery would be revealed.

In all, five new works were premiered in the two spectacular February Repertory concerts of 1931: "Primitive Mysteries," "Bacchanale," "Two Primitive Canticles," "Rhapsodics," and "Dolorosa." The last three were solos for Graham, the first two were for herself and the Group. The concerts had been her most remarkable to date. The day after the concert, the *New York Telegram* printed a sympathetic feature story on Graham, who increasingly had begun to attract popular curiosity if not popular acclaim:

> Miss Graham is a serious student of Terpsichore, a personable young lady with ideas and a finely trained body. Miss Graham intends that they should come together through the medium of the dance. Her effort in that direction results in angular, cold, stylized movement. . . . To a layman in the world of dance, Miss Graham reveals herself as an artist on the right track, a master of her art who has let ideas overwhelm her. Mellowness is no part of her. The freshness that is newness consumes her.

The reporter, Ben Washer, who was new to dance, like most of those who would be asked to write on Graham at the time, was a general feature writer not prepared either for the stark world of Graham's choreography or for her intelligent verbal presentation of her work. However, he was not too surprised at the "angular, cold, stylized movement" to realize that she was "an artist on the right track" and that she was engaged in an exploration of a new dance form. It was this restless investigation that was to give each of Graham's seasons a freshness and unusualness that made her company permanent revolutionaries of style for the next twenty years.

No new works were premiered in the performances following the February concerts. The Dance Repertory Theater, a temporary alliance at best, was allowed to become dormant. In March the Group gave a single concert in the Washington Irving High School series, and in April a single concert at the Guild Theater. By April, however, there had been changes in the composition of the Group, with several new dancers replacing those who had left. As a result Graham redid some of "Mysteries" to accommodate the newcomers. She also decided to rework her own solo dance, "Dolorosa."

A Graham dance, whether a solo or a Group work, did not necessarily achieve its final form by the time of its premiere. It was almost always altered, polished, redone. In large measure the premiere of a Graham work had to be considered its final dress rehearsal. Not only would a piece be sharpened or changed in subsequent performances; it might even be recostumed, as was "Dolorosa" within the brief period between its first appearance in the February concerts and its performance in April, where, in the eyes of one reviewer, it nonetheless retained its "uncompromisingly ugly" appearance.

In 1931 Graham joined John Martin, dance critic for the *New York Times,* to demonstrate her theories of movement as part of a course that Martin was giving at the New School for Social Research in New York. At the time Martin was the most serious and vocal of the critics who championed the cause of modern dance. Not only did he cover all dance concerts that were given in New York, but, with missionary zeal, he wrote several books explaining the aims and intents of modern dancers. The idea behind the New School courses was to reach the public in yet another way with the message that modern dance was a serious form of dance theater and ought to be of concern to people who took an interest in artistic matters.

In 1931 Martin's course was held in an oval room beneath the main floor of the school. It became the scene of a dramatic encounter.

Graham sat on a platform in the center of the intimate room, backed by two rows of her dancers, also seated and wearing sweaters, and they were surrounded on all sides by the audience.

After explaining her theory of movement, based on the contraction and release of the torso, Graham invited questions from the audience and began answering them. One balding man, obviously agitated by the direction the talk had taken and the movement that was being shown as examples of dancing, finally asked whether Graham had the intention of developing "natural" movement in her art. Her answer did not satisfy him. He repeated his question and again was dissatisfied. But he was insistent, and to refute Graham's idea of body movement offered an exaggerated and humorous demonstration of an ordinary gesture. This exasperated Graham, who blurted, "You don't know anything about body movements!" The man persisted, and Martin stood to say that the discussion had been interesting but that the lecture had to move along. He then for the first time addressed the man by name: "Mr. Fokine"—Michel Fokine, the distinguished Russian ballet choreographer. Graham was stunned but recovered smoothly to apologize that she hadn't known to whom she had been speaking.

But Fokine was furious and wrote an angry article for the Russian-language publication *Novoye Russkoye Slovo,* in which he asserted, among other things: "Ignorance and amateur interpretation of art are not new. They have always existed, but in our times they seem to flourish more profusely." The encounter was symbolic of the mutual dislike ballet and modern dance had for each other and it earned Graham a fervent detractor.

Fokine never forgot or forgave a slight. Several years later he elaborated on his earlier Russian-language attack on modern dance, this time in an article for the widely read *Literary Digest.* He raised a furor by quoting Graham as having stated that Pavlova bowed well, period. Graham's press agent, Frances Hawkins, who then had recently joined the Graham forces and now spent most of her time attempting to explain Graham to an uncomprehending public, wrote the *Literary Digest* offering free tickets to the editor, so that he could see for himself that Fokine's allegations were untrue. Hawkins also pointed out that Fokine had misquoted Graham. The editor did not bother to attend the Graham concert, and perhaps it would not have mattered if he had. With Fokine's article Graham moved into the forefront of the modern dance world's *enfants terribles,* who would provide material for dozens of humorous and not-so-humorous attacks. The clash with ballet was inevitable, and Graham and Fokine, with their respective supporters, were both hard-headed enough not to give an inch. Later the audience would decide the question simply, by patronizing both forms of dance.

In May 1931 Graham had her first opportunity to work with actors in a legitimate play, as opposed to the musical theater or the choric dramas that Irene Lewisohn had directed. She appeared in a production of the play "Electra," cast as The Dancer. The producing company was associated with the University of Michigan in Ann Arbor and did a short tour of Eastern colleges before appearing in an American drama festival. Graham created three solos for herself: "Dance of Fury," "Lament Over the Urn," and, in the concluding scene, a dance to lead the Chorus. One admirer felt that the first two solos looked excellent in context but that the last dance relied upon a Chorus that lacked the requisite skill to present the movement properly. Regardless, her solos possessed a look of completeness within the folds of the drama. To the observer they seemed to provide a "dance impression of the shifting moods of the play."

The experience was valuable for Graham theatrically. And it touched something more as well, for it influenced her to use Greek drama in her work. The first instance of this appeared in the fall concert in the dance "Dithyrambic." In another two years there would be "Choric Dance for an Antique Greek Tragedy." But more significant than these isolated pieces was the cycle of dances that emerged a decade and a half later, a cycle that used Greek myths and that culminated in the towering full-evening dance drama "Clytemnestra."

As she did regularly, Graham traveled West to Santa Barbara during the summer, first to visit her mother and stepfather and rest from the long grind of the year, and then to stay with Horst near Santa Fe before the fall season. The past season had been enormously satisfying, and in the fall she and Horst would assume full teaching positions at the Neighborhood Playhouse. She could afford to relax with a greater feeling of accomplishment than she had had since the start of her career. She still had to teach to support herself, and recitals were still an expensive affair in which box-office receipts could be counted upon only to cover the basic costs of the production, with perhaps a few dollars for each of the dancers. But the group of dancers that she was training could do the movement that she was creating out of her intense individual conception of what dancing ought to be. And she could look at the accomplishment of five years of creativity that had brought her from sexy wiggling in the Follies' "The Garden of Kama" to "Electra." No chorus girl, which was always the public's image when it heard the word "dancer," would ever have been asked to participate in a drama festival, but Graham had been asked. Her audiences remained small, but they were growing.

The exotic Spanish-Indian brand of Christian ritual that Graham had used for "Primitive Mysteries" reminded many observers of the Mexican muralists who were attracting considerable attention in the art world. Inevitably the question about influences was put to Graham in an interview. With her characteristic flair, she allowed that she had been influenced by the painter José Clemente Orozco but that she had not used him as a model to be copied or even approximated. Graham also might have observed that she was in the process of laying the foundations for a new art form, while the painter was merely adapting to nationalistic ends a European tradition of painting; and that if any comparisons to painting were to be made, the structural revolution of Picasso was closer to her achievement than was the social-action school of Mexican artists. But this was 1931, and social action was very much in the minds of many.

The Neighborhood Playhouse Studio, where Graham and Horst taught full time that fall, had instituted expanded courses in drama and dance. Like her work at the Anderson-Milton School, the Playhouse brought her in contact with actors whose experience of dance usually had been tap dancing or, in the case of some of the women, lessons at a neighborhood "tap and toe" academy. For most actors dance training was show work, a means to the end of getting into the theater and earning the chance to become an actor. Contemporary dance training at the time was not what Graham eventually would help to make it: a medium of dramatic expression in itself.

There was also a December concert to prepare for. For this concert Graham created three solos: "Dithyrambic," "Serenade," and "Incantation." The composers, selected as usual by Horst, were, as usual, uncompromisingly modern: Heitor Villa-Lobos ("Incantation"); Arnold Schoenberg ("Serenade"); and Aaron Copland, whose Piano Variations accompanied "Dithyrambic." Of the three, Copland's eccentric and broken rhythms elicited the most creative response from Graham. The solo was a tour de force in the minimal style that she employed to sketch rather than fully flesh-out movement. The dance was spare, uncompromising, fearsomely difficult to perform, and, from an audience standpoint, difficult to follow.

"Dithyrambic" demanded utmost concentration from both performer and onlookers. Since Graham had decided to strip her dances of ornamentation and of any kind of superfluous movement, the burden of concentration that she placed on the viewer was enormous. It was difficult to watch everything that Graham included in a dance. She was profligate with movement, displaying the easy fluency that characterizes master choreographers. "Dithyrambic" relentlessly moved ahead with flicks and touches of movement, each of which bore a relationship to the one that came before. This moment-to-moment relationship was, in effect, the theme. Without a viewer's total concentration, the work became a collection of individual phrases that had no relationship to one another. Needless to say, audiences found "Dithyrambic" very difficult. Graham reworked it during the next several seasons, as was her custom, but it remained a dance for the few and not for the many. None of her Group ever performed it. The Pierrot dance that she created to the Schoenberg music in "Serenade" was a more easily assimilated work, light in tone and readily recognizable. Graham could smile, too, sometimes, but her audience did not give that any special attention.

A week after the December concert, the German expressionist dancer Mary Wigman made her first American appearance. She had been brought over by theatrical impresario Sol Hurok, who threw a party to celebrate her arrival and introduce her to the leading American modern dancers. Humphrey, Weidman, and Graham dutifully attended, but they had little enthusiasm for an artist they considered an interloper. The attitude toward foreign artists remained. For modern dancers it was difficult enough to make their own way without the added stumbling block of foreigners, who always seemed to receive more favorable box-office attention from audiences. Matters were exacerbated when Hurok announced that he was going to establish a Wigman School of Dance in the United States. Wigman herself, as it turned out, had no interest in remaining in America and intended to return to Europe to continue her work there. When Hurok had insisted on the necessity of a school,

Wigman offered one of her pupils the opportunity of becoming its head. Thus Hanya Holm, a German, found herself in New York, faced with a cool if not hostile world of modern dancers and without even a sure command of the English language.

To the consternation of Graham and other modern dancers, the Wigman School was immediately popular. Some students who might have found their way to Graham and to others now went instead to Wigman and Hanya Holm. But the school, in turn, ultimately helped to create a greater awareness of modern dance. Several years would pass until the modern dance world became used to the idea that the Wigman School was not the threat that it originally was imagined to be, and that there was room for everyone. For Graham in particular, the school became helpful in another way. Hanya Holm, in endeavoring to explain the Wigman method and technique, created the expanded lecture demonstration, a type of presentation that Graham later elevated to a minor art form. Meanwhile, the initial touchy response of the modern dancers to Holm was evidence of the month-to-month struggle for solvency that was part of their existence.

In the early part of 1932, Graham and Horst again did some touring. It was one of their sources of income. During the last week of January and the first week of February, they made a short tour of the South, starting in Washington, D.C., and touching Tallahassee; in South Carolina, they appeared in Columbia and in Rock Hills at Winthrop College.

Graham's next concert with the Group was scheduled for the end of February. For this concert she prepared a new group work, "Ceremonials," to a score commissioned from the young American composer Lehman Engel. Running about thirty minutes, "Ceremonials" was the longest piece that Graham had yet attempted. Like "Primitive Mysteries," it was based on Indian material, but it was not nearly as successful and, indeed, in a way seemed jinxed. Graham had been feeling ill while readying "Ceremonials" and had not been able to prepare it properly in rehearsal. In addition, the first performance was danced at the theater (the sympathetic Guild) that was presenting Eugene O'Neill's "Mourning Becomes Electra," and the Group hardly had any time to rehearse on stage because the play's set had not been struck. It was finally removed just prior to the dance concert, but then the theater's house curtain proved inoperative and could not be lowered; so the play's front drop, on which a New England house was painted, had to be brought down tardily at the end of "Ceremonials." Finally, Graham curiously, or perhaps understandably because of her illness, had provided herself with relatively little to do in the piece. It was as if she had been seized by uncertainty. "Ceremonials" had three sections, with a light humorous dance in the two interludes, but the piece did not have the simple vigor of "Mysteries."

"Ceremonials" was not praised and its poor reception troubled Graham. Her anxieties about her talent worsened, and Horst spent much time and energy trying to comfort her. He even suggested that there was a rhythm to creativity, likening her experience to Beethoven's, whose lesser Eighth Symphony followed the powerful Seventh.

In April she and Horst went out once again on a short tour; and then special recognition and a burst of support came in the form of a Guggenheim fellowship, for which she had applied the previous year. Graham was the first dancer ever to be awarded a Guggenheim, and she immediately announced that she was going to spend the summer in Mexico, in Yucatán. With any luck, further travel in alien exotic locales might fire her imagination, as had her trips with Horst to Taos and Santa Fe. After two June recitals in Ann Arbor at the Lydia Mendelsohn Theater, where she had performed in "Electra," the summer was hers.

The Depression had struck hard at America's working population and was even crueler on American artists, so the Guggenheim money was exceptionally helpful. Graham always economized on the cost of everything, from costume material to the music she used, having most of the latter played in piano reductions or by small ensembles. Horst, in "Mysteries," had restricted himself to flute, oboe, and piano for more than one reason; similarly with another score that used only percussion and trumpet. But even with such economies money was always a serious problem. And because it was, in a sense it eventually was bypassed. Since there was no possible way of solving the problem, Graham worked out a way to ignore it. She simply refused to consider money in any serious relation to what she was doing. Her attitude was that, if one devoted oneself to modern dance for the money, then one was in it for the wrong reason. She gave her dancers whatever payment she could when she could, but she relied on personal loyalty, not a paycheck, as the cement to keep her organization together. That attitude never changed in her mind. To discuss money was to betray art, and later in her career, when substantial sums were available for her company, she still refused to consider money of any importance. Her simple view was: Crusaders don't expect paychecks. And she saw herself as a crusader, a revolutionary. The grueling experience of the Depression and her own refusal to cater to public taste placed an indelible stamp on her soul—as, indeed, it had on the whole of the modern dance movement.

The usual Guggenheim fellowship at that period offered between $2,000 and $2,500 for twelve consecutive months. Because of her performing and teaching commitments, Graham could not afford to take an entire year off; so her fellowship was arranged to run for four months, in the amount of $800. The sum gave her the opportunity to have a fiscally secure trip in which she need be guided only by her interests. She and Horst, equipped with a camera, sailed on the *Morro Castle*, which was destroyed in a horrible fire at sea a few years later. In the Yucatán peninsula they visited ruins and outside of Mexico City climbed the Pyramids of the Sun and Moon. Graham and Horst took rolls of snapshots and thoroughly enjoyed their touring. Though the trip did not immediately inspire any new dances, it reinforced the feelings she had about the Indian culture that she had already observed in the Southwestern United States.

But Graham could not regain hold of the deep impulses out of which she created "Primitive Mysteries." In the fall of 1932 she gave a concert with her Group, showing three new pieces. The first, "Salutation," with music by Carlos Chavez, was a little dance in a low-pressure march time. Graham used it to begin the program, thereby effectively retiring the usual program opener, "Dance," which had served since 1929. The "opening dance" was a curious custom among modern dancers, who ordinarily made no concessions to audiences. The assumption was that the theater's usual starting time would find the audience full of food and drink (possibly an unwarranted assumption in the Depression) and, perhaps, a bit too restless to settle down into the more serious part of the program. So choreographers would prepare a trifle of a curtain raiser to ease audiences into the more substantial work that was to follow. It was an oddly practical practice for the instigators of a revolution.

Another of Graham's new works was "Dance Songs," a suite of

solos of varying moods, starting with a ceremonial and ending in a song of rapture. In keeping with frugal orchestration favored at the time, composer Imre Weisshaus's music was scored for baritone, flute, and drum. The final new work was "Chorus of Youth—Companions," a reflective piece looking back on the past, with music by Horst.

None of these works approached the level of rigorous purpose that drove Graham to do "Primitive Mysteries." She was at a distance from her richest powers, although she was in command of her craft and was entering a significant new phase of her career in which she would work only with commissioned scores. Her creative work would be based on active collaboration with musicians, and she would not use standard repertory music in an illustrative way. Horst, of course, encouraged her; and as a result of the commissions and the association with her, several American composers, among them Riegger, Copland, Cowell, Barber, and Schuman, would advance their careers.

In December came the announcement that Graham was preparing "Six Miracle Plays," with medieval texts arranged by Natalie Hays-Hammond. They were to be presented at the Guild Theater in February 1933. But before that Graham had two other unusual dates to fulfill. The first of these was the Group's first well-paying date: to appear on the opening-night bill of the Radio City Music Hall.

The Music Hall was the idea of Samuel L. Rothafel, known familiarly as "Roxy," one of the great showmen of the period, who had known Graham from her Denishawn days in Los Angeles, where he had once hired her. He undoubtedly expected similar dancing now. His concept in creating the Music Hall was to build the most magnificently equipped theater in the United States and to present there the best attractions to be found in the fields of vaudeville and concert performance. The plan was incredibly ambitious, and on the opening night bill, in addition to Graham, were, among others, comedians Weber and Fields, the dancer Ray Bolger, the singer Jan Peerce, the acrobatic Wallenda family, and an adversary of Graham's, the German expressionist dancer Harald Kreutzberg.

The whole bill was a grandly mixed bag of entertainers. Opening night, December 27, 1932, the performance, which started at nine o'clock, ran terribly late. It was well after midnight when Graham and the Group came on to present "Choric Dance for an Antique Greek Tragedy," a new work. Long before, the 6,000-seat house had begun to empty, but devotees of Graham, who had seated themselves close to the stage, were unaware of the dwindling audience. John Martin stuck out the long wait, and in his review of the evening for the *New York Times* admired the volume of movement that Graham created upon the vast stage.

The performance was a worrisome experience for the Graham dancers. The elaborate stage machinery, not the thinness of the audience, caused them the most distress. The Music Hall stage could be split in half, with one part descending while the other rose or remained stationary at viewing level, so that the show's acts, regardless of how elaborate, could follow each other without interruption. Graham and the Group went on after a horse act, and the only barrier between the dancers and a fall into the gaping pit behind them, left by the descending back half of the stage holding the horses, was a black curtain. Since the dance required a lot of backward movement, the dancers understandably exhibited throughout the performance a certain edgy quality quite apart from that within the dance itself.

During rehearsals the appearance of the Group backstage, with their long dark costumes and reserved demeanor, had caused a stir. The dancers never went anywhere individually at the Music Hall but always walked together, escorted by the rehearsal pianist, Deny De Rimer. They spoke to no one—a matter of both shyness and a sense of superiority—and departed immediately after their own rehearsal. The rumor was that they didn't know English and were foreigners . . . possibly Greek. Graham was not so reserved and chatted with Roxy, who once took the Group for a tour of the facilities, showing them off like a proud householder. He referred to the dancers as "little ladies." Later on detractors would call them "Graham Crackers."

The opening of the Music Hall made a big splash, but the show could not draw sufficient customers to sustain the theater. Rothafel suffered a heart attack, and a few days later Graham and the Group were off the bill that boasted artists of the "highest reputation" in the realm of music and dance, sixty ballet dancers, forty-eight Roxyettes (later Rockettes), and an orchestra of one hundred. But Graham was not going to go without the promised fee, not in the depths of the Great Depression. She and the Group returned nightly to the Music Hall to await reinstatement. Each night they were told that they were not needed, to which Graham patiently replied, "We'll wait." Eventually the contract was settled according to the terms agreed upon, and the Group, with its money, returned to the small halls of high art. Beyond the money and a few choreographic bits that Graham extracted from "Choric Dance" for other concerts, the most notable aspect of the experience for her was that the Music Hall was the biggest house in which she had ever played—and ever would.

The Music Hall, Rothafel's experiment in providing serious and diversionary entertainment on the same program, had proven, in effect, the last gasp of vaudeville. Like the legitimate stage, only worse, vaudeville was disintegrating before the inroads of the talking picture. Nothing that either the stage or vaudeville could offer compared with the spectacular and inexpensive entertainment presented by the movies. Vaudeville died slowly but uninterruptedly. As for the stage, the number of new productions appearing on Broadway eroded steadily from the peak of 264 in the 1927–28 season to about one hundred a decade later. The owners of the Music Hall foresaw these signs and booked its first movie two weeks after the hall opened. Thus was created the successful formula of long films and short but mammoth-scaled stage shows that has endured and prospered.

The second of Graham's outside projects to be completed before the presentation of "Six Miracle Plays" was also removed from the usual dance domain. One of the best known and most successful performers on Broadway was Katharine Cornell, who was beginning to fulfill the expectations that she had aroused in audiences for a decade. In February 1931, the same month that Graham had brought forth "Primitive Mysteries," Cornell had triumphed in *The Barretts of Wimpole Street*. Though the larger audience was not aware of Graham, Cornell was; and for her next production, *Lucrece*, an adaptation of Shakespeare's dramatic poem, "The Rape of Lucrece," as prepared by André Obey, Cornell asked Graham to stage the movement. It was a remarkable collaboration of two of the greatest women of the American stage.

Some members of Graham's classes at the Neighborhood Playhouse at the time, in the winter of 1933, could not quite understand Graham's admiration for Cornell, whom they considered only a "voice actress." But in *Lucrece*, under Graham's guidance, Cornell would use volumes of movement. Graham explained to her classes that she choreographed a pavanne for the production. "Katharine

Cornell learned it in two rehearsals, but it took two weeks to teach the company."

As *Lucrece* was ultimately staged, Cornell did not speak until the final scene of Act One. The work was carried forward by two narrators in gold masks, who recited the story as the actors mimed it against the decor and in the costumes of Robert Edmund Jones. *Lucrece* enjoyed a modest success, and Cornell looked forward to another collaboration with Graham, with whom she had formed a relationship of mutual respect and friendship.

Graham now turned to the "Six Miracle Plays," which were to open in the second week of February. The "Miracle Plays," which proved to be a departure from her current development toward an increasingly spare use of movement, were something of a throwback to her Denishawn days. Compared with the hard percussive style of her work in the concert dance, these pieces were pretty, decorative, and in one case (influenced probably by *Lucrece*) straightforward mime to the recitation of poetry.

Through working on the "Miracle Plays" Graham had the opportunity to control the entire stage presentation. She was the director and was responsible for the realization of the script. She chose Horst to compose the incidental music, cast members of the Group (including her sister Geordie), choreographed the movement, and also danced herself. Until now she had always been responsible to another; as a performer with Massine or collaborator with Cornell in *Lucrece*. That the plays were not a success was of less importance than the fact that she had made progress in the theatrical hierarchy.

Her next important date was a Group concert in May. Lehman Engel, for his second Graham commission, had written the score for "Ekstasis." Graham prepared a beautiful solo for herself that was full of changing dynamics and altered balances. This dance made imaginative use of the in-and-out pulse that had become the cornerstone of her teaching method—the contraction and release of energy, the organic development of one movement continued, but slightly modified, into another. This had been her subject the evening of her encounter with Fokine. Her art was steadily evolving toward a more lyrical presentation of movement, away from the intellectual rigor of her earlier works. She was now using transitional movements unselfconsciously, whereas previously she would give a few essential parts of a movement and allow the viewer to fill in the missing elements. It was, in its way, like a drawing that consists of dots that the viewer himself has to connect with lines to make sense out of.

During all this activity, classes continued at Graham's studio, now located in a loft on 66 Fifth Avenue, between Twelfth and Thirteenth Streets in Greenwich Village, around the corner from Graham's new apartment at 29 West Twelfth Street. She taught a company class nearly every day, and she or her assistants would also teach student classes. One of the unofficial duties of the assistants was to wipe up the floor after Graham's and Horst's trio of incredibly fluid dachshunds, who wandered around freely making puddles. Group members were always on the lookout for little dry, crystallized patches in corners of the studio.

The Group now had been in existence for nearly five years, and some of its members were impatient to present their own choreography. They had been studying dance composition with Horst, who was beginning to establish the fundamentals of a course for which he would become well known, and they naturally wished to create and perform dances of their own. Graham, mostly at Horst's behest, decided to show these pieces to the public in a series of studio performances. Graham acted as general supervisor, and a Group member was responsible for assembling the programs. Each dance was costumed and staged by the choreographer or someone of her choice.

The studio series was very much Horst's idea, and he assigned each of the choreographers a specific type of dance. Sophie Maslow, who was to appear on the first program, prepared a Bach sarabande. After finishing it, she danced it for Horst, who criticized and then approved it for performance, a practice he followed with all the pieces. Graham remained aloof until the series was ready, then viewed the dances and tore some to shreds. Maslow was told that the choreography for her sarabande was not original, that it was something she had seen somewhere, and that she should try again. Maslow went home, restudied Horst's criticisms, and that night entirely rechoreographed her piece, which then proved so first-rate that for years thereafter Horst used it in his classes to demonstrate what a sarabande was all about.

Others of the Group responded more emotionally that day to Graham's uncompromising standards. One dancer answered back sharply and Graham slapped her. Another began to weep, and others broke down too, so roiled had the atmosphere become. Graham paid no attention. Standing the angered offender atop a chair seat, she draped her with a skirt so long that it stretched down over the chair's legs to the floor. The dancer was then ordered to repeat her whole dance, moving only atop the confines of the chair. Remarkably, as everyone saw, the dance was transformed into a sounder work.

Although the studio concerts were a useful showcase for the dancers, the series did not really interest Graham and was therefore allowed to die. The first studio concert illustrated how Graham and Horst differed in their approaches to finished work. Horst addressed himself to the structure of a piece, offering a general analysis of its defects and suggestions as to possible specific improvements. In contrast, Graham, who was accustomed to drawing her work out of her deepest feelings and rationalizing afterward, reacted to a dance as a total experience. She often did not know the direction a particular dance was going to take until she had completed it and was able to look at the finished product. Hers was the instinctive approach that proceeded from feeling, not thought. She had not realized the greatness of "Primitive Mysteries" until Horst and then her audience's excitement told her.

As members of her Group discovered, Graham could not accept mediocrity in any form. Her fury at what she considered inferior material sometimes drove her into a rage. Anything less than maximum effort was not permitted, and when Graham became angry she lashed out at the offender with an unreasoning passion. For the dancer who chose to remain with Graham, there were two choices: improve or be destroyed. Later in Graham's career she remarked coolly to Robert Dunn, "I never destroyed anyone who didn't want to be destroyed!" Graham either brought out the best that dancer possessed, or that dancer didn't survive with the company.

Graham could mesmerize her company members into achievements of which they did not think themselves capable. In her sallies of rhetoric, she drew on everything from mystical evocation to philosophical speculation to weave her spellbinding case. In every instance the images were vivid. And dancers who were moved to the depths of their beings to do better later were often at a loss to remember any of the particulars of what Graham had said to gain the effect that, in a sense, she had created.

In his appreciation of the underlying framework of a dance,

Horst was by far the more analytical of the pair. His method of analysis and teaching was based on a study of musical tradition, and for modern dancers trying to avoid the gigantic roadblock of balletic tradition, Horst encouraged the study of preclassic forms of dance. In sharp contrast to Graham's emotional intensity, he had a didactic manner and at times a bawdy wit. Horst's own deep feelings about, and his understanding of, the importance of modern dance were what sustained Graham and others in the tide of ridicule and misunderstanding that met their appearances before the general audience. That Horst accompanied the modern dancers on the piano and found talented young composers to create music for them were only the surface signs of the support he provided.

Graham was now forty, but as usual she was purposefully discreet about her age. Ordinarily, she placed her birth within the twentieth century, dropping at least six years from her age but occasionally, to a novice reporter, she suggested a date that gave her a generous nine-year padding. Graham had come a long distance: She had created a vocabulary of clear, forceful gesture full of the angularities and gruff athleticism that had absorbed her. In "Primitive Mysteries" she had achieved one of the pinnacles of modern dance. She had even become something of a symbol. To many, Graham was modern dance. Since "Mysteries," however, she had not produced a comparable achievement, and in all she had not taken secure hold of the themes that her work would mine.

In February 1934 Graham again presented several new works. One, "Celebration," had a score by Horst. The choreography was in the blunt style of movement that had worked so well in "Primitive Mysteries," with the Group divided into units. Like the austere "Mysteries," "Celebration" had no story line, but it did have an exuberance expressed in many passages of jumps, which in turn were contrasted with slow, graver passages. The piece was the first in which Graham turned her dancers loose to jump extensively. She also did a satiric trio, "Four Casual Developments," for three of her dancers (Sophie Maslow, Anna Sokolow, and Lillie Raidy), using a score by Henry Cowell. The piece poked fun at innocent Victorian maidens. The knowledge of a Victorian upbringing that the dance displayed came from Graham's own firsthand adolescent experiences, a fact that probably would have surprised most of her partisans.

Soon after the February concert, Horst brought out his new

publication, *Dance Observer*. A magazine of modest thickness, tabloid-sized and selling for an affordable ten cents, its aim was to document the comings and goings of the modern dancer, since the existing magazines and newspapers would not. *Dance Observer* was favorably disposed toward the modern dance and generally hostile to ballet and anything else that could be considered mere "entertainment." Horst, as editor, was open to all forms of modern dance and had only one inflexible rule regarding reviews—that Graham remain comfortably beyond question.

5

The Dance and the Academy

"... Martha Graham has a marvelous
technique. I won't take that away ...
from ... her."
Ruth St. Denis

The year 1934 was a watershed for modern dance. In its long struggle for recognition and acceptance as an art form, the appearance of Horst's *Dance Observer* early in the year at least provided the dance with an alternative to the know-nothing criticism it had generally received. Then another development occurred. Martha Hill, one of Graham's early admirers and pupils, helped organize a summer festival of modern dance at Bennington College in Vermont. Not only would the festival prove to be the salvation of many of the modern dance companies in the usually nonexistent summer season, but it would offer the kind of focal point that the field of modern dance had not been able to establish for itself.

In 1926, Hill had attended the first concert Graham gave. She enrolled with Graham as a student and had even been an early member of the Group. When Hill left the Group for a position in the physical education department of New York University, she began to introduce dance movement into a curriculum that until then had not included dance. Hill's first step was to nestle music courses amid sports instruction. Since NYU's music department did not want to teach music to the sports department, Hill went outside and hired the composer Norman Lloyd to be her instructor. The physical education department was relatively large, so Hill's departure from previous practice was not particularly noticed. Thus modern dance gradually made its stealthy entrance into the Eastern academic world.

With her academic connections and her deep appreciation of the new dance forms, Hill began scouting for a summer home for the dancers and choreographers whose sporadic employment halted during the summer. She found the answer in Bennington, where an adventurous, newly established women's college was seeking a way to generate revenue from its unused campus during the summer. Martha Hill and Mary Josephine Shelly of Columbia University's Teacher's College proposed a six-week summer workshop in dance to Bennington's president, Robert D. Leigh, who was willing to try any venture that might ease his school's financial burden in the depths of the Depression. Though the workshop might have seemed a gamble to President Leigh, it turned a profit in the nine years of its existence, and Bennington became synonymous with the modern dance movement.

The staff for the first year read like a who's who of the movement. Graham, Humphrey, Weidman, Holm, and Horst (who for the first time in recent years did not go to the Perry-Mansfield Camp in Steamboat Springs, Colorado), along with John Martin, were the visiting staff; the permanent members were Hill, Shelly, and Gregory Tucker (music), with Bessie Schönberg as their assistant. The enrollment was subscribed to the limit, mainly by physical education teachers from throughout the United States. One hundred three students were registered, all women. Their average age was twenty-seven, not exactly ideal for aspiring dancers, although the spread in ages ranged from fifteen to forty-nine. After paying all administrative expenses, including rental, to Bennington, the festival had a surplus of $694.06.

The plan for the Bennington festival was simple and did not alter for the first five years, although it was somewhat refined. The intent of the organizers was to expose all of the students who attended to all of the new currents in modern dance. The core elements of the program were the classes in fundamental techniques.

The first year these classes were divided into three segments: Graham conducted the first two weeks, Humphrey and Weidman the second two, and Hanya Holm the final two. In addition to the opportunity to work directly with the movers and shakers of the world of modern dance, students were offered courses in teaching methods, history and critical theory, music and dance, and the chance to compose their own dances. The first year Holm conducted this workshop.

Students were told that the work costume was the washable leotard and that they should bring some informal and sports clothes as well. Students worked all over the campus, including the chicken coop, where piano practice was held. The local armory, where dance recitals were given, held about 500 people, with temporary bleachers, and everyone was encouraged to buy tickets early to avoid disappointment. In addition to the students registered for the whole summer, others dropped in to audit one or another course for a few days or a week.

Bennington ran a taut and tidy ship that fulfilled everyone's expectations. The universities from which the women came paid their fees ordinarily, and the teachers returned to their schools with firsthand experience of the newest trends in modern dance. Each of the choreographers had the opportunity to give a recital. Bennington College derived some revenue, the career dancers had a place to work, and modern dance had found a marvelous way of proselytizing its cause at no expense.

What no one among the organizing group quite realized at first was that the students, for the most part, were never going to be professional dancers. Only three or four years later did younger students come to Bennington in sufficient numbers, these then to be recruited for the various companies. But the first groups that emerged from the North Flyer train at the North Bennington station were mature women, physical education instructors, most of whom had a channel-swimmer sturdiness. Modern dance was not by any means designed for sylphs, but neither was it right for those women at Bennington the first year. But through them and the others who came in subsequent years, modern dance was to enter college curriculums, through the gymnasium in most cases, and later through the performing arts departments.

Though the workshop students were not destined for the professional stage, they showed enormous zest for the instruction. At the end of each two-week session, they displayed in performance the techniques they had been studying. Not the type of lecture demonstration that the individual choreographers could show with their own thoroughly trained companies, the presentation nonetheless included the basic elements of the different styles. Graham instructed students in her idea of floor work, the varieties of falls that could be accomplished (from the relatively short fall on one count to the falls of longer counts, in almost slow-motion descent), and the vigorous, knees-up running-in-place. For her own Group, as her technique developed in tandem with her creative expansion, Graham would add more and more elements to the demonstrations. But with the Bennington students she kept the technique presentation to a few basic movements and repeated them over and over.

Internally, the Bennington workshop was not quite one big happy family. Though the choreographers did make efforts to get along with one another, woe betide the hapless student who, attending a Humphrey-Weidman class, took up a Graham preparatory stance learned the week before. The inadequacies of the technique taught by a choreographer other than the one then in charge of the class would be explained to the confused student. The old competition among choreographers remained. Nonetheless, the Bennington experiment was a success. Modern dance now had a home, if only for six weeks in the summer, during which the staff received not only a fee but room and board.

Graham and Horst returned to New York full of vigor and worked first on a long, exhausting solo, and then on a dance for the Group, possibly most immediately inspired by the New England summer but drawing on much more. Graham was now moving toward an accomplishment that would compare with "Primitive Mysteries." The solo, "Dance in Four Parts," was to an extant score by George Antheil; the Group work, "American Provincials," had a new score by Horst. A concert was scheduled for November 2, but because of an injury she postponed the opening of her fall season to November 11.

The solo lasted twenty minutes. Anyone who has worked in the theater knows that solos of five minutes or more are difficult to sustain, and that twenty minutes of unadorned dance places an extreme burden upon the artist, not to mention the audience. The challenge, however, was the sort Graham repeatedly laid upon her audiences. She gave them what absorbed her (as she did with her dancers), and it was their job, in effect, to provide the rest of the experience. "Dance in Four Parts" was performed, as were all of her dances at this period, on a bare stage, and in this case with only a single shaft of light picking her out. In line with her work up to this time, Graham was intent upon eliminating transitional movements and simply presenting essential and dynamic bits of significant activity; she had no interest in prettying up the movement and making it easier for an audience to follow. In the hands of anyone else, such a dance probably would have disintegrated into its component parts, but Graham's performing intensity was able to supply audiences with interest enough to keep them attentive. Generally speaking, even those in the audience who did not respond to the message of modern dance often were bowled over by the sheer performing intensity that Graham brought to the stage. Insiders thought of Graham and Humphrey as fire and ice, indicating theatrical electricity on the one hand and cerebral dance structure on the other.

More important, in terms of the dances to follow, was the Group work, "American Provincials," in which Graham returned to the exorcizing of the past, the theme she had taken up in "Heretic," with the forebears ranked against one of their descendants. Now this theme had an American context. The first part of the new work was Graham's solo, "Act of Piety," and the second part, "Act of Judgment," which was designed for the dancers of the Group, showed Graham lashing into them to expose their narrowness. In "American Provincials" Graham demonstrated the force and power of the Puritan heritage and made a furious attack on it. As was noted at the time: "But here is no supernatural ordeal or omniscient judgment, no formal defiance or cabalistic ritual. This is the personal fury, the direct attack, the veritable lashing of the tongues of dance." Graham was still tethered by her background, and she fueled many of her dances with hauling and tugging against it. The specifically American past had begun to stir Graham's deepest resources.

By now Graham's work was attracting wide attention. The magazine *Vanity Fair*, in its December 1934 issue, used her in one of its "Impossible Interviews," presenting her together with the curvaceous blonde stripper Sally Rand. In the accompanying illustration Rand is hiding herself behind a peekaboo stratagem of large, pink, feathered fans, while the adjacent Graham is covered from nape to instep with a shapeless black dress. Graham's hollow-cheeked face is rendered in bile green and her eyes are watch-spring spirals. Her body is contorted in cubist angles with fingers and arms at bizarre tangents. Sally poses delicately on her high heels, looking vacant and sexy. Part of the interview dialogue reads:

> GRAHAM: You should learn to bare your soul.
> SALLY: Say, I got to keep something covered.

Elsewhere Stark Young, an admirer, was to say that, if Graham ever gave birth, it would be to a cube. As the scourge of traditional theater dance, Graham with her name alone automatically registered the idea of dissent among those who knew her work or only knew of it. The position had its advantages as well as its disadvantages. Though she was not a commercial success, she had a moral integrity that gave her stature.

One example: In January 1935, Fiorello LaGuardia, then the mayor of New York, appointed Graham to the Municipal Art Committee, which was aimed at bringing "culture to the masses." Committee work was abhorrent to her. The defunct Dance Repertory Theater showed how working to Group ends concerned Graham. She was out to create a form of dance in which she was the center—a personal expression of the greatest intensity—and nothing else could challenge that intent. Still, Graham accepted the mayor's appointment. It was a mark of the public position she had achieved.

She continued to be engaged in a variety of activities, one after the other and sometimes simultaneously. Cornell's production of *Romeo and Juliet* opened in December 1934 to good reviews, although some critics did not even notice that Graham had done the stage movement. Edith Evans, the English actress, was extravagantly praised for her Nurse, with an interpretation that profoundly moved Graham, who shyly approached to ask Evans what lines of text had set her interpretation. The question stemmed from personal interest, in that Shakespeare's Nurse reminded Graham of Lizzie, who had brought up Graham and her sisters and exercised a strong influence on them, providing spontaneous warmth to a household of calm probity.

In the early part of 1935, Graham and the Group were scheduled to give several lecture demonstrations for academic organizations. In February the Group performed for the Conference on Modern Dance held at Teacher's College; and then toward the end of the month, they demonstrated in Washington, D.C., for the National Conference of the Progressive Education Association.

The lecture demonstrations had evolved out of necessity. The whole of modern dance was considered so beyond the realm of understanding that, defensively, each of its major figures would go in front of an arranged audience and offer illustrated explanations. In the course of the talk, the elements of the choreographer's style would be demonstrated by members of the company. The "lecture-demo" was, in effect, like a slide lecture, except that the images were created in front of the audience by live performers. During the talk, the choreographer might or might not give a short history of modern dance. Ordinarily, Graham concentrated on showing what it was that her Group did, explaining why she used these unorthodox means. Basically, she related her movement to the society from which it sprang—a rhythmic, vigorous society, she said, in which machine technology had played a large developmental part. She emphasized that though her dancers did not dance like machines, they could not help but be affected by the rhythms of machinery. She also emphasized that she, in fact, was inventing nothing but rather was rediscovering what the human body could do.

As she was discovering movement, the theater was discovering her, and she was engaged to stage the movement of Archibald MacLeish's *Panic,* a documentary about the effects of the financial crash on individuals and society. This was an unusual production in several ways. To begin with, with twenty-five speaking parts, it was extravagant. In addition, Graham was to work with a chorus of twenty-three. But money was extraordinarily tight in mid-Depression 1935, so mounting such an expensive play could be accomplished only through the most adroit maneuvering by producer John Houseman and co-producer Nathan Zatkin. To minimize expenses, Houseman and Zatkin stipulated that *Panic* would run only three performances, and they asked Actors Equity to waive the usual fees applying to unlimited-run productions. Virgil Thomson accepted a modest $50 to compose a score requiring only a metronome and a telegraph key, and Jo Mielziner designed the décor for no fee. To cover the time needed for rehearsals and the three-performance run, Houseman rented the Imperial Theater for ten days. The director, James Light, worked with the cast, headed by Orson Welles, independently of the chorus. The chorus was the responsibility of Graham, who was regularly exhausting it with her energy and demands. Not until a few days before the opening would chorus and cast be joined together. Graham needed to rehearse her chorus on the Imperial's stage and thus spent most of her time working in the theater. The crowd scenes she devised took place on the fifteen-foot-wide strip of stage closest to the audience. Beyond the chorus, the speaking actors delivered their lines from a raised platform of the set. The performance was generally acclaimed, and Houseman, reflecting on it, felt that the use of the crowd was *Panic*'s most "challenging" element. But he could not resolve in his own mind whether Graham's crowd movements helped express or diverted attention from MacLeish's poetry.

Within a week, Graham and Horst were off on a tour of six scattered recitals that took them from Connecticut College in New London to Omaha. Then in April came her final concert of the spring season, for which Graham had prepared the brilliant solo "Frontier," another dance in the American vein. This would be one of her best-received works and foremost accomplishments. It was six years after the blunt brutality of "Heretic," and Graham had begun to soften the thrusts of her movements somewhat. She was still uncompromising in her rejection of flossy decorative gestures, but now emotional warmth rather than strict intellectual rigor was allowed to govern movements as well. There was strength in the delivery of gesture, but it was allowed to subside rather than be broken off abruptly.

For the score she had her usual collaborator and confidant, Horst, and, as he had done so superlatively in "Primitive Mysteries," he once again provided Graham with precisely the measures and cadences she needed. She also had a new collaborator. For the first time, Graham asked for décor. To prepare the design of "Frontier" she sought out the sculptor Isamu Noguchi, whose sister, Ailes Gilmour, had danced with the Group from 1930 to 1933. Thus commenced the highly distinguished Graham-Noguchi theatrical collaboration, which would produce some of the finest blends of dance and stage design in the history of the American theater.

"Frontier" was premiered on April 18, 1935, at the Guild Theater. It was the first of a two-part dance called "Perspectives No. 1 and 2." The second part, "Marching Song," with a score by Lehman Engel, was markedly less successful. Graham quickly separated the dances, dropping "Marching Song" and keeping "Frontier" in her active repertory for many years. The theme of "Frontier" is the conquering of space, the mastering of the frontier. Graham is first seen in profile, seated on a section of fence post placed at the rear of the stage. Two ropes extending slightly forward from the fence and disappearing up into the flies overhead form a broad V, giving the illusion of a limitless plain. Graham is gazing off to one side. With her first movements, a series of tiny steps, she delineates a large square area. The steps almost form a visible perforation, marking the area she regards as her own. She returns to the fence, then bounds forward in a straight line, conquering the space in another way. Later she moves forward again on the same direct line, but now she jumps up and extends her leg at a right angle to the side, like the tolling of a pendulum measuring off the time in a confident and secure manner. The wildness of her first assault on the area has been replaced with a calm exploration of her zone of mastery. At the end of the dance, she again rests on the fence post and gazes off in profile, but now makes a folding gesture of the arms that reminds one of the closing of a gate.

In "Frontier," which was praised for its simplicity and emotional strength, Graham celebrated the vigor, the tenacity, and the character of the settlers of the West who conquered an area of wilderness. In this case, the civilizing process was seen in its brave beginnings and not in its later repressive strictures, which are inherent in fence-building.

Merle Armitage, a theatrical agent, was stunned by the accuracy with which the dance evoked his own childhood on a ranch. It

> took you back into the whole nostalgia of the early America, the prairies, the women who were old when they were forty—bearing the children and doing the laundry and all their cooking and nothing and no money and everything; and all this was in there in the most amazing way, and yet the triumph of the frontier was in there, too. The ascendency, the pulling out. . . . I recognized my own setting.

Armitage was an extravagant and pungent personality who had been an engineer and stage designer, and who was also a writer and publisher. As an agent he had represented artists such as the singers John McCormack and Amelita Galli-Curci and the Diaghilev Ballet on its first tour of the United States. He had first seen Graham in the Greenwich Village Follies and had been immediately struck by the force of her dancing. After "Frontier" her impact was enormously magnified. "For her to come out of Denishawn was like a leghorn chicken giving birth to an eagle." Armitage began working to have her presented to as wide a public as possible. Although he himself placed her in the category of the major attractions he had presented, he recognized the difficulties in making her art a great popular success.

In several months' time, Graham had created "Dance in Four Parts," "American Provincials," and "Frontier." Now she prepared for a second summer at Bennington and, without knowing it, for a work in which she would not achieve what she set out to accomplish.

The 1935 summer course was again to last six weeks. The choreographers invited were, again, Graham, Humphrey, Weidman, and Holm, but Holm could not attend and delegated one of her assistants, Tina Flade. Horst would teach composition. The students were still predominantly physical education teachers, and the average age was twenty-eight. Two male students were enrolled, and a black girl was given a scholarship. Tuition fees were increased to provide additional revenue for support of the enlarged staff. Graham brought her entire Group with her.

There were several changes in the workshop's program, notably more stringent rules regarding participation in the various classes, particularly composition. The summer session having proved itself the first year, its sponsors now felt they could more rigorously screen the students. Other changes were made to ensure that each of the students would be able to work for longer than two weeks with each of the resident choreographers. To accomplish this, two-a-day classes in different techniques were scheduled in an overlapping arrangement, so that at the end of the six-week session every student would have at least four weeks' exposure to all of the techniques taught. As in the previous summer's session, this general program proved to be the most popular course.

The course in which students had the opportunity to work creatively with the choreographer was formally established as "The Workshop" and put under Graham's charge. The idea of the workshop was to have an active choreographer create a piece, working with professional dancers and students. At the end of the six-week session, the new dance was to be given a public performance in the Armory. Graham's Group formed the nucleus of the workshop, and after auditions twenty-four of the students, all women, were admitted. These were aspiring dancers, and, as such, they were set apart from the rest of the physical education–oriented students.

The task that Graham set for herself and her collaborators during the span of the six-week summer session was to create a complete piece of theater. Norman Lloyd was to compose the score; the designer Arch Lauterer was to devise a set; and Graham, working for the first time with both of them, was to choreograph the dance. In addition, sculptor Alexander Calder, whom Graham had met at a friend's home, had been asked to create some décor elements. He intended to adapt his mobiles to a live theatrical performance, a first-time venture for him also.

Among the students in the workshop was Jane Dudley, who had quit Hanya Holm's group to be at Bennington. As she did on dancers and nondancers wherever she went, Graham had exercised on Dudley the magnetic pull of the Graham personality. Dudley was determined to join the Graham Group, and she worked so fiercely in Graham's class that she was too overcharged to sleep at night. Yet she wanted a daily double exposure to Graham's teaching. Taking extra classes required permission, and when Graham was told of Dudley she made a point of visiting her in her room one evening to tell her she could take the additional class work if she wished.

A few years earlier, when Dudley was a teenager but already considering a dance career, she had been warned against modern dance and Graham specifically. The counsel had come from none other than Ruth St. Denis, one of the mothers of it all, who nonetheless was echoing a popular feeling. "Now . . . my dear," St. Denis had said, "you mustn't get into this . . . modern . . . dance. It's not . . . American. Americans love what is beautiful. This is not . . . beautiful. Now Martha Graham . . . Martha Graham! I saw Martha Graham, and everybody around was laughing, and they had a right to because . . . it was not beautiful." St. Denis did add: "Now, Martha Graham has a marvelous technique. I won't take that away . . . from . . . her." Dudley had not been dissuaded.

Another student in the workshop was Muriel Stuart, a teacher at the School of American Ballet. Lincoln Kirstein, who had once criticized Graham so literarily and who was still enlisted as one of the chief foes of modern dance, was in the process, with George Balanchine, of establishing a ballet company, for which he was drawing upon the school's energy. Intensely curious about the activities at Bennington, Kirstein enrolled Stuart in the workshop. The work, hard and demanding in any case, was particularly so for Stuart, who did not have much experience dancing in bare feet. With great determination, she worked to master everything Graham taught. To keep the punishment at an acceptable level, she eventually had to affix soft pads to the soles of her feet.

Driving everyone as hard as she ordinarily did, and perhaps more so, for hours Graham had the workshop dancers do "pleadings," for example—a shallow V-shaped configuration of the body with back and legs cleared from the floor and palms facing upward, all one's weight resting on the buttocks. And for hours and hours, it seemed, the students did "runs in place." Graham was committed to creating forty-five minutes of choreography from scratch, an audacious act—attempting that much work in so short a time with three dozen dancers of whom two-thirds were strangers.

"Panorama," as the dance was called, marked the first time that Graham tried to work seriously with strangers since forming her own Group. The Group was, in effect, a personal creative "instrument," accustomed to Graham and supple enough to pick up the smallest hints and touches of her gestural vocabulary. Precious time did not have to be wasted explaining every individual phrase and gesture. Because the Group had been trained to move as an extension of Graham's own body, she could communicate with it in a motion equivalent of shorthand. This was impossible with new dancers, no matter how diligent and hard-working they were.

While the choreographic work on "Panorama" moved along in fits and starts, Lloyd completed the score and Lauterer devised the set. The Armory had a small picture-frame stage, but Lauterer used only a part of it. He completely re-created the interior space of the Armory, building an open, three-level set on the floor, with large baffles at the sides so that the center could be flooded or emptied of performers quickly. The set's topmost platform was so near the ceiling that a dancer standing on it could place one leg atop the proscenium arch of the smaller conventional stage. Calder's "mobile" contribution was overhead discs, which were to be tugged and pulled by the dancers with lines attached to their wrists. The "Panorama" production was in no way simple.

In content, Graham's dance was a sweeping overview of American history subdivided into three themes: the "Theme of Dedication," which dealt with the Puritan pioneers; the "Imperial Theme," which examined slavery, superstitions, and fears; and finally the

"Popular Theme," which displayed a people with an awakening social consciousness.

"Panorama" was presented on August 16, the evening before the close of the summer session. John Martin's review for the *New York Times* was kind but unenthusiastic. For him, the most interesting part of the dance was Graham's use of the three levels. He thought that the work, in the sweep of its concerns, showed a development in her talent toward the theater rather than the concert dance, and he felt that the decorative elements enjoyed more success than did the choreographic ones. He particularly liked Calder's wrist lines and discs. Most devastatingly, Martin referred to parts of the dance that "give evidence of the haste with which it was composed."

Apart from "Panorama," at the performance Graham herself had offered two solos, the brilliant "Frontier" and "Sarabande." Although Martin praised these, Graham was not consoled. She was always mostly concerned with the newest work, as is any artist, and was unable to regard it with a balanced judgment, no more than a mother is able to view her newborn child dispassionately. Perhaps with "Panorama" Graham recognized that some of the criticism was justified.

The following morning Graham went with Lloyd and his wife to the small café in the Putnam Hotel, where they saw Martin at breakfast. A friend had already telephoned Graham and read Martin's review, and she entered the café in a silent fury. She restrained herself for a while but finally rose and flew at him. Her frustration and, in all likelihood, the knowledge that "Panorama" had not been up to her own standard drove Graham to vent her hottest anger on Martin. It did not change anything, of course, except to upset Martin. Graham in a rage was monumental.

Even the left-wing press, in the form of *New Theater* magazine, which only the month before had praised Graham for some of her early social protest dances ("Vision of the Apocalypse," "Immigrant," "Poems of 1917"), found "Panorama" heavy going. It was a piece that pleased no one, not even Graham, who felt very hurt by the criticism. After the achievement of "Frontier," this was a bitter pill. Graham never repeated "Panorama," and it was left interred in the mountains of Vermont as testimony to a failed experiment. In later years (it was a defeat she remembered for a long time), she blamed the failure on the visitors who came in to watch her work during rehearsals. Whether true or not, she never again permitted visitors to watch her choreographing. However one assigns the blame, "Panorama" appears to have been too ambitious a project to attempt with an unknown group. The one positive result of "Panorama" was that it brought together Graham and Arch Lauterer, who would later collaborate on some of Graham's finest pieces.

In addition to its first summer home at Bennington, modern dance was gradually finding a year-round institutional home in the colleges. Martha Hill's classes at New York University were an early example. The foothold became more secure when Sarah Lawrence College instituted a dance major in 1935, the year Graham taught there.

Since the popular theater was closed to serious-minded modern dancers, the move to the academy was an alternate route to survival, but it had its drawbacks. No matter how hard college dance and dramatic departments try, they never manage to capture a thoroughly professional air or level of performance. At times, their utter disdain for the practical necessities occasioned by commercial pressures produces admirable results that can be attained in no other manner, and there is no question that modern dance as it developed would not have been possible without the generous assistance of the universities and colleges. But it is also likely that, had the dance come of age outside the academy, it would not have grown up with such a pedagogical attitude toward developing its audience—the attitude, in a sense, of a teacher who will not go out of his way to popularize a course or advertise it in any manner that might be construed unfavorably as implying enjoyment. In the eyes of the educational world, fun meant a lack of seriousness. Modern dance found it hard to laugh, and this was one reason it was exceptionally difficult to fill a hall outside of colleges.

At the colleges, students and faculty formed groups called Orchesis societies, which became a network of interested persons who would arrive and turn out faithfully for visiting modern dancers. The system was in a way like a giant alumnae group that provided a net of connected and interconnected way-stations along which modern dance traveled from one city to the next. Gymnasiums became a way of life for modern dancers whose first intrusions into the academic world were through the physical education departments, where the only performing facility was the basketball court.

Whatever the long-term disadvantages, in the short term the colleges provided shelter for the fledgling art and aided in its survival at a time when it could not afford to take a longer-term look at its ultimate goals.

There were partisan pulls on modern dance as well. Artists like Graham, who were outside the cultural establishment, found themselves continually wooed by radical causes to perform homilies about, and ultimately conform to, a specific line of political thinking. At times the temptation to meet this demand to shape the line of her own art for material gain was probably strong. Radicals were an important part of Graham's audence. Sometimes the demand to accommodate was not so subtle. Graham once found herself faced with the threat of a picket line from a union that did not feel her art was political enough. Encountering the situation in the rawest box-office terms, she still refused to change her programing. "Do you know who I am?" asked the activist. "Yes, you fill my balcony," replied Graham, with an assurance that she could probably use to still riotous halls and, one suspected, storms at sea if necessary. The performance went on without any change of programing.

Still, she sometimes participated in left-wing occasions. In October, for example, she joined a rostrum of speakers, including Clifford Odets and Archibald MacLeish, at a dinner for *New Theater* magazine. She went as a guest, despite the fact that the magazine had found "Panorama" lacking. Presumably her earlier works, perhaps the staging for MacLeish's *Panic* in particular, still spoke for her. One of the activities of *New Theater* was to support those artists whose work it liked. Indeed, it had bought all the tickets for one benefit evening of the three-evening run of *Panic*.

At the other end of the political spectrum there was also interest in Graham, but she did not welcome it. In 1936 an aggressively assertive Germany was preparing for the Olympic games, to be held in Berlin. In addition to the sports events, the government had decided to ask for the cultural participation of nations that were entering the games. Accordingly, a letter from the Ministry of Propaganda, over the signature of Rudolph von Laban, the teacher and theorist, was sent to Graham inviting her and her Group to be the guests of Germany and to perform as part of the cultural Olympics. The magnitude of the offer was stupendous. It was, in effect, international recognition for her Group, her creative talent, and for the rightness of her artistic struggle. The letter meant that she was considered a first-rank cultural representative of her country, a position that had not yet been accorded to her by her own government, which had neither supported nor in any way encouraged her efforts. To accept the offer meant that she would be the recipient of international publicity and in the course of a few weeks would probably receive more sympathetic attention than she had gathered in a decade. She replied:

> I would find it impossible to dance in Germany at the present time. So many artists whom I respect and admire have been persecuted, have been deprived of the right to work for ridiculous and unsatisfactory reasons, that I should consider it impossible to identify myself, by accepting the invitation, with the regime that has made such things possible. In addition, some of my concert group would not be welcomed in Germany.

The signature in her bold, slightly backward-slanting hand closed the matter.

Graham's pre-eminence and moral fiber proved an immoderate attraction for causists in the 1930's. But where they wanted political commentary, she provided moral parables. Her vision was directed to unlocking the fetters that bound the spirit, not those twisting the social fabric.

The years 1936 and 1937 were to be transitional for Graham. Basically, she was turning away from the abstract starkness of great works like "Heretic," "Lamentation," "Primitive Mysteries," and "Celebration" and moving toward a new theatricality. In effect, she was trying to bring together the resources of the theater and the vocabulary of movement she had hammered out.

The use of stage properties was a matter of primary importance to Graham. Until "Frontier," she had worked with the black drapes that recital dancers had traditionally used from the time of Isadora Duncan. She had, however, evolved some striking lighting designs for herself as far back as "Adolescence" (1929), in which she sat in a pool of light surrounded by a slightly menacing darkness. Now it was time to graduate to décor, and she set about exploring how it could best be used for her purposes. Her increased interest was, in a sense, part of her gradual turn toward theater.

Graham was strongly against large flat painting and strongly inclined toward the three-dimensional object that would occupy space on stage and in effect become a part, or "character," in the dance. She liked very much the sculptural possibilities of Noguchi's set for "Frontier," as she liked Arch Lauterer's three-tiered set for "Panorama" with its baffles for exits and entrances. With Calder, however, she had sculptures that moved, and the possibilities of this intrigued her. The problem was to get moving pieces into a dance in an organic way.

For her first concert of the spring season, Graham asked Calder to do designs for a group piece, "Horizons." The piece was programatic, a popular historical-artistic rendering of the story of the colonizing of new territory, and it did not contain much of Graham's strong inventiveness. Martin panned it more in sorrow than in anger. It was divided into four sections, "Migrations," "Dominion," "Building Motif," and "Dance of Rejoicing." Calder supplied circles and spirals that spun around on an empty stage to set the mood of each section, and blocks for the dancers to dance among. However, Graham found the mobiles so unsatisfactory that she never again collaborated with Calder (she once mentioned his name slightingly to Lauterer in telling him what to avoid in designing), and never again did she try to use kinetic stage properties. For her next new work, at the end of the year, she turned to Noguchi for the setting.

Meanwhile, for the remaining part of the spring, Graham and Horst, with the help of Merle Armitage, who lived in Los Angeles, had scheduled their first transcontinental tour. The first time that Graham attempted to put together a cross-country tour since leaving Denishawn a decade previously, this trip was also in the nature of a trial run for an anticipated Group tour the following year. The schedule averaged out at two performances a week and easily ate up whatever money was realized.

The bulk of the concert tour was booked for the West Coast, and of course included Santa Barbara, which would have the opportunity to see how Graham had evolved in the years since she had last performed there as part of Denishawn. After two concerts in Michigan, she and Horst traveled to Washington for appearances in Seattle and Tacoma, then to Portland, and then to a special reception by the Orchesis Society on the University of California's Berkeley campus. The physical education majors and the Orchesis Society had arranged an afternoon tea, with several hundred students and a solid representation from the faculty attending. Graham spoke encouraging words and basked in the friendly reception.

In the Detroit *News* of March 17, at the beginning of her tour, she received a critical review that was more typical of the reception she was generally accorded:

> Miss Graham is the most perplexing of American dancers and her programs stir controversy. A reporter who expresses bewilderment over Miss Graham receives letters comparing him, unfavorably, with Ivan the Terrible. It is perilous work, reporting on Miss Graham, for nobody is dispassionate about her. There is no tranquil twilight zone of opinion. If you set down dissatisfaction with any of her doings, you should, according to the various schools of thought, either be crowned with laurels or boiled in oil. However, here goes. She was just as puzzling Monday evening . . . moving from downright ugliness to an occasional cold beauty.

Working slowly down the Coast from Berkeley, she arrived in Santa Barbara for a concert at the Lobero Theater during the first week of April. Everyone curious about Martha turned out to see what the new art of modern dance was like, but even sympathetic relatives found themselves at somewhat of a loss. The same mutterings that had been heard in the East turned up in her home town, to the effect that, if this was what dance was all about, then it wasn't much. She had made no concessions for her home town audience and gave them a straight dose of repertory. In Santa Barbara, as elsewhere, Graham had assaulted the eyes with bodily configurations that it would take a generation to become accustomed to.

In Los Angeles a few days later she gave two concerts at the Philharmonic Auditorium. There the memory of Denishawn was strong, and the reviewer sought to find the elements of Denishawn training still existent in her dancing. Able to point only to her costuming as being reminiscent of Ruth St. Denis, he detected "the magnificence of the 'Peacock' [a St. Denis solo] with an American moral." An interview she gave had little effect in persuading people differently. Stressing that her work sprang from the American experience, she cited the spaciousness of the West as a very strong influence on her and said that wide steps and broad lines were natural ways for an American dancer to move and that, in her own mind, she associated leaps with the European ballet tradition.

The previous year Graham, on her way back east after visiting her mother in Santa Barbara, had given another interview to the *Los Angeles Times* that tried to prepare the way for her work. It was a remarkably succinct and clear statement of what she was doing and of her creative regimen. She was forty-two when she gave the interview: "A dancer of today leads a completely regimented life. . . . I get up at six to practice two hours, and I know that if I stay out too late the night before, the first half hour of practice will be worth very little. . . . After my own work there is practice with the company for me, several hours each day. Then teaching so that I may make my living—few dancers can live on recitals—and after that, creative study for performance. . . . The lift of the arm does not mean that it represents a tree or anything else. The arm is raised in an uplift that is graceful, presents the beauty of an arm in motion. It is enough. America is not interested in impressionism. Our dramatic force lies in energy and vitality. Symbolism is alien to it. That is theatric and not good theater, for it does not communicate itself directly to the audience from the dancer." Referring to Horst, she said, in affection and admiration: "He really dances with the dancer, although he weighs 250 pounds and doesn't move from his piano bench." Graham's words about her work made sense, but the public still sought the lyrical and flowing gestures that Denishawn had accustomed them to. To a great extent even the gauzy memory seemed far preferable to most than did the stark percussive actuality of Graham with her pale cheeks and deep-set, intense eyes. The reviews continued to be harsh.

When they returned to New York, Horst and Graham were asked to participate in a fund-raising demonstration performance at the Neighborhood Playhouse for a distinguished and wealthy invited audience. Among the guests was Eleanor Roosevelt, invited by Rita Morgenthau, who afterward spoke warmly to Graham about the recital. The following week, Graham's press agent and manager, Frances Hawkins, sent off a letter to the White House, along with a souvenir booklet that Graham and Horst had had prepared for the transcontinental tour and a broadside of favorable newspaper notices (at the time very hard to find) culled from various sources. Hawkins included a one-paragraph history of the uphill struggle of the modern dance:

> I think that the broadside is particularly interesting because it reveals the very favorable reaction of the American public to an American artist. It has been a very long and weary struggle to get the public not to be so completely dazzled by foreign

> glamor that it is blinded to native genius. This is particularly true in the case of the dancer, but I am certain that this recent tour of Martha Graham's, during which both audiences and managers found this country had at last developed the dance as a native art, will do much to further the public's pride in our artists.

Mrs. Roosevelt's reply that week, through her secretary, was cordial and commented favorably on the material that Hawkins had sent. Though it seemed a routine letter, it was to have an important consequence.

Meanwhile, after the completion of the annual four-week June course in technique at the studio, which she began in 1934 just prior to her first July at Bennington, Graham returned to her third summer at Bennington. The festival had clearly become the most important single event in the year's modern dance calendar. Bennington in 1936 was a success in terms of enrollment, finances, and reputation. As in the past two seasons, the students were mostly teachers, and again reflecting the male-female imbalance in modern dance, primarily women. Graham scheduled no new work. She and the Group would teach, and she would perform a program of solos. Doris Humphrey and Charles Weidman were in charge of the summer workshop.

In the rest of the dance world, significant changes had taken place that were reflected in the concerts at Bennington. Lincoln Kirstein, who the previous year had sent Muriel Stuart to Graham's workshop, was having severe difficulties with the American Ballet Company that he had formed with the choreographer George Balanchine. Kirstein was an admirer of the Diaghilev Ballet, and his ambition was to establish a comparable American company that would build on the work of teachers and choreographers living permanently in the United States. An intensely patriotic man, Kirstein wanted an American dance, but he envisioned it as ballet within an American style, whatever that might turn out to be. The School of American Ballet was established in 1933 (Kirstein had originally intended to locate it in Hartford, Connecticut, away from the feverishness of the New York theater world, but Balanchine had insisted that the school be in the city), and a small company was duly formed in 1935. Shortly thereafter it was asked to become the resident company of the Metropolitan Opera.

From the beginning of the school, Balanchine, in his choice of music and thematic material, had inclined toward the classical ballet tradition. He might do a ballet like "Alma Mater" on an American theme, but basically he was not interested in ballet with either stories or plot development in the usual sense. This meant that the subject matter Kirstein was interested in rarely was handled. In addition, Kirstein saw that the Ballet Russe touring companies were having more success than his own American Ballet, and he was also aware of the burgeoning success of the modern dancers who not only concentrated on American themes but made a point of the "home-grown" character of their art as distinct from the European-dominated ballet. Since Balanchine was not inclined to create large numbers of ballets on "native" themes, Kirstein decided to create a small touring company of dancers drawn from the School of American Ballet. The company was called Ballet Caravan. Its policy was to have American dancers perform American dances choreographed for American audiences. Despite the opposition of Kirstein, an active polemicist and a litterateur of accomplishment, to modern dance, there was no more logical place to launch such an enterprise than Bennington, and so on July 17, 1936, Ballet Caravan made its first appearance before a vaguely hostile group of modern dancers in Bennington.

Although modern dancers disliked ballet in a somewhat doctrinaire and blanket fashion, without dealing with the particular merits of any one dancer or company, the presence of a strong contingent of male dancers in Ballet Caravan gave it a pleasingly balanced appearance and made a distinctly favorable impression on the Amazonian world of modern dance. The Caravan company included, among others, the brothers Lew and Harold Christensen, Eugene Loring, Fred Danieli, and Erick Hawkins. The program included "Harlequin for President," "Yankee Clipper," and "Pocahontas," all with scripts written by Kirstein and choreography by members of the company. After the performance, Graham visited the company backstage in the Armory's basement dressing rooms and made a point of greeting one performer in particular, Erick Hawkins. An admirer of Graham's (he had worked with Muriel Stuart to learn Graham's technique but had come to feel that he was seeing it only at second hand), Hawkins was especially pleased.

After the departure of Ballet Caravan, the summer settled back into its accustomed frame of classes in the various modern dance techniques. The general program continued to be the most popular

Rehearsal snapshots of the 1964 reconstruction of "Primitive Mysteries."

Left: Section I, "Hymn to the Virgin."

Below: Section II, "Crucifixus."

Above: Reconstruction of "Primitive Mysteries" (cont'd).
Section III, "Hosanna."

Below: Martha Graham, the Group, Louis Horst, and dachshund at rehearsal of "Primitive Mysteries." New York, 1931.

Pre-Bennington years:

Martha Graham and Louis Horst.

Neighborhood Playhouse
productions with
Charles Weidman, New York.

Trip to Yucatán, Mexico, on Guggenheim Fellowship, 1933.

Louis Horst and Martha Graham at Bennington College.

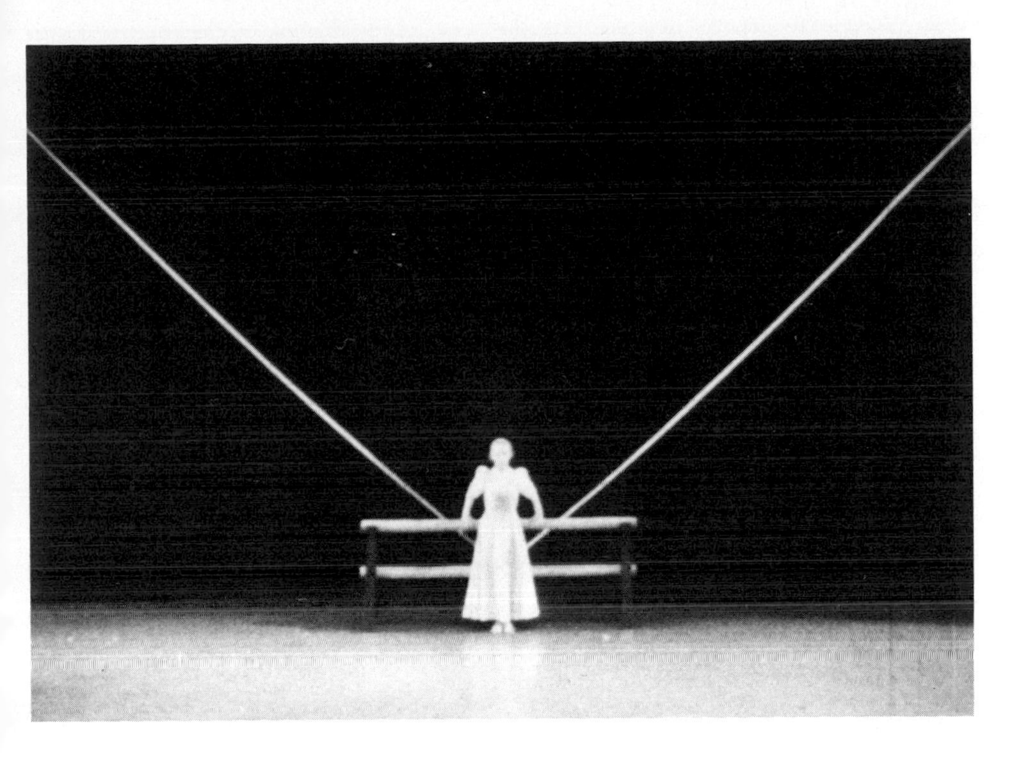

Rehearsal snapshots of 1964 reconstruction of "Frontier," originally produced in 1935.

Reconstruction of "Frontier" (cont'd).

course. Horst's informal class in music for modern dance had become a regular part of the curriculum. Weidman's group in the workshop performed the premiere of "Quest," and Humphrey created "With My Red Fires." As part of the concert series, Graham did a program of solos. At the end of the season it was announced that Hanya Holm would take charge of the workshop the following year.

In July, the Spanish Civil War began. Though other modern dancers often used political themes, Graham rarely did. On this occasion, however, she felt sufficiently involved to prepare a dance; indeed, she may have been influenced to do so by the intense left-wing agitation demanding that artists deal with the subject. For the fall season, therefore, she prepared "Chronicle," a work that ran for about an hour and traced the course of the Spanish Civil War—its inception and its consequences. Graham attempted to use her feelings of pain and outrage as material, but the dance lacked the imaginative fire that infused those dances in which her emotions became translated into significant motion. "Chronicle" was an act of sympathy, but it did not flare out from the core of her interest in the mythic and the well of unconscious feelings upon which she drew for her major pieces. Yet, despite the failings of "Chronicle," it was a clear sign that her attention was moving away from the highly introspective pieces that had first brought her to public attention. She was beginning to survey the terrain of the outside world and reflect it through the prism of her sensibility.

Frances Hawkins took the occasion of "Chronicle" to follow up her earlier letter to Mrs. Roosevelt, offering to provide her with tickets for the December 20 or the December 27 performance, with the explicit understanding that no attempt would be made to draw any publicity value from her appearances. Hawkins undoubtedly was sincere in her promise not to inform the newspapers, but it seems highly unlikely that the appearance of the President's wife at a theater in New York, the media capital of the country, would not have been noticed by someone, even without any prior alert. In any case, Mrs. Roosevelt replied that she was already engaged and sent her regrets.

However, her interest in Graham was not idle, and about a month and a half later, in the first week of February, Graham received a letter on White House stationery sent to her in care of the Neighborhood Playhouse:

My dear Miss Graham,
. . . I am wondering if you would like to come down on February 26. I am having a birthday party for Mrs. Henry Morgenthau, Jr. It will not be a large party. Miss Sidney Thompson, an old friend of Mrs. Morgenthau's, is going to do some recitations and I thought if you could come down and give us a few dances it would make a delightful evening. There will be some people here who will be well worthwhile meeting, besides the fact that we can give some publicity for your appearance. Be quite honest, if you do not care to come for a small group. I do not know who travels with you on these occasions, but I am quite sure I can put you up for one night and perhaps one friend.

Cordially yours,
ELEANOR ROOSEVELT

Horst, when he saw the letter, muttered about following a "disease," the diseuse (reciter) Miss Thompson, but of course he was enormously pleased. The invitation conferred on Graham a respect and recognition that had not yet been given to any other American dancer. She had passed up the international hoopla of the Olympic games in Germany the previous year but now was recompensed by the chance to appear at the White House. Horst and she had to scrape together train fare. A snowstorm delayed their arrival, but fortunately a limousine met them at the station and took them to the White House. Horst shared a room with James Roosevelt, and Graham dressed alone in Lincoln's bedroom. While Graham was waiting to perform after the 7 P.M. dinner, one of the White House guards looked disapprovingly at her bare feet. Among the two dozen guests were the President in his wheelchair, who greeted the artists and thanked them for attending. Declining the invitation to stay the night, they returned to New York that evening and taught class the next day.

Mrs. Roosevelt carried an account of the evening in her syndicated column, "My Day," in which she reported Graham's saying that she worked four hours each day to keep herself in good physical condition and that it took her two months to recover from a six-month vacation. (Exactly when Graham had taken a six-month vacation was not clear.)

Toward the end of March, Graham prepared the transcontinental Group tour for which she and Horst had, in effect, practiced the year before. Again, Armitage helped with the bookings. The Group had not toured before, and the cross-country plan made the trip all the more special. Because the company was to dance in Canada, it would also be the first Graham company ever to dance outside the United States. For many in the Group, it was, in fact, the first time they had traveled so far from home.

The tour, like the earlier one, had a leisurely quality that flew in the face of all economic reason, all the more so now that the entire Group, fifteen people, was involved. Appearances averaged out at two a week, so for many of the dancers the trip was like a paid vacation. They had enough time in each place to be tourists and spend nearly every cent they earned. Horst, who was a veteran traveler, read detective novels and saw to the details of music and production with avuncular good humor.

The tour started out in March in high anticipation with a date in Madison, Wisconsin. From there it went to Chicago, and then to Billings, Montana, where the audience thought that the Group looked more like a girls' basketball team than a group of dancers. None of the local boys would ask the young women for dates because they thought they were too masculine. Immediately after Billings the company went to Canada to play a date in Vancouver. The naïve young women from New York had expectations of Canada similar to those they had of England. They all wanted to have tea and crumpets or scones, and were disappointed to find Canada so much like the Midwest. They also had to adjust the pitch and energy of their dancing to compensate for a raked (deliberately slanted) stage that they had not encountered previously. All in all, the trip was an adventure for them, but not for Graham, who now had a full Group to take care of.

More, she was still facing audiences that did not comprehend, and she was still gathering know-nothing notices from whoever was assigned to cover the programs. Reviewers complained about the relentless pounding of modern dancers while admiring their "gymnastic ability." Reviewers found little grace and even less structure in the dances. They saw instead hops, antic jumps, and shuffling, and found the pieces as much of a mess as they assumed Miss Graham saw the world was in. They wondered why she didn't dance Einstein's theory or the story of vitamin D. It was a difficult time.

As a matter of brutal fact, while she was being castigated by her enemies, the supposed comfort of her ostensible disciples was almost as severe a trial. When the group played a date in any city that had a sizable college, the local Orchesis society would invariably arrange a social to show Graham the movement that they had learned either firsthand or from a faculty moderator who herself had studied at Bennington. Graham had had her share of such socials the year before and often delegated Horst or some of her assistants to go. Once one returned and told her that Bennington had created a Frankenstein. The big awkward girls, whom she described as "sergeants," were taking every little exercise they had learned and making a dance out of it. The more awkward and the more horrible the dance, they better they would say it was. Graham had certainly changed their views about Denishawn's flowing loveliness, but not the way she had intended. One is reminded of the story of Isadora Duncan who, late in her career, attended a recital at a Russian school that was supposedly utilizing her technique. After watching the recital, she stalked onstage and put the flowers that had been given her on the floor as she announced that what she had seen was the grave of her hopes.

Graham did not go so far in public, but she was tormented inwardly by each fresh report about an Orchesis reception. Her technique without her presence to direct and guide the dancers had been made a caricature of itself. This was one of the strongest impressions that she carried away from the tour. In later life she rejected the filming of her dances for future reference in part because she did not want enthusiasts using the steps without understanding their origin. The members of her Group knew that they were living with a genius whose verbal images illuminated meaning in a way that the simple repetition of steps could not. However, at the time of the tour, they were living and traveling with an unhappy genius.

For the rest of the Group, though, it was all an adventure. In Seattle, they hit another raked stage and took it in stride. At the Opera House in San Francisco, they were presented with the largest stage that they would encounter on the tour, and they had to cover more space than they were accustomed to. Everyone ended up with leg cramps and most spent a restless night with little sleep. Two nights later, at Sunset High School in Carmel, they had the opposite problem, a severely restricted stage space. Here they made the simple adjustment of reducing the number of dancers in individual pieces. Some of the dancers went down to the ocean to dip their feet in the Pacific, and the next night they were right back on the huge stage of the San Francisco Opera. It was taxing.

At least the Lobero Theater in Santa Barbara was reasonable, and Graham's mother, friends, and relatives all turned out again to see Martha. They were kind, but few understood. Graham's mother never really grasped the import of her daughter's work, but she was a staunch supporter nonetheless and had the Group out to enjoy the house with its orange tree in the yard. Few of the group had ever seen oranges growing on trees, and Gertrude Shurr saved her souvenir orange until it withered. To some, Mrs. Graham appeared very New Englandish, as did the interior of the house in contrast to its exterior and the warm sunshine outside. The house, like Graham, possessed that strange amalgam of stern Yankee mixed with the hedonistic emotionalism of Southern California.

California was pleasant, but Graham was tired, and the Group still had five performances to give, the next being in Los Angeles, where Merle Armitage was waiting to greet them. The tour had not been what Graham had hoped it would be and, although she tried to conceal her feelings, Armitage felt that there was something noticeably wrong. It seemed to him that she was in a state of uncertainty bordering on depression.

Two weeks later, on April 30, the Group played its last date in Pittsburgh. However, instead of waiting a day or so to take a leisurely train trip back to New York, leftish members of the Group insisted that they leave that night after the performance, catching a very late train so that they could be back in the city in time to march in the May Day parade the next morning. Graham wearily acceded, and they all returned on a slow, uncomfortable train.

Armitage had been brooding about Graham. It seemed to him that unless she had a complete change of scene, she would be in serious trouble. He shot off a telegram, inviting her out to the Coast for a rest. In his bluntest, but kind, style, he told her to come back to California, that he would rent a house for her to recuperate in. This she owed to herself, to him, and to her public—and he suggested that emotionally she had reached the bottom of the barrel. Graham wired back: "I can't accept that much from anybody." Armitage wired: "Tickets on the Chief will be delivered to you day after tomorrow. No answer required." Not a word came from New York. Not knowing whether Graham had accepted or not, Armitage went to Pasadena to meet the Chief on the appointed day and found to his great relief that Graham was aboard. He embraced her emotionally.

Armitage was living in the middle of Los Angeles in the Silver Lake district, and he had rented a house for Graham at Redondo Beach on the coast. At the time he was working on a book about Graham (he had already published books on Picasso and Stravinsky), and he was consulting with Ramiel McGehee editorially and had taken on a young artist named Carlus Dyer to prepare a series of sketches for the Graham book. McGehee lived in Redondo Beach and Dyer was a frequent visitor. McGehee, as fabulous in his own way as was Armitage, had traveled around the world and was particularly knowledgeable about the cultures of China and Japan. Among other things, he had met the Empress Dowager of China and had been the English tutor for the young Emperor of Japan, Hirohito. Graham was fascinated by him, as Armitage had hoped she would be. She also soon became passionately infatuated with the handsome Dyer. Her sexual life had been sporadic; their affair was intense. Except for discussions with McGehee about the Orient, she spent practically all her time with Dyer, swimming in the morning and evening and, in Armitage's pungent recollection, "fuckin' all night. They'd invite me down to breakfast, and they'd crawl out of bed, both of them, you know, they'd come out on their hands and knees, practically."

Armitage banned all talk of dance at meals and cautioned everyone not to think about it. The ban seems to have worked. For Graham, there were conversations with McGehee on Lao Tze, and there was the sea and the handsome Dyer. The holiday provided a respite from thoughts of dance. The two-month vacation seemed to dissolve the psychic and physical kinks that had made Armitage so anxious about Graham. When she left to return to New York, Graham told him simply, "This is a rebirth."

In July, Graham and the Group went again to Bennington. The workshop this year was taken by Hanya Holm, who created "Trend." Graham offered two new works at her Group's performance. The first was a solo, a new opening dance, called just that, "Opening Dance," which Martin dismissed in the *New York Times* as something that "belongs in that thankless category of the recital dancer, something to raise the curtain with." The second new work, "Immediate Tragedy," showed her mulling over the tragedy of the

Spanish Civil War again. The piece had some conviction, but, as in "Ceremonials," not enough of Graham's deepest feelings were engaged to make a really tight work out of it.

The Group concert was more important for the happy scene in the Putnam Grill after the performance when Graham appeared with Ruth St. Denis. St. Denis, who was paying her first visit to the dance festival, appeared as part of an effort to bury all factional hatchets in support of a Dance International Series, a demonstration of contemporary ballet and modern dance that was to be presented in December.

St. Denis was to appear in the modern section of this demonstration, but not Shawn. Since his professional split with St. Denis in 1931, he had toured the country and abroad with a group of male dancers and had established his own summer festival and school at Jacob's Pillow in Becket, Massachusetts. He had no use for Bennington, nor did the Bennington group have any regard for Shawn. While the Dance International programs were being presented, Shawn and his group were touring, and they returned to play New York with their own solo concert the month after the Dance International programs were completed.

Although neither St. Denis nor Shawn ever liked modern dance, both publicly came to live with its developments more or less well. In private conversation, though, they continued to be disdainful. St. Denis's remarks to Jane Dudley about Graham are a harsh example, though conceivably they were as much the result of St. Denis's attitude toward Graham as toward modern dance. She was, in any case, kinder toward Humphrey, whom she had taken touring with her in the early days of Denishawn, and she even sent Humphrey and Weidman a congratulatory letter after their first independent concert.

St. Denis's and Shawn's attitude toward modern dance, unlike the attitude of the modernists to European dancers, was not intensified by the minor competition it offered. In the early 1930's when modern dance audiences were very small, St. Denis and Shawn filled the vast outdoor stage in Lewisohn Stadium in New York. Their sexy and quasi-mystical style of dance was very much in public favor. St. Denis also staged annual dance pageants at the Westchester County Festival in White Plains, for which each dance studio within fifty miles would turn out its students. It was there that St. Denis had taken aside Dudley, whose mother taught dance rhythms and several times sent her daughter to be in the pageants, and cautioned her about Graham.

But now the differences between Graham and St. Denis were to be publicly reconciled. The first reconciliation had been attempted in 1928, when the Denishawn house was opened near Van Cortland Park in the Bronx. Shawn and St. Denis invited all of the prodigal dancers who had left them, and St. Denis gave Graham a pink and gold sari bought on the company's Oriental tour. Graham made a spectacular entrance in a low-cut black dress with a red velvet ribbon from which dangled an icon, but the goodwill dissipated quickly, since it was clear that Denishawn's children were competing with Denishawn. Only years later, when St. Denis and Graham were in a cooperative presentation, did they become reconciled.

Curiously, despite St. Denis's basically cool attitude, Graham over the years continued to court her favor. She spoke well of St. Denis in her classes at the Neighborhood Playhouse, while she never had a good word for Shawn. The psychology behind Graham's feelings about the stunningly beautiful St. Denis appears to be quite complex: St. Denis was the figure who inspired her and the authority who rejected her. Still, when St. Denis visited Bennington and went backstage to speak to Graham after her performance, Graham was ready to welcome her. Graham invited St. Denis to accompany her to the Putnam Grill, and when the two of them entered, there was a spontaneous expression of enthusiasm. Graham, in her grand style, gracefully turned it from herself and indicated that it belonged to St. Denis. Perhaps Graham could afford to be magnanimous, for she was the cutting edge of a movement that had achieved acceptance among serious dance enthusiasts. For herself, she had been to the White House and no other American dancer ever had. Still, she gave the applause to St. Denis. The gesture was taken as the healing of a breach.

In her autobiography St. Denis appears a bit puzzled about Graham's feelings for her: "Most of the time in my class she sat very still and listened. When she spoke it was only to ask an intelligent question. My direct work with Martha was very slight. She soon joined Ted's classes, and she owed her professional development to the deep concern and affection that Ted had for her during these early years. But she is kind enough to say that the influence of my personality and work was a large factor in her life."

At the end of the year, the staff of Bennington School of Dance congratulated itself, observing in its report that Bennington was "the outstanding single agency for promoting the growth of the dance as an art in America." The report noted: "A no less direct and no less important influence of the school is that it has given to a new and still struggling art a center which publicly identifies it as an independent art." The festival, which had started on a budget of $7,000, had run it up to five times that amount in a scant four years, the past year even offering fellowships to younger dancers (José Limon, Esther Junger, and Anna Sokolow, a member of Graham's Group), and still it could show a profit at the end of the year.

The festival had provided the backing that enabled modern dance to hold its head up in the intellectual and academic world. The Dance International Series was an attempt to find it a place in the public's favor. Not only were there to be performances in the Center Theater, but the Radio City Music Hall was to present a pageant glorifying dance and NBC Radio was to broadcast information about the series. Exhibitions of paintings and stage designs were also planned.

The modern dance evening included St. Denis, Graham, Humphrey, Weidman, Holm, and Tamiris, all of whom were appearing together for the first time. Graham presented her Group in a new work, "American Lyric," and she also performed "Frontier." As its title suggests, the new dance was another of Graham's American pieces, like "Frontier" and "Panorama," but again, as with "Panorama," it was not successful. Graham, however, was working her way toward a dance of Americana that would change her life. The evening was long, well attended, and favorably reviewed. But only St. Denis, who presented two solos and a piece called "Balinese Trio," was asked for an encore. Given a choice, the popular public taste still opted for the pretty Orientalisms of Denishawn rather than the seriousness and severity of modern dance. The primary place of modern dance was still in the world it had made for itself.

In November, Merle Armitage's book on Graham appeared. He designed it himself and had drawn on an illustrious set of collaborators to create what was, in effect, a celebration of Graham. Among the contributors of essays or articles were drama critic Stark Young, art historian and museum curator James Johnson Sweeney, composer George Antheil, and dance critics John Martin, Margaret

Lloyd, and the volatile Lincoln Kirstein, who had done a complete about-face. Barbara Morgan, a painter-turned-photographer who had been taking pictures of Graham and the Group since the mid-1930's, contributed some of her finest photographs; and Carlus Dyer did diagramatic drawings of various dances to head each of the chapters. The book was handsomely produced and privately printed by Armitage in a limited edition of 1,000 copies.

Graham of course, knew that the book was being prepared, but the reality of it did not strike her until she had it in hand. It was testimony of a special sort. She wrote of her feelings thirty years later in an introduction when the book was reprinted for general distribution.

> This book was very important in my life. When Merle Armitage first came to me to say that he wanted to do it, I was honored of course and very pleased, but not at all prepared for the impact of it later when it was there in print in my hands. It seemed to be about someone else whom I did not know at all. I was stunned and shaken and forced to think of many things I might never have thought of, and I was very grateful for that. Now, so many years later, I am grateful still.

Money was still scarce. Graham and the Group went to Washington, D.C., to do a single concert in January 1938, and at the end of the month, back in New York, she and the Group appeared on a benefit program to raise money for medical supplies for Republican Spain. The concert, sponsored by the American Dance Association, gathered together as many dancers as there then were in New York. The evening included Anna Sokolow, Tamiris, Hanya Holm's company, Paul Draper, and Ballet Caravan, which, by coincidence, offered "Show Piece," a work choreographed by Erick Hawkins and one of the dances that Graham had seen him in at Bennington when she had gone backstage to congratulate him.

A few concerts were lined up for the spring, but altogether there was not more than one performance a week for the next four months. As in the past, Graham was forced to mix solo appearances with the Group's performances on tour. She traveled out to Westfield, New Jersey, with Horst early in February, and then with the Group a few days later to Northampton, Massachusetts. The Washington Irving High School series in New York continued to be one of the Group's regular appearances, and Graham with one or two members of her Group participated in lecture demonstrations at the Neighborhood Playhouse. These were presentations that showed the range of instruction available at the Playhouse. The students, all unknown at the time, were either assigned a scene by Sanford Meisner, who headed the drama department, or given a dance assignment by Horst or Graham. The demonstrations had little value for Graham, but they gave students who had been instructed by her the opportunity to use the lessons she had taught them.

While on tour and when at home, Graham read voraciously (she once said to an interviewer, "I owe all that I am to the study of Nietzsche and Schopenhauer"), and during the months of March and April she was jotting down notes and ideas for a work to be based on interpretations of American historical documents such as Lincoln's Emancipation Proclamation and the Declaration of Independence. She intended the dance to be performed at Bennington. A spring tour found her appearing with her Group in Cleveland for the first time, and she and Horst played a concert recital at the Wellesley Club in Columbus, Ohio, where a cousin of hers, Mrs. Frank S. Prescott, was part of the sponsoring committee. For the rest of the tour, the Group played Ann Arbor and in Missouri—Kirksville, Fayette, and St. Louis finishing up at the vast but somehow atmospherically intimate Auditorium Theater in Chicago.

The honor of being the host of the World's Fair of 1939–40 was accorded to the United States and by 1938 plans were well enough along the way to construct the fairgrounds. Flushing Meadow in New York was chosen as the site, and in May of 1938 the Fair committee decided to have a celebration that would precede by one year the official opening of the Fair. The country was beginning to make some progress in pulling itself out of the financial chasm into which it had fallen with the stock market crash of 1929. Though it had taken nearly a decade, there now were flickering signs of life in the economy, and the feeling of bleakness that had gripped the country in 1933 had disappeared. In its stead was a growing sense of confidence. It was this upsurge that the committee wanted to celebrate and take as the theme for the fair, which was being presented as a guidepost to a better future.

Grover Whelan, who was in charge of handling the Fair's public relations, set May 1, 1938, as the preview day and invited the public to a free entertainment at the Fair site. The program was designed to have a strong dance component, and Graham and her Group were asked to participate in the finale. They were preceded by groups of Polish, Ukrainian, Swedish, and unspecified Balkan dancers, and by a selection of classical music and popular songs and operatic arias. In the finale, Graham and the Group appeared in Grecian-looking costumes with banners and performed a small pageant-like dance with music by Ray Green, specially arranged by Robert Russell Bennett. To end the program a chorus of 100 high school students carrying a model of the Trylon and the Perisphere, the fair's architectural symbols, sang the Fair's theme song, "Dawn of a New Day," composed by George Gershwin, and all 500 singers on the program rendered the American premiere of Sibelius's anthem, "Onward Ye Peoples." The crowd was vast and the newspaper coverage heavy.

Graham and the Group had no further concerts that spring, and they worked on the new dance that Graham had in mind for Bennington, a dance that would use the spoken word. The script that she had prepared for the work was culled from her readings in American history and literature, and it followed the use of American documents employed by William Carlos Williams in his book *In the American Grain.* Williams's book, even now not especially well known, was then very much of a book for "the happy few." That Graham used the book is some indication of her alertness to contemporary works. Graham decided that a reader would declaim texts during the dance, and that the whole piece would be presented in the form of a traditional minstrel show. It would open and close with a parade, with various episodes in between. The dance was to be called "American Document."

Graham by this time had firmly established the pattern of using new music for each of her dances. It was Ray Green who now composed the score for the new dance. By way of testing some of its movements, she had used some of the music of this young composer in the fanfare at the World's Fair. To design the piece, she called on Arch Lauterer, and for the first time in her career she asked someone else to do the costumes. This was Edythe Gilfond. Graham had in mind a major theatrical work.

6

Graham Smiles

". . . the Beatrice Lillie of the
dance and she's been hiding it
from us all these years."
Walter Terry

"American Document" was well along by the time Erick Hawkins showed up at Graham's Fifth Avenue studio to take the June course. Hawkins, whom Graham had first seen and complimented at Bennington and whom she had seen several times since, possessed one of the more inquiring minds in the dance world. With Balanchine's American Ballet he had made it a point to watch rehearsals and to analyze the work Balanchine was doing. From Muriel Stuart he had learned something of Graham's technique. Without any specific plans, but somewhat dissatisfied with what he was doing under Balanchine's direction, he went to the Graham studio with Kirstein's blessing to see firsthand what she was doing and whether there was anything in her work that would be of help to him. Hawkins was not the first male dancer to study with Graham, but he was one of the first few. He was also one of the few *ballet* dancers to take her course.

The Group was working on "American Document," and Hawkins, not at all a shy person, asked for permission to watch rehearsals as he had done with Balanchine. Surprisingly, Graham allowed him to do so. It was a permission she had given only rarely at any time and not at all since "Panorama." The Group murmured.

After watching for some time, Hawkins said to Graham, "I'd like to come to Bennington. Maybe you could even find a place for me to walk across the back of the stage." Hawkins did not expect that Graham would ever use him in any "serious" way, but he now felt that Balanchine's sense of dance, which he admired, did not hold any great possibilities for him as a performer and that perhaps exposure to Graham's creative work might provide him with something more individually suited to himself. To his surprise and the amazement of everyone else, Graham took him on immediately to become part of "American Document." The minstrel-show structure of the dance was loose enough to accommodate changes in the individual parts, and so fitting Hawkins into its framework did not really necessitate any broad revision of the work. But Graham made broad changes anyway. She not only made Hawkins a principal in the piece, but she made him her partner. All this happened in a period of four weeks.

In Bennington, during rehearsals, the Group was not happy. As usual, Graham banned all husbands for the rehearsal periods when, for the first time, a man was dancing with the Group. Then she insisted that none of the dancers go out in the sun unprotected. She herself wore a broad-brimmed hat and went around with a parasol. After that, she banned the wearing of slacks. Some thought it silly; others were docile. But the circumstance that caused the most irritation was the designation of Hawkins as a principal dancer. The simple fact of the matter was that he had been with the Group only since the beginning of the June course, about four weeks, and there were dancers who by 1938 had been with Graham for ten years (and still others who had been there for at least five years). Not only had Hawkins been elevated above them, but he was also instructing the Group. The types of corrections he offered added insult to injury. His approach was quite alien to the manner in which Graham made a correction. Where she would explain the growth of a gesture from the movement that had preceded it, using emotional or psychological images, Hawkins would be likely to talk of holding the arm at a forty-five degree angle. He spoke in terms of established poses and givens that Graham had always disregarded.

The Group was irritated, but Hawkins's handling of the dances that had been almost completely set in New York gave Graham time to work on her solos.

The advent of "American Document" caused shock waves in the sensibilities of modern dancers. The piece itself, with its extensive use of the spoken word and quasi-play format, was unusual. The appearance of a man in one of Graham's works was revolutionary. Moreover, the dance itself turned out to be overtly sensual in certain aspects, and in the Puritan high seriousness of modern dance, sex was not a subject for dancing. The piece was cast in six sections. Its characters were an Interlocutor, End Figures, the Chorus, and Two Principals. The first portion was the "Entrance," consisting of "Walk Around" and "Cross Fire"; this was followed by "Declaration," "Occupation," "The Puritan," and "Emancipation"; the piece concluded with "Hold Your Hold!" Housley Stevens Jr., the Interlocutor, was called upon to deliver quotations from the Declaration of Independence and the Emancipation Proclamation. Continuity passages were written by Graham herself. After everyone entered and bowed to the audience, Stevens stepped forward to say:

> Ladies and gentlemen, good evening.
> This is a theater.
> The place is here in the United States of America.
> The time is now—tonight.
> The characters are:
> The dance group, led by Sophie [Maslow],
> You, the audience,
> The Interlocutor—I am the Interlocutor,
> And Erick and Martha.

The music composed by Ray Green picked up again and the dance began its several episodes. Hawkins and Graham did the first duet, then Hawkins and the Group performed "Declaration," and Graham and the Group danced "Occupation," in which one of Graham's most memorable solos emerged as she created the figure of an Indian girl, the Native Figure, with her long hair drawn back at the nape of the neck and braided to hang down the back. Photos of Graham in this role were used on program covers during the subsequent touring of the piece. The "Puritan" episode was a duet for Hawkins and Graham in which the Interlocutor alternately spoke lines from the fire-and-brimstone Puritan minister Jonathan Edwards and the sensuous Old Testament "Song of Songs." Thus the cutting observation "Death comes hissing like a fiery dragon with the sting on the mouth of it" is followed immediately with "Let him kiss me with the kisses of his mouth/For thy love is better than wine"—New England Puritanism versus lusty abandon, a motif that was to be expressed many times in Graham's subsequent work. The "Emancipation" had a large Group dance and another duet for Hawkins and Graham. In the final section, Hawkins and Graham each had a solo, the Group joined for the final "Walk Around," and then exited after the Interlocutor's leave-taking: "Ladies and Gentlemen, may we wish you good night."

"American Document" took a theatrical form, the minstrel show, designed for popular entertainment and infused it with Graham's own preoccupation with the formation of the American sensibility. Through the Declaration of Independence it showed the country's break with Europe, which was followed almost immediately by a form of domestic imperialism, which took the country away from the Indians who inhabited it. It showed the strength of the Puritan heritage and some of the inhibitions that this heritage entails. It touched briefly upon the economic difficulties of the time of the Emancipation and ended with an affirmation of democracy. A morality play of a special sort, it was patriotic but also demonstrative of the problems of the individual as regards the moral and institutional demands of the system. "Document" was a compressed social history of the United States, and in it Graham was at last able to do a major work on an American theme for her Group.

"Document" was very much a fulfillment of the large-scale documentary on America that Graham had earlier attempted in "Panorama" and "Horizons." Now she was faced with none of the elements that had interfered with the realization of those works. She was not pressured by time as she had been previously, for she had accomplished much of the work in the New York studio before going to Bennington that summer. Further, she was working with her Group, and not, as in "Panorama," with large groups of unfamiliar students. It is true that she had to work harder with Hawkins than with anyone else, but he was eager and willing and worth the trouble. He brought something to Graham's work that she very much wanted. Working with a ballet-trained dancer had its technical problems, and, before her style of movement became habitual for him, Graham spent three years telling Hawkins to restrain and not to "reach out" or "spill." But, in the larger scale of things, such technical problems were minor.

In terms of Graham's own career, the significance of "American Document" was that Graham, tired of being an outsider, whether an honored one or not, let Hawkins serve as the instrument through which she would enter the theatrical mainstream. Hawkins was a tall, handsome man, as firm as an oak, and he exuded an American solidarity that was perfect for this dance. As an epic of American life, an all-woman version of the country's development would have been a curiosity. With a good male dancer, "American Document" had a chance to become popular entertainment.

A pivotal dance in Graham's career, "American Document" not only was a major work on an American theme but also marked the opening of a whole new phase in her work. She had always been interested in drama, and now she had created a dance work that used words, producing a hybrid form that partook both of dance and drama, thereby making the work accessible to a broad public beyond the still limited number of modern dance partisans. The declamations of the narrator offered a comprehensible structure within which the dances could be seen and more easily understood. In part, therefore, by not intimidating audiences into a hostile or mocking response, this work helped remove some of the public's reluctance to accept this new type of dance that had tried so industriously to create a place for itself in the cultural life of the country. For the next decade, the success of the piece prompted others to try similar experiments, though with less success. At the very least, for those who did not know dance it was patriotic—which, indeed, is what Graham intended. Later, when interviewed about "American Document," Graham commented that she had heard the propaganda from other countries and had wanted to counteract their hostile effect with words.

Every aspect of the dance received attention from the critics. Lincoln Kirstein, who called it "an ambitious work in its combination of speech, music, and movement," also noted that it "had spectacular scenic touches." The example he gave came from the "Declaration" section, "when four doors opened at the back of the theater and four of the company in blue appeared suddenly like a 'blare of trumpets.'" The Armory was not an ideal plant for either equipment or furnishings, but Graham got from Arch Lauterer a set that would allow for exactly the kind of entrance she needed. Beginning with "American Document," Lauterer collaborated with Graham on some of her most spectacular dances. Their collaboration was one of friendship and respect, so much so that Graham became godmother to Lauterer's son.

Having three duets with Graham and one solo, Hawkins was a highly visible presence in the dance, and the objections to him were strong. First, he had come from the enemy camp, ballet, and had penetrated the redoubt of modern dance with consummate ease. Second, the presence of his sheer male physicality in what had been a Group of artistic vestals was a source of jealousy. Hawkins, big-boned and broad, was assertive in his style of dancing. He danced bare-chested in one section, and a reviewer, accurately but in a tone of shock, referred to him as being "naked except for white shorts." Since in that summer of 1938 he had the best tan of his life, he certainly made a striking figure. Further, not only had Graham, the tough-minded leader of the dedicated band, taken a man into her Group and given him precedence, she even created a dance about sex for the first time. It was unheard-of.

Jack Cole, reminiscing years later about modern dance, acknowledged that though he had taken a few classes in the mid-1930's at the Graham school, he left its Amazonian atmosphere for the more congenial confines of the Humphrey-Weidman school. Graham had been Diana, the virginal goddess of the hunt, running with her creative hounds in pursuit of ideal dance form. Now she had suddenly detoured to dally with a male personage. The *New York Times* dourly observed that the erotic duet in the "Puritan" episode was "distinctly weak." It found only the company parades at the beginning and at the end worthy of praise.

Graham could not have cared less. She was clearly doing exactly what she wanted to do, and it was she, after all, who had decided that Hawkins should dance bare-chested. Speaking just in terms of her dance, she had found a means of achieving a theatricality in her work that otherwise would have been impossible. She needed a man to inject dramatic conflict into her work, and Erick Hawkins, in effect, came along at just the right time. He provided the opportunity for Graham to deal with personality differences and thus to go beyond the examination of her own isolated individual experiences. He offered her the chance to develop plots. She would remain the center of her dances, but, if she wished to, she could replace an examination of states of being with a narrative unfolding. It was a whole new universe. It was also the end of an era for the Group. Gertrude Schurr, Anna Sokolow, May O'Donnell, and Kathleen Slagle, dancers with, collectively, thirty years of experience with Graham, left. Within three years four more male dancers joined Graham, and her original concept was replaced by the more conventional Company comprising both men and women.

Historically, whenever Graham took a new creative direction some of her followers were unable to make the transition with her. For some the adjustment to her first independent concerts after leaving Denishawn was too much to endure, and then the shift to abstract dances caused some of the more social, action-oriented groups to find fault with her. Similarly with "American Document," simply because it was experimental and unquestionably a turn toward a type of theater that had not previously been seen in her work. After working for over a decade to forge a creative body of movement, she was now seeking to expand her audience to include those who did not interest themselves in the purely formal consideration of watching a choreographer form her vocabulary. While the great pieces of that early period remain some of her finest achievements, her largest following among the public would be built by the intensely emotional and dramatic dance theater pieces that followed.

Thus "American Document" was the forerunner of a whole line of dramatically based dances that for many became the hallmark of Graham's style of theater. In effect, it blocked off the vision of many people to what had gone before. But the transformation was a development, not a radical change. Though she acceded to the audience's fondness for stories, she did not attempt to prettify her movement. Yet, after the summer of 1938, some of the austerity that kept the public at arm's length began to disappear, and her creative focus soon revealed a radical shift. She began to modify her technique away from the percussive line that she had used during the previous decade. In her classes, her students and the Group had been instructed to come down hard directly on the beat and to hold for an infinitesimal moment. Now she began to soften the transitions between movements and to place the accent of the movement just prior to the beat of the music. Oversimplifying, the hard "one, two, three" attack was becoming "*And* one, *and* two, *and* three," so that lyrical flow was induced in the combinations and sequences of the dance. Graham, an instinctive artist, changed her technique to suit her creative needs. She was not bound by any rules, not even ones she had made herself; the stylistic look of her dances grew out of her own artistic direction. She moved in the directions she had to, despite any objections.

She also began to script her works in a new way. From this point on, she would have an elaborate scenario prepared to give to designers and composers. Earlier she had explored various ways of working with music, and once even without music. At the start of her career Horst had encouraged the use of little-known composers, like Satie and Koechlin, among others; and then, to emphasize the modern dancer's independence from the music, he had her choreograph the dance before the composer wrote the music, so that the composer fitted the music to the dance as Horst himself had done for the early masterpiece "Primitive Mysteries." With this new practice of preparing a script to send to the composer, she formed a pattern that she would retain, with few exceptions, for the rest of her career. With a script in hand, the composer no longer had to come to the studio to watch the dancers working (and sometimes turn out music by the yard). Instead, he could take the ideas set out in writing and create a musical score that, though it drew its shape from the narrative, was, in effect an independent structure. Only after this point would Graham work with the score. It was the act of an independent and strongly creative personality in full command of her craft.

The response to "American Document"—the fact that it was popular, that audiences liked it—was quite startling to Graham, who had become habituated to popular abuse. Her first concert after Bennington, at Carnegie Hall, was sold out. On this occasion she presented "American Document" under the auspices of the magazine *New Masses*, and the response foreshadowed the reaction throughout the country. Thematically, theatrically, and emotionally, the work had caught the attention of the broad public. In its themes, "American Document" spoke to the hopefulness of the times, as Graham had intended. As theater, it was full of excitement. And emotionally, in the sexualized interplay between Hawkins and Graham, it had a special sort of electricity.

Although she and the Company had only five other performances that fall, because of the success of "American Document" Frances Hawkins (no relation to Erick Hawkins), Graham's manager, assembled substantial additional tours. Erick Hawkins was still a member of Ballet Caravan, but its performing schedule was not so heavy that he could not make the performances Graham needed him for. It was obvious, however, that he eventually would have to choose between the world of ballet and the world of modern dance.

Graham continued to give her time to political causes—benefits for Spanish Civil War victims and meetings against fascist governments. In December, she appeared at a rally along with Dashiel Hammett and several others to protest the excesses of the Nazi regime in Germany. But from this point on she no longer considered using contemporary political events as subject matter for her work. Though Graham was in sympathy with the politics of the underdog, she was not artistically motivated by them as many of her dancers were. She was, however, interested in history and, at this time, particularly in American history. Underlying history was the myth common to all peoples, despite their individual differences. Graham found the myth of America in the concept of the frontier, in the lives of the Indians who predated the European settlers, and later in the ruminations of a New England poet whose life was expressed in her poetry. History, reaching toward myth, and the mazes of the human heart now became intertwined themes.

The new popularity of Graham's work even brought her to the attention of furrier I. J. Fox, who asked Graham to appear in an advertisement wearing one of his coats. It may seem odd that the woman pictured in *Vanity Fair* in 1934 in a shapeless tube dress should be asked to do fashion modeling. But in private life Graham was a smartly dressed woman even to the point of being a clothes horse. She was, of course, an exceptionally skilled seamstress who could run up a dress for herself overnight, and who, until "American Document," had designed all the costumes for her dances, from the little "lotus blossom" look of her earliest works to the floor-pounding aggressiveness of her "long woolens" period. So now it was nothing for her to model. With her hat poised rakishly forward, she posed in front of a mirror displaying Mr. Fox's mink as pertly as anyone who had earned such a badge of distinction.

A woman of forty-four, she looked absolutely splendid, appearing to be in her mature but unspecified thirties. She carefully cultivated an indefiniteness about her age (most people did not know how old she was, and those who did loyally remained silent) and was exceptionally careful about having her picture taken. She discouraged members of her Company from taking candid shots of her. In the theater she was as young or as old as she wanted to be, but offstage, casual snapshots could reveal what theater arts could conceal. Except for that, she could have been the age she appeared to be. As a performer, Graham was an absolute marvel. She possessed a quickness of movement and a precision that gave no indication of age. She pushed herself intensely, pursuing her daily schedule of private rehearsal, public teaching, and creative work with her Company. The intensity of her activity seemed to work as a tonic for her.

In the spring of 1938 the Company, accompanied by Erick Hawkins and Horst as musical director, went off on a six-week transcontinental tour that averaged two performances a week, not especially good in itself but twice the exposure of the Group's first transcontinental tour. The first tour had been a bitter strain, but now she had Hawkins and she had "American Document" as the central piece on the program. In contrast to the half-empty houses of the first tour, large crowds were attracted wherever the Company went. The tour swung through the South, up the California coast, where it included a performance in Santa Barbara, and back through Chicago, ending in Ithaca, New York. In Chicago, 2,500 people turned out at the Civic Opera House. The performance was sponsored by the Chicago Civil Liberties Committee, and the audience observed a half-minute of silence for the fate of Czechoslovakia, which had been partitioned the year before and now had been completely absorbed by German expansion. As had been her custom, in Santa Barbara Graham brought members of the Company home to meet her mother. This time she brought Hawkins as well. He had become vitally important to her, professionally as her creative foil and personally as her lover.

At the beginning of May, Graham and Horst, who in a sense

had moved out of her personal life but who would remain with her professionally for another ten years, performed a rare solo concert at Notre Dame University in South Bend. Solo work was to become almost unheard-of for Graham in the next several years. Indeed, the level of her concert activity had already diminished to the point where it made up scarcely 10 per cent of her appearances in public. The bulk of her work was now with the Company. The fact that she had just about fully graduated from the recital stage was a significant measure of her changing fortunes.

Though the outlook for the Company was bright, the outlook for Bennington was not. Rather than return to Vermont in the summer of 1939, the dance festival decided to transport itself to Mills College in San Francisco. The first five years of the festival had been brilliantly successful. Bennington College, however, became less open to the interplay of disciplines—such as music and stagecraft—that in earlier years had been partners in dance productions. Reacting against this new rigidity, the school's directors, Martha Hill and Mary Josephine Shelly, accepted an invitation from Aurelia Reinhardt of Mills to transfer the school to San Francisco and attract a student body primarily from the West Coast. In this they were successful, and the summer school at Mills was generally a good one. Because, however, of the expense of the transfer, the directors were able to present at the end of the course only a demonstration of techniques, rather than a festival week of modern dance. This had also been the case in the first year at Bennington in 1934. It seemed to leave the school hanging.

Horst and Graham made the trip west, but without the Company. San Francisco was Horst's home town, and his wife Betty still lived there and ran a dancing school. One unanticipated consequence of the trip was the discovery at Mills of a remarkably talented young dancer named Mercier Cunningham. Cunningham, who shortly afterward shortened his first name to Merce for professional reasons, drew immediate attention to himself in all his classes. He was extraordinarily quick (he had already achieved proficiency in tap dancing, of which he was fond) and had a great jump. Graham was sufficiently impressed with him to invite him to become a member of her Company. The second male dancer Graham worked with, Cunningham thus had immediate entry into the forefront of the modern dance movement. He joined Graham in New York that fall.

When Graham and Horst returned to New York, Graham began working on several new pieces, one a solo for herself, "Columbiad," and the other a Company work, "Every Soul Is a Circus," in which Cunningham would be included. Horst, who had an appointment for a year at Teacher's College as an associate in dance, composed the music for "Columbiad," and Paul Nordhoff did the music for "Circus"; Edythe Gilfond did the costumes, with assistance from Graham; and Philip Stapp created the décors. Graham now had a full constellation of collaborators. The works were scheduled for the last week in December at the St. James Theater.

During the middle of the month, Graham took time off to contribute her services to the third annual "Stars for Spain," a benefit for the refugees of that country's civil war. Ironically, among those on the program was the stripper Gypsy Rose Lee, who was enjoying considerable success at the time. The sight of Graham and Lee on the same bill may have jogged a few memories back to the satiric pairing of Graham and Sally Rand in *Vanity Fair* some years earlier.

Professionally, Graham was now in possession of two men of contrasting but excellent physical qualities. Hawkins was forthright and strong; Cunningham was airborne and elusively quick. Graham decided to pit them against each other in "Circus." With the arrival of Hawkins in "American Document," she worked with a popular form, the minstrel show, as well as (on a less emphasized level) with sex. In "Circus" she decided to try her hand at humor—not the bitter mocking of her past-oriented "Heretic" or satire designed to demolish some real or imagined foe ("Four Insincerities"), but good-natured, genuine humor designed to illuminate some corner of experience through fanciful incongruity.

The full title of the dance, "Every Soul Is a Circus," came from a poem by Vachel Lindsay, and Graham placed herself in the center of it as a dizzy woman, flirting and playing parts. For her, it was an abrupt transition from high tragedienne to comedienne, but she was to manage it marvelously. She cast Hawkins as a domineering ringmaster and Cunningham as an acrobat with whom she flirts and from whom Hawkins ultimately saves her. In an intriguing twist, she created an alter-ego for herself, a modishly dressed woman who sits in a box observing the goings-on. Philip Stapp's settings were spare and yet had all of the elements essential to a miniature circus ring. At the start of the dance, the entire set was visible, including the structure containing the alter-ego's "observation" box and, on the right-hand side of the stage, the couch on and around which Graham lolled and kittenishly kicked up her heels. In front of the stage hung two long red ropes. Two girls entered to part them and create the illusion of a curtain being opened on the circus. At the end of the dance, when all was settled, the two ropes were brought back to center front where they once more hung straight down.

In its own light-hearted way, "Every Soul Is a Circus" was remarkably revealing as an emotional self-portrait. It put Graham in the position of choosing between acrobat and ringmaster and showed her as someone so flighty that she needed to be watched. In the end, in an attempt to escape from her flightiness, she chose the ringmaster, the dictatorial figure whose whip she fingered inquisitively, rather than the bounding acrobat.

Walter Terry, writing in the *Herald-Tribune*, expressed the feeling of a generation that had grown up in Graham's austere works when, commenting on "Circus," he called her, the "Beatrice Lillie of the dance and she's been hiding it from us all these years." She could do comedy, not only satire, but had never felt motivated to. Now she felt secure enough to laugh at herself. Horst had been good for her head and kept her working when other distractions might have stopped her, but Hawkins was good for her heart. Though she might fear being without restraint, as the inner elements of "Circus" suggested, she could nonetheless play and have fun. Her work did not immediately become frivolous, but it did acquire a warmth that had been absent previously. Audiences that had gone to Martha Graham concerts in the grim 1930's went, broadly speaking, for an inspirational movement parable; but those who wandered into the theater at this point in her life could begin to smile and enjoy themselves. Though it would be years before she could alter the hollow-cheeked, iron maiden image into something more appealing to the general audience, she had made a beginning.

Hawkins decided to sever relations with the Ballet Caravan as soon as possible. In two years Graham had created two good roles for him and had used his dancing abilities in a meaningful way. That was more than he had been given in four years with the American Ballet and Ballet Caravan. He had moved from his own apartment on East Fifty-eighth Street to her apartment at 29 West Twelfth Street, right around the corner from the school, and they had a personal and professional relationship that lasted, through some extremely painful interludes, for twelve years. Graham was forty-four years old, he was thirty.

Aggressive, bold, ambitious, Hawkins stepped into Graham's life not only as her lover and a star in her Company but as her part-time manager and publicist. Hawkins also took over responsibility for the Company's luggage and bookkeeping, and he tried to organize its operations on a more systematic and rational basis than so far had been used and, for the most part, had been needed. Now that Graham had begun to create "theatrical" pieces there was more to worry about than just costumes.

Modern dancers all started as concert recital artists with a minimum of props. A few black drapes sufficed for background, lighting established the mood of the piece, and the single piano and perhaps one or two instrumentalists constituted the musical ensemble. When Graham started to use scenic collaborators and to make large architectural demands on them, the organization of the properties became a larger problem. And with the substantial spring tour that Frances Hawkins had arranged (increased fees and more dates, averaging four a week, with some at places where Graham had never before appeared—all essentially the result of the Company's success with "American Document"), a firm hand was also needed on the finances. While functioning as Graham's lead dancer and working on dance pieces of his own, Hawkins also watched over all of these arrangements. He had, in a way, become the ringmaster in actuality; and, although years later dancers then with the Company could comment on the positive influence that he had had, in general he was resented and unappreciated by those surrounding Graham.

The Company's spring tour started in Philadelphia, went into the South and then the Southwest, worked up the West Coast, and returned through the Midwest to finish in Hartford. The program contained two solos by Graham, the new "Columbiad" (a patriotic solo in a heroic but less successful vein) and the older "Frontier," and the two new theater pieces, "American Document" and "Circus." In Dallas, where the Company had never before appeared, it attracted an audience of 2,000. At Baton Rouge, where the Company was brought in by Louisiana State University under the prodding of the dance department, Horst and Graham were honored at a luncheon. In the early afternoon, one designated member of the Company gave a lecture demonstration, then Horst and Graham addressed the students and interested spectators. In the evening they gave a performance. It was a pattern followed in any college town with a large, interested dance department.*

Armitage greeted the Company when it arrived in Los Angeles to appear as part of a dance series that he had prepared for his audience. He had settled into the life of an impresario and had ceased going around the country representing individual artists. Graham, well received in Los Angeles, explained to a local interviewer her concept of dancing. The creation of a new style "was not done perversely to dramatize ugliness or to strike at sacred tradition [or] to destroy from sheer inability to become proficient in the technical demands of a classical art. The point was that the old forms could not give voice to the more fully awakened man. They had to undergo metamorphosis . . . in some cases, destruction, to serve as a medium for a time differently organized."

After Los Angeles Graham went up the coast to Santa Barbara and was able to introduce to her mother yet another man, Cunningham, as a demonstration of the enlarging scope of her work in theater dance. When the Company reached Corvallis, Oregon, it gave "American Document" alone as a matinee program for students and then played a full program for adults in the evening. Cecil Smith in Chicago, an appreciative and perceptive critic, endorsed wholeheartedly the shift of Graham's creative

* Horst, who conducted the music, also saw to it that the Company always had enough time to eat. Years of touring had taught him that local sponsors rarely prepared anything like the substantial meal dancers need after a strenuous performance, especially since they eat lightly before appearing on stage. Horst carefully checked the train schedules and the closing times of local restaurants, and at times he would surgically extract fifteen minutes or more from a dance in order to keep the running time of the program to the necessary length.

direction into the theater dance drama. Referring to the contrast with the past, he noted, "A Martha Graham recital in those days was an affair to be viewed as seriously and clinically as a surgical operation. I shall never forget the solemn, almost religious hush that enveloped the small audience at my first Martha Graham recital and the fearful mental effort I put forth in the partially vain hope of grasping what was going on. How different it all is now!"

Critically and in terms of audience size, it was the best tour that the Company had ever experienced. There were still pockets of resistance to the Graham aesthetic, but in the United States the vitriolic denunciation of her art was becoming rarer. The scourgings of the 1930's were the price that she had to pay. She had endured.

When the Company returned to New York, there were two new works to be prepared for the summer festival, which had been shifted back to Bennington. But the festival had made changes. Despite the good enrollment and the generally satisfactory services at Mills, the directors had decided that they really did need a festival week. Thus they returned to Bennington, but they found that the conditions for returning were that the Bennington School of the Dance, the former official sponsor of the program, be absorbed as a department into a larger entity called the Bennington School of the Arts. Further, the new organization formalized all of the disciplines into separate compartments and in effect isolated the members of each discipline from one another. What had been a free and easy interplay among disciplines was lost and never to be regained. As a result, the Bennington idea was ultimately killed as effectively as if its death had been planned.

Graham had had nearly two months to get her new pieces ready. One of the works was "El Penitente," the flowering of the Southwestern trips she and Horst had taken in the early 1930's. The other dance, "Letter to the World," typically emerged from her reading, in this case of Emily Dickinson. Horst did the score for "El Penitente," and Hunter Johnson was commissioned to compose the score for "Letter to the World." Arch Lauterer designed both productions, and Edythe Gilfond did the costumes.

"Penitente" was a trio for herself, Hawkins as the Penitent, and Cunningham as the Christ figure. For "Letter," a Company work, she needed additional men and so added David Campbell, Sascha Liebich, and David Zellmer. She intended this dance to be another of her theatrical productions, and it promised to be different from anything she yet had done.

Writing to Lauterer about the set for "Letter," she explained what she had in mind:

> I wish the stage piece could be something not quite so recognizable as part of a house. . . . Perhaps a structure of a summer house to make it dreamlike, in a sense using differing colors of transparencies perhaps to give an unreality—perhaps using in large scale the idea of the fan-shaped windows over the door or perhaps a roof [line sketch of inverted **V**] just poles or very light frame. . . . For a while I even saw a little bridge-like thing I walked over into reality. I love the arm of the bench so much. Could it be anything like that?

The bench referred to was a wonderfully evocative piece of odd furniture which had an arm like a roller coaster and looked like a combined couch and work table, suggesting perhaps a small storage cabinet or an end table. It was a piece, painted in pristine white, that combined all of the elements in "Emily's" cloistered life. One of the most successful pieces that Lauterer designed for Graham, it had the strength of utilitarian furniture and the sensitivity of imaginative sculpture.

But by the time of the Bennington festival Graham was still having difficulties with "Letter." In "American Document," Graham had previously used words as a narrative continuity spoken by an actor who was given some stylized but not elaborately choreographed movement. In "Letter" she wanted to have one of her dancers recite the verse of Emily Dickinson so that the poetry would be part and parcel of the dance fabric. Somehow the different elements did not cohere, and everyone else's part was complete before she worked on her own. Like most choreographers, she felt she could work more rapidly on her own part, and aside from logic she had the choreographer's usual utter confidence in her stage powers. In actual fact, the choreographer often has little or no real time to create a role and even less time to rehearse it with the company and integrate it into the rest of the production. This is roughly what happened to Graham.

On opening night she found herself with half to three-quarters of a dance piece that was revolutionary in approach but had been insufficiently prepared.

The newness and the partially finished state of the dance helped defeat it in the eyes of the audience and critics. "El Penitente" was seen as a well-crafted minor piece and "Letter" as an experiment that did not achieve its intent. The harshest comment came from the *New York Times* critic, John Martin, who suggested that the piece be left in Bennington—just as "Panorama" had been five years earlier. It was an infuriating experience for Graham and the Company. "Letter" was not a dance she was willing to drop, but there was nothing to be done at the time. The Company completed its second performance, after which everyone separated to reassemble in New York in the fall. Martha's mother was then on one of her periodic visits to the East, and she, Martha, Georgia, and Georgia's husband, Winthrop Sargeant, took an auto trip to Boston and then to New York to see the World's Fair, in its second and final year.

During the fall in New York, the Company had only two concerts, and "Letter" was presented at neither. Graham reworked and revised the dance, concentrating for the most part on the light-toned middle section, "The Little Tippler," and her own solo, which came at the end. By the end of the season, she had reworked "Letter" to her own satisfaction.

She also made changes in the presumably completed "Penitente." Feeling that Cunningham had too young a face for the role of Christ, she asked Isamu Noguchi to prepare a ritual mask and cloak for the Christ figure. Eventually she had him redecorate the entire production. Like the changes in "Letter," this also was a step toward, and not away from, the audience.

Speaking to an interviewer prior to the Company's appearance at the Mansfield Theater in January, when "Letter" was presented, she made the clearest statement up to that time about the change in direction that her work had taken. "We must win back our audiences," she said. "We have alienated them through grimness of theme and a nontheatrical approach to our dancing. Now that we modern dancers have left our period of 'long woolens' behind us, we must prove to our audiences that our theater pieces have color, warmth, and entertainment value. We must convince our audiences that we belong in the American Theater."

It makes one smile to think that Graham, who went on stage with "a whip in her hand," now by her own admission was holding out an olive branch. Her imagination was so fecund that she could alter direction and, in some cases, do an about-face without any loss in creative intensity. There was no doubt that Graham was the grimmest of the grim when she wanted to be, and now that she no longer wanted to be, she was going to be the most theatrical.

The subject of "Letter" is the inner life of the New England poet Emily Dickinson as expressed in her poems. The character of the poet was a beautifully congenial one for Graham. Our knowledge of Dickinson's life is to a great extent based upon conjecture. There is a little correspondence and some autobiographical information available, but the life basically has to be guessed at through a reading of her verse. A shy, retiring person, Dickinson created an important body of artistic work which was the objectification of her life, as dance was the objectification of Graham's. Graham created the character of Dickinson as a dual role: She played "One Who Dances," and Jean Erdman (the observer in "Circus") played "One Who Speaks." The setting was an abstracted scene with a bench on one side and the trellised front of a house on the other. Real and dream events mingled easily. Time was broken sequentially, so that the "Now" and the "Then" became present in a new combination that inhabited the same space.

Graham was the center of the action. A flow of memories and a sense of her obligations swept around her in her stillness. She would find herself reproached directly by the Ancestress, danced sternly by Jane Dudley, a figure who recurrently drew her back from her emotions of love and desire to considerations of family tradition. The yearnings of feeling and the reproaches of tradition tugged her in opposite directions. The section in which she loses her lover is reflected in the line, "There is a pain so utter, it swallows being." But Dickinson endured through her poetry, and Graham's heroine endures through her art, her "letter to the world."

The music by Hunter Johnson had no special distinction. But the dramatic intensity of the work and its high degree of movement invention—in Graham's solos, in Cunningham's rollicking prancy movement, and in Hawkins's solid, well-chiseled variation—combined to make the piece one of her great achievements. Having decided to point herself in the direction of the theater, she was strengthening her hold on the creative line she was pursuing toward the area of legend and myth where local events can be abstracted to a broader, more universal plane of meaning.

Just as "Letter" was complex and allusive in its relationships, so "El Penitente" was sunny and clear. The dancers entered as strolling players, ready to enact a primitive morality play, and they exited after the dance had run its course. Graham split her own role into three distinct segments. She was in turn the Virgin, remote and unapproachable in a blue veil; the Magdalen, eminently approachable as she caressed her body with an apple; and finally the comforting Madonna. The piece was a play within a play. One could see the dancers as people who take the parts of characters. The whole became not so much a Passion play as a comment upon those who can create one. The three strolling players were simple, uncluttered people who shared and identified with the biblical themes of sin, penance, and redemption in a way that transcended time. A part themselves of their own Southwestern desert ritualism, they managed also to transform themselves and their emotions into remote characters and to cleanse themselves of guilt feelings about temptation and remorse. This process of redemption fascinated Graham, but for the time she could only create a dance about other people's ability to accomplish it. She could not place herself in the center of such a dance. The score by Horst had just the right simple lilt that the tone of the piece required. After the disappointing "Columbiad," his score showed again the creative rapport between him and Graham.

On repeated viewing, "Letter" was hailed as the masterpiece that it had become, thus nearly eclipsing "Penitente," which previously had been considered the stronger work.

"Letter" brought Graham the first substantial financial gift that she had yet received from a private source. One might say that it was Graham's turn to a new theatricality that brought it to her. She received an anonymous check for $1,000, a gift without strings. The donor suggested that Graham continue to produce works like "Letter" but added that she should do anything she wished with the money.

Interviewers were now requesting Graham's opinions on everything under the sun, from the latest fashions to the latest dance craze—at that time, jitterbugging. She had become a minor celebrity. She fielded all questions with great aplomb and granted quot-

Martha Graham and Erick Hawkins in "Every Soul Is a Circus" (1939).

Rehearsal snapshots of 1964 reconstruction of "El Penitente."

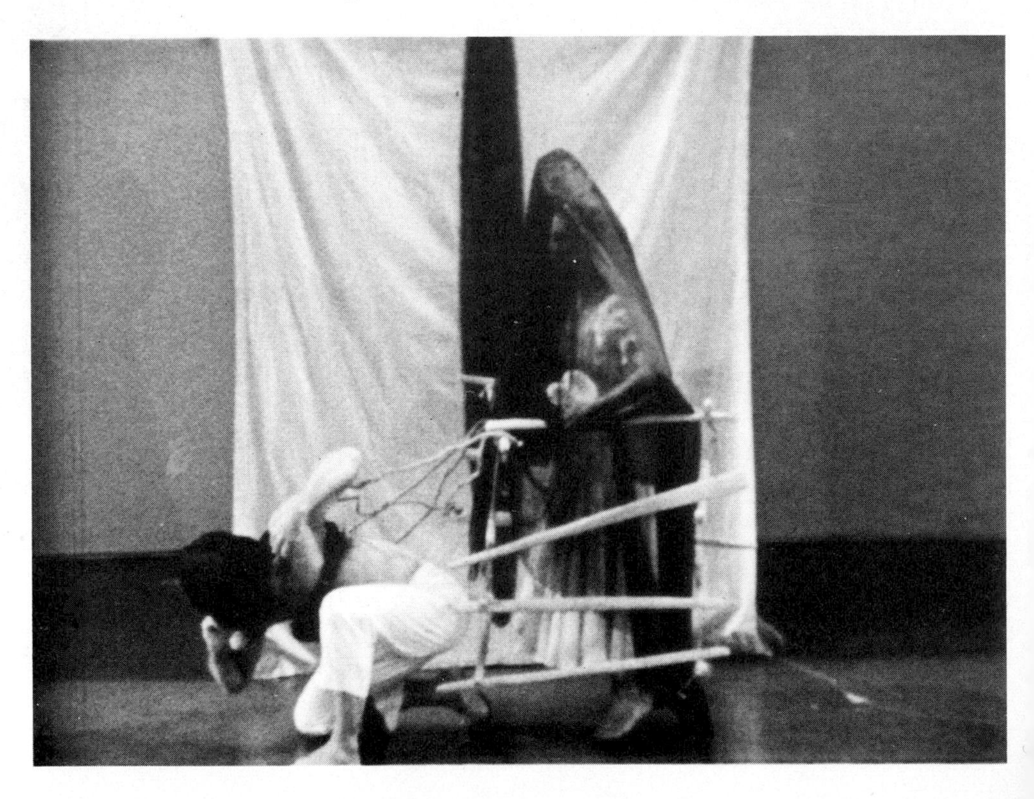

Rehearsal snapshots of 1964 reconstruction of “El Penitente” (cont'd).

Left: Martha Graham modeling mink coat for I. J. Fox. New York, 1939.

Below: Martha Graham's mother at Bennington, 1942.

"Deaths and Entrances" (1943).

Martha Graham and Erick Hawkins: "Deaths and Entrances" (1943).

"Appalachian Spring" (1944).

"Salem Shore" (1943).

able interviews to anyone who made a request. It was delightful to be at the center of things rather than to be considered an eccentric for creating the basis of an art form that, a half-dozen years previously, no one seemed interested in. In jitterbugging she found an "ugly beauty." To another interviewer she confided that while on tour with her Group she had been approached by a football coach in Missouri who wanted to buy the secret signals she used in "Primitive Mysteries" to get the dancers to follow her around. It was all good fun, and Graham handled the news media with more skill than might have been anticipated from a cult figure whose audiences had been made up of fervent followers. She clearly seemed to enjoy her turn toward the public.

An interviewer chatting with Graham about clothes would have no inkling that, much as Graham adored good clothes, she could afford few and made many of her own. "A dress must be built with two purposes, to look well when still and to look well in motion." This was the principle she followed when dressing her dancers. "A woman very seldom thinks of both [situations] when she buys a dress. If I wear a dress in which I can't move freely, it makes me inarticulate and self conscious." She added: "Another point, which I believe is just the same off the stage as on, is that no woman should wear a dress she cannot top. No matter how beautiful the dress is, it gives a mechanized impression if the wearer's personality cannot come through it." The only thing about Graham's clothes that changed later, when she no longer needed to scrimp, is that she was able to afford to buy the clothes and shoes that she adored from designers like Norell and Dior. She always regarded clothes, however, as sculptured objects that had to be "built" or "well constructed," and in later years rare was the class, when her school was thrown open to visitors, in which she did not appear in a new dress.

Also as part of finding herself the object of curiosity and some acclaim, Graham, along with Doris Humphrey and Charles Weidman, narrated a radio program dedicated to tracing the history of modern dance. The program, "On With the Dance," featured a survey of the development of dance in the United States. It brought Ruth St. Denis together with her most famous pupils.

In addition to the passing notice of publicity, Graham was also the subject of the profoundly scrutinizing gaze of the photographer and painter Barbara Morgan, who had been observing her work for a good portion of the preceding decade. Morgan, who had given up painting in favor of photography with the birth of her children, had started to take pictures of Graham and the Group in the mid-1930's, and by 1941 had assembled a sufficient number to prepare a book of photographs about Graham: *Martha Graham: Sixteen Dances in Photographs.* In their field the pictures are unique. Morgan was vitally interested in capturing the nature and the feeling of each of the dances, and in the process she was able to capture much of the personality of Graham as well. The photographs were painstakingly prepared. They were not simply performance shots, but the distillation of the essence of the dance into several frames. It was a magnificent achievement that pleased even Graham, who was notoriously difficult about pictures. On the occasion of the publishing of the book, the Gotham Book Mart, presided over by Graham's longtime friend Frances Steloff, gave a reception for Graham and Morgan in Gotham's series of receptions, "Modern American Artists."

As a performing artist, Graham had been extraordinarily well served by the publishing industry. Compared to concert singers and other dance personalities, especially in the world of ballet, her popular reputation was modest, but she had had two excellent books published about herself and her work that kept to the most rigorous standards of production and taste, each in its own way a testimony to the ideals and standards that Graham had set for herself. She was hard-headed and hard-driving, impossible to live with when things were not going well, and at times given to rhetoric of the most obscure type in class or rehearsal when she wanted to make a point. Her temper was already of legendary proportions. But her unquestioned dedication and talent attracted designers, musicians, and dancers to her as to no other figure in her world. She became the magnetic center of the most advanced experimentation and at long last was beginning to receive the recognition that was her due.

The round of her year, however, was still much the same. After the spring season, there was the June course at her studio, where Hawkins was now teaching ballet, and then she and the Company would repair to Bennington for the six weeks of the summer course. For Bennington, that summer of 1941 furthered the process of deterioration that had begun with the school's compartmentalization of the different arts. The number of paying students dropped under a hundred, the smallest the student body had ever been, and teachers' salaries were cut. The result was the ironical situation of the Bennington summer program's being in financial difficulties when the rest of the country was beginning to pull itself out of the economic hole. The festival was now held in the tiny attic theater in the Commons Building, a further reduction in scale from the Armory. Bennington, which had made money in the depths of the Depression, was sliding under as the massive resurgence of the American economy was about to begin. The approaching war would finish it off entirely.

Graham's finances were still perilous at best and nonexistent at worst, and with an expanded Company and the demands of theatrical production she was pushed to the very edge. What Graham needed was a source of financing that would be sustained on a yearly basis and not applied like a bandage to cover a particular fiscal wound. She herself was unable to raise money. She could demand a dancer's lifeblood in rehearsal and performance, but she could not bring herself to attempt any systematic bid for money. This job Hawkins took on. In addition to his other duties, he began to search around for ways in which to tap private funds for the Company.

Graham had new dances to think about, more theater to make, more stories to tell. She had been working on a new production, developing it with Arch Lauterer, and by the festival week in August was ready to show the world her latest humorous dance, "Punch and the Judy." Every choreographer is concerned primarily with the organization of stage movement, and, in considering other aspects of the production, some pay more attention to the scenic and costume designs than they do to the music. Despite the fact that Graham worked with hordes of new composers, she always seemed to regard the contribution of a designer like Lauterer or Noguchi as having more weight than the contribution of a composer, and she designated designers "artistic collaborators," something she never did with musicians.

For "Punch and the Judy" (costumes by Charlotte Trowbridge, the wife of Carlus Dyer), Lauterer created a superlatively suitable and assorted series of props and settings. The dance had six parts—a prologue, three "dilemmas," and two "interludes"—and explored the battle of the sexes as seen from an epic theater point of view. The dilemmas were those of a man and wife, who have contentions, quibble, and then make up. They are meant to be the archetypal couple of all time. He is the braggart and she is the alternately ecstatic and despairing woman.

In the prologue, the fates set the stage, and then the first dilemma for Punch and the Judy is posed in the appearance of a child. The Judy flees the trouble in the first interlude through a flight of imagination symbolized by the appearance of Pegasus, the mythical winged horse, describled in the program note as "that force which enables us to imagine or to escape or to realize." The Judy escapes to dally with ideal heroes—a soldier, a scout, and a highwayman—and then realizes that she must return to actuality. In the second dilemma, Punch is attracted to Pretty Polly and sets the Judy to raging, which brings on the second interlude and again the flight from the here and now. From life's pain, one turns to the imagination but then must return to the ordinary again, despite the ameliorating transport of the imagination. In the third dilemma, Justice is blindfolded and Punch triumphs, but, when he is overthrown later, the Judy intervenes for him. Punch goes back to his bragging, and the whole cycle begins again. There is no resolution to this war. It is continual and without end and has its extremes of affection, reconciliation, and disaffection. Hawkins danced Punch, and Graham, of course, the Judy.

It had been three years since Graham had met Hawkins, and the tumultuous nature of their relationship was already established. Graham had thrown things at Horst when rehearsals had not gone well in the past, and now she raged at Hawkins in their private life and sometimes in public. Their private and public lives were thoroughly intertwined. Some of Graham's Company never accepted the presence of Hawkins, and one suspects that the Victorian ladies who "direct the lives of others" were more than just the mythic ancestor figures that Graham had used in many of her dances. Hawkins, an energetic, restless, dedicated man, who was fifteen years younger than Graham, found himself caught in the web of aspiration that surrounded her.

For many in the Company, Graham was a woman who had accomplished something vitally important, something that should not be interfered with by a mere man. Rumors about their relationship circulated wildly. Possibly the most extreme was that Hawkins had attempted to push Graham over the edge of the Grand Canyon. In the Company's superheated atmosphere, anything was possible.

After all, Graham had already done the impossible, emerging from nowhere to become a national figure in the arts.

More, Graham's intense emotional voltage, the fuel for her dances, was never turned off but only moderated from time to time, and no one could be expected to withstand its intensity easily on a daily basis. To a great extent, Hawkins lost his bearings in the egotistical vortex that surrounded Graham. For her own part, it seems clear that Graham loved him as much as she could love anyone or anything outside of her work. But there is no doubt that their relationship was a difficult one from the start, and some of that difficulty is reflected in "Punch and the Judy."

In "Every Soul Is a Circus," the dithery woman danced by Graham was compared, as we have seen, to Bea Lillie by one reviewer. In "Judy," Graham's performance was characterized by another as being "almost Chaplinesque." When she premiered the work at Bennington during the 1941 festival week, it was praised, but, as usual, the piece did not achieve its final form until subsequent performances. In September Graham wrote to Lauterer from California, where she was vacationing with her mother. She was full of enthusiasm for the piece and for their collaboration, but she was also aware that the dance still needed some touching up. "I have to do a little work on 'Punch' before we give it in New York. I still think that the weakness begins after my angry dance [in the second dilemma, after Pretty Polly catches Punch's eye], and I must work that and the angry dance out." But this was only polishing. "I am so happy about Bennington this summer. I feel that you and I have learned to work together and we are in the beginning."

For all the pleasure that Graham felt about the reworked "Punch," she had overlooked a difficult practical problem—the cost of transporting the scenery from place to place on her concert tours. And so had Lauterer. No doubt in response both to Graham's suggestions and to his own enthusiasm, he had let himself go creatively without giving this problem any thought. Now money problems forced Graham to find some way to make the set more transportable. Two weeks before an out-of-town date (impossibly short notice), she wrote to Lauterer asking for changes in the set. The letter vacillated between her need to resolve practical necessities and her reluctance to ask someone to modify creative work with which they both were pleased. It was a strange role for Graham, to ask a fellow creator to do something less, in effect, than the person could do. "We find that we cannot carry so much. . . . I know how thankless it is to do things over with compromise. . . . Do not despair. I will not make this mistake again. . . . I only hope that you will not think it impossible to go ahead on any future project." Lauterer did as Graham asked. He also penciled a note to his new bride on one of Graham's intense letters, saying that he recognized that she was strange and unlike anyone else he had ever worked with and, in that sense, uncomfortable. But for the time being, like others who fell into the magnetic gravitational pull that Graham exerted, he found himself caught up in a situation that, at its creative level, was impossibly attractive.

The month of December was heavily booked for Graham and the Company, with dates throughout the South and even a trip to Cuba for two performances in Havana sponsored by Alicia and Fernando Alonso. Other than the single date in Canada during the unhappy transcontinental tour of 1937, it was only the second time the Company had played outside the United States.

The Company played its first date in Rome, Georgia, on a Saturday evening and took an early Sunday train to Miami to make the boat connection for Havana. On the ride down the coast of Georgia, the conductor hurried through the train announcing that Pearl Harbor had been attacked by the Japanese. Everyone was shocked, and Company members Jean Erdman and David Campbell, who came from Hawaii originally, were exceptionally agitated. The tour became very unimportant, but there was nothing to do except continue to Miami and fulfill the dates that had been contracted for. The following day, while waiting for the Havana boat in a greasy-spoon restaurant on the pier, the Company heard President Roosevelt ask for a declaration of war on Japan. All the way over to Havana, there was an anxious feeling about submarine attack. Nothing happened.

Havana, where the Company stayed at the Nacional Hotel for the two days of its engagement, was an alien world. There were bullet holes left over from political upheaval in the walls of the hotel. For many in the Company the heat was enervating. Outside there were trees and birds singing in the bright sun. For a company that spent most of its year in and around New York City, it was a marked change. Even before the announcement of the war, Graham had been highly nervous about the whole trip. She worried about the Company's reception and about the appropriateness of including "Penitente" on the programs in a Latin Catholic country. In addition, Cunningham had been unable to make the trip because he had to report for an army physical. He was replaced in "El Penitente" by Welland Lathrop (Horst's assistant in his composition course) and in "Circus" by Sasha Liebich. Lathrop was not at all successful as far as Graham was concerned. Graham's misgivings were not too far wrong. In terms of audience response, the engagements were not particularly successful. They were typified by an incident in an afternoon concert when someone in the audience casually rolled a Coca-Cola bottle down the aisle of the theater. The Company returned to the States and worked its way back to New York for a couple of performances in the week between Christmas and the New Year. Cuba had been a fittingly unsatisfying transition to a year that, apart from the war, would be awkward and difficult for Graham.

7

The War Years

"Some days I have spent
in the depths of the earth."
Martha Graham

In the year 1942 the Company had a fairly busy schedule, and Graham's popularity, if anything, increased. The Company spent the early part of the year preparing for another tour to begin in February and run through March. Starting in Philadelphia, the Company worked its way west and returned for its last performance in Virginia. The war was beginning to take its toll of male dancers throughout the country, and Graham's Company, which was still largely female, by almost three to one, filled in for the Littlefield Ballet in Columbus, Ohio, when the latter had to cancel because most of its male dancers had been drafted.

In Chicago, Graham encountered Katharine Cornell, and the two had a breakfast that made the gossip columns of the papers. There was even a "strange-as-it-may-seem" item about Graham in one of the Chicago paper's cartoon sections, in which it was averred that she carried around for good luck a bit of relic cloth that was thought to be five hundred years old. Graham premiered "Land Be Bright," a dance that had obvious structural parallels to the patriotic "American Document" and included an Indian, Chingachgook; Betsy Ross; and a Yankee. But it was not a successful dance; reflex political pieces had never really worked for Graham. The sympathetic Cecil Smith noted, "The solo dances tremble on the brink of pantomime with an unresolved conflict between seriousness and a mood of half-expressed whimsicality. The intellectual content of the whole work is not well organized as yet nor is the intended emotional tone altogether clear." C. J. Bulliet commented in the *Chicago Daily News,* "I wish Martha Graham had in her makeup less of Delsarte and more of the priestesses of Isis and the Peruvian goddesses —more of Little Egypt, of Carmen Miranda, and Carmen Amaya. Intellect, I have been told, is a grand phenomenon, but it can be overworked in an evening dance divertissement." Hawkins later commented, "Martha got trapped into it and wasn't committed to it." Others in the Company considered it a potboiler, and Graham herself was not interested in keeping it long enough to present in New York. After a second performance on the tour, it was dropped. Indeed, she so thoroughly dismissed it from her mind that in writing to Lauterer about the year she said that she had done no new work at all, completely omitting the hapless "Land Be Bright."

In Cincinnati, the Company's next stop, Graham told a local reporter a story about herself that was currently making the rounds. The story concerned two dowagers. After seeing a recent Graham concert, one called the other and said, "My dear, you should have gone to Martha Graham's concert last night. Either she is deteriorating or we're getting better, because we liked her." During the same month *Harper's Bazaar* published a poem by William Carlos Williams, "War the Destroyer," which was dedicated to Graham. In the poem he suggested that neither writing, music, nor prayer could change the war but that, if anything could, it was the force of dance, which in itself was an affirmative expression of the spirit. For Graham it was a beautiful tribute.

The country, meanwhile, was beginning to mobilize itself for full-scale war. Terrible as it would be for the next several years, the war thoroughly cut through the Gordian knot of economic deprivations and intellectual constrictions that were part and parcel of the 1930's. For many years Graham and her colleagues had hammered out a style of movement in an atmosphere of revolution rather than evolution. The movement was full-blooded, strong, and sinewy, and reflected the American experience through the intuition of the individual artists. Now the revolution achieved its time. The period of World War II brought changes that allowed the future dancers of that generation to flourish. The restless young men and women of the war years were exposed to more new ideas and innovation than their parents' generation had been. The sheer mobility of the country, increased a hundredfold, was an important factor. Troop trains crossed and recrossed the country bringing men from quiet towns to large cities, and in many cases to New York City, where USO tickets provided many men and women with exposure to an art form that they had never before known.

The June course at the Graham studios preceded the Company's move to Bennington in July. The Bennington Summer School of the Arts was even more a shade of its former self. Graham was the only choreographer present from the glory days. Humphrey, Weidman, and Holm each sent representatives, but there was no money for productions, and courses in science, government, and economics were being offered along with instruction in theater arts. Martha Hill, the co-founder of the institution, who had taught composition, technique, and dramatic movement, now found herself teaching square dancing and functioning as a "caller" for weekend dances. The students were encouraged to donate their services to the 200-acre farm that the school ran as its part of the war effort, and they were also exposed to lectures on the war and the future. For the presentation of modern dance, Bennington no longer had anything to offer. The festival that had served so brilliantly in the years 1934–38 was over.

Graham, though, received an important compensation. When the summer school was officially closed, it became in effect a workshop for her and Lauterer. For the next three years, Graham and her Company were established as artists-in-residence at Bennington, and there they worked on various productions. The college kept the Company together and able to function through the difficult summer period. Although Bennington's horizons, once so grand, had been narrowed to being the summer home of modern dance's most powerful and fecund creative talents, it was ideal for Graham, who would have Lauterer and the proposed new Bennington Theater *

* Designed in 1940–41, the theater would have housed the dance, drama, and theater design workshops, but it was not finished even thirty-three years later.

all to herself. There she could mine the student body at her leisure.

Hawkins, as well as Horst, accompanied Graham to Bennington. Although Hawkins was still nominally a member of Ballet Caravan, since the beginning of the war that company had ceased to exist. Kirstein, its organizer, had entered the service and eventually wound up on the Continent tracing works of art that had become separated from their owners through chance or systematic thievery. At the same time, Balanchine, its primary choreographer, was doing shows on Broadway and later would go to Hollywood to do musicals. The ballet world that Hawkins was a part of simply suspended operations for the "duration," and Hawkins would not return to it.

The year, with its changes and sense of incompleteness, continued to be unsettling. A peacetime nation was adjusting itself to a wartime situation. Graham had very few dates to play in the fall. There was little money for artistic work, and modern dance, at the leading edge of the dance world, suffered most. Some members of Graham's Company went on tour (Sophie Maslow and Jane Dudley, for example, formed a trio with William Bales); others found work in the Broadway theater. Graham did not appear on Broadway for over a year, not until the fall–winter season of 1943. And not just Graham: Neither did Humphrey, Weidman, Tamiris, or Holm appear. Humphrey and Weidman presented studio recitals on a continuing basis. Graham managed a couple of appearances in New York at Central Needle Trades High School Auditorium and at the Kaufmann Concert Hall of the YMHA at Ninety-second Street and Lexington Avenue. But it all had a fitful quality.

Reading, as always, Graham became increasingly interested in the work and the world of the three Brontë sisters. Slowly a dance began to develop. As she read she would mark passages and make notes of things that interested her. Passing on to something else, she would find that a particular phrase or an aspect of a writer's work would recur to her, and she would again examine the text or refer to another text. Then, after more thought, she would begin to prepare a scenario of the texts and the images that she felt were appropriate to encompass the form of the idea that was beginning to take shape in her mind. "I get the idea going. Then I write down, I copy out of any book that stimulates me at that time any quotation, and I keep it. And I put down the source. Then, when it comes to the actual work, I keep a complete record of the steps. I keep notes of every dance I have. I don't have notation. I just put it down and know what the words mean or what the movements mean and where you go and what you do and maybe an explanation here and there."

Graham called the new dance "Deaths and Entrances." In May 1943 she wrote Lauterer about the progress on the new dance:

> I have not quite finished the thing I am working on. I hesitate to say the Brontë because it is really no longer that I feel. It has become something else more general, I think. I see how far I am away from my scenario when I read it again. Partly that's because the music [by Hunter Johnson] is far from it too. It is frenetic and in places quite marvelous, although Louis [Horst] does not like it. But then he never does at first. . . . But it has become an experience of the emotions involving that part of us that is responsible for the creative dream. It is only this weekend that I saw light at all.

Her sense of the work's theatricality was very strong. "It will be strange and frenetic and at times very simple with a kind of acting technique removed from dancing." She also had a comment about her lack of work over the previous year, unconsciously damning "Land Be Bright." "I have committed a sin of omission rather than a sin of commission . . . and I feel ashamed and cowardly as a result."

"Deaths and Entrances" was ready in time for the summer workshop at Bennington, and despite the lack of production money for new work Graham and Lauterer managed to present it as a workshop performance with limited props and costumes. The women dancers made some black jersey dresses, and Hawkins bought some black trousers at an Army-Navy store. Hawkins was understudying both Curly and Judd in the ballet sequences of *Oklahoma!*, so the premiere was set for a weekend to enable Hawkins to return to New York to fulfill his contract. *Oklahoma!* offered him some of the easiest money he had ever made, and he was naturally reluctant to give it up.

"Deaths" ostensibly is the story of the relationships of three sisters who live with their memories in a large gloomy house. At times the sight, or handling, of symbolic objects—a shell, a vase, a goblet—sets off trains of memories in which the past replaces the present and whole sets of relationships are acted out with incredible intensity. Cunningham was the Poetic Beloved and Hawkins the Dark Beloved, while Dudley and Maslow joined Graham as the sisters. Frustration and contention exist among them, and periodically men and women from the past come forward to dance with them. Of the three sisters, Graham is the strongest and at times appears to be the only living person on the stage, with everyone else, including the sisters, an extension of herself. She appears to be engaged in a lonely struggle with herself as much as with her sisters. The two lovers from her past, the Dark Beloved and the Poetic Beloved, fight a duel. Memories flicker in and out of focus. The transitions between the remembered events cause a certain whirl of dizziness that is expressed by the rapidity of the dancers' comings and goings. Graham does a frightening solo portraying a mind losing control of itself. Finally, at the end, she pulls events back into order and triumphantly places a chess piece on a board near where her two sisters are sitting. The exact nature of the struggle is never explicitly stated and remains in a dark corner of the mind. The final gesture of triumph is totally ambiguous, since the nature of the conflict has never been clarified. The work, however, has a compelling, haunting quality. There are glimmers, dim flashes of illumination, but no real explanation. One is aware that the trio of sisters is undergoing an emotional storm and that by the end of the dance the storm has passed.

During the performance, which was held in the tiny rooftop theater of Bennington's Commons Building, a late summer thunderstorm brightened the interior of the hall with flashes of lightning. Halfway through the performance the lights failed. Helen Lanfer, a pianist who had recently joined Graham, was so engrossed that she continued to play. The dancers stopped and waited for the power to be restored and then repeated the performance from the beginning. It was an eerie and appropriate accident.

"Deaths and Entrances" was a form of surrealist theater in which time was handled in a discontinuous fashion and not as a narrative thread connecting consecutive events. Events were associative, not sequential. Thus an occurrence in the past could assume a place in the immediate present because it was related to a current event or existing object. This was a form of dance theater in which the tyranny of progressive time was suspended in favor of the selective process of the human memory, reorganizing experience in accordance with its own priorities.

Since the appearance of "American Document," Graham had been actively engaged with the handling of time and the penetration of the past into the present. In "American Document," she assured everyone that they were present in the here and now. "Ladies and Gentlemen," the Interlocutor says, "this is a theater. The place is here. . . . The time is now. . . . The characters are . . . Erick and Martha." Because from time to time the characters were able to stand aside from the roles that they were playing and then re-enter them, the production also made clear that, although it presented scenes from the past, it was very much of the present. In "Every Soul Is a Circus," Graham split the major character, a woman, into two people, one an observer in a box and the other the actual protagonist, thus presenting a curious division in which one part of a person, or one layer of time, judges another. Again in "Punch and the Judy," the heroine would escape from the reality of her errant mate, Punch, through flights of fancy, and these imaginings would replace the actuality of the here and now. After each of the "ideal" heroes failed her, however, she would return to the here and now and to the silly, erring reality of Punch, bragging and parading around.

In the duality of vision that seemed congenial to Graham's thought, man was at one moment the pure ideal "poetic beloved" and then again the forceful, strong, sexually attractive "dark beloved." He could be the aerial and lofty "acrobat" at one moment and the disciplined and domineering "ringmaster" at another time. She played with the twin conceptions of man and kept both in her work, at times having one dominate and at times the other, always leaning, however, to the physical, sexual explanation of man's motivation. For Graham, men were much like powerful but clumsy creatures who occupied a place in one's heart but always with reservations. The serious people, in terms of carrying responsibility, were women. They endured and had to make sense of the awkwardness of men. Male behavior was to a great extent less complex than that of the female, who had to weigh, balance, and judge courses of action.

The arena of decision for Graham thus was the present as it was interpenetrated by the past. She had a view of a recurring rhythm in the life force, a view that at times came close to determinism. She always, however, stopped short of sheer mechanistic compulsion as an explanation for action. Accepting the existence of forces that move outside of a specific time and place, Graham tried to decipher these broad patterns of impulse and action in relation to the specifics of the individual person. Time feeding back upon itself became a real dimension in the lives of the characters she created. In "Deaths and Entrances," Graham invested the intensity that she had previously shown in "Letter to the World," but it was the darker side of her powerful imagination that now dominated. The lack of activity in 1942, stretching into much of 1943, had been a constant irritant to Hawkins, who felt that something had to be done to raise money to prevent dances like "Deaths and Entrances" from being interred at Bennington. In bed one evening, as night thoughts flooded in, he announced, "I'm going to get $2,000." It might just have been one of those wayward thoughts that vanish with the sunrise, but Hawkins remembered the name of a rich woman involved in local philanthropy in Santa Barbara, a name Graham had mentioned to him. He was willing to try, and he was strongly motivated. He wanted Graham to create dances again, and he wanted to appear onstage himself. Hawkins wrote Mrs. Max Schott, included press clippings, and told her of their extreme need. The whole incident was no more carefully thought out than this. Within a week a check for $2,000 arrived. This money meant that the Company could have proper sets and costumes for a New York presentation of "Deaths and Entrances." The 46th Street Theater was therefore rented for two Sundays.

Hawkins then decided that, in addition to full sets and costumes, he wanted to have the score for "Deaths and Entrances" orchestrated. Graham had never had an orchestral accompaniment for her concerts and had thought it a great improvement when she was able to afford two pianos instead of just one. There was no money for the orchestration, but Hawkins was having a run of luck. The first $2,000 had been easy. Why could he not just as easily find the additional money, $500, necessary for the orchestration fee?

For several years, an unassuming woman had been taking class at the school at 66 Fifth Avenue. Hawkins had scarcely noticed her, and her name had not registered especially strongly with him, until one day he realized that Bethsabee de Rothschild was a member of the wealthy banking family. She was the one he decided to approach. Pulling together his courage, Hawkins waited on the street for de Rothschild after class one day and asked her for $500 to have "Deaths and Entrances" orchestrated. After a slight hesitation, she agreed to give it to him. The small bequest given in 1943 by de Rothschild was to culminate in her exceptionally generous support of the Graham Company for nearly twenty years and later in the founding of two full dance companies in Israel.

Bethsabee de Rothschild fled France before the German occupation at the beginning of World War II. Upon arriving in the United States, seeking a teacher of ethnic dances, she found the studio of the well-known teacher La Meri at 66 Fifth Avenue, just one floor above the Graham school. De Rothschild had taken some yoga lessons in Paris but had not in any way interested herself in a professional career as a dancer, though she was attracted to the raw physical pleasure of systematic movement. She started taking classes at the Graham studio and soon fell under the spell of Graham's creative power. It is possible that de Rothschild might have been asked to assist Graham earlier had she made herself known. But she was a shy, retiring person, working quietly and efficiently, and did not at all give the impression of being the enormously rich heiress she was. She made no special demands for herself, and Company members found it hard to reconcile her great financial resources with the idea of the sight of de Rothschild doing manual labor, repairing an ancient electric shaver, or being pleased with an exceptionally inexpensive dress from Fourteenth Street (which she wore with fine jade that most mistook for costume jewelry). She was simply a quiet, industrious, unassertive person who took class at the Graham studio. Until Hawkins suddenly realized there was a "de" in front of her name, he had thought no more about it than he did about the name of the Rothschild Department Store in Kansas City, where he was born.

The concert made possible by Mrs. Schott and Bethsabee de Rothschild was strongly acclaimed. It was Graham's first Broadway appearance in over a year. In addition to "Deaths and Entrances," Graham decided to do a solo that would express the longings and frustrations of women left at home while their men were away. Graham put the situation in the past, in a beautiful lyric solo called "Salem Shore," but the piece had an obvious application to the wives and sweethearts of those in the service whose lives had become a routine of patient waiting as their men traveled across oceans to strange islands and continents whose names they had scarcely noticed in school geography classes. Lauterer designed ritual and historical objects: the parasol used on the bride's wedding day, the fragment of the prow of a ship, a bit of a "widows' walk" that is so much a part of the architecture of New England whaling villages. In assembling these appointments of a way of life, Lauterer created a world in microcosm. As Graham danced, phrases of the wedding vow were spoken from the wings by an unseen narrator, and from time to time there is the worried question, "Will he come back from—?" The dance had an immediacy that was readily apparent to all who saw it.

Although the 46th Street Theater had been rented for two consecutive Sundays, only one concert had been announced. Graham, perhaps anxious after so long an absence from Broadway, was not sure that she could fill the house, and therefore held back to see the response. The theater was so jammed for the first performance on December 26 that people had to be turned away at the box office. "Salem Shore" was applauded, but not until Graham heard the strong applause for "Deaths and Entrances" did she permit the announcement of the second concert. With a keen sense of showmanship, Hawkins sent out their press representative, now Isadora Bennett, during the second intermission to announce that, because of popular demand, the same program would be repeated the following week at the same theater. It was the type of canniness that is ordinarily thought of as "show biz," and Graham, though she rejected Denishawn's "commercialism," was not beyond it when she thought it was to her advantage.

There were new students entering Graham's school now, students who possessed a sleekness very unlike the hefty strength of the dancers who had made up the earlier Graham companies. The younger dancers were growing up in a different atmosphere, one not filled with the contentions of the embattled generation that Graham represented. Although they were devoted to Graham and her style, they saw no reason not to go off to take a ballet class several times a week in addition to their instruction at the Graham school. Of course, since they knew that it would anger the older generation, Graham no less than the others, they did not do so openly. Though they went secretly, they nevertheless went.

As a result, the look of the Graham dancer was beginning to change in several ways. The feet, which had been rigidly held in the normal "parallel" position, now began to display a certain amount of "turnout," a position that was most strongly associated with the classic ballet. Some of the teachers of the Graham technique resisted any such change and did not permit it, but slowly the emphasis changed from a posture that represented dissent from ballet's dominant position in the dance world to one that took from ballet the advantages it had to offer. As a systematic form of strengthening exercise, there was no other dance technique that could match it for the completeness and thoroughness of its workout of the entire body. A good ballet class touches every muscle from the instep to the nape of the neck.

Of course, Graham herself had changed—that is, what she strove for creatively had changed, and this in turn changed her dancers. They were no longer the hard percussive movers that they had been at the start of her Group; they now were able to insert more flow and sinuousness into their execution of her works. Graham did not repudiate the "hardness" of earlier pieces like "Heretic" and "Celebration," but she had seen additional possibilities, and she added them to the original movements that she had evolved. In time, toward the end of her career, the dancers who would emerge from her school would have a lyricism entirely foreign to the dancers with whom she had started.

The Graham technique, as it evolved, developed the body for those things that Graham wanted to do choreographically, and it was therefore an expression of her creative direction. Even in the beginning of her work, she did not pretend that her company classes were complete. She expected members of the Group to take other classes (though not ballet) in order to complete the exercise of their bodies. She knew that she could not simultaneously forge a creative vocabulary of movements that were completely original and provide a well-rounded class for each and every person in her Company. She always chose to do what gave expression to her individual creativity—and this was a decision that she inevitably made throughout her career, whether it was a question of personal relationships, modifying a technique, or accepting some dates and refusing others that were creatively less interesting.

In developing her Company style, the training of male dancers had been something of a special problem for Graham. Just when she had her dancers, all of them women, moving in the right way, Erick Hawkins came along, and she had had to teach him what she wanted. Because he had already had a significant amount of ballet training, she caused him to modify much of what he had learned.

Then, when she started working on "Letter to the World," she had several male dancers new to the Company and also fairly new to dancing. Since they did not have enough professional training, she had to bring them up to the level of the women in the Company in a relatively short time. Though it required a great deal of work, she eventually created a homogeneous Company style. But the effort to blend the men into the whole changed certain of the accents and styles of attack that had been developed for the women alone. For one thing, men didn't settle as easily into the pelvis in floor work as did women, but they did have more exciting potential in air work.

If Graham had been rigidly inflexible, if she had established a certain cut-off point, announcing that thus-and-such was the true Graham style and that none other would be tolerated, she would have consigned herself to a creative backwater, something she had no intention of doing. With each new piece, there were adjustments and modifications to be made in the technique, for, after all was said and done, technique was the servant of creative intelligence and not the determinant of the possible. Technique necessarily would change as Graham's ideas changed from one period to the next.

The modern dance company was, and is, an extension of the creative individual in a way that few ballet companies are. When all else fails, ballet can get by on sheer technique which has been theatricalized to please the eye. Modern dance, on the other hand, is nothing without something to express. It does not exist without the infusing intelligence of a good choreographer. In modern dance content determines form: Form does not exist independently in modern dance as a good ballet technique can exist apart from anything of choreographic significance.

It can be said that the emergence of modern dance as a viable and serious form of theater art is the result of the sustained efforts of a group of intolerant, individual egos, each of whom felt that his or her own approach was the only valid one, or at least the best one. John Martin referred to the early days of the dance as "days of divine indiscipline." He did not, of course, refer to any lack of dance technique, but rather to the fact that in the earliest days of modern dance many different kinds of techniques were being experimented with by many different kinds of dance performers. There was as yet no standardized technique.

What we know today as classical ballet also evolved over a

considerable period of time—in this case, over a period of several hundred years. In creating its own special vocabulary of movement, the ballet drew on the folk and social dance forms of Western Europe from the sixteenth century onward. At times, ballet dancers fought as violently with one another about the necessity, say, of the turned-out position of the leg as did various modern dancers who emphasized different comportments. But, in time, varying views were resolved as standard ballet technique as we know it gradually evolved from the work of both choreographers and performers. So, too, did modern dance evolve from the creative experiments and unfettered spiritual quests of modern choreographers and performers.

The historical resolution of any artistic contention has been that the most creative talent carries the day. Certainly, in the case of modern dance, it is likely that, when a standard technique evolves, it will probably have at its core the broad principles that Graham evolved for herself—the maximum utilization of the torso and the acknowledgment of the floor as a source of energy and not simply a platform from which to escape into the air.

Of all the choreographers who emerged in the first decades of the serious modern dance tradition, Graham was by a long measure the most talented. Like her fellow artists, she had first to establish the type of movement vocabulary that was congenial to herself; then, again like the others, she began to use this vocabulary in a series of works that expressed her feelings about herself and the world she inhabited. The special quality that made her stand out was the breadth of vision that she brought to any subject she chose to examine. Other dancers were as seriously inclined as she, and others were, in fact, more musical in their use of dancers, but the depth of Graham's understanding of motivation was unmatched. She would play with a theme and exhaust it, examining it first under one aspect and then under another, and then reversing it or turning it completely upside down in order to expose all of the facets within. She was able to do this because of the inexhaustible flow of movement invention that poured out of her. It is true that she never worried about a step—thus the revisions that her dances underwent, sometimes for season after season. She felt that there would always be another step or series of steps to replace those that did not quite draw the viewer's attention as she wished. If necessary, she would throw out whole sections of a dance she had created. She was profligate with movement in a way that no other choreographer of her generation dared to be.

By the time Graham was working on "Deaths and Entrances," she had so completely trained her company that she was able to have individual dancers work out sections of their own parts. To an extent, this was a matter of Graham's confidence in her choreographic powers. Less secure choreographers often consider a collaboration between themselves and their dancers a threat to their creative authority. Graham could be strict and even cruel in rejecting movement that she felt did not express the correct emotion, but she could at the same time be open and generous in accepting what the dancer had worked out. In "Deaths and Entrances," Graham set the general pattern for herself and the other two sisters and then let Dudley and Maslow work out many of the details. While it is always pleasing for a dancer to be able to work creatively with the choreographer and offer suggestions that fit in with the mood and style of a role, the satisfaction derived from assisting someone as rigorously demanding as Graham was all the more special.

After a few successful concerts in the spring of 1944, with strong encouragement from Hawkins, Graham boldly decided to take an entire week in a Broadway theater, unheard of at the time, and to hire an orchestra. Graham was the first of the modern dancers to attempt a full week on Broadway and to subject herself to the commercial competition that inevitably followed. This was a far cry from both the cooperative programs of the Dance Repertory Theater and the Sunday afternoon recitals in a Broadway house that were possible only because Sunday was drama's usual day off. In Graham's week at the National Theater, the black drapes that had been the traditional background for the recital artist were replaced by actual décor. Horst, who used to play and observe from the wings and sometimes cue the electrician and the curtains, now found himself in charge of a small orchestra in the pit. And the lighting was directed by the most accomplished lighting designer in the theater, Jean Rosenthal, who became part of the Graham "family" of artistic collaborators.

Even during the great creative days of the late 1930's and early 1940's, when Graham's reputation as an innovator was at its height, the Company had been too poor to have a lighting designer and even too poor to take the requisite lighting equipment on tour. Then the production would be lit with whatever equipment was available. When it was exceptionally skimpy, Hawkins would have to search for bits and pieces of equipment with which to execute the light plot for the evening's works. The advent of popularity at last enabled Graham to have specialists handle the various aspects of production. Popularity, of necessity, brings the technically trained, but in Rosenthal's case it brought Graham a genius.

Rosenthal regarded her art as something that should enhance the choreography and establish a partnership with it. This was similar to the way Horst regarded his music. It was a question not of dominating or being placed in a subservient position to the movement, but of presenting it to best advantage by setting it off against (in Horst's case) a musical score of easy rapport, or (in Rosenthal's case) by shifting gradations and intensities and directions of illumination.

For Graham, the week on Broadway would give her the opportunity to show her growing audience an anthology of both her early dances, created in the 1930's, and her newer, more theatrically dramatic works. The season ran from May 7 to May 14. The earliest Group piece in the program was "Primitive Mysteries." Graham revived the solos "Frontier," "Lamentation," and "Deep Song," her 1937 dance about a woman's suffering during the Spanish Civil War. She asked Lauterer to do a setting for the dance, which originally had been performed on Graham's then customary black-draped stage, and though for her the entire week proved a terrific success, Lauterer's experience of working on "Deep Song" contributed to his eventual decision to end their working relationship. In the commercial theater, away from Bennington, Lauterer felt compromised and Graham did not. Conditions on Broadway were not ideal, but Graham accepted the difficulties and Lauterer could not. Meanwhile, the encomiums and the audience poured in. Graham was back on Broadway, and in a much different capacity from that of a performer of sexy little numbers in the Greenwich Village Follies twenty years before. Like the good descendant of pioneer stock that she was, she had hacked out a living space in the thicket of the theater world by force of will, energy, and prodigious talent.

Financially, the week at the National Theater was, of course, the most ambitious thing that Graham had ever attempted. She obviously had no conceivable way of producing the necessary money from any of her own resources, and the task was thus handled by Hawkins, who was still slightly cocky from the success of his fund-raising of the previous year.

Hawkins was driven by an ambition that was nearly the equal of Graham's. He wanted to dance and he wanted to choreograph. Graham provided him with roles as long as she was able to keep the company working, and the promotion of the Company became a way for him to advance his own career. But, more and more, the amount of time required to raise and oversee money ate into the time he could devote to his own choreography.

To guarantee the week at the National Theater, Hawkins mounted a full-scale effort to raise funds. He had previously intended to ask Katharine Cornell for money and had drafted a letter to her requesting assistance. Graham saw it and absolutely forbade him to send it. Asking Cornell for money was not acceptable to Graham; their relationship was not that of benefactress and beneficiary but of artists who shared a mutual respect. Such a request, she believed, would have changed their relationship. Hawkins tore the letter up, though it irritated him to do so. Now, however, he insisted on approaching Cornell, and Graham agreed. Cornell not only contributed money of her own but also asked friends in the theater world. At a Sunday afternoon gathering at her home, a substantial $26,000 was raised. It turned out that the week of performances in May was sufficiently successful to recoup all the operating costs—that is, the rental, house and company salaries, and publicity. But for the cost of the productions, Graham needed the funds that came through Cornell. The sum was large enough to enable the Company to draw upon it for several years to come.

It was also through Hawkins's efforts that Graham received a major commission to do three new works for a concert in the fall of 1944. The concert was sponsored by the Coolidge Foundation and was to be held at the Library of Congress; it was one of the most prestigious series in the country. Hawkins had written the previous year to Elizabeth Sprague Coolidge, a vigorous octogenarian and discriminating patron, encouraging her to see Graham's performances. Mrs. Coolidge moved with the decisiveness customary to her when she was impressed, and promptly commissioned three musical scores, one each from Darius Milhaud, Paul Hindemith, and Aaron Copland, and she commissioned Graham to choreograph three new dances.

The October concert in Washington was an enormous challenge, but Graham was delighted with it, a sign of the creative strength and vigor she felt within herself. The first person she contacted was Arch Lauterer, whom she wanted to create the décors for all the dances. Writing him a long letter, she explained the financial arrangements in detail and asked whether the money was sufficient for his time and energy. It was a very large undertaking, and she apologized for being able to offer so little. She emphasized that she was giving him a guarantee of what she was assured of having and that if more money was available she would see that he received it. She wanted to work on the dances with him in Bennington, when she and the Company were in residence, just as they had all done the previous year on "Deaths and Entrances."

Lauterer wrote her a shattering reply. The letter was couched in the usual friendly terms of their correspondence, but its import was that he was not at all satisfied with the products of their artistic collaboration. He envisioned his place in the theater as being more than a scenic designer, which is what, so far as he was concerned, their collaboration made him. He felt that his wishes had been given short shrift for the most part, and that the collaboration was, in effect, in the service of her creation, with his décor simply a background to a triumph that was hers. Lauterer wrote that he had had complete artistic responsibility for over a hundred productions at the Cleveland Playhouse before coming to Bennington. Citing the necessity of having to earn a living for his family, he said he could best provide for them in the academic world (he was then on the faculty of Mills College), where, additionally, he felt he could do some work. He did not feel a part of her successes, for the final product of their collaboration had always borne her special stamp. The critics who reviewed the dances he had designed had not even felt it necessary to praise his work, and even had criticized work that he felt represented his precise idea of theater. Lauterer's dissatisfaction was a total surprise to Graham. Their relationship had been more than that of colleagues, and now it was as a hired designer that he was objecting.

She delayed answering, hoping that the situation would right itself without any further complicating statements from her. But since the issue eventually had to be faced, she sat down to compose a reply. Like a well-balanced oration, the letter began with a confession of her insensitivity to his needs. She admitted feeling guilty for her oversight and her inattention to the things that were of importance to him.

As the long letter progressed, it moved from contriteness to shrillness and anger, at times assuming the tone of a rant:

> You say it is now possible to engage someone to do things for me [things she was asking of Lauterer]. You know that is not true and when you say that you slap my face and make me intensely angry. That you have no right to say. I do not "engage." I work with someone I trust and whose vision I revere, as I do yours. It is the way a mind works that is beautiful, precise, and precious. And then you say that I can "engage" someone. There are dreams to be placed before the world. The world may hate them but that is not important. It is important that each of us raise the standard of civilization the tiny fraction that is immortal law. I am doing [it] as best I can, however wrong I may be. If you say that you cannot realize your dreams, your potentialities with me I am grieved but I see how that is. If you say it will not work or that it is money, then you are not fighting, Arch, and I could kill you for that. The faith I have in you makes it necessary that you fight or I shall come perilously near to hating you. That may not matter.

By the end of the letter she regained her composure and said that she did not want be accusatory but did want to know definitely whether or not he would be available for work on the Library of Congress series. She wrote: "You are one of the few that dare not fail, I know you will not unless you do not fight. I wish the need were not for that but it is a law of birth that has never been changed, I guess."

Concluding with the information that she would be in Bennington for an additional week in August, she added a final note about her progress. "I am working on the Hindemith ["Mirror Before Me"], the hardest job yet. Some days I have spent in the depths of the earth. I send this with love always, Martha."

Lauterer's reply was negative. He could no longer work with her. Thus he became the first of Graham's major collaborators to leave her. His problem was one that others who worked closely with Graham, whether dancers, musicians, or costume and scenic designers, would have to face—namely, the difficulty of retaining a sense of personal identity in the face of her creative presence. Everything in a Graham production was subordinated to the creation of a work that would be as perfect an expression of her idea as possible. Everything was subordinated to her own vision, her way of doing things, her will. Coming from obscurity to a position of eminence by the exercise of that will, which dismissed outside opposition as foolish, she overrode any hesitancy on the part of a collaborator or Company member. To achieve her ends, Graham could be solicitous, kind, understanding, and compassionate; she could also be mean, cruel, vicious, and unyielding if she thought it necessary. Graham, in this sense, wielded power with the brutal but necessary force that she felt each individual situation required. When Lauterer left, he did so out of necessity, for personal artistic survival. Others left for the same reasons. Some lingered too long and became chained to the wishes and needs of her ego. Sustained, independent, creative association with Graham was possible only for those with a temperament that allowed them to stay disentangled from her. For many, too close an association over too long a period of time produced a form of artistic enslavement, which cannot have have been intended by Graham but which was the result of her own strength. It depended on the individual whether he or she would be able to live a life apart from Graham and whether the demands made by her were acceptable to his or her own sense of achievement. For Lauterer, the answer was no.

With Lauterer's refusal, Graham needed another designer whom she respected and with whom she could collaborate on the productions for the Coolidge music festival. Her choice was Noguchi. He had done "Frontier," her first set, and she felt that he was temperamentally attuned to her. The collaboration would prove to be a long and fruitful one. A strong sculptor in his own right, Noguchi was able to exercise the artistic judgment that removed his work from the category of an also-ran in the collaboration.

With the Coolidge Commission, Graham was attempting to work on a series of projects more quickly than she had ever done before. Hawkins had assumed the burden of production, and with comparable energy she responded to the task of creating three large-scale new works. She was least successful with the Milhaud, a score that was not particularly congenial to her. She choreographed a dance for the Company, "Imagined Wings," but did not include herself. This piece was composed without any creative exchange between Graham and the composer. Not since her earliest concerts had she worked with pre-existing music.

For the Hindemith she decided to create an evocative, mysterious work for two persons, herself and an attendant, who wait and prepare in an anteroom for an encounter that is never specified. The public responded to it warmly.

For the Copland piece she had the opportunity to work out a script in complete conjunction with the composer. Graham and Copland each made suggestions and revised his or her conception slightly so as to take into consideration the wishes of the other. The score was "Appalachian Spring," and of the three pieces it was by far the most successful and the most popular. It won the Pulitzer Prize for music for Copland and it became a signature piece for Graham—so much so that thirty years later, at a benefit performance, when the first bars of the music were heard the audience applauded, seeing once again in memory the small ecstatic woman suffused with the joy of a wedding and the making of a covenant. The commission brought Copland the national recognition that none of his previous scores had achieved and provided him with a suite that was given frequent concert performance. It was the cap of Graham's Americana period. She did not return again to personages of American history or to the events of the American expansion for subject matter. She had started her exploration of these concerns with "Heretic," in which she expressed a strong sense of revolt against the country's Puritan heritage; in "Appalachian Spring" she closed her chapter on the American experience with a strong affirmative response to its history and development.

Graham had wanted to work with Copland on a theater project for some time. When Graham sent him her script, without a title, Copland conceived the dance first in terms of Graham's personality. The few suggestions he made for changes in the script she accepted without hesitation, and Copland began to work on the score in June of 1943, finishing it a year later. It was perfect timing. She completed the successful week at the National Theater in mid-May and then had sufficient time to absorb and work with the score for the October premiere date. By the time the work was ready for presentation, Graham had found a title for it in one of Hart Crane's poems—his long epic of America, *The Bridge*. Copland's music, however, was in no way programatic to the text of the poem. The title was drawn from a section of Crane's poem called "The Dance," which told of an Indian maiden and her lover, the land she ruled over, and her passions and joys. In this dance, Graham came to terms with her American past.

What she responded to in Crane's poem was the passion of the mythic native who lived in this country before the land was settled. In the dance Graham made this drive domestic and at the same time accessible to her audiences by transferring it to the life of the settlers rather than focusing on those who passed across the land before there were fences and boundaries to hinder the free roaming of game and hunter. Graham domesticated the passion that once drove her outside organized society and changed it into the motive force that generated an organized society.

Noguchi's setting for the dance—a farmyard, created with lean economy—was the most socially domestic of locales. A section of fence rail indicated all of the territory that the young couple possessed, and the house was nothing more than a peaked entrance and a clapboard wall. The Revivalist had an inclined stump for a pulpit, and the four poke-bonneted acoyltes who followed his ecstatic lead had a bench to sit on at the side of the house when they were not clustering about him. For the Pioneer Woman, Noguchi designed a rocking chair of such slimness that it was almost like the profile of a chair rather than the actual thing. This entire collaboration among Graham, Noguchi, and Copland occupies a special niche in the theatrical history of the country. Each contributed elements that meshed perfectly with the ideas and conceptions of the other.

On the surface, "Appalachian Spring" is the story of a Husbandman and his Bride (danced by Hawkins and Graham) taking possession of their new house and starting a new life together. The work is a masterly amalgam of piety and passion, of hesitancy and resolve, of the spirit of adventure and the doubts that dog the steps of the venturesome, causing temporary hesitations in their forward progress. The two young people are observed, examined, and ultimately approved of by the older generation, represented by the Pioneer Woman (danced by the beautiful May O'Donnell) and a fire-and-brimstone Revivalist (danced by Cunningham). The action is set in the early days of America.

The Husbandman's first entrance brings him to the side of the cabin where he and his Bride will dwell, and he runs his hand reflectively over the surface of its overlapping boards. There is a sense of both possession and questioning.

As the work progresses, the Husbandman and his Bride dance a warmly joyous duet that reveals their shared hopes for the future. The Revivalist with his broad-brimmed hat is a formidable figure, more concerned with rectitude than with love and warmth. He represents one aspect of the experience the young are entering. His sternness is softened by the Pioneer Woman, who has already experienced the emotional joys and pains that will become the lot of the young woman.

The simple tale of the man and his bride examining their farm gives no inkling of the ramifications of gesture with which Graham composed the dances for her principals. The Bride's joy is not simple hopping up and down but a surge of happiness that seems too good to be admitted, so that she draws back from the full expression of her happiness for fear of driving such pleasure away. The slow expansive gestures of the Pioneer Woman indicate her sharing of the younger woman's joy, though tempering it with wisdom. The Bride has steps that are buoyed up with hope for the future, while the Pioneer Woman, like a ship breasting waves, sweeps along with calm resolution. The Husbandman settles his feet into the ground like one who is drawing sustenance from it in the way that any living thing might. He is as solid as the fence posts that hold up his railings, but he appears to be someone who could grow. He is open and firm. The Revivalist, filled with fervor, is equally firm. He, in effect, carries around with him a congregation-audience which listens to and applauds his words. In a beautiful fusion of two different types of gesture, Graham had the congregation of four small girls cup their hands as if in prayer and then clap together as if applauding. Surrounding it all, Aaron Copland's singing score wrapped itself like a benign thread, while Noguchi's setting, more like a spatial drawing than a sculptural block, gave indications of place without obtruding.

In "Appalachian Spring" audiences recognized a story that was simultaneously personal to a couple and their kin and an expression of a country's growth. The musical quotes from a traditional hymn that Copland incorporated into his score emphasized the warm, religious, and joyful values expressive of the sinew and heart of a young country that, though still struggling, was confident of a happy outcome.

There was another affirmation in the work as well, one that informed the more abstract social theme. Graham was at this time fifty years old and in the flood tide of her creative energy. A mature emotional relationship had come to her at a time when most women of her generation had been married for twenty years. Because of her feeling for Hawkins, she had been able, in "American Document," to articulate her fear of the danger that the preacher Jonathan Edwards warned against in his sermon against fornication. She had turned her gaze upon herself as the dithery, flighty woman in "Every Soul Is a Circus," and she had played with the idea of the woman as madonna and temptress in the hot Southwestern climate of "El Penitente." "Letter to the World" showed her losing love and creating art out of the loss. In "Punch and the Judy" she despaired of and ultimately embraced the vagrant braggadocio, Punch, who could be neither relied upon nor entirely dismissed from one's life. In the darker, unresolved world of "Deaths and Entrances," she wandered in the coils of past love. Then, in "Appalachian Spring," she emerged into a world of light in which there were no nagging shadows of the past but only the joyous present as she and her mate assumed control of their lives and proceeded together. This was an affirmation that had not been possible previously either in her work or her life.

8

In the Public Eye

"You may challenge her method
of projection but not her
artistic integrity."
Robert Coleman

The war years were a fulfillment of what Graham had struggled for ever since leaving Denishawn. That company had passed into history, and Ted Shawn and Ruth St. Denis had long since parted, each to pursue individual interests. When one now thought of modern dance, one thought of Humphrey, Weidman, Holm, Tamiris, and, in a special category, Graham. She was the most characteristic representative of the group, so much so that a satirist at the Rainbow Room, when caricaturing a radical meeting, presented it "in modern dance style, as Martha Graham would have done it."

In her increasing status as a public figure, Graham sometimes became subject to public manipulation of her name. In 1940 an artist, Paul Meltsner, had contributed a portrait of her to the Argentine National Museum, and now, because of the fascist sympathies of the government in power, he was asking that it be returned. Claiming to have raised $3 million in bond drives already, he pledged the sale of the portrait to another bond drive. Thus Graham, without any control over the situation, found herself being used. The State Department finally defused the situation by suggesting to the artist that he regard his painting as a gift to the people of Argentina and not as a gift to the current regime.

The war years were also a time when a certain "deification" of Graham began to accelerate. The original source of the cult feelings was Graham's own intense view about dancing. She considered dancing a special form of life fulfillment and had remarked frequently to prospective students that, if they had to ask whether dancing ought to be their career, then it was probably not for them. It was only for those who could not conceive of any other way of life. As early as the days of her first Group, when she was giving classes to small numbers of students in Carnegie Hall, she began to develop loyalty of an exceptional sort. Sabin and McDonald, saving the ravelings of Graham's dance costume, were one example. Another comes from the experience of Michio Ito, a fellow tenant in the Carnegie Hall studio building and choreographer of one of Graham's dances in the Follies, who dropped into her class one day looking for dancers to take with him on tour. When he saw a girl whose feet were bleeding continue to dance, he decided that this type of devotion and intensity was not for him. Later, in the 1930's, members of Graham's Group tailored their lives around her creative needs. When they occasionally were given a weekend off without rehearsals and they made plans to date, relax, or visit families, they immediately canceled any activity if it was hinted that perhaps Martha might be working in the studio and could use a little help. The dancers considered themselves an elite, and Graham was the leader who occupied a special niche removed from the mass of people. As the earlier years receded into memory and the older dancers retired, Graham's myth grew.

The process of deification was also encouraged by Graham's personal vanity and the element of mysticism in her make-up. She spoke of life forces and Indian philosophy and was profoundly serious. She was "cosmic." By 1944, when she was fifty years old, she had outlasted all of the dancers with whom she had started. Among the women, there were now new dancers like Helen McGehee and Yuriko Amamaya (who ordinarily used only her first name). Everyone in the Company was her junior—in some cases, although they did not know it, thirty years her junior. Her first little trio of dancers, Thelma Biracree, Evelyn Sabin, and Betty McDonald, called her "Miss Martha," a polite reflection of nineteenth-century address.

To her current Company she was simply "Martha." There was no other, and no one could mistake who was being referred to. Physically, Graham was remarkable. In the mid-1920's she had achieved an individual, dramatic look which she retained almost unchanged for the next thirty years; the hair drawn back severely, the mouth a full scarlet notch, the upper lip flared over slightly protruding teeth, and the high cheekbones were instantly recognizable. Through carefully posed photographs she took care to protect the image she presented to the public. Candid photographs could reveal only the moment—perhaps not a moment Graham cared to show, and certainly not the theatrical dream.

Graham still had her detractors, although even they respected her. Robert Coleman, reviewing her concert of May 10, 1944, for the *New York Daily Mirror*, wrote:

> As for Miss Graham's art, it is difficult to evaluate. There are no standards for it other than those of her own making. It might variously be described as neurotic posturing, strained plastic movement, and bodily pantomime. . . . They were morbidly fascinating like watching a mother in labor or an unfortunate doubled up with acute appendicitis on a curb, writhing wretchedly in anticipation of the arrival of an ambulance. . . . Miss Graham is not one to seek cheap effects. She never mugs, in fact she relies almost entirely upon her body, rather than her mask-like intriguing features, to convey meaning. You may challenge her method of projection but not her artistic integrity.

In large measure, the year 1944 established the pattern that the Company would follow for the rest of Graham's working life: the spring or fall season in New York, limited engagements outside the city, the summer at Bennington or another school, and regular teaching assignments at the studio-school or outside schools like the Neighborhood Playhouse. The publicity that followed the Coolidge concert in Washington enabled the Company to assemble a few dates outside New York. Then it settled in for the next year's spring season at the National Theater. Soon the war in Europe would be over, and shortly after the war in the Pacific would end, releasing from the service hundreds of thousands of men who were eager to begin a civilian life, and, in the case of many, to embark on a theatrical career.

The new season proved to be quite important. Within her own

Company there was a certain restlessness that Graham tried to satisfy by having various dancers present their own works on the spring program. Hawkins, for one, was very anxious to do this, and so was Cunningham. Graham allowed each dancer to prepare a single work for an official premiere. It was an intelligent step. So long as the Company remained a personal choreographic tool for the head of the group, anyone with choreographic ambitions would have to leave in order to form his or her own group. Indeed several of Graham's dancers did this, some with outstanding and some with indifferent results. Sophie Maslow and Jane Dudley, who earlier had teamed with William Bales to present their works, were now enjoying successful touring. Other dancers, like Nina Fonaroff, prepared works for recital concerts in cooperation with other choreographers. But the opportunity to present work with the Graham Company, with its reputation and audience, was a special advantage for any choreographer and a strong inducement to stay.

Hawkins prepared "John Brown," a dance inspired by the antislavery crusader, and Cunningham offered an odd solo for himself called "Mysterious Adventure." Both men had been working choreographically for several years, but Cunningham's individual inclinations expressed themselves earlier and in a more complete fashion than did Hawkins's. "John Brown," with its concentration on an American theme and the use of spoken text, bore a strong resemblance to Graham's work, and it was impossible to beat her at her own game, both intrinsically and in the eyes of others. Works using her choreographic vocabulary and her philosophical groundwork were doomed to be treated harshly by the critics, as was "John Brown," and were to prove creative blind alleys for those who stayed with them for any length of time.

Cunningham had been strongly influenced by the ideas of the composer and musical theorist John Cage, whom he had first met on the West Coast and who now was living in New York. Cunningham, who felt limited by the straight story line of Graham's works, tried to produce dances that were nonlinear in development and that drew attention to themselves in terms of the motions themselves rather than through any symbolic or narrative content they might have. If Cunningham were a wordy person, he might have explained what he was doing in the very terms Graham herself used some ten years earlier in discussing her own work: "The lift of the arm does not mean that it represents a tree or anything else. The arm raised in an uplift that is graceful presents the beauty of an arm in motion. It is enough. America is not interested in impressionism. Our dramatic force lies in energy and vitality. Symbolism is alien to it. That is theatric and not good theater, for it does not communicate itself directly to the audience from the dancer." When Graham left Denishawn she was reacting against the use of dance to imitate ethnic forms of movement or the movement of natural phenomena, like dawn or the flight of an insect. She wanted to stop pretending that she was something other than a dancer—an American dancer—when she performed, and her solution, ultimately, was to emphasize the dramatic side of her person. Cunningham took the process one step further and became a person moving in space without any dramatic accents. But just as the world had not been ready for Graham's movement, so it was not ready for Cunningham's. A review of Cunningham's solo in the *New York Times* called it "a cutish solo and exhibition piece quite without content, belonging to the dance recital category" and suggested that perhaps it was "more kind than wise for Miss Graham to sponsor young choreographers."

The season as a whole, though, was quite successful. The program included "Letter to the World," "Salem Shore," "Appalachian Spring," "Deaths and Entrances," and "Mirror Before Me," now renamed "Herodiade" at the request of the composer. Attendance was large and enthusiastic. Most significantly, the season caught the attention of the impresario Sol Hurok, who offered to represent Graham the next year on a national tour. This was recognition of an especially gratifying sort. The Hurok organization had a reputation for handling only the most important names in the performing arts, and his willingness to represent Graham was not just a plum for her but another step upward in the acceptance of modern dance. Previously Hurok had handled foreign artists almost exclusively. Having made its reputation and secured its operating base outside of the commercial theater, for the most part in colleges and universities, modern dance was now being sought by the commercial world.

Indeed, a number of modern dancers had moved to Broadway in the role of show choreographers. Charles Weidman, Doris Humphrey, and Helen Tamiris were very active in show work, and soon Hanya Holm would make a professional theater name for herself by creating the dances for *Kiss Me, Kate.* Modern dancers proved to be ideally suited for work in Broadway shows, possessing as they did a strong dramatic technique that lent itself to expressing psychological complexities of character. Agnes de Mille scored a tremendous success with her dances for *Oklahoma!*; her "dream sequence" made such a scene a requisite dance number on Broadway for the next decade. The whole of the popular performing world was caught up with the idea of psychological insights into behavior. Surrealism was rampant in the arts, and the unconscious mind became a hit overnight. Popular attention struck modern dance like a plague.

At first, the effect was not really notable. But gradually more and more energy was siphoned off into popular entertainment and less and less was directed into the concert or company recital. The full toll would not be apparent until the early 1950's. Then the old formulations of dramatic dance began to wear thin. They spoke less directly to the time than they had in the late 1930's, and thus modern dance, which had been so alert to social currents, seemed to lose touch with the society it once reflected so accurately.

In the flood tide of success and popular esteem, however, little appeared on the horizon, professionally speaking, except a rosy glow of hope and enthusiastic enterprise. Katharine Cornell, hearing about Hurok's offer to represent Graham, was overjoyed and sent off a telegram to him: "My regard for her as a person in the theater as well as the dance is the highest. As a creative artist at once produced by America and expressing America she is without peer. My best wishes to you both."

Graham's new enterprise was the creation of a new dance with music by Carlos Chavez, who was being extremely slow in delivering the score. The new work, which was to be premiered in New York in January of the next year, would start the association between herself and the Hurok organization and would break the fifteen-month hiatus since the presentation of her last new works. That summer Graham went again to Bennington but performed only "Appalachian Spring" and "Herodiade" at a recital for the students.

The state of Graham's private life was not as encouraging as that of her public life. In the seven years that Graham and Hawkins had lived together there were few times without difficulties, but by 1945, for Hawkins, their difficulties were beyond control. He swallowed his pride, went for psychological counseling, and moved out of his and Graham's apartment and into the studio. He remained a member of the Company but taught class at the studio no more, teaching instead at Adelphi College in Garden City, Long Island. The separation lasted for nearly a full year and caused Graham sufficient torment to seek psychological therapy herself from one of the people to whom Hawkins had gone for help, Dr. Frances Wickes, a dedicated Jungian.

In a book by Dr. Wickes, *The Inner World of Choice*, the therapist describes a dream of one of her patients, a dancer, who felt she was losing the emotional support on which she depended. Dr. Wickes related the dream:

> "The tide is out. I am walking on a seemingly endless strip of white sand, carrying in my hand a chalice? a casket? On one side is the withdrawing ocean, on the other an unscalable cliff. I see far out across the waters a great wave gathering in towering, menacing force. It approaches with incredible swiftness. I throw myself upon the sand just as it is about to break over me. It encloses me in a cave of clear jade. Then there is utter unfathomable darkness." When the wave recedes she sees a narrow opening in the cliff where the wave broke through. Beyond the rocky passage is a meadow with a green and leafy tree in the center.

This resolution was interpreted as a hopeful sign.

The new dance, called "Dark Meadow," that Graham was working on for the January 1946 season took her beyond the second period of her creative life, the period of the great "American" dances, and provided a transition into the next phase of her artistic journey, her profound exploration of ancient myth. Graham's instincts throughout her career had pushed her toward using mythic materials, and it seems clear that her contact with Dr. Wickes helped to confirm her new direction. Eventually her attention would be drawn to myths of classical antiquity, both Hebraic and Greek, but for the moment she was deeply into myth of an unspecified time and place. "Dark Meadow" took the problems of daily existence and expanded them to heroic size, acting them out through characters with generic names. The work was like a saga with a life-affirming cyclical force. By the time it was presented, Graham and Hawkins had effected a reconciliation.

In preparing the set for "Dark Meadow," Noguchi created cone-shaped mounds that looked like a biomorphic Stonehenge; he supplied a second shape with a white face into which various shafts were placed during the course of the work. In its effect, the set was baffling but beautiful, like an abstract painting that suggests figuration but stops short of delineating any details sharply. In all, it was a far cry from New England or the Appalachian hills, but, as was her custom, Graham was a few paces ahead of her audience.

In the program note prepared for the dance, Graham wrote: " 'Dark Meadow' is a re-enactment of the Mysteries which attend the eternal adventure of seeking." There were four sections, and each of the incidents was bridged by transitional dances by five women and four men, collectively called They Who Dance Together. Graham created for them some of the most intricate and lyrical ensemble movement to be found in any of her dances. The lead role was a woman (Graham), One Who Seeks, who was contrasted with the second major female role, She of the Ground, a graceful earth-mother figure, and He Who Summons, the godlike male lead, which Hawkins danced.

At the opening of the work, Graham stood on an inclined rock faintly resembling a Druid's pulpit, and the action of the chorus moved in front of her while she was self-contained in meditation. The first section was entitled "Recurring Ecstasy of the Flowering Branch," the second "Terror of Loss," the third "Ceaselessness of Love," and the final again "Recurring Ecstasy of the Flowering Branch." After her thoughtful immobility, Graham involved herself in a long solo dance with a black cloth that seemed to represent the many things that could cloud the meadow. She continually seemed to be returning to some singular incident and mulling it over, first from one viewpoint and then from another. She was comforted by She of the Ground, who possessed the serenity so conspicuously lacking in the questing figure danced by Graham. The air of the piece was grave but not in any way painful. These were epic characters whose motivations were shadowy but whose comportment was that of those who are involved in a ritual designed to expiate or placate a disturbance in the deeper flow of vital movement—life. "Dark Meadow" was a dance of root causes and responses rather than of specific incident. It was greeted enthusiastically.

The rest of the season, which lasted two weeks, centered upon what the promotion called "Hits from the Graham Repertory." Graham was nervous, and Hurok himself was disquieted when she told him that she could not be reached by telephone since she was too poor to be able to afford one. She finally exploded only hours before the opening curtain, declaring that it was impossible for her to go on. Some misguided functionary had painted the floor of the stage, and Graham, who did not like the feel of it, declared it unusable for her dance. Hurok accepted her agitation with calm—he had already endured decades of comparable spasms of anxiety and self-doubt—and assured her that the paint would be removed and the floor restored to her full satisfaction before opening night. It was, and to make sure that the fumes of the paint remover were not overpowering, Hurok sprinkled perfume on the stage floor just before the curtain opened.

The two-week New York season was almost completely sold out, and thus the tour began with great prospects. This was Graham's first opportunity to bring such a varied repertory to so many different cities. The accommodations were the best that the Company had ever enjoyed; in fact, the Graham Company had never had it so good. As the Company worked its way west to Chicago, south to Texas, and up to Los Angeles, the Hurok press office prepared the way with pictures, releases, and advertising. But for all the advance notice and the good accommodations, the tour did not fulfill the original high expectations. In Los Angeles, for example, the Company played four dates to disappointing houses. One night, when Hurok visited Graham in her dressing room, he found her terribly agitated over the size of the houses. In addition to the low turnout, she had been suffering from a cold and had been in bed until three o'clock in the afternoon, and, perhaps most important of all, she and Hawkins had been squabbling. Though she danced with a red nose, the performance went well. Still, even though critical acclaim everywhere was far greater than it ever had been in the past, it was clear from the tour as a whole that, outside of New York City, there was still public resistance to the form of theater that Graham presented.

After the tour ended in Chicago in April, Graham had to prepare a new work for presentation a month later. The Alice M. Ditson Fund of Columbia University had asked Graham to premiere a new dance for the first program of the Festival of Contemporary Music. The score for this new work was by Samuel Barber, and together she and Barber had selected the legend of Jason and Medea as their subject. Graham had prepared a script, which she and the composer agreed upon. They did not use the legend literally, but instead created a situation in which the characters were both allegorical and contemporary figures.

The new work, which Graham called "Serpent Heart," suggested that the squabbles between herself and Hawkins were matters not easily put to rest. A small-scale work for four dancers, it examined the jealousy of Medea when Jason preferred over her the daughter of the king of the city in which they were staying. The young Princess was the first leading role given to Yuriko, a deft, delightfully quick dancer who immediately made a strong impact in the part as well as in the remainder of the Graham repertory in which she appeared. May O'Donnell, now a guest artist, danced the part of the Chorus and commented on the actions of the principals in their triangular affair. Hawkins was Jason. For herself, Graham created one of the most venomous parts in her repertory—a woman driven by jealousy to murderous revenge. Because Jason prefers the young Princess, Medea kills him. Her solo, in which she extracted a long red ribbon from herself, simulated the spewing up of a vile liquid having the corrosive power of acid. For décor, Noguchi prepared a rough gray, textured block for the Chorus to stand on and a brass harness with quivering brass rays emanating from it, which Medea took upon herself after the murder. Moving about the stage in it, she was like a glittering, malevolent presence. The piece was the incarnation of jealousy and signaled a turn on Graham's part to another examination of the role and effects of passion. This dance was a far cry from "Punch and the Judy," in which Graham took Punch back after he had strayed with Pretty Polly.

Barber thought of his score and the orchestra suite he drew from it as "Medea," but Graham entitled the piece first "Serpent Heart" and then "Cave of the Heart."

In June, Louis Horst received the warmly complimentary letter that he usually received from Rita Morgenthau after another year of teaching at the Neighborhood Playhouse, but this time he also was informed that he had been awarded a fellowship for $3,500 for his contribution to the creative arts. It was the first such tangible award he had been given in recognition for his incredible devotion to the world of modern dance, and, in particular, to Graham. By his own choice Horst remained in the background and allowed the various dancers he assisted to accept the praise that began to accrue to modern dance. It is doubtful, however, that the movement would ever have taken the form it did without Horst's devoted interest.

Composition courses are common in music academies, but until Horst began to teach dance composition no one had systematically offered choreographic study. As a musician, Horst had strong ideas about how a piece should be structured, and he communicated them to his students with a rough and ready wit that was the enemy of pretension and affectation. He was not overly concerned with the particular movements that a student developed and was continually delighted with fresh material, but he always insisted that a dance piece have form. He did not want the form to become so rigid that it inhibited the development of the dance, but he did want the student to have an idea of how to structure a piece and carry it through to logical completion. In line with his ideas about flexibility, he did not encourage symmetrical development, which he believed would leave the viewer bored, but encouraged his pupils to try asymmetrical development in their work.

Horst liked dancing and the energy it represented. There is no question that he had a special sympathy for dance movement that made him unique among the composers and accompanists of his day. He possessed a rhythmic sense that accommodated itself to the movements of the human body in an almost caressing way. Once Horst had found the right tempo for a piece, he would always remember it, as well as the exact needs of the individual dancer. His ability is extraordinarily rare and requires both precise musicianship and an intuitive understanding of dance movement. Beneath Horst's bulky exterior lurked a dancer.

His energy level was phenomenal, and he carried on a full teaching load in both winter and summer. The only difference between his regular work year and his vacation was that on vacation he taught in places like the Perry Mansfield camp in Colorado, at Mills College, or, for many years, at Bennington. His normal position at the piano was a somnambulant slouch, with a cigarette ready to drop its ashes drooping from the corner of his mouth. To the casual observer it would seem that he was half asleep and not paying attention to the dancer's demonstration of an exercise he had assigned. Generations of students were startled to have him suddenly make a piercing observation about the development of the work they were displaying. He not only was paying acute attention but could place exactly the point where he thought the student had let the thread of the dance slip away or where he had not logically followed a course of development the dance seemed to be working toward. His criticisms were pointed but not cruel; his humor took the edge off many of his harshest corrections. He began to have a reputation for having eyes in the back of his head. A resolute and methodical teacher, he evolved from his classes a series of principles that he eventually incorporated into a formal course.

One of the things that Horst felt strongly about was what he considered the mammoth presence of ballet in modern dance. Deciding that modern dancers should not be trapped by the romantic forms of ballet, he had them study what he called preclassic dance forms—dances like the allemand, gigue, passepied, and so on, that preceded the formal development of the ballet. Whenever he saw a particularly felicitous use of one of these forms he would incorporate it into his course. Sophie Maslow, for example was delighted to have a saraband that she had created for the early studio dance series used as an exemplar of the form in his courses.

For all of the first generation of modern dancers, Horst was the champion who would help them in any way he could, whether by playing at their recitals for the most minimal of fees or by perhaps translating into English articles about German expressionist dance for them to read. He regularly visited museums and art galleries and bought Klee and Marin when these artists represented an elitist and minority taste; he became for the dancers he helped a kind of window into the developments of the other arts. But always his special energy was saved for working with Graham. He encouraged her when criticism was particularly harsh or when she felt that the battle was too much for her to wage any longer. He would take her rehearsals, giving her a little breathing space when it was needed, but he also compelled her to keep working when her own inclinations were to leave the studio and "go to the movies."

Although Graham was given a great deal of credit for using the work of contemporary American composers, in large part this credit must be given to Horst, who set Graham's pattern of commissions and directed her toward the musical generation that was growing up around her. In some way, the commissions Graham made were more important for her reputation than the dances she did. The Coolidge Foundation and the Ditson Foundation gave her commissions out of their interest in music, not dance. Music was an established and recognized art, and modern dance was not, so that the lever of music was a very useful one for her. That aside, it is unlikely that without Horst she ever would have made quite the use of contemporary music that she did. It is also unlikely that her career would have taken her in quite the direction that it did.

Horst was an unusual revolutionary. He took all sorts of chances in his career and yet remained conservatively married to a wife he hardly ever saw. His taste in artistic matters was advanced, but his style of life quite conventional, reminding one of the remark of the pioneer family-planning advocate, Margaret Sanger: "The more radical the message, the more conservative should be the dress." Horst enjoyed eating and drinking well, and he relished a cigar. But there was a restlessness in him that belied these comfortable inclinations. There really was no good reason for a musician, first, to leave his birthplace, where he was reasonably well known and had a variety of paying jobs, to join a dance troupe like Denishawn at a point when its fortunes were extremely variable; and then to leave that company, just when it arranged the longest and most lucrative tour of its history, to become the musical director for a recital dancer like Graham. The second move, especially, was slightly short of lunacy, but it was logical for a musician who loved dance.

The career that Horst chose in accompanying Graham, and all the others of that first revolutionary generation and succeeding ones, brought him the respect of his colleagues and a measure of popular success, but, essentially, Horst's role was that of the beloved uncle in the dance family. Having chosen a highly speculative career by casting his lot with dancers, he then set about securing his future in the most conservative and methodical way. He created teaching positions for himself in a variety of schools and brought dance instruction to a level that it had not previously reached. The composition course awakened dancers to the idea of structure in a way that had not been apparent to most before Horst pointed it out. His mind was analytical in its basic thrust, and he enjoyed examining in the most exhausting way the dancers who came under his scrutiny. To outsiders, his teaching method was admired even more, if that is possible, than it was by his dance students. Drama students in his course at the Neighborhood Playhouse who were being exposed to the dance for the first time did not understand how dances were organized or the logic of the completed work. It was precisely this concern that Horst emphasized during his entire career. A man who grew up playing in the orchestra of a vaudeville house pit, he graduated to the faculty of the Juilliard School of Music when it installed a dance department.

By the mid-1940's, Horst's days of composing for Graham were over. This eventuality he undoubtedly foresaw when he encouraged her to work with young American composers. Horst earlier served as Graham's musical director, but with the arrival of Hawkins in her life, he less and less exerted the dominant influence he once had in her decision-making. More and more, Graham would consult him in only a pro forma manner. Their relationship, which had begun, at least on Graham's side, as a passionate involvement, had cooled to an artistic and a business association. In practical terms, nothing had changed in his affiliation with the Company. He still accompanied and conducted and traveled with it. But in effect, everything had changed between Graham and himself.

During the summer of 1945 he went off to Mills College for a month and then spent another month teaching at the Perry-Mansfield School in Steamboat Springs, Colorado, while Graham and Hawkins spent the summer by themselves, camping part of the time in the Southwest in a section of the country they both loved. As much as Graham romanticized the Southwest in her work, Hawkins found her an uncomfortable camper, uneasy in the outdoors and terrified by the rustling and crawling creatures of the open air.

In the fall several aspiring male dancers newly returned from military service found their way to the school at 66 Fifth Avenue. In a short time, Stuart Hodes, Robert Cohan, and Bertram Ross would become members of the Company. They would become, in effect, the third new Company that Graham created. Earlier, Cunningham left the Company to begin his own career, one that would have as much effect on the next generation of dancers as Graham's had on his.

Along with her teaching at the school, Graham continued to work at the Neighborhood Playhouse, which was bursting at the seams with young men out of service who were itching to make up for lost time and carve themselves a place in the theater. One of these young men was Richard Boone, whose eventual career would take him to the movies and a highly successful television series based on the exploits of a sophisticated gunfighter. At this time,

Boone's vision was directed toward the Broadway stage, and the Neighborhood Playhouse was going to be his entree into the theater world.

"The first time I came into the Neighborhood Playhouse," he relates, "I was two weeks out of the Navy, and I rode up in the elevator, and somewhere between a brassiere factory and shoestore was the Neighborhood Playhouse School. As I opened the door of the elevator, there was a door right across the way, and there were forty girls on the floor doing contractions. I didn't know what a contraction was at that time, and here I was two weeks out of the Navy. I thought, 'I don't know what this is, but it's where I belong.' I later told Martha that story and she laughed."

It was an exceptionally exciting time for the Playhouse and everyone connected with it. Graham had been elevated to the level of the "high priestess" by her cult followers, and, along with her actual success, there was the scent of success for all of the aspiring actors and actresses enrolled at the school. The economic constrictions of the 1930's had finally disappeared as the country entered a period of prosperity. There seemed to be no limit to the possibilities for upward movement. The generation that successfully fought World War II possessed an energy that could not easily be contained.

Boone remembered his first encounter with Graham:

> This strange little lady came into the classroom. And she spoke in a whisper. Martha speaks very softly, and you have to listen very carefully. And she said, "Now, what I would like you to do is go from this side of the room to that side of the room, and I would like you to do it in your most expressive way."
>
> Well! There were eleven—animals—in the class and here we went. We went bounding around the room like kangaroos. And we looked around and this little woman was collapsing and laughing. "My God, I've never seen anything like that in my life!" She was hysterical. "It's so great and so terrible what you're doing."
>
> Hell! I could jump six-two, and I was doing leaps, but my feet were flying out like boards, it had nothing to do with dancing. I was just jumping because somebody said OK, go ahead and jump. When she finished laughing, she was really collapsed, and then she began to talk to us about what the body means in terms of expression. And some of us learned as actors things that nobody else could ever have taught us.

In Boone's case, some of the things he learned were to have very specific uses. When he later played Western gunfighters, for example, he used the Graham fall on the count of one to simulate being shot. He had an even more profitable lesson. In class one day Graham stressed the importance of natural movement and gave as an example the walk of the cat. She herself had been fascinated with the movement of animals since childhood, and the walk of the cat was one of the examples she regularly offered to her students. Fifteen years later, the example surfaced in Boone in a way undetectable by anyone without prior knowledge of his background: Boone used the walk of the cat to pattern the stance of the character of Palladin in "Have Gun, Will Travel," his extremely popular television series. At one point Graham asked Boone if he were interested in becoming a member of her Company, but he declined, although he once danced in a concert with Nina Fonaroff, one of Graham's dancers.

As a teacher, Graham was indeed unforgettable. She entered a class as if it were the first one she had ever conducted and as if the people taking it were, potentially, the most talented group she had ever faced. In a word, she taught each and every class as if it were the most important ever. Walking in one day on Jane Dudley, her assistant, at the Playhouse, she took over the class because it did not have the right "feel." There was no "kundalini"—the energy that, according to Hindu belief, travels up and down the spinal column between the genitals and the brain, the most potent of the forces that can be unleashed in the human being. Dudley adored Graham both as a choreographer and as a teacher and, even though she was a long-time observer of her, she still considered a Graham class a special experience. She learned as much as she was able from watching Martha teach.

Graham always had complete authority in her classes. As Boone recalled, "With Martha, you get it right away or jump out the window. Get out. She has no patience. She whispers louder than most people scream." Spontaneously, Graham told them one day, "I think it's important, it really is, that you should say words." She then held in her arms one of the girls in class while speaking Hamlet's soliloquy, "To be or not to be . . ." All the while she looked at the student's hand as if she could read the universe in it. The impact on the class was incredibly forceful.

Graham, by this time, delegated a great deal of her teaching load to trusted members of her Company. For one thing, she simply did not have enough time to handle all of the teaching assignments offered to her. She was a dynamo, but, at the age of fifty-three, she was beginning to slow down and was allowing those of her dancers who understood what she was doing to take those classes she could not. Usually she designated Nina Fonaroff, Jane Dudley, Hawkins, or Marjorie Mazia. She put in a regular appearance at almost every class, so that the student would have the benefit of her fiery presence at least a couple of times during the course.

But no matter who was doing the instruction, there was a feeling of utter dedication to the class and the type of training being given. Though every teacher had a different style of instruction, the message was the same: Bring out the potential movement that lies within. Graham had surrounded herself with, and had helped create, a group of committed dancers who were passing on to the outside world some of the amazing dedication that characterized her entire career and the work of those who stayed with her.

The Neighborhood Playhouse was as close to Graham as anything outside of her own studio. It had an atmosphere of freshness that was increasingly rare at her studio, where she was revered as if she were removed from the sphere of mortal men. At the Playhouse she was one of the staff, albeit a famous one, but not a goddess, and she thus had to prove herself in a way she did not with the adoring pupils of her own school.

At the Playhouse, moreover, she was faced with another department, the acting department, which felt that *it* had the answers to the prayers of the aspiring actors, something Graham was not allowed to forget. Sanford Meisner, who headed the acting department, was a strongly opinionated person who wished to bring out the best in students in terms of acting first. He acknowledged dance's validity, but felt that his section of the school was the most important. Since Graham and Meisner joined forces to provide the school with productions of one sort or another, their different individual assessments of whether dance or acting should lead often caused difficulties. Still, their work together also often generated intense excitement.

Part of the success of the Playhouse was due to Horst's patient attention to the students and to his great understanding and sympathy for Graham's intentions. During one of his classes in 1947, he had the first-year students doing some movements in preclassic Greek forms, and from this came the idea for the end-of-the-term recital—*The Eumenides.* Horst worked with the students, explaining over and over the basic Graham principle, that in order to move here, a preparation or an accommodating movement had to be made there. In addition to his intelligent stringency, Horst could also break the tension in a roomful of students all trying to do Etruscan-style movement by observing pointedly, "That's a crock of shit!" The calculated use of coarse observation was one of his teaching tools, and he applied it in varying amounts and strength as necessary. With the postwar veteran group, it was used liberally to establish contact and a sense of rapport. Thirty-five male and female students were involved in the production of *The Eumenides.* They worked on it for four months in order to dance strenuously on stage for twenty-eight minutes. Graham and Meisner spun off suggestions to one another, and each would adapt or modify the resulting situation to fit into the over-all production. For the students, a production such as this was the most important part of their professional lives at the Playhouse in that the effect of Graham's and Meisner's teaching could be seen in operation and the students at last could demonstrate onstage what they learned in class.

The influence that Horst and Graham together had on the acting profession is difficult to assess directly, but when one looks at the roster of people they worked with—Bette Davis, Lorne Greene, Henry Fonda, Betty Garrett, and later Tony Randall, Richard Boone, and Gregory Peck, among others—it is obvious that the infusion of dance intelligence into the acting profession was steady and continuous at critical times in the American theater. Their influence was felt also in a secondary way through Graham-trained students who imparted their knowledge to others. After being graduated from the Neighborhood Playhouse School, Boone, for example, got a bit part as a soldier in the John Gielgud–Judith Anderson production of *Medea.* His role, though, was secondary to the after-performance demonstrations of Graham movement that he gave for Gielgud in the deserted theater. Together they would go through the play with Boone creating the gestures for Gielgud's role as he would interpret it with his Graham training. And Gielgud then studied the movement approach to make his own interpretation richer.

For her second season under Hurok's management, a tour that included several weeks up and down the East Coast and then a full week in New York, Graham premiered "Errand into the Maze," a duet for herself and Mark Ryder. Graham had by now established her audience as an adventurous and chic assembly that included many from the theater as well as other arts. In "Errand," she follows a tape lying tangled on the stage. This leads her into a maze, and, ultimately, to a large bony V shape through which she can escape. Crossing a dangerous area, she is menaced by a man wearing a bull's head (later eliminated), whose hands are held in a yoke that lies across his shoulders. The yoke was an unusual device to harness the man's menacing energy. Though he could still rush around the area, he could not hold onto the woman. The idea was of a powerful but not overpowering presence. It came under control only when the woman exercised her own strength of character to dominate it. Read allegorically, the dance had little to do with the story of Ariadne, which was referred to in the program notes, but was a representation of unconscious fears, symbolized by the Minotaur-like creature. A strong and effective work, "Errand" indicated that the real enemy of the individual is fear, which can be vanquished only by facing it down. The décor by Noguchi was spare: a wishbone shape at the left of the stage and some small shapes suspended in the space above center stage, giving the impression of a vast plain topped by a limitless sky.

Graham's second season under Hurok included several changes in costuming and casting. All of Cunningham's roles were distributed to members of the Company—Mark Ryder and John Butler took over most of them—and Graham, for the first time, relinquished two of her own roles. Ethel Winter took over Graham's solo, "Salem Shore," and Pearl Lang took Graham's role in "El Penitente." Several of the dances were also recostumed, among them "Punch and the Judy" and "Dark Meadow." The Company was full of talented young performers who were slowly replacing the original group. She was now in her fifty-fourth year, but her own energy was seemingly undiminished, and in the now renamed "Cave of the Heart" she could perform her demonic solo with the verve and vigor of a woman half her age. The season was so well received that Hurok added four more performances to the originally planned week in New York and might have added more if the musical *Brigadoon* were not scheduled to open in that theater. But despite the warm reception, the economics of the tour, as was the case the year before, did not balance out satisfactorily.

Meanwhile, the Coolidge Foundation, which had received such

exemplary value for its money in commissioning new ballet scores for Graham, had again given her the opportunity to choose another composer to work with. This time she picked William Schuman. The commission was a major one for Schuman and became an important landmark in his career. It undoubtedly gave him some sympathy for dance as well, for, when he subsequently became president of the Juilliard School of Music, he established a dance department.

Graham was now at the beginning of a period in which she would explore the possibilities of expressing herself through the myths of Greece. As usual, the subjects of all the myths she chose seem to arise out of her sense of her own experience.

For this commission, Graham created "Night Journey" for herself, Hawkins, Mark Ryder, and a chorus of six women. This dance revolved around the Oedipus legend. Hawkins played Oedipus, and Graham, Jocasta, his mother. The décor, again by Noguchi, was a metal bed shaped like the reclining figures of a man and woman. For the Seer, who vaulted around almost like a child on a pogo stick to warn Oedipus and Jocasta of their impending doom, Graham devised a beautiful, eccentric hopping motion. For herself and Hawkins, she used a bit of rope to bind them together, sometimes tightly, sometimes loosely, but always in a way that made one think of an umbilical cord. Graham took the story of Oedipus and made it the story of Jocasta. It was she who was the focus of attention in the dance and not her errant son-husband, Oedipus, as in the legend.

The occasion of the first performance of "Night Journey" was a music symposium sponsored by Harvard's music department. The performance used members of the Boston Symphony with Horst conducting. At the first performance, the dance had considerably more detail about the history of Oedipus and Jocasta than at its next performance, in New York, where Graham revised it so as to concentrate on the moment when Jocasta realized that Oedipus is her son and the murderer of his father, her former husband. One of Graham's most imaginative sequences of movement is the alternating caressing and cradling motions that she finds herself making to encompass the lover-child reality of the man who has become her husband. The initial reviews in Boston were mixed, but subsequently, with revisions, the dance had a better reception. Eventually it was filmed, one of the few Graham dances to be recorded by a professional crew.

Since Hawkins and Graham had resumed living together (still in the Village, but now at 257 West Eleventh Street, several blocks west of the studio), the situation from Hawkins's point of view had progressed relatively well. The doubts and difficulties that Hawkins had experienced in his relationship with Graham had been put in abeyance for the time being, and, with his customary energy, he again was beginning to organize and promote the Graham Company.

When Graham returned to New York, she was given a reception by the National Association of American Composers and Conductors at the Waldorf-Astoria Hotel, where she was presented with an award for her work with contemporary composers. She was toasted, and famous, and honored, and adored by her followers—but still not financially stable. Hurok estimated that he had lost $35,000 on the Company. The sum was a drain that he was unwilling to accept, and he therefore declined to represent the Company after the conclusion of their contract. The lack of substantial management prevented another coast-to-coast tour for the next twenty years.

One of the most successful radio programs of 1947 was Ralph Edwards's "Truth or Consequences." One of the most successful features of this program was a guessing game in which the public tried to identify a mystery personality from a set of rhymed clues. The show would select the name of a person who would be given the opportunity to guess the identity of "Mister" or "Miss Hush" from all those who had written in and sent along a contribution to the March of Dimes fund appeal. Each time the program went on the air without the identity of the mystery guest being discovered, more prizes would be added to the pot. Jack Dempsey had been the first mystery figure, Clara Bow the second. A publicist, Louis Craig Barton, suggested that Graham would make a splendid third.

Graham was hesitant, whatever the appeal of being considered the "equal" of Jack Dempsey and Clara Bow. Hawkins encouraged her to accept, citing the amount of publicity the contest would give, which might make it easier for the Company to get bookings. Who knows how many contestants might come to a Graham performance once they knew her name? Despite misgivings, Graham accepted the offer. Accordingly, the writers on the show prepared a little jingle to be read to the listening public in dribs and drabs for as long as it would take to identify her. The quiet intense voice of Graham began the clues line by line. The full rhyme read:

> Second for Santa Claus, first for me,
> Thirteen for wreath, seven for tree.
> Bring me an auto, a book, and a ball,
> And I'll say Merry Christmas in spring, not in fall.

In its cutesy arcane manner, the jingle gave her profession in the first line (dancer), her initials in the second (thirteenth letter of the alphabet, "M"; seventh letter, "G"), the actual last name (Graham auto) in the third, and the movement of jumping in the last line. Graham, who had not been entirely enthusiastic about the project from the beginning, loathed it by the time she was identified in December.

People began to suspect that Graham was "Miss Hush" long before anyone called by the program identified her. Strangers came to the studio at 66 Fifth Avenue just to look, and if they caught sight of Graham, would call out, "Miss Hush!" The studio had to install a special switchboard to handle the volume of incoming calls. The situation became so uncomfortable for her that she had to go to another studio in order to rehearse the Company in peace and quiet. It was publicity but publicity at a price. Graham even found herself cornered in the alternate studio by an enterprising United Press reporter, who had tracked her down. His report of the encounter gives a lurid but reasonably accurate sense of her feelings.

> "Good morning, Miss Hush," I said. "I beg your pardon," she said, with all the warmth of ice cubes falling in the sink. "Come now, Miss Hush. You know . . . dancer . . . graham cracker . . . thirteen and seven." Miss Graham's complexion began to take on the purplish-black hue of her ballet costume. She said "Arrggh" quite clearly, thought a moment, and added, "Arggh."

Ruth Ann Subbie, who won the "Miss Hush" contest and its $21,500 worth of prizes, was not at all disturbed. She, like thousands of others, had listened to the clues, made guesses, and never missed the "Truth or Consequences" show. For listeners to the show the game was splendid good fun, but Graham was not used to being the quarry in a popular chase and cursed the day she agreed to do it.

Not only did listeners to the program try to track Graham down, but also *The New Yorker* magazine, which wanted to do a profile on her, and *Who's Who,* which wanted to include her in its listings. The biographical sheet in *Who's Who* requests birth date information, and Graham avoided filling it out for over a year. *The New Yorker* was another thing, and its reporter, Angelica Gibbs, made a determined effort to find out as much about Graham as possible. This was not easy since the inclination of those who knew Graham was to close ranks and not give out information that would in any way diminish her public and now near "mythic" persona. With perseverance Gibbs did manage to write a good profile. Among other things, she was only six years off in her estimate of Graham's age, and she gave an accurate impression of the air that surrounded Graham at the studio:

> There may also be half a dozen feminine members of the Company, some seated on the floor and some on a bench that flanks one wall, as they sew away on their costumes and chat with Mr. Horst, who, white-haired, corpulent, and calm, is sipping a glass of elderberry wine. From the rehearsal room come muffled snatches of dissonance, musical and oral. Presently the door opens and several perspiring, barefoot dancers totter out. Miss Graham, in a long, black robe, appears for an instant behind them, glances Medea-like at the strangers, and then closes the door on the whole bunch with a good deal of emphasis. The members of the company go on sewing industriously, but through their ranks, between sighs of admiration, runs the well-worn tribute "Martha's terrific today!"

This was one of the few solid pieces of reporting ever done on Graham since the beginning of her career; the Gibbs profile became the curious world's only real source of information about her. In one form or another, the information in the Gibbs profile was quoted and used for the next twenty years by journalists assigned to write about Graham.

More and more Graham voluntarily withdrew behind a constructed personality that diminished the womanly side of her life in favor of the public "high priestess." For one who had been scorned in the 1930's, the adulation of the 1940's had a sweet taste indeed. One result was a smaller and smaller circle of friends.

Graham's old friend Merle Armitage had accepted the job of art director at *Look* magazine in New York, and one of the first things he did after reaching the city was to re-establish contact with Graham. He had recently had his first (and only) child, Chama, who was named for the area in New Mexico where he and his wife calculated the child had been conceived. Graham liked the little girl—perhaps her feeling was akin to her happiness several years earlier when Arch Lauterer asked her to be the godmother of his child—and on some preverbal level of communication the affection was reciprocated.

Indeed, children were one of Graham's genuine soft spots. She always seemed glad to establish a relationship with them, even in the most hectic surroundings. Once when she was still in stage make-up while receiving visitors after a performance, she noticed that the make-up frightened a little girl. "Would you like to know why I wear make-up like this?" Graham asked the child. "It's so that people in the audience will be able to see better. They're so much further away than when sitting in a room together. But it is frightening when you see it close up." On another occasion Graham tripped over choreographer Brian McDonald's son, who was playing on the floor. Everyone was set for a display of temper, but instead Graham asked the boy what he was drawing and showed genuine interest in him.

As ever with Armitage, she could relax with him as she could with few others. Thanksgiving, Christmas, and New Year's were strongly family-oriented occasions at Armitage's home, and Graham would often visit them. "She would come into this very domestic, bucolic atmosphere," Armitage recalled, "the Thanksgiving turkey and all the regular things that Americans love and enjoy, and she enjoyed it as much as anybody. I used to look at her and marvel. Hell, she was out there doing the dishes." On these occasions Graham became a person that she rarely showed to others, if at all.

Once after the war, during one of the Hurok-sponsored tours, Hawkins and Graham visited Armitage when he was still living in a suburb of Los Angeles. "We had a fantastic house out there in groves of trees, with three balconies," Armitage recalls.

> It was like a Chinese pagoda, or something. And I remember so well one afternoon we were sitting out there, drinking, and in drives Erick with Martha. My wife made chop suey, and we all got roaring drunk and had a wonderful time. I remember we had a big conversation about whether they could find their

way back to Los Angeles from El Monte. Apparently she was very upset then [she very likely was worried about the tour, which was not proving financially successful], but they were both in marvelous spirits.

On another occasion Graham accepted the invitation of Cady Wells, one of Armitage's friends and a rich amateur painter, to visit him in Santa Fe, along with Armitage. Wells had a party one night to which he invited four atomic scientists from Los Alamos, which was only thirty miles away. None of them had ever heard of Graham. The meal was pleasant, and after dinner Graham went dancing with one of the handsome young scientists at the La Fonda Hotel in Santa Fe. When Graham and her escort returned, Wells and Armitage, quiet and unseen, were sitting on the veranda. "So we saw them parting, when he very gallantly brought her up, and said, 'Ma'am, I just wanna tell you you're an awfully good dancer.' I don't know whether he ever found out or not who he'd been dancing with."

Another day Graham and Armitage went about twenty five miles northwest of Albuquerque to watch the Zia Pueblo Indians dance for rain. It was 9:30 in the morning of a beautiful day, with a clear blue sky and magnificent sun. Going into the Zia Pueblo they came across a broad wash of sand, in which a big ranch wagon and another large passenger car had stopped to change a tire. Armitage asked if they needed help. "As we were pulling away," Armitage recalls, "one of those people in the party—obviously Easterners—said, 'Goddamn Indians think they can make it rain.'"

When Graham's group arrived, the Indians were in church, and they heard Palestrina and Bach on a wheezy old organ. Soon the church doors opened and out came the Indians, who then went to a dressing room to change into their Indian dress. Starting to dance, one line of women and one of men, they went around in a circle, making intersecting patterns. The piñon logs had been set afire, and the air was spicy. The drums were beaten continuously. The sight, the sounds, and the seductive odor became hypnotic. Graham sat as in a trance during the hours the ceremony continued. Then the sky did cloud over, and by 4 P.M. it started to rain. Though the ceremony had gone on since 9:30 A.M., the time had passed very quickly.

Armitage, remembering the wash, suggested that they leave, since a quick rain can produce a flash flood. Graham was very excited and agreed, saying, "I've had just about all I can stand." By the time they got down to the wash, it was running lightly, and the people who had changed tires earlier now were having difficulty crossing the wash. "And I came across there at forty miles an hour," Armitage says, " 'cause then you're all right. And I couldn't resist—this was petty—I couldn't resist shouting out, 'Goddamn Indians think they can make it rain!' "

The whole quality of life changed for Graham when she was with the goodhearted Armitage. He had a rough gallantry that was a wholesome tonic to the intense world in which Graham normally lived. Work in the theater is demanding. The energy required to get "up" for a performance requires a psychic "hype" so that everything connected with a performance is brought into a heightened focus. In this kind of situation minor irritations are often broadened into major confrontations, and, in the case of a dance company, controlling the situation and keeping the company in a state of relative calm is a major job.

To this usual intensity, Graham brought her own. At crucial times in her life, Armitage provided her with the necessary shelter and encouragement to escape her professional tensions. This kind of assistance was invaluable to Graham. As a titanic figure in her field, she had great numbers of associates but few friends. There was a social distance between her and her Company, no matter how dedicated they were. In terms of close relationships, Horst was first in line because of his long-time staunch support of her work and because he was the one who for so long had been closest at hand. Bethsabee de Rothschild, who was becoming increasingly involved with the Company and would soon step in to be its sole support, had also become a confidante of Graham. Finally, there was Hawkins, who represented an involvement that was comforting as well as vexing. There were very few others. Armitage was one of them. Graham was in her mid-fifties, an age when new friends are often difficult to acquire and relationships based on work and common interests supply the bulk of the people inhabiting one's world.

9

High Priestess of Myth

"There is a pain so utter that
it swallows being."
Emily Dickinson

Interest in Graham's career was at full flood. There were even rumors that a movie studio was to make a film of her life, but first and foremost, now that Hurok no longer represented her, she had to secure another New York season. ANTA decided to sponsor the Company at the Maxine Elliot Theater during the last two weeks of February 1948. This engagement gave her the opportunity to show "Night Journey" in New York for the first time. The Company had performed it only once so far, during an appearance in Boston the previous spring. Also for the February run, Yuriko created a new work. All in all, it was a successful season. In New York Graham had a faithful public.

Two days after the close of the season, Graham appeared with others at a benefit for the *Dance Observer* at the YMHA. Twenty-five years after Horst had founded the magazine on a shoestring, it was still going strong and still advancing the cause of modern dance, although everyone agreed that the war with ballet was over and modern dance was getting adequate representation from other dance publications. But the combative habits of the times of trial were not easy to give up, so that even when the need for its advocacy was past, *Dance Observer* continued to present the case for modern dance as forcefully as it could.

Martha Hill, who had been so instrumental in setting up the Bennington College school of dance, had been quietly but efficiently at work to create another summer home for modern dance. Although the economic stresses of the 1940's were not like those of the 1930's, dancers still did not have a major performing house that they could consider their own. A summer center would in part answer their need for an anchor. It would also help to focus attention on the early generation of dancers that survived—Doris Humphrey had retired from active performing in 1945 because of an arthritic hip—and give the younger dancers a chance to work with them at a time of year that was best for students. With the assistance of Rosemary Park of Connecticut College and the co-sponsorship of New York University, where Hill was still on the faculty, Martha Hill helped bring into being the Connecticut College Dance School.

The first summer session, in 1948, featured Graham and her Company. Humphrey was gone, her work to be carried on by José Limon. Charles Weidman, who no longer had a concert group with which to work regularly, was enjoying a popular success on Broadway, as was Holm, with the latest Cole Porter hit, *Kiss Me, Kate.* Tamiris was in a series of Broadway shows, *Up in Central Park, Showboat,* and *Annie Get Your Gun.*

Many of those who had been part of the Bennington scene went to Connecticut College: Horst, of course; Lauterer, who had made his peace with Graham; the composer Norman Lloyd and his wife Ruth, accompanist and teacher. In addition to selected works from repertory, Graham created a new dance for the Company called "Wilderness Stair: Diversion of Angels." Inspired by a line from the work of the poet Ben Belitt, whom she had first met at Bennington, this dance had a score by Norman Dello Joio. Amazingly, the choreography did not include Graham.

The dance celebrates the state of being in love and has a sunny, warm emotional climate that is in great contrast with most of the works Graham was producing about the same time. Noguchi, who created the setting, produced a large burlap cloth that was held taut by rope threaded through the edges. Behind this set dancers with long poles pushed the tightly stretched cloth into peaks during the course of the dance. Graham later discarded this set as too distracting, and in fact she made several revisions of the choreography as well before the work was exactly as she wished it. Retitled "Diversion of Angels," this dance then took its place in her repertory as one of the most durable and joyful dances she had ever created.

Hawkins prepared a new work, "The Strangler," which took the Oedipus legend as its subject matter. Unlike Graham, Hawkins focused on the earlier part of the legend, when Oedipus solves the riddle of the Sphinx (played by Anne Meachum). Hawkins created the dance as a ritual of an individual's coming of age. Thus, in the space of a year, both Graham in "Night Journey" and Hawkins in "The Strangler" had concentrated on widely differing aspects of the same myth. Graham saw tragedy and Hawkins rebirth. As in "John Brown," "The Strangler" used an actor (Joseph Wiseman) to read lines as the dancers performed. The dance was not received well.

It was at this time that Graham lost Horst. During the summer session, Horst had difficulties with the Juilliard student orchestra that was playing at the festival. His irritation with them disrupted rehearsals so much that Graham interrupted him one day and said simply, "Louis, this has got to stop." Horst, stunned at being rebuked in front of students, put down the baton and left the rehearsal. Helen Lanfer thought that he had aged twenty years when she saw him walking toward his rooms just afterward. Horst wrote Graham a letter of resignation and even took the extreme step of sending a copy to his union. He wished to be Martha Graham's musical director no longer. Graham wasn't even sure that Horst would conduct the performance that evening, and she told Lanfer to conduct if Horst did not. A true professional, Horst conducted for Graham that night, but for the last time. The violence of Horst's reaction to Graham's relatively mild statement, whatever the context, indicated how strained relations between them had become. Hawkins, Horst, and Graham were all drawn to the finest edge. The smallest incident could disturb the precarious balance, and in Horst's case one had.

After the close of the school session in August, Hawkins and Graham traveled west for their vacation and stopped off to visit Cady Wells in Santa Fe, arriving in time for the fiesta celebration. After the agitated, tumultuous years of 1945 and 1946, both Graham and Hawkins were readjusting to their new relationship. Previously Hawkins had been a young aspiring dancer who was working and learning, but recently he had begun to assert himself both privately, by his temporary withdrawal from Graham's personal life, and professionally, by starting to choreograph. Whatever Graham may have felt about the value of his work, she wanted and needed him as a man and was willing to accept his aspirations within limits.

Hawkins, as a choreographic novice, had the usual doubts about the worth of his work and was nettled at its poor reception, particularly at the booing he had endured at Connecticut. He was achieving perspective on his own life, but needed a more settled relationship with Graham. In the Southwest, away from the contentions of the theater world of the East, in a section of the country they both loved, they decided to get married.

This decision was urged by Hawkins, as he put it, to "clarify the ambiguity" of their relationship. It was a spur-of-the-moment decision that conceivably might have come at any time, but for its own reasons, given the dynamics of Graham's and Hawkins's difficult relationship, it happened in the summer of 1948. There were no elaborate preparations, and friends and relations were not consulted or told beforehand. Since they made their decision in the middle of a local fiesta celebration, the town clerk's office was closed and had to be opened to issue them a license.

The ceremony took place on September 7, 1948, in the First Presbyterian Church of Santa Fe. With Wells and the church organist, Ruth Grant, as witnesses, the Reverend Kenneth M. Keller pronounced them man and wife. Hawkins stated his age of thirty-nine correctly on the license, and Graham put down forty-six, deducting eight years from her actual age. Stories went out on the national wire services, but all after the fact. It was the first marriage for both. After visiting Graham's mother for a few days in Santa Barbara, they returned to New York.

In New York, life went on as always, which for Graham meant work. Her marriage was absorbed in the steady flow of activities. The city had decided to create a high school of performing arts that would be open to all students in the school system who wished to pursue a career in the performing arts. Graham, Martha Hill, and John Martin were asked to oversee the dance auditions that were required for admission. They spent the better part of a morning and

and an afternoon rating more than a hundred candidates. Graham's time was well spent in that she began to draw to her Company students who might otherwise have not been available to her.

Graham's fame was at an extraordinarily high peak. She was so much the public figure that some misguided promoter in Atlanta placed the name "Miss Hush and Dance Company" on the marquee of his theater. Flying into a rage, Graham announced that she would not dance unless it were removed immediately. It was, and the performance went on as scheduled, but there was another irony. The audience turned out to be as intimidated by Graham's reputation as a serious artist as the promoter was not. During "Circus," one of her lightest and most humorous pieces, a few members of the audience naturally laughed. They were immediately shushed by those sitting nearby, and the rest of the work was received in respectful but disconcerting silence. For the Company it was an eerie feeling. Yet the incident reflected the status that Graham had achieved. She was not funny in the way others might be, she was serious in capital letters—and indeed she regarded herself in this light. A dance satirist, Iva Kitchell, created a satirical dance about Graham, "Soul in Search." Though audiences found it amusing, Graham did not like it at all. It did not fit in with her idea of herself. No longer was she to be the object of derision that she had been when she was struggling for recognition. She was now beyond that. Her position as high priestess was not to be tampered with.

From the beginning, Graham had chosen serious subjects because, in her eyes and the eyes of others in the heroic generation that broke away from Denishawn, ballet was frivolous. A "divertissement" on a Graham program would have been sent back where it came from after having its ears soundly boxed. Then, when she first met Hawkins and did "American Document," "Punch and the Judy," "Every Soul Is a Circus," and "Appalachian Spring," a brief period of sunshine entered Graham's life. Her mind, however, always returned to its religio-mystical, tragic sense of life, and this did not encourage comedy. Graham became identified with grimness in the popular mind. The sober, "searching" image that she projected to the public prevented it from laughing at a genuinely funny production. They were inhibited, and the bulk of her work tended to encourage this attitude.

It was precisely because of her pre-eminence that Graham drew the friendly and sometimes unfriendly attention of satirists. This sort of pre-eminence makes a snowball-throwing child in the comic strips seek out a man with a top hat. It would be funny to knock off anyone's hat, but hilarious to knock off the hat of the man at the top of the heap. One of the better satirical efforts appeared in the Danny Kaye movie, *The Kid from Brooklyn.* In one scene he made a spectacular entrance down an aisle preceded by bloused and kicking Russian folk dancers. He then launched into a song about the changing dance world, first becoming coy when describing the beautiful mood pieces in which a ballerina wafts across stage, and then suddenly being convulsed into angular deformity, crying, "and then there was Marta Gra-ham." He alternated from gauzy to gutsy, describing "Marta Gra-ham" and her "six little graham crackers" in greater detail. He created a number called "Diesel Engine 45," in which "Gra-ham" was the engine and the six little crackers were sparkplugs. He grimaced as he described the dance and its "significance." It was an extremely good routine, probably the best of the references that were made to Graham by the movies. In other pictures, although Graham often was not mentioned, the situation clearly referred to her. An artistically soulful director pushed a musical comedy in the direction of Greek tragedy, and the production was saved only when he returned to his senses and created a popular entertainment. So much for "Marta Gra-ham"!

But for all her fame, Graham could not afford a Broadway season for nearly two years, from February 1948 until January 1950. Nor could any other major figure of the modern dance world. Money was extremely scarce. In 1949 there was another attempt, this one sponsored by Bethsabee de Rothschild, to bring together the various elements of the modern dance world for the purpose of presenting a strong selection of works so that the public could see a broad grouping of its various forces. The series was held at the New York City Center, formerly the old Mecca Temple. Typically, Graham did not participate, although several of her dancers did. Nina Fonaroff, Merce Cunningham, and Sophie Maslow all presented works, as did many dancers not associated with Graham—José Limon, Katherine Litz, Iris Mabry, and Charles Weidman, for example. Indeed, Graham's nonparticipation went so far as to take her on tour at the time of the series.

The tour that the Graham Company undertook was in complete contrast to the fairly luxurious Hurok tour that had them all in Pullmans. This was a bus tour with long hauls between one-night stands, and the pace put the Company on edge, no one more so than Graham. A review in Texas praising Hawkins infuriated her. She blamed everyone, starting with Hawkins, and her anger seeped into every seat in the bus. No one was exempt, and anger was in the air for days. It was the type of tour that can bring out the worst in anyone. Since their reconciliation and marriage, things had not gone at all well for Graham and Hawkins.

Hawkins felt a proprietary interest in the Company. He had worked hard for its success and wanted to see himself get more publicity, which naturally still centered upon the person of Graham. If it was an understandable wish, it was, given Graham's views, an extraordinarily unrealistic one. She saw her Company as an extension of herself, and she did not have any intention of sharing with anyone else. Though she had permitted members of the Company to choreograph pieces that were included in the repertory, she was not going to have her own pre-eminence challenged. A clash was inevitable.

Because of Graham's indifference to business matters, Hawkins had often taken to acting on his own in this area, and after the Company returned to New York he disappeared for a time on a fund-raising trip without consulting Graham. Taking the money remaining in the Company account, he traveled first to Boston, calling the Company manager, Gertrude Macy, when leaving Boston to ask her to tell Martha that he was doing something important, but not what he was doing. He then flew to Houston and subsequently to Dallas, where he stayed with Craig Barton and Leroy Leatherman, using their apartment as an office. Finally, on New Year's Eve he contacted Blevens Davis, who agreed to give the Graham Company $5,000 with which to open a season in New York. Hawkins felt that his gamble had paid off handsomely. Triumphantly he returned to New York only to find Graham stony-faced despite his success. When the season opened, his name did not appear in the billing outside. What for him had been an act in both their names looked to her suspiciously like a whittling-away of her authority. The lack of appropriate billing outside the theater struck Hawkins as a spiteful gesture and a poor reward for his efforts.

With money assured for the season at the 46th Street Theater in late January, Hawkins, undaunted by Graham's coolness, encouraged her to think beyond the United States to the rest of the world. Though Graham was not especially eager to make a foreign tour, she did not strongly resist the idea. When Hawkins asked de Rothschild, she actively supported the idea with a pledge of $10,000, and with that guarantee Charles Green, who had booked the 1949 bus tour, went to Europe to arrange dates. Meanwhile, in New York, Graham was seen with her Company for the first time in nearly two years. It was the first season since 1926 that she did not have Horst as her musical director.

Also about this time, Graham received a commission from the Louisville Orchestra to create a new dance with a composer of her own choosing. Graham, who had been pleased with her collaboration with William Schuman on "Night Journey," asked him to collaborate with her again. And she also collaborated again with Noguchi, who designed the sets for this new work. Entitled "Judith," this dance was a solo for Graham. In style, it was a concerto for dancer and orchestra. Between opening and closing orchestral statements, Graham danced sections devoted to various aspects of Judith's life. Both Graham and the orchestra were onstage, the orchestra hidden by a translucent curtain.

The dance was received very well, both when it was first presented in Louisville and later at a New York concert in Carnegie Hall. The new work was important for everyone connected with it. It gave Graham national coverage and kept her name in the public eye; it was a good credit for Schuman; and it even helped to save the Louisville Orchestra, which needed public interest and support. It eventually got the new support it needed because Robert Whitney, the conductor, had been willing to take a chance when Louise Kane, one of orchestra's strongest backers, suggested the Graham commission. For the occasion, the mayor of Louisville, an advocate of modern activity of all sorts, had even dipped into a municipal contingency fund to finance the new production.

For her 1950 season, Graham prepared two new works, "Eye of Anguish," a vehicle for Hawkins based on the story of Shakespeare's Lear, and a solo for herself, "Gospel of Eve." The latter was in the vein of "Punch and the Judy" and "Every Soul Is a Circus." It featured a woman gazing into heart-shaped mirrors and trying on improbable hats, vainly trying to preserve outward appearances. Both dances focused on the question of age: old, mad Lear bedeviled by his young daughters, and a perennial Eve keeping up appearances while loneliness ate away at her. This season was the first in which

Graham featured several dances in which she was not the central figure. Her solo was well received, and the week of performances started the year strongly.

In April, the Woman's National Press Club awarded Graham and Olivia de Havilland citations for work in the theater—an especially sweet award for Graham, who was presumably so far beyond the realm of popular entertainment. The awards were presented by President Truman at the club's annual dinner in Washington. At the end of the month, Graham announced the European tour, which was scheduled to start in Paris and continue in London. In large measure, it was the support and enthusiasm of de Rothschild that had persuaded Graham to undertake this tour.

De Rothschild was absolutely fascinated with American modern dance as an art form. She had never seen anything like it in France or in Europe, and, as a matter of fact, had herself originally thought of American dance forms as being those of the popular films or some sort of social jazz dance. She was a convert, and with a convert's passion she wanted to win over others.

De Rothschild's infatuation with modern dance had grown so that she wrote a book about it. This was one of the most level-headed and clear-eyed accounts of modern dance to appear, bringing a strong French analytical approach to an art form that had not as yet been subjected to such analysis. *La Danse Artistique aux U.S.A.* was printed in Paris (1949) in a limited edition of a thousand copies, and de Rothschild never bothered to have it translated into English. The book not only articulated her own keen understanding about modern dance but also served to introduce the subject to an audience that was almost totally unknowledgeable about it. Because she had not toured abroad, Graham's reputation was based on secondhand reports outside of the United States. On only two occasions had she appeared outside the country—first on the 1937 transcontinental tour when the Group danced in Vancouver, and the second time in 1941 when the Company was in Cuba. Graham planned to take a different sort of Company to Europe—a host of men as well as women, orchestral instead of a single piano accompaniment, and a substantial amount of scenic material.

As he helped to design a program for the tour, Armitage noticed that Graham was nervous and not the cool performer he remembered from the past. He knew, though, from previous experience the kinds of tension she sometimes worked under and the effect that a bad reception could have upon her. Armitage was working with Craig Barton, who had suggested Graham's name as "Miss Hush" and who had joined the Graham administration at Hawkins's invitation. Both Armitage and Barton thought it would be a good idea to have Alexander Calder design a cover for the program, since he was well known in France, had lived there for long stretches of time, and would lend the proper cultural credentials. Graham refused even to consider the idea. Her experiences with Calder on "Panorama" and "Horizons" were still vivid, and she wanted nothing to do with him.

Despite the anxiety, or perhaps because of it, the programs Graham selected were long and taxing and included "Letter to the World," against Hawkins's advice. Hawkins, recalling the trip, thought Graham was pushing herself and being "greedy." After arriving in Paris, they were soon overtaken by the first in a series of brutal mishaps. During the opening program, which Eleanor Roosevelt attended, Graham twisted her left knee toward the end of "Every Soul Is a Circus" and was unable to dance further. It was immediately obvious to her and to Hawkins that the injury was severe, although it was not entirely clear how long she would be incapacitated. Hawkins canceled the performance scheduled for the following evening and, putting together repertory works in which Graham did not appear, quickly rearranged the programs to try to save the season. It seemed theatrical suicide not to have major roles "covered" by an understudy, but the modern dance world had never admitted to the possibility of a performance for which the principal dancer would be unavailable. For modern dancers the idea of a company as a vehicle for personal expression was so strong that it completely dominated good sense. To Graham, in bed in Paris, in pain and unable to appear, it made no difference. She declared, "If I can't dance, I don't give a damn if anybody dances." The Company appeared without her for only one performance. The critical reception was poor, and the Paris season was canceled. The Company mood was depressed. De Rothschild did the best she could to keep spirits up. She continued everyone on full salary even though they were not performing, and she had Hawkins and Graham stay with her and her husband, Donald Bloomingdale. Though they rested and dined well, nothing could change the injury that Graham had sustained. The cartilage in her knee was torn. Graham received electrical treatments for the knee (the odor of these treatments caused Hawkins to faint at one point), but still the flexibility of the knee was not restored. Relations between Graham and Hawkins were severely strained. The trip, there was no forgetting, had been his idea.

Three weeks later the Company arrived in London for the second part of the tour. Graham went to the Piccadilly Theater to test her knee. During rehearsal it was obvious that it had not healed sufficiently for her to appear. At a press conference on July 17, it was announced that because of her injury Graham could not dance, and that the opening therefore would be postponed. After receiving contradictory advice from two physicians who examined Graham, Hawkins concluded that the only thing to do was cancel the season. The decision infuriated Graham to near incoherence and precipitated the worst argument she and Hawkins had ever had. Things were said that could not be taken back. The argument was so extreme that, in effect, it ended their marriage, although they were not formally divorced until four years later when Hawkins obtained a divorce decree in Mexico.

Two days after the first announcement, a second announcement explained that the season was definitely canceled and that the Company hoped to be able to return to England in the near future. The trip was over. Gertrude Macy's contingency policy with Lloyds of London covered most of the loss from the trip. The Company members scattered and eventually made their individual ways back home. Hawkins rented a car and drove around the countryside, stopping at Stratford to see a few plays. Macy tidied up the loose ends, and de Rothschild tried to comfort Graham.

This had been the worst disaster for Graham since the 1930's. Not only had her attempt to conquer Europe failed, but her personal life was shattered. She was left, in a sense, entirely alone: Horst gone, Hawkins gone, the old companions from the early days of her career no longer actively performing or with their own companies, and therefore competitors. From this point on, the people most intimately associated with her career would be dependent on her, not she on them. Now, in place of a personal life, she had a professional family. A line of Emily Dickinson's, included in "Letter to the World," might describe her condition: "There is a pain so utter that it swallows being." Graham's life began to mirror the tragic myths of Greece she so admired.

The European disaster stopped Graham dead in her creative tracks. When she returned to New York, it was only to pause before going on to Santa Fe to recuperate in solitude and isolation at Cady Wells's ranch. Wells was a sympathetic and considerate host. He provided her with a haven and a secluded retreat. Indirectly, because it was Armitage who had brought Graham and Wells together, this was an extension of the hospitality offered by Armitage most pronouncedly at another depressed period in her life. Although periodically Wells would send Graham money for her seasons, it is doubtful that he ever helped her more than he did by offering his hospitality in the months after the European disaster. The situation again recalls the character in "Letter to the World." The loss of her lover forces her to face her destiny as a poet, and she realizes that she must find happiness in the intensity of her work. With her incredibly strong body and will, Graham began weightlifting to strengthen her leg.

After several months of isolation, she returned to New York. Hawkins had moved out of their apartment, although he was still teaching at the school. It was to be an interim period for them both. Hawkins was earning his living at the school that he and Graham had worked very hard at making a success. Both tried as much as possible to stay out of each other's way, although each inevitably encountered the other from time to time. Graham had regained little of her spirit. Her classes were a mere shade of the vibrant experiences they had been for generations of students.

For the next two years she and Hawkins taught under the same roof. De Rothschild then bought two small buildings at 431 East Sixty-third Street, which she established as the headquarters of her foundation and as Graham's school. Hawkins retained the studio at 66 Fifth Avenue and began to work exclusively on his own choreography while developing his own approach to movement. Eventually he rejected the Graham technique, which was based on stressed energy, and evolved his own movement, which emphasized flow. Working with the composer Lucia Dlugozewski, he formed a small company, and, after old wounds had healed, he even won Horst's praise for his new direction.

In the meantime, in the first year of the separation, Graham gradually began to display more interest in her work. For one thing, the Louisville Orchestra wanted to repeat "Judith" in New York. This would get her back to work again. As was customary, the Company disbanded between seasons. Graham had no urge to work with them, in any case. Her knee still bothered her. She continued the analytic therapy that she had started during her separation from Hawkins. She even tried to effect a reconciliation with him but found that their relationship could not be restored.

Although her knee had not completely healed, the December performance at Carnegie Hall with the Louisville Orchestra was a success, and the Louisville Board invited her to do another work for them—another solo, to music commissioned from Norman Dello Joio, with whom Graham had previously worked on the joyful "Diversion of Angels." She and Dello Joio chose the character of Joan of Arc as the subject of the new dance, and Graham asked the avant-garde artist, architect, and designer Frederick Kiesler to create the settings. Like the protagonist of "Letter to the World," she was immersing herself in work.

Dello Joio had been involved with the character of St. Joan for some time and had gone so far as to write a three-act opera called *The Triumph of St. Joan.* Although it was given a performance at Sarah Lawrence College in May 1950, it was not an entirely satisfactory score, and Dello Joio did not allow the manuscript to be published. When the Louisville Orchestra gave him a commission, he decided to draw from the opera a three-movement symphony. Like the opera, the new composition handled Joan in three aspects—as The Maid, The Warrior, and The Saint. At its premiere performance in Louisville in 1951, the piece was called "The Triumph of St. Joan." Several years later Graham rechoreographed the solo into an ensemble work called "Seraphic Dialogue."

In creating "Triumph," Graham returned to a device that she had used in "El Penitente" and "Letter to the World." She took aspects of her heroine's character and presented them as individual portraits. In the character of Joan she found someone who had been seemingly crushed but who ultimately triumphed. Though she was not entirely satisfied with the dance, it enjoyed a warm public response.

The experience of working again was tonic for Graham. She

picked herself up and decided after a year's hiatus to reassemble the Company and have a New York season. She was now fifty-six years old.

Once again Graham's contacts in the musical world came to her aid. William Schuman, who had collaborated with her on "Night Journey" and "Judith," had been appointed president of the Juilliard School of Music and had decided to establish a dance department there. Recognizing that there were two major branches of dance, he created a department with both ballet and modern dance instruction. Horst's early inclinations had proved sound in a major way. Schuman invited Martha Hill to head the administration of the department, Horst to teach his course in dance composition, and, of course, Graham to be part of the faculty.

This seemed to be an excellent opportunity to create a repertory company in which prime examples of the work of selected choreographers could be seen. At the very last moment, when everything seemed to have been agreed upon, Graham balked and decided that she was not interested in the project. Everyone knew that she was the central figure in such a venture, because she had the requisite masterpieces that any repertory company needed, first, to be truly representative, and second, to establish the aesthetic credentials of the form. But the repertory venture was dropped, and Graham, in effect, was back in force with her fiercely intense, fiercely personal art.

During the third week of April, however, she and the Company gave a series of performances for the benefit of the Juilliard dance department's scholarship fund. Graham created "Canticle for Innocent Comedians," a Company work in which the dancers formed and re-formed an elaborate series of curved panels (designed by Frederick Kiesler) in and out of which they danced. The dance contained a fresh and joyous choreographic attack that showed Graham at full strength as master of a theater that fused all of its parts into an integrated structure.

The academic world was beginning to discover Graham and besiege her with offers to speak at symposia and commencements. In March, she was one of the speakers chosen to address the Sixth Annual Symposium of the International Federation of Music Students held at Juilliard. In May, Rutgers University held a symposium at the inauguration of its new president, Lewis Webster, and Graham again was one of the speakers invited to participate. She offered the Rutgers students the advice that she had given to her own pupils over the years and that now, perhaps, had a new meaning to her: "The only freedom in life is that of the discipline one chooses."

When the Connecticut College Dance School, launched in 1948, was entering its fifth year, Graham went up as part of the faculty with several of her dancers. After some benefit performances in New York, the school survived the initial deficit of its first year and had grown nicely. This year Horst, in his methodical way, instituted a lecture series to open the program, and Graham was asked to give the first lecture. Her talk, a quasi-mystical evocation of a dancer's value, never failed to have an effect on audiences. "It is not enough to be called a marvelous technician; through strength and vitality, the dancer must realize the wonder of his body and his awareness of it."

The dance school at Connecticut had entered a secure phase of its existence, just as the Bennington dance school had in the worst days of the Depression, and there were courses on everything from actors' movement to creative composition. But the glue that held this dance school together was the same that had made Bennington such a success. Stated simply, the school was an opportunity for students and faculty alike to maintain association and make new acquaintances in a common field. The student who was unsure of what type of modern dance company or techniques would be the most rewarding for him had the opportunity to try courses in several of them. The faculty, for its part, could observe new developments in the field and establish a network of relationships that might produce concert dates throughout the country. It was an extraordinarily useful world for the modern dance, a forum for the exchange of ideas, and a very efficient way to get necessary business done. It was a world that, out of deference to Graham, Hawkins was not invited to participate in for a dozen years. Though the exclusion necessarily slowed him down, it was not an ultimately debilitating snub.

During the summer, de Rothschild announced that she again would undertake a cooperative season to show the public a representative selection of dances that would display the individual talents of modern dance. The reasoning behind the season was absolutely sound, and the linchpin, as always, was Graham. Although she had always resisted being part of any such cooperative venture, to refuse de Rothschild after all that she had done would have been the grossest sort of ingratitude.

Graham's relationship with de Rothschild was based on a secure and respectful friendship. De Rothschild repected Graham as a great talent and wished to be part of the process by which Graham's genius would be allowed to show itself. Erick Hawkins had, in general, handled the raising of money for the Company and had initially secured de Rothschild's support. When he left, the problem of money was solved by de Rothschild's largess, which was given without histrionics. Indeed, during the twenty years or so of their active collaboration on tours and the creation of new dance works, Graham herself never asked de Rothschild for money. It was simply a matter, as de Rothschild put it, of sensing what Graham needed and then providing it. The people who helped Graham financially always respected her feelings about her art and what she was attempting to do. They did not force her to modify her personal quest in any way, but gave her the money on an as-needed basis. If she wanted to have a season, the money would be found. If she wanted to move her studio to another, larger location, the money would be found. And always operating at the center was Graham, herself, restlessly pacing, balancing one need against another, driving herself forward and bringing along in her train those who wanted to work with her and who respected the quality of her creative powers. The only plan in her career was to fuel the creative urge that drove her on from one work to the next.

So Graham agreed to become part of the season that de Rothschild was planning for the following spring. Graham, however, did extract a price for her cooperation: a week of her own at the Alvin Theater in 1953, following the two-week cooperative company season. She did not demand this from de Rothschild; she simply let it be known that she would like to have it. De Rothschild in any case had her own two-week season, with several companies sharing the limelight.

In a sense, despite de Rothschild's efforts, it was too late to form an institutional framework for modern dance. By the mid-1950's there were only two functioning companies of major proportions—Graham's and José Limon's. All others were small performing ensembles or were completely dormant because the choreographer had gone off to work on Broadway. The other companies in de Rothschild's series had to be revived especially for the occasion. It was a classic example of commercial success destroying the achiever. The movement that had begun penniless in lofts was installed on the "Great White Way."

For the occasion Graham gave Yuriko her own part in "Dark Meadow" and introduced a new work, "Voyage," for which William Schuman did the score. Commissioned by the Katherine Cornell Foundation, the dance was an erotic frolic with three men. Graham could still see herself in the principal role even though the three men—Robert Cohan, Stuart Hodes, and Bertram Ross—were young enough to be her sons. As the dance progresses, the relationships among the four characters degenerate to a stage more primitive than the civilized level at which they began. At the end, one of the men returns to his senses, and civilized behavior again becomes the norm. Noguchi designed the set with an archway. He originally gave Graham a garishly vulgar design in which the portal, lit up with naked light bulbs, resembled the female genitals. Although this caught the essence of the piece quite accurately, the effect was more than Graham wanted and was consequently toned down. Later the dance was revised and retitled "Theater for a Voyage." It was eventually dropped from repertory.

Graham had enormous difficulty deciding upon her own costume for "Voyage" and at the last minute chose a dress from her personal wardrobe. Using a street dress for a theatrical costume was an exemplary practical demonstration of the remark she had made years previously to the effect that a dress should look good both when hanging still and when in motion.

The Company that Graham assembled for her week at the Alvin was one of her finest and a tribute to her continuing artistic vitality. Graham had a name and a school that attracted students from all over the country. For the modern dancer in New York, some class work at the Graham studio was considered an essential part of one's dance education, whether or not the student wanted to go on with the Graham Company. Graham therefore had a large number of students to draw upon for the Company.

Initially, Graham had wanted all the men in the Company to be about six feet tall and broadly built. Hawkins fitted the ideal exactly. At one point in the late 1940's and early 1950's, the four men in the Company were within a quarter of an inch of one another in height. With regard to the women, she had always been quite eclectic, having tall and short women. As black dancers showed up at her school, she included them in the Company. Unlike ballet, which has remained almost exclusively white, modern dance has showed itself hospitable to the aspiring black student. Also, though the point hardly needs making, for years prior to the women's liberation movement, modern dance was a field in which women were more than equal—they dominated. Graham herself was in the forefront, as far as equal opportunity for talented dancers was concerned. She demanded only one thing of her dancers, and that was total dedication.

As a teacher Graham became more guru-like. She was always more likely to explain what she wanted in terms derived from yoga or Zen than in Western terms, as when she took over Jane Dudley's class with the comment that the students were not displaying "kundalini." At other times, she would use the Zen example of the onion in explaining to students that, while she was asking them to strip away layers of behavior, she was getting them to do so in order to more fully realize their true inner selves.

As always, she did not understand the words "I can't do it," and she worked repeatedly with a student, using both the most menacing tone and strong stretching or pushing motions to prove that it could and would be done. A pupil with a slumped back could elicit the threat of expulsion from the class with the admonition not to return again. A student who was unable to put the proper flow into a movement might find Graham herself spread-legged on the floor, demonstrating precisely the manner in which the gesture was to be performed. Graham continued to drive herself and her students to do things that only seemed beyond their reach.

As in the past, she was concerned with the look and flow of the costumes that were designed for the Company. She now, of course, had costume designers to work with her. Nonetheless, she nearly always took an active interest in the costumes, to the point of pinning them on in fittings. She could even use a fitting session as a game. She was not above driving a pin through a bit of flesh. During one session, while working with Stuart Hodes, who had become her partner, she was fitting the leg of one of the costumes and inserting pins into his leg as regularly as into the cloth. Hodes, having decided to find out how painful it could be, said nothing and gave no sign of feeling anything. After he had moved around a little in the costume, she told him to take it off. He replied matter of factly, "I can't."

"Why not?"

"Because you pinned it to my leg." Graham gave him a friendly punch and removed the pins.

She found that at times shock tactics were useful to get the results she wanted. Since she believed that the urge to dance represented extreme desire in some way, she would often use sexual references, sometimes with an edge of cruelty, to make a point. With one girl who was not doing one of the floor exercises correctly, she spread the girl's legs and said, "Some day a man will do this to you and you'll remember it." The girl was shattered and stayed away from class for some time. To another girl, who never seemed able to do as well onstage as she did in the studio, Graham said, "I won't have virgins in my Company. I don't care if you have to stand on a street corner to get a man. I don't care how you get him, you have to get a man."

The competition for Graham's interest and attention was strong. Without Horst or Hawkins on the scene, there was no one man in Graham's life. She relied upon one or another of her dancers as a confidant, usually picking someone on whim. Awareness of this situation created tension within the Company, so that all found themselves vying for Graham's ear—more out of self protection than anything else, for she had great intuitive skill in reading human beings and would startle people with statements about themselves that often exposed fears they thought they had hidden from view. These insights about others she would pass on from confidant to confidant. Intrigue and chaos grew. Simple business dealings regarding booking dates would be protracted wildly beyond normal lengths because no one other than Graham would make a decision for fear that the wrong step would bring down her wrath. Contracts remained unsigned, bookings tentative, and everyone on the edge of anger. As she had torn costumes to shreds for years before her opening nights with her small Group, she now lacerated everyone's emotions to get the requisite working atmosphere for herself. She needed a certain amount of indecision and turmoil in order to operate, but now the turmoil went beyond the older device of costume destruction. As always, Graham could still the emotional water that she roiled with gestures and words of kindness and concern. But nothing was lasting. The only sure thing was uncertainty—and of course, the privilege of working with one of the great geniuses in the history of dance.

An important element in this atmosphere of turmoil was Graham's deep reluctance to leave the stage in favor of younger performers. As long as she stayed actively in public view, her roles were, for the most part, denied her senior dancers. The effect of this was felt all the way down to the youngest dancer in the Company, who could not hope for solo parts until the senior dancers moved up to the principal parts. This situation produced quiet desperation, and sometimes not so quiet desperation. In modern dance, with its economically inadequate rewards, roles were the real coin of satisfaction, and there was unremitting competition for them.

In class Graham was ever the grand lady. She treated each encounter with a class in the studio almost as an encounter with a lover for whom one wants to look one's best. Her own flawless appearance was achieved with good everyday make-up, slightly heightened; her hair was always perfectly composed and in place, her apparel perhaps accentuated by a piece of jewelry. She particularly liked the young woman in class to wear jewelry. She had little patience for straggle-haired girls who did not look their best.

The spring Graham appeared at the Alvin Theater, directly after the de Rothschild–sponsored dance series was also the occasion of the twenty-fifth anniversary of the Neighborhood Playhouse. The Playhouse had started as scattered classes in apartments, loft buildings, and empty studios on the Lower East Side, and after several changes of address, it had arrived at more glamorous surroundings in midtown. During the time it was moving and growing, Horst and Graham had been faithful members of the staff. A quarter-century had passed almost without anyone having realized it. The board read into the minutes of its meeting a special citation for both Graham and Horst in recognition of their efforts and successes at the school.

It was a time of milestones. Horst was seventy years old and Graham, de Rothschild, and Rita Morgenthau collectively threw a party for him at the B. de Rothschild Foundation offices. It was a time for friendly recollection. The *Dance Observer* had celebrated its twentieth anniversary, the Graham Company was over twenty-five years old, and Graham had choreographed well over a hundred dances. They had all weathered the storm.

10

Ambassador of Dance

"She is one of the great creators of
our time. . . . she has enlarged the
language of the soul."
Richard Buckle

Events totally outside of the dance world brought Graham to the attention of the government. The cold war with the Soviet Union had entered a new phase, and the weapons used by Russia included cultural presentations in addition to the increases in armaments. The Soviet Government, which had thousands of dancers and musicians on its payroll, decided that they could further its efforts to win the allegiance of nations and governments. Accordingly, it began to send folk troupes of chubby-cheeked girls and bounding young men to various indecisive nations in much the same way that a nineteenth-century government might have dispatched a gunboat. Evidence of the Soviet Union's energy, it was also a much nicer way of trying to influence foreign governments than by brandishing weaponry.

Deciding to counter the Russian cultural effort with its own, the U.S. Government began to search for the best ways to present the country in a culturally favorable light. That the nation had a cultural history as well as an economic and political history was almost totally obscured by its material success. The government did not have a ministry of culture as did most East and West European nations, nor did it have any established way of bringing artists under a governmental wing. The emergency Works Project Administration of the 1930's, which helped actors and dancers to survive the Depression, had long since been disbanded. The strategy chosen by the government was the development of a program whereby the cultural efforts of the United States could be applied to "trouble spots" through the sponsorship of an agency on the scene—embassies, consulates, and the State Department in general. A department of cultural affairs was created to handle transportation and local appearances of theatrical, musical, and dance organizations that would appear under State Department sponsorship.

Since the Russians emphasized dance in their own country, dance became an important part of the U.S. presentation. Active in the cultural affairs division of the State Department were several people who were familiar with Graham's work. Because modern dance is an indigenous art form, it was logical that Graham was among the first to be asked to represent the United States abroad. She accepted with misgivings, and preparations for her second tour of Europe began. Representing the United States was a special honor.

In agreeing to travel overseas, Graham put herself in something close to the position she had had at the start of her career. Though she had an international reputation, it was uninformed and based on hearsay. In effect, she had to prove herself to a new audience at the age of sixty, when most artists have a secure reputation and can afford to relax.

So in February 1954 Graham, a Company of fourteen dancers, and the musical director Simon Sadoff sailed from New York on the *Queen Elizabeth.* The Company took with it ten productions plus a dance which it was going to premiere in London, the scene of Graham's bitter humiliation four years earlier. The new piece, "Ardent Song," with a score by Alan Hovhaness, was incomplete when the Company sailed, and Graham planned to finish it in London. The Company would be appearing there for two weeks, and "Ardent Song" was scheduled for the second week. From London, the Company would move through Europe, stopping in Holland, Sweden, Denmark, Belgium, France, Switzerland, Italy, and Austria.

The penetrating London cold caught the Company unprepared, and to warm up, many of the dancers soaked in tubs of hot water into which they kept the hot water flowing. They learned later that, as they sat in their baths, the overflow ran through vents and down the side of the building onto the sidewalk, sending cascades of water onto Shaftesbury Avenue.

The opening at the Saville Theatre in the first week of March was almost universally panned by the critics, who found little merit in "Dark Meadow," "Canticle for Innocent Comedians," or "Appalachian Spring." An occasional kind word was written in one or another column, but the initial reaction was incomprehension and condescension toward what critics insisted upon calling "barefoot" dance or "free" dance. They regarded it as a kind of obscure ritual. Whatever it was, most of them took no pleasure from it. "The unceasing effort required to deduce from these dance dramas even a hint of Miss Graham's abstractions and philosophies," the critic of the *Sunday Times* wrote, "leaves one exhausted rather than entertained." "It is impressive but not designed for enjoyment," declared one magazine. Another paper inquired politely after the opening night performance, "Was this trip necessary?" There was an occasional favorable comment—"It's a new language in which she says new things"—but the voices of disapproval rang far more strongly.

Then after a week came a forceful statement of appreciation from Richard Buckle, whose critical star was ascending. In an article in the weekly Sunday newspaper, *The Observer,* he said: "Now I conjure every idle habit-formed fellow, in need of a third eye to see new beauty, that he should visit the Saville Theatre and watch Martha Graham. She is one of the great creators of our time. . . . I hope all thoughtful people will see her, for she has enlarged the language of the soul." It was a welcome affirmation, but it came a full week after the Company opened, and the theater was nearly empty. Only a few persons were having their eyes opened to a new form of theatrical dance, though, in some cases, the experience would change the course of their lives.

Meanwhile, Graham had great difficulties in finishing "Ardent Song." She did not like to be bound too tightly into the rhythm of a piece, but the rhythmic character of Hovhaness's score kept pressing her. "Ardent Song" was designed to last fifty minutes, and she had finished only three-quarters of it. There were gaps here and there throughout the work. The pressure was intense, and the hostile critical reception had taken its toll of energy and confidence. The day before the scheduled premiere she assembled the Company at five in the afternoon to tell them that because she could not finish "Ardent Song," it would not have its announced premiere performance the following evening.

Although Company members knew that Graham had been having trouble and were almost relieved to have the dance canceled, the news shocked Gertrude Macy, who was producing the season. She ran up to the top floor of the theater where Graham was still addressing the Company to attempt to change her mind. She was winded and puffing as she spoke, but Graham held to her announced decision. Unable to believe that Graham was going to cancel, Macy continued to press her. Pointing out that some of the press had been sympathetic, she admitted that the attendance had been poor but insisted that presenting the premiere was the only way to salvage something of the season. In making her points she used the word "unprofessional" several times to describe such a last-minute cancelation. It was a highly potent term. Graham exploded in rage; she had been called everything during the course of her career, but never had she been accused of being "unprofessional." She dismissed the Company to continue her argument with Macy in private. At the end of the performance that evening, Graham told the Company that there would be a rehearsal in the theater the next day at 8 A.M.

Afterward a small group of dancers led by Robert Cohan gathered in the rehearsal studio of the theater without Graham to try to get a jump on the next day's work. One of the unchoreographed sections in the dance revolved around Yuriko, who was the soloist, and four couples. Knowing how Graham had positioned the couples in relationship to Yuriko, Cohan began to choreograph patterns for the couples. As the leader of the group, he started a pattern of movement. From that opening position, each of the other three couples would follow him. When all had repeated the sequence, he devised another movement and the couples again repeated it, until, in all, they filled a six-minute gap in the work. At eight the next morning, the group showed Graham what they had worked out. Thinking it suitable, she included it in the dance and went on to do as much else as was possible in the short time available. Although most of the dance somehow was finished, there was still a serious gap in a portion that Mary Hinkson, Linda Margolies, and Matt Turney had to perform. This fast-moving section the three women simply improvised in each performance.

It was in this form that "Ardent Song" toured Europe. With the help of her Company, Graham set the rest of the sections except for the one wild portion that the three women danced. And every time the piece was repeated, they would come offstage furious because the entrances and exits were difficult and they were never entirely sure of what they were doing. Margolies finally snarled at her husband, Stuart Hodes, as she came off, gasping, "When is she going to set this fucking dance! When the hell is she gonna . . . ? Goddamn it, why don't you give us some steps to do?" Later, after returning from Europe, Graham changed the dance radically by inserting a new character.

Despite the improvisation and the haste with which the dance was finished, the London critics reacted with reasonable positiveness to "Ardent Song." "For technique alone 'Ardent Song' is worth watching," one paper noted. With the response to the premiere, and most likely because of the Buckle article, the houses picked up during the second week. But their appearance had not been the unqualified success that Graham and the Company had hoped for, and Graham especially felt taxed and tired.

The next stop on the tour was Holland, followed by Sweden and Denmark. In Holland, Graham gave a lecture demonstration that was so successful that she decided to add it to her other appearances. To anyone who has never seen the Graham lecture demonstration, it is difficult to characterize its precise feeling. It is, in essence, an informal performance. The dancers turn out as for an actual performance, but at times they allow themselves to relax into their roles as individuals as well as performers. Graham's descriptions of the life of a dancer and the detailed comments she makes about the movements have an elevated seriousness, at times marked with humor, that is both witty and touching.

At the Century Hotel in Antwerp, Graham took the time to write to Horst, telling him about her reception and reaffirming her appreciation for all he had taught her. The letter was affectionate, gossipy, sad, and hopeful:

> I think of you many times here in Europe and speak of you all the time . . . every press conference carries your name some place in it. Praise be the A-B-A form, to say nothing of the others. I have had a curious time here . . . a time of re-evalua-

> tion. . . . I have had such fatigue as I have never known. London was so hard. It was mixed but a critic named Richard Buckle . . . a ballet fan turned the tide for me. The houses were small at first but then we did finish with filled houses and bravos. He is a power. It seems that the thing most amazing is that we as Americans have a culture other than the movies or Russian ballet transplanted. . . . This has been something, Louis. The [important] thing has been the work and the public relations things as well. Now the U.S. Embassies are asking for us as they say we are the best cultural relationship thing that has happened. . . . Curious that so "dead" a thing as the "modern dance" should have importance. *Pace* some dance critics I could mention. Well. Well! . . . One man rode on a motorbike from Hanover to Amsterdam to see us. One rode on a motorbike to Stockholm from the Polar Circle to see us. I think the world is hungry. . . . All has not been easy for my heart or for my body but it has been wonderful. I only wanted this to tell you that you are doing a great and valuable work in training the creative instinct to express and make manifest what it feels is urgent. And it is important. . . . I return for the June course and Connecticut. I have no money, of course. Vienna is from June 3–8. Then I probably fly back. I shall call you when I arrive. I hope you are well and that the year has been good for you. All love. Martha

In Antwerp the Company was praised, and the reviewer from *Le Matin* admired the music, complimented the dancers, and liked "Diversion of Angels" as well as "Letter to the World" and "Errand into the Maze." Afterward the Company went on to Paris, to a reception that was a complete contrast to the disastrous visit four years previously.

The invited audience of the first evening was a little restless because of the length of the program, so subsequent programs were cut down by trimming bits and pieces out of various dances. Beyond that, Graham and the Company were received as great artists. Of the dances on the program, only "Letter to the World" did not meet with general approval—which was ironic, because Graham had pushed herself to exhaustion and eventual injury in order to be able to include this work in her first Paris season in 1950. Otherwise, the dances—especially "Deaths and Entrances," "Diversion of Angels," and "Canticle for Innocent Comedians"—got their best reception. Attendance was good, particularly at the last two performances.

On the opening night, Baroness de Rothschild, Bethsabee's

mother, gave the Company a party at her house on Avenue Foch and presented pocket mirrors with a little map of Paris on the back to all the women. For Paris itself, it was time of mixed emotions. It was the happy anniversary of the end of World War II, but the period of the Company's stay also saw the surrender at Dienbienphu. The Russian ballet company decided that it would be wise to cancel its Paris opening. Before the Graham Company left, there was a ceremony at City Hall at which Graham was given a diploma and a medal from the City of Paris as an acknowledgment of the quality of her art. In the history of Paris, it was the first time that a dancer had been so honored. Paris, the scene of her first disastrous attempt at a European season, had now honored her, attended her performances, and presented her with an official notice and citation. It was a wonderful springtime to be in Paris.

Although the Swiss reaction was good, nothing could match the reception in Paris. In Italy, the next stop, the Company had to share four of its six programs with an opera company. Opera and ballet were a traditional pairing in Europe, though the Graham Company was unused to it. The occasion was the Maggio Musicale in Florence, which usually had a conventional and conservative bent. The audiences were some of the worst the Company had ever encountered. They did not like what they saw, and, perhaps even more, they did not like the music. Not even Copland's "Appalachian Spring," popular almost everywhere, found favor in their eyes and ears. Graham found that she had to exercise all her stagecraft and a bit more to keep the performance tone for some of her appearances.

One evening the Company was scheduled to do "Night Journey," Graham's intense retelling of the Oedipus legend, right after an opera buffa in which the devil set all the town clocks back so that everyone ended up in bed with the wrong person. As the performance began, with Graham swaying with a length of rope over her hands, the audience found it hard to believe what they were seeing.

"There was a sense," Stuart Hodes recalled, "that the whole audience was cracking up like an ice floe that was just about to turn into slush. They weren't an audience anymore, they were just a bunch of raucous, confused, embarrassed, surprised, and annoyed people. And just at the point where they would get close to the outer limits, Martha would stop and she would turn to them, walk out to the edge of the stage and throw a gestural curse at them. It was the evil eye! And I mean those people knew when they'd been hit with *il malocchio*. She shot a bolt at them! And they stopped. They knew it. Watch this one! She's got it!"

The dance had one of the most exciting and unusual entrances for a male in her repertory—a pole-thumping hop for the Seer, danced by Hodes. The choreography called for him to circle the stage, sometimes with his back to the audience. Waiting for his entrance, Hodes decided that it would be a mistake to turn his back, so instead he hopped around the stage with his eyes fixed resolutely on the audience at all times.

Graham, of course, was not pleased with her reception but rather than sulk in the hotel she dressed up as smartly as she could and, acting triumphantly, proceeded to enjoy the city. The basic source of the difficulty did not lie with Graham. The Italian attitude toward dance simply was not serious, and the Graham Company above all else was serious. Florence and Graham were a cultural mismatch.

For its last stop the Company went to Vienna, and the much more positive results there ended the tour happily. Though many of the Company stayed on in Europe, Graham flew home almost immediately afterward. She returned with a sense of satisfaction. She had wiped out the debacle of 1950. She had met the test and again won. This time she had, in a sense, done it alone.

In some countries she had been a great critical success; in some she had aroused the interest of talented individuals; in some she had created a great stir among dancers; and in still others she had become a pet of the intellectuals. There had also been a great response to an art form that had been created by American artists out of desire and determination. Western Europe, which formerly had been willing to acknowledge the supremacy of the American musical but little else, now hailed modern dance as a serious American cultural development.

In July, at Connecticut College, where she addressed an audience of eager students, Graham spoke of the dedication required to make dance a career. Saying that "Europe needs American dance," she encouraged each student to "become, through hard training, an acrobat of God."

If Graham was content, the State Department, once it examined the various reports about the tour, was ecstatic and immediately started planning another tour. Whether Graham cared or even thought about the motives of the government in sending her around the world is irrelevant. To her, the important thing was that she had managed to do something that had eluded her the first time around. Now the government was talking about a tour of the Far East, which would wind up in the Middle East. Because of her fascination with the East, it was an irresistible challenge. The trip was scheduled for the fall of 1955.

In the spring, de Rothschild again sponsored a festival of modern dance similar to the one held two years earlier. Ten companies in addition to Graham's had agreed to appear. For her own performance Graham restructured the solo, "The Triumph of St. Joan," first performed with the Louisville Orchestra in 1951, into a group work.

Keeping the three aspects of Joan—The Maid, The Warrior, and The Saint—she assigned them to three different dancers. These three Joans became aspects of the Joan formerly danced by Graham. "Seraphic Dialogue," as the revised dance was now called, was to be the first of a series of dances that would find the heroine in the center of action thinking back over her character's life as depicted in episodes portrayed by other dancers.

When Graham asked Noguchi to think about an appropriate design for "Seraphic Dialogue," he returned with the most beautiful décor he had ever created for a Graham dance. It was so strong and and startling that it caused her to think through her approach to the dance and revise it according to the new possibilities it offered her. What Noguchi provided was a polished brass set that shone like gold. On the right were three seats upon which the dancers who portrayed aspects of Joan perched while one or another of them danced. To the left, opposite them, was an anchored stand on which hung a cross and a sword in the same polished brass. To the rear of the stage was a structure of circles, triangles, and rectangles resembling the tracery of a stained-glass window. It contained no glass, however, just the outlining metal. The shape at the back was a place of retreat, of rest and security, and entry to it was gained through a gate that opened out.

At the beginning of the dance, Joan is seen before this structure, and her patron, Saint Michael, is fluttering his hands above her head in a gesture of beatitude. The three dancers who play the various aspects of Joan's life are behind a screen, and as Joan retires they enter and seat themselves at the front of the stage side by side. Saint Michael enters from time to time to dance with each of them—offering the cross to The Saint, comfort to The Maid, and the sword to The Warrior. Joan herself dances dialogues with these various aspects of herself, as she considers various periods of her life and puzzles over the events and the fate that brought her to the stake. Finally, as a sign that the voices she obeyed were indeed correct and her actions blameless, she is taken by Saint Michael into the sanctified retreat behind the tracery.

The dance is a stunning balance of elements, each finely turned and set into place to give viewers a completely rounded picture of the protagonist's public and private character. Joan's "conversations" with herself are the matter of the dance, in which the flashback technique is used with a precise knowledge of its strengths and a delicate avoidance of its pitfalls. In a sense, the content of the dance is self-justification. And Graham, of course, had listened to her own "voices" as did Joan. "Seraphic Dialogue" was received with great enthusiasm.

For the Far Eastern tour—a mammoth, sixteen-week project lasting from October 1955 through March 1956—the twenty-member Company traveled in one plane, and the costumes, scenery, and technical equipment (together totaling six and one-half tons) traveled in another. The advance man, Craig Barton, examined the technical facilities of every theater a week or more before the Company arrived, to see what adjustments would have to be made before the time of the performance. Graham preceded the Company to Tokyo, arriving there on October 18. The Company left New York to join her a few days later. Their first appearance, in a lecture demonstration, was on October 29, but the publicity work had to come first.

When Graham arrived, the immediate shock of being surrounded by reporters and cameramen was great. As one who had always been extremely careful about having her picture taken, her experience in Japan, where everyone in sight seemed to have a camera that he used almost constantly to record her every gesture, was one of the severest trials of the tour. This was a culture shock she had not anticipated. After her initial reaction, she learned to ignore the constant clicking. In Tokyo the Company was being partially sponsored by the Sankei newspaper chain, and the press coverage of its comings and goings, not to mention Graham's, was therefore extensive.*

In the United States the Company was loaded aboard a plane named *Disneyland*, which made its first stop in San Francisco. Bethsabee de Rothschild traveled with the Company ostensibly as wardrobe mistress: because of the uncertainty of airline connections and local transportation, she decided to travel with the tour, and on a State Department tour everyone had to have a job. However, as usual, everyone took care of his own costume. Stopping in Honolulu and Wake Island, they lost a full day when crossing the international date line. The last lap of the trip brought them into Tokyo, where they were met by newspapermen and a small crowd carrying banners saying "Welcome Martha Graham"—but Graham was not there.

The picture-taking was constant. After a quick trip through customs, the Company was loaded into convertibles with tops down and bunches of balloons attached to them. On the way into town, the newspaper arranged to photograph the Company as it stopped to look at a shrine or a historic building. Then back again into the cars and downtown to the newspaper offices, passing the Imperial Hotel, where they would stay. More pictures were taken as they wandered about the modern offices of the newspaper, and then all were brought back to the hotel and allowed to go to their rooms. Still no Graham. After lunch the photographers were brought on again, and more pictures of the Company strolling around the hotel gardens were taken. Finally, all of the publicity for the day was over. Still, no one had seen Graham.

The next day the Company saw Graham for the first time at a luncheon. Stuart and Linda Hodes greeted her and complimented her on looking well and rested. Graham replied that she was able to relax as soon as she was away from the Company. Whatever else was intended, the remark was a home truth. The Company enabled Graham to do what she needed to do creatively, but it was nonetheless a weighty responsibility that at times rested very heavily on her. Years later she commented, in a conversation about Ruth St. Denis, "I saw her do the great ones—'Cobra,' 'The Nautch'—the great ones, before she became what I am now, which is to carry a

* The sponsoring newspaper, with sublime tact, gave the actual date of Graham's birth from which any child could deduce the truth, and in the same paragraph maintained that she was fifty years old.

company." The reception by the audiences on the Asian tour lightened her burden, at least for a time.

In the Daichi Seimei Hall on the morning of October 29, Graham and eight members of the Company gave a lecture demonstration to familiarize the audiences with the new dance style they were going to see. As Graham spoke, the dancers demonstrated the various aspects of her technique, and after the demonstration Graham answered questions. One member of the audience wondered why the Company wore shoes before and after the performance but not during the performance. Graham had always wanted students in her school to keep their shoes on while walking around the halls and to take them off only when working in the studio, but this was the first time she had ever been asked to explain. With her usual aplomb, she created an explanation on the spot to the effect that when dancers meet an audience or accept applause they like to be dressed formally, and that by working without shoes they enable the audience to enter into the performance. It was a good explanation, one that she continued to use whenever she was asked about her dancers' bare feet.

The next day the technical crew unpacked the equipment and set up the house for the first evening's performance, and on November 1 the Company opened with "Diversion of Angels," "Night Journey," and "Appalachian Spring." The audience covered the stage with streamers and flowers, and the critical reception was warm. By the end of the week of performances, the audiences were reluctant to let the Company leave the stage. By this time, the critical notices were unreservedly enthusiastic.

Seiko Takada, a Japanese woman who had been a student at Denishawn with Graham's sister Georgia, told the newspaper that sponsored Graham's appearance in Tokyo: "I have seen Miss Graham when she was young, and I studied in the same class at the Denishawn school with her sister. So I have a special feeling to appreciate her performances. To my great surprise and delight, I find her young, just the same, after long years. It must have been a tremendous effort for her to develop her dance to such a high standard as shown at the present performances. Usually a dancer fails in expressing his inner self when he pays full attention to formal beauty of movement. But it was not the case with her. She succeeded in uniting both the sublimity of her thought and the grace of her movement. She made a real art of the body."

The Company's enthusiastic reception in Tokyo was matched almost everywhere they went. There was some political hostility to the American dance company from several left-wing newspapers, but in general audience reactions to the Graham choreography and performance were quite unpolitical and enthusiastic throughout Asia.

Just prior to the triumphant appearance of the Graham Company, Alexandra Danilova and a ballet company were given an excellent reception in Tokyo. One newspaper critic compared the two companies on the broad basis of their talent and their dancing skill and mentioned how impressed he was with the long working career of foreign artists. In Graham's case it may have been longer than he knew.

After closing in Tokyo, the Company received a surprise: a week off with pay. Barton had written from South Korea that it was totally impossible for the Company to perform on the stage that was available. The Company traveled with a floorcloth to protect the dancers' feet from splinters, but the theater in Seoul was in such disrepair that there were actually holes in the stage. The State Department was disappointed, but the dancers were delighted. Some stayed in Tokyo while others scattered to Kyoto.

When the Company reassembled after the week's vacation, they flew to Manila, which after Tokyo was a bit of a letdown. It was certainly a less cosmopolitan city than Tokyo, and the local Catholic bishops had expressed some opposition.

As was the custom, performances started later than in Japan and concluded at 1 A.M. The wife of the local sponsor of the week in Manila, who sent a box of iced mangos backstage after one performance, sent a roast suckling pig on the last night. No one wanted to eat it, but no one wanted to offend their hosts either, so the Company took it back to the hotel with them, Stuart Hodes holding it outside the taxi window. At the hotel, the cook in the coffee shop cut it up in small squares, and the Company proceeded to dine while Graham sat at an adjoining table, saying reproachfully, "He hasn't lived very long."

The Company continued the custom of giving lecture demonstrations, and in Manila, during the day, it performed at an armory before an audience of thousands. The Company stood in the middle of the hall on an elevated platform somewhat larger than a boxing ring. The members of the Company spread out, facing in all directions, because there were people in every direction. The audience was very quiet until the demonstration came to a standard gesture in a Graham class, in which the dancer extends the leg with the foot at a right angle, then points the foot, extending the line of the leg, and then flexes it again. At that the armory filled with laughter. Hodes recalled, "It was a great experience—something unfamiliar but enjoyable brings on laughter." The reaction of the lecture-demonstration crowd was quite different from that of the evening crowds. The wealthier theater patrons gave the Company a perfunctory reception even on the last night of the season.

Still, for the Company, being in Manila, like being in Asia, offered a wonderful chance to see new things. The dancers went to local dance schools to give a Graham class and to observe the dancing of the region, and, just before they left the country, the U.S. Ambassador invited them for morning coffee.

On November 19 the Company left the Philippines and headed for Bangkok, where it was greeted at the airport by people holding strings of flowers. The requisite press conference was held, with Graham answering questions and the members of the Company ranked around her as in a family portrait.

Thailand, which had maintained its neutrality and independence for nearly a thousand years, received the Graham Company with calm dignity. The Thais were gracious hosts. Tours were arranged for the Company to visit local temples, and to take a boat trip upriver to see the Temple of the Dawn. A prince of the royal family arranged for a display of dancing on his lawn, where he kept a baby elephant tethered. The performances, which were well received, were attended for the most part by rich Thais and wealthy European residents. As in the Philippines, there was an enormous gap between the audiences at the evening performances, which tended to be the established elite of the country, and the audiences at the afternoon lecture demonstrations, which were attended by vast numbers of young students and other interested people. Not until the last night of the week did the Company have a sold-out performance.

Although the tour was only five weeks old, stresses and strains were beginning to show. These were largely the product of the virulent edge that Graham had developed over the past several years. The companies she worked with and the administrators who surrounded her were held together by her own ruthless determination.

Creating an atmosphere of Byzantine intrigue around her, she controlled the Company through cunning, cajolery, and castigation. There had already been several arguments with members of the Company, and on the way from Kuala Lumpur to Singapore it became obvious that one woman, who was at the breaking point, would probably not be able to continue with the Company. In addition, aside from the relatively innocuous diarrhea that could be held at bay with a few gulps of medicine at least long enough for a performance, various ailments were beginning to plague members of the group. The Company manager, Leroy Leatherman, had to have his appendix removed. In Ceylon, Craig Barton hobbled about on crutches after injuring himself. Eventually, nearly everyone in the Company missed one performance or another because of illness. The only two exceptions were Matt Turney and Graham herself. Although at the start of the tour she had had severe reactions to the typhus and cholera inoculations, during the tour itself she blossomed and made every performance.

For the State Department the most important parts of the tour were yet to come. Indonesia had an independent-minded government, as did India, and because both were extremely critical of the United States and its posture in Southeast Asia, it was especially desirable that the Company make a good showing there and display American culture in a sympathetic and artistically accomplished manner.

Preparations for Jakarta, Indonesia, were meticulous and extensive, and created a certain tension. The representative of the United States Information Service had prepared very detailed itineraries for the Company as well as "fact" sheets, and he tried in every way to prevent any untoward incidents. The attitude of the Indonesian Government toward visitors, as reported by Barton, did not help the Company's state of mind. Barton informed them of requirements that sounded much like those imposed in a police state: two passport photos to be presented when arriving, entrance and exit visas, currency declarations, inspection of incoming and outgoing mail, and a curfew that might or might not be in effect. If it was and one was arrested for a curfew violation, it would be nearly impossible to get out of jail before the next day. All in all, the Company felt more like a group preparing to go into enemy territory than a touring theatrical attraction preparing for performances. Barton also told them that there were no taxicabs, only bicycle cabs; and because there were lots of mosquitoes, everybody must take malaria pills.

To further complicate matters, in an effort to prevent unhappy incidents the Company did not stay in hotels but was quartered instead with resident Americans connected with the embassy. Though the embassy tried to settle everybody comfortably, the arrangements required a series of intricate automobile pools so that everyone got to the right spot at the right time. If it happened that someone did not get to the right place, he or she would be missed only when it was too late to do anything about it.

Despite the special cautions, the week that the Company spent in Jakarta followed the schedule that was used in each of the full-week stayovers. On the first day, the Company arrived in the afternoon and met with the technical director and the local sponsor to iron out any problems connected with the performances. On the second day there was a lecture demonstration and the official press conferences, at which Graham was becoming ever more adept in fielding questions. The third day was spent socializing with important local people and attending an evening party at the embassy. The regular performance schedule started on the fourth day, which was also the first opportunity to rehearse the productions. The fifth and sixth days were spent in rehearsal and performance of the two programs not yet given. The seventh day was one of rest, with some further socializing with people the embassy wished to entertain. The eighth day the Company left for the next stop, where the schedule repeated itself.

During the week, an Indonesian woman who had studied at the Graham school in New York arranged for the Company to see performances of local dancing. Suti Arti Kailola, called Pil by everybody, turned up at the airport when the Company arrived. "Her reunion with Martha at the airport was a weird contrast," Hodes recalls. "We were surrounded by photographers, of which Martha is always terribly aware. She was met first by the impresario, who greeted her, welcomed her, and handed her a bouquet of flowers. It was instructive to watch the way Martha drew out the taking of the flowers, reaching forward with her long neck and passionate profile, holding gracious expressions on her face, looking raptly for long moments while the flashes went off. Then Pil came through the gate and toward Martha. She had that intense pained look that people have when they are very happy and very moved, and Martha held out her arms. They embraced, Pil unconscious of everything except the reunion, and there was Martha holding the pose, turning the famous profile, putting on the performance until the flashes stopped popping."

A memorable moment occurred during an obligatory social gathering, a morning coffee reception with the wife of the vice-president, Mrs. Hatta, and her mother. They had been in Tokyo shortly before, when the Graham Company was due to arrive. Knowing that Graham would be coming to Indonesia, they got tickets for a performance, which left them quite baffled. They mistakenly had been given tickets for the Danilova ballet company and for a while had thought that Danilova was Graham. Graham laughed and said that they were very different: "After all, Danilova wears point shoes," she began—"And you are the barefoot contessa," Mrs. Hatta's mother concluded, alluding to the title of the then current movie.

The entire week passed with quiet pleasantness and no political "incidents," and the Company scored a great success in a country that had a strong dance tradition of its own and thus accorded dance a major place in its theatrical and cultural life. Reflecting on the Graham Company, the *Times* of Indonesia commented, "If ever this paper came perilously close to forgetting its policy of leaning neither to the East nor the West, it was during the Martha Graham week, because this talented woman presented something of the United States that we could wholeheartedly approve of." And so a major hurdle for the Company was cleared more successfully than anyone had supposed possible.

The stop after Jakarta was Rangoon, Burma, which had an easier and more relaxed atmosphere. The various countries the Company had visited were beginning to reel past in a blur of moneychangers, strange-looking alphabets, and theaters with less and less technical equipment. And not just equipment. Bathrooms were scarce in the theaters, and dressing rooms almost as rare. The tour was becoming more wearing, and, with conditions edging toward the impossible, irritation became increasingly magnified. Graham had one more large test to confront before she could allow herself to relax, and this was India, which had one of the oldest dance traditions in the world.

With her strong inclination to Eastern philosophy, it might have been understandable had Graham taken dance forms of the Orient and used them for her own ends, but this was something she never did. In Tokyo, when she had been asked specifically whether she would borrow Japanese modes, she answered that she would not copy Japanese dance forms unless she knew their spirit, that copying only the surface of something would be pointless. In a profound way, Graham's answer articulated the difference between herself and her first teachers, Ruth St. Denis and Ted Shawn, who went all over the world collecting dances and using them in their own brand of eclectic programing. Graham would not borrow anything until she understood the core of the art, and then what she produced would reflect the original source only tangentially. When Graham did "Frontier," a dance about the plains of the United States, she included nothing of roping or horseback riding in it. Rather, she evoked the spirit of the people who conquered the plains. Similarly, when she did "Appalachian Spring" she did not introduce, say, hoedown movements into her dance narrative about farm people; rather, she went to the core of the task that faced them: the uniting of a man and woman for the purpose of creating a new home and a new family unit distinct from the ones that they had come from. In India, Graham would be exposed to a great volume of dance material that, in its antiquity and variety, would seem almost to mock the efforts of anyone trying to create a "new" art form in dance. She would present works in a fifty-year-old art form to a country in whose history fifty years was like the blinking of an eye. Graham watched the dance of India with great respect and analytical interest, and she presented herself and her art, despite its youth, with confidence in its soundness.

This portion of the tour opened in Dacca, East Pakistan (now Bangladesh), and then proceeded to Calcutta, to Madras for a week, to the island of Ceylon, up the west coast of India to Bombay, then to New Delhi and Karachi for a final week before leaving for Iran. Graham's poise and the dancing of the Company carried them through India and Pakistan with the same ease and success that they had displayed in Indonesia.

In general, the left-wing press was politely hostile, and at each press conference—in addition to the usually innocuous, "What is 'modern dance'?"—would manage to ask what might have been at least one embarrassing question. At one press conference, with her Company bright and shiny for the occasion, she was asked, "Why are there no dances in your Company in which the subject is universal brotherhood?" Graham paused for only a moment before making her grave reply: "There are no dances in my Company in which that is not the subject. I could not do a single step if I did not believe in brotherhood. But I am not a propagandist. I don't need to make dances that say they are about brotherhood. All of my dances are."

The critical reviews were friendly and at times ecstatic. In Dacca, the local press commented, "Miss Graham brought a new idiom of expression, vitality, drama, and sense of adventure in the modern dance, abandoning realism for abstraction." When the Company played in New Delhi, Nehru, who rarely went to the theater, came to see them perform. In Madras the Company visited a compound run by the Theosophical Society for artists and musicians who had lost their court positions as the maharajas lost much of their income. At the colony lived an old musician in his eighties, attended by a young man. When the old man composed a song or remembered an old melody, the young man would memorize it. Both had attended a Company performance, and when the group visited he welcomed them with a song that Graham immediately recognized and members of the group gradually realized was a variation on the Shaker melody from "Appalachian Spring."

The tour had been so tightly organized that no provision was made for the Company to see the Taj Mahal. When de Rothschild realized that they were going to leave India without being able to see the most famous landmark in the country, she arranged out of her own pocket for a day's visit. This gesture was one of her many quiet generosities.

After their week in New Delhi, during which they witnessed an Independence Day parade, the Company went to Karachi and then left for the Persian Gulf port of Abadan, where they played in a well-equipped theater which had hot and cold running water, fully equipped dressing rooms, and even air conditioning. The change came as a great relief. Here there was no need to set up makeshift bathrooms or to wonder whether the light was going to fail, or which day the water was shut off, or how many guards would be required to keep the costumes from being stolen, or where to hide the electric irons so that they would not disappear, or whether the floor would be so dirty and splintery that they would have to use the floorcloth.

From Abadan the Company went to Teheran, and then to the last stop—it was now February—Israel, where Graham had a striking success. There were enthusiastic audiences for all performances. Here Graham met a former member of her Group from the 1930's and an unknown painter, Dani Karavan, who in a few years was to design several productions for her. In order to see her performances, he had hiked into Tel Aviv from his kibbutz. Like many others, he was entranced.

The Company contract expired on March 4, but the technical crew stayed on salary for an additional day to pack up the equipment and ready it for shipment back to the United States. Like everyone else, Graham was exhausted, but at the age of sixty-one she had come through a sixteen-week tour under the most arduous conditions with a level of energy equal to that of anyone in the Company. For the State Department, the tour had been a complete success.

After relaxing in Israel, Graham flew home toward the end of April. Gone for an entire theatrical fall and spring season, she came home to mend another personal fence. The occasion was offered when the Capezio Dance award was given to Ted Shawn. There had been something akin to bad blood between Graham and Shawn ever since the time Graham left Denishawn. She had made up with Miss Ruth, but Shawn had been a more difficult problem. To Graham, Shawn represented the kind of practicality she despised—the kind she explained in her letter to Arch Lauterer that she might hate him for. Shawn, from Graham's point of view, compromised with the artistic realities of a situation, and compromise infuriated her because it negated all that was most meaningful to her. For his part, Shawn, apart from his initial disdain for modern dance, had been bitter about what he considered Graham's ingratitude.

However, they both had survived difficult times and now decided to forget their differences and concentrate on areas of agreement. A photograph was taken of them smiling and toasting one another. She was delighted with his award, and he had even mellowed somewhat in his attitudes. He no longer considered modern dance "morbid" and, as a matter of policy, regularly presented it along with ballet and ethnic dance at Jacob's Pillow. Graham had never appeared there, but now the door was opened for her, and a few years later she gave a lecture demonstration at the festival.

Again on the international scene, Graham received an invitation to perform in Germany, which had been conspicuously absent from

Performance of "Clytemnestra" with Helen McGehee and Bertram Ross.

"Clytemnestra" (1958). Studio rehearsal with net instead of red cloak.

State Department tour
to the Far East, 1955.
Above: Arrival in Tokyo

Left: Martha Graham rehearsing
"Errand into the Maze"
with Stuart Hodes, Rangoon.

Studio shot, 1952.

"Judith" (1950).

"The Triumph of St. Joan" (1951).

Above: Sewing costumes in studio. Standing, Linda Hodes and Geordie Graham.

Left: At Company party with Richard Buckle, 1963.

Below: Teaching at Connecticut College.

Edinburgh, 1963.

her 1954–55 European itinerary. She had declined to appear there on the tour because, as she said, she did not wish to offend the Jewish members of her Company. On the occasion of the opening of the new Philharmonic Hall in Berlin, another invitation was extended to her, and she finally consented to appear at the opening along with other American artists, among them Eileen Farrell. She went without her Company, however, and performed "Judith," the solo she had created for the Louisville Orchestra.

Graham at this time also overcame somewhat her deep and long-standing reluctance to make films of her work for public display. In the mid-1930's she had allowed a documentary filmmaker, Julian Bryan, to film her solo "Frontier" and to photograph the Group in several short excerpts from other works. The film was made on a shoestring—in black and white and without sound—and for lack of money it remained unedited for nearly forty years. Graham was not much interested in this or in any similar effort to provide an independent record of the past. She had allowed extensive "record" films to be made, as an aide-memoire for herself and for anyone who was studying a role, but otherwise she had strongly resisted the idea of preserving her work in any permanent form. She was fortunate that her accompanist, Helen Lanfer, also functioned as a choreographic amanuensis, notating Graham's dances in a method of her own directly on the music scores. Graham's reluctance stemmed from her unwillingness to create any type of record, film or notational, that would allow a stranger to restage one of her works without her supervision. Her attitude was based in part on her understanding of the old tradition of ballet in which choreographic patterns were passed from teacher to pupil in a connected series of links that stretched back, in some cases, one hundred and fifty years.

Now, however, with de Rothschild's encouragement, she relented and allowed *A Dancer's World* to be made. This film, cooperatively sponsored by the B. de Rothschild Foundation, the Mellon Foundation, and the facilities of WQED, an educational television station in Pittsburgh, was a record not of one of her individual dances but of her training methods. It consisted largely of excerpts from several lecture demonstrations. The specific problem that Graham faced in allowing the film to be made was the fact of her diminished physical skills. The director of the film hit upon the idea of using her as the narrator, and the result, which shows Graham reflecting on and explaining the requirements of a dancer, is one of the most outstanding dance films ever produced.

In all, of the more than one hundred fifty dances that Graham created during the course of her career, she allowed only a tiny handful, fewer than ten, to be filmed and preserved. They were by no means all representative of her best. Graham's attitude was an expression of the vain megalomania that had always been in evidence but that now was dominating more and more both her own feelings and her relations with others. She was interested in herself in the present. Because she was strong, she could keep everything under control as long as she was around. What happened afterward did not matter. From time to time, she would feign interest in preserving her works, but always she managed in some way to frustrate the project. In the same way she always scuttled any real attempt (as with the Juilliard dance department) to create a modern dance repertory company that would perform the works of many different choreographers.

Even her attitude toward her own work displayed the same characteristic. To a large extent, Graham ignored anything that was not immediate. When great dances that she had created no longer served as vehicles for herself as a performer, she dismissed them and went on to create new works in which she could have a performing role. With such a ruthless attitude about herself and her own work, it is not surprising that she had so little interest in the work of others.

From the outset of her career there never was a question of standing apart from her work; she was always the center of it. She did not readily design a dance for others, nor did she look upon the relinquishing of a role as a performing necessity. Her art was a personal one that was not easily shared. When she lost creative interest in one dance, she created another. Performing was the one activity that gave Graham vitality. It was the only way in which she could deal with the conflicts that gnawed at her.

Graham held onto roles so jealously that discouraged members of her Company began to leave, since it appeared that there was no other way they could extend themselves and further their own careers. It is not surprising that Graham's desire to control all aspects of her Company and her work should have intensified after her break with Hawkins. Perhaps even worse—though in matters that cut so deeply no measurement is really valid—was the loss of certain of her dance skills and the lessening response of her own body. Such attrition was inevitable, but to Graham it was the key to everything.

As her ability to control life through dancing decreased, she came to rely more heavily on alcohol to sustain her. Alcohol had entered her life seriously when Hawkins left. The social drink became a social necessity and then an essential anesthetic. Because Graham had always taken extraordinary care of her body through exercise and her sometimes odd diet, her health was not greatly impaired by her drinking for a number of years, and she always managed to accomplish anything that was important to her.

Despite all this, Graham's creativity continued unabated. For some time she had been preparing the most ambitious performing vehicle that she had ever created for herself—a full evening's dance about the passions and murderous conflicts in the House of Atreus after the Trojan War. The opera-length ballet was commonplace with choreographers of the nineteenth century, but few choreographers had tried it in the twentieth century, and, among modern dancers, only Alwin Nikolais had been able to sustain such length. Noguchi was asked to do the décor, and Halim El Dabh, an Egyptian composer, the music. Graham planned to work on costuming with one of her lead dancers, Helen McGehee. Graham's old friend Katharine Cornell commissioned the music through her foundation, and de Rothschild commissioned the choreography. Not only did this piece climax the line of dances for which Graham drew special inspiration from the myths of Greece, it became the crowning achievement of her theater works.

Graham chose as her central character Clytemnestra, who murdered her husband so as to remain with her lover. The story of the dance starts as Clytemnestra's restless spirit wanders through Hades after her death. Though she had passed from life into death, not even that radical transformation could grant her rest, for she was dishonored in the eyes of the shades surrounding her.

"Clytemnestra" is divided into four parts: two acts, a prologue, and an epilogue. In the prologue, the protagonist is seen sitting in the underworld, dwelling on the events of her past. The spirits of those with whom she was involved during her life pass by in a long procession, without regard for the chronological order in which they appeared during her lifetime. By trying to understand the meaning and motivations of her life, Clytemnestra will discover the key with which to free her spirit from its wandering.

In the first act, the time is set back to the actual events of the queen's tragic life. All of the characters who passed by in her imagination in the prologue now appear in a narrative sequential order and perform the actions that lead eventually to the doom of Clytemnestra. The city of Troy has fallen, and, though the people of Mycenae rejoice over the news, Clytemnestra, their queen, receives it with bitterness. Her liaison with Aegisthus, begun while her husband Agamemnon was away at war, she must now give up. She recalls the passionate love of Paris and Helen, the cause of the war, and then the sacrifice by Agamemnon of their daughter, Iphigenia, to secure good winds for his ships to sail to Troy. The dance of vengeance that Graham created to express Clytemnestra's reaction to the death of her daughter is one of the strongest creations in the dance.

Graham gave the role of the young queen to one of the younger members of the Company, who danced while Graham herself remained intensely quiet on the stage, asserting a tremendous theatrical presence. The transitions were so skillfully done that one accepted the substitution as being entirely natural. The queen was, of course, a younger woman in those days, and the contrast made good dramatic sense. It also helped that Noguchi designed the production in isolated units, like islands in the sea, so that a time change could be effected merely by having a character move to a different area of the stage, which would then be illuminated while the rest was dark. When Agamemnon returns in triumph, it is Graham herself who greets him, lures him into the house, and kills first him and then, to complete her revenge, his mistress Cassandra.

The second act finds the queen and her lover Aegisthus in charge of Mycenae, but in a dream Clytemnestra is troubled by the ghost of Agamemnon. His own revenge is accomplished through their son Orestes, who escaped Clytemnestra's wrath through the efforts of his sister, Electra. Orestes kills both his mother and her lover, thus avenging his father and sending Clytemnestra into the kingdom of Hades. In the epilogue, once again set in the underworld, Clytemnestra, by examining the chain of passion and duty that has resulted in the wasting of the household, is granted rest through the understanding that the chain of revenge may be broken by a rebirth of the individual through an acknowledgment of guilt. Clytemnestra finally acknowledges her lustful passions and is granted the privilege of having the curse of dishonor lifted from her.

Technically, the complicated story of the dance was always made dramatically clear by two singers, a man and a woman, one at either end of the proscenium. Dressed in contemporary evening clothes, they rendered the songs and narrative in a half-spoken, half-recited manner. The first aria set the chilling tone of the story as the male intoned a low ah-h-h-h-h-h-h-h and then elided into an upper register e-e-e-e-e-e-e-e. The score was programatic in the best sense of the word. The men's costumes were simple translations of Grecian styles showing maximum physique. The women, for the most part, wore the long dresses that Graham traditionally used for her heroines. She created a dark dress for herself and an enormous red cloak under which to murder Agamemnon. Noguchi's décor was ambiguously simple and convertible to many uses. His large crossed spears were at one moment used as a platform to transport a triumphant warrior and at another as a litter to carry a corpse. When the Messenger of Death first appears he carries a Noguchi-designed staff with a serpentine spiral running down its length. This suggested both the menace of a snake, and, as a grace note, the healing symbol of the medical profession, but, in all, the staff was designed as a contemporary interpretation of a Greek herald's caduceus. All of Graham's collaborators, including her long-time lighting designer, Jean Rosenthal, exerted a sympathetic and superb effort for "Clytemnestra," and it was with their help that Graham created a masterwork.

Running through Graham's work, as through her life, was the theme of unruly passion versus the constraints of duty. This theme was expressed in "Heretic" in the simple hammering against the wall of a closed society. Here was passion speaking to duty. It was also expressed in the contrast between the "dark" and the "poetic" beloved in "Deaths and Entrances," and in the more humorous "Punch and the Judy," where the Judy in a mature, responsible way endures and pleads for the wayward Punch. The war between the pagan and the Puritan began for Graham in the sensuous climate of Southern California, where she received from her family a rigorously strict and unsensuous upbringing. That she did not enter her theatrical career until after her father's death is an expression of the same conflict. Later, when she created a dance for herself and Erick

Hawkins in "American Document," in which the words of life-giving Ecclesiastes alternated with the punitive tirades of Jonathan Edwards and she stood alone onstage listening to the words of damnation, the top half of her body was held stiffly correct as her pelvis rolled sensuously. For Graham, the price of passion was punishment, and there was nothing to be done about it. And punishment could be absolved only by a confession of guilt.

Graham's life was the ebb and flow of energy pent up and released. Her technique was also based on the contraction and release of tension. Designed on the basic in-and-out breathing motion of the body, it was not a cerebral ordering of human movement, but a flesh, bone, and marrow solution to the problem of forming a vessel for passionate movement, and it was firmly rooted in the passionate animalistic aspects of man. She once said, "Desire is a lovely thing, and that is where the dance comes from, from desire. And the thing that makes you turn, for a dancer, is the desire to turn, first, so that everything comes out in desire; and where does desire reside but between the legs, for most people."

The tension that existed between Graham's upbringing and her instincts was the fuel that kept her creative effort intense for over five decades. When asked about her profession by interviewers, she would always answer that she was a dancer first and a choreographer second. It was the dancer's passionate response to experience that came first with her and the choreographer's ordering sense that came afterward. "Clytemnestra" was a summation of roles that she had played in her school, in her work, and in her life.

But only onstage could Graham be the arbiter of what should and could happen. Offstage, psychiatry and alcohol deadened the wound of loneliness. Although she was surrounded by people, she had no one. Her mother, to whom she had been particularly close, died in the summer of 1958, and, seemingly in an effort to bury the past as well, Graham methodically destroyed all of the letters and notebooks that her mother had saved over the years. Increasingly, Graham cloaked herself in an oracular pose, just as onstage she covered herself with theatrically stunning robes. Horst never came to the school, though she would see him from time to time, as often as not at a dinner to which both had been invited. She found it difficult to establish any kind of personal, passionate relationship with others. She had become the hostage of her own fame. The

Company depended on her, her administrators depended on her, and the modern dance world depended on her. She was the chief spokesman for the profession, she had a reputation that was universally recognized. Ask a man to name the most famous modern painter and he is likely to answer Picasso; if queried about modern music, he probably would answer Stravinsky; and if asked about modern dance, he would answer Martha Graham. But how much of that fame was now for Graham a punishment would be difficult to say.

11

Acrobat of God

"I don't have to defend myself.
The public will defend me."
Martha Graham

The darling of the State Department's Department of Cultural Presentations, Graham continued to be in demand for interviews, and every spring another college or university wanted to give her an honorary degree or have her address the graduating students. She had become a regular feature of Connecticut College's summer school lecture series. Surrounded with attention, she was fixed in the pose of the great lady. There was almost no one with whom she could relax. Students regularly came to worship at her feet, and strangers were kept at bay with a mixture of hokum and *grande-damerie*. The Company enjoyed periods of intense intimacy with her, and then periods of reserved silence. Her high-energy personality tended to absorb the people around her, and she created a suitable role to play for each of the people in her life. At the school her private room was just off the kitchen, and students and younger Company members would be brought in for little inspirational chats that were distinctly mystical in tone. If a visitor was coming to the school and some crisis threatened the good impression that Graham wanted to make, she would turn on to an almost performing level of alertness in order to smooth things over. Nothing was allowed to be commonplace in her life. In moving around the school, she was in effect giving a series of small performances. This was one of the ways she got through the day. The bottle of whiskey that the staff assistant was sent out to get from the local store also helped.

Whatever, it was a remarkable performance. She maintained a grueling schedule that would have exhausted someone half her age. Graham not only was creating excellent dances, but at the age of sixty-four she appeared in them and toured extensively in addition to fulfilling her teaching commitments. Her drinking was chronic, yet, however heavily it intruded into her private life, causing missed parties, forgotten engagements, and postponed publicity events, it hardly ever interfered with her professional work. When will and sheer determination alone did not suffice, she had vitamin injections.

Bethsabee de Rothschild began at this time to take an increasing interest in Israel. First she established in Tel Aviv a boutique for Israeli crafts, and then she made grants to individual dancers who were working in Israel. In the summer of 1958, after "Clytemnestra," she arranged for the Graham Company to return to Israel to give a series of performances in celebration of the tenth anniversary of the founding of the country.

While in Israel, Graham saw Dani Karavan's design for the Inbal Dance Company's production of "The Story of Ruth." The décor showed talent and originality, and Graham took the time, as always, to compliment him. Karavan himself was not happy with the look of the production. Though pleased with Graham's appreciation, he told her how bad he thought it was. When he returned home, he realized what he had done. "Martha Graham tells me she likes it and I tell her it's bad; how foolish I am." Two years earlier, he had hiked from his kibbutz to see Graham's performance, and in a few years there would be several commissions from her. For the time being, however, he had a tribute and an invitation to visit her at de Rothschild's home, where she was staying.

In December Doris Humphrey died. This was the first loss from the heroic generation of Graham, Weidman, Holm, and Tamiris. Ironically, Ruth St. Denis and Ted Shawn were still alive, and on occasion even gave a public performance. The modern dance world expressed its grief for Humphrey in a memorial program at Connecticut College the following summer. Graham and Horst were there, and despite the sadness of the occasion Graham was able to relax and turn back the clock to the less artificial days when she and Horst worked together to establish Graham's reputation. At the traditional faculty dinner meeting at the end of the session, Graham sat on the arm of Horst's comfortable stuffed chair and put her arm across his shoulder as she listened to the various reports.

She continued to be surrounded by activity. In the beginning of 1959, she somewhat surprisingly joined with George Balanchine of the New York City Ballet to work on a common project. It was to be a unique experience for both of them, since neither had previously worked with a choreographer of stature from a totally different dance discipline. Balanchine was a pure classicist, the successor to the school of ballet established by Petipa, and in his own way quite as revolutionary as Graham. His work within the more established vocabulary of movement that is ballet had set the style of American ballet just as Graham's own work had created the style of modern dance movement that had been adopted most often by dance departments in American colleges. Their collaboration, in fact, would be the first between two leaders of their respective disciplines. The collaboration had been proposed by Lincoln Kirstein as a cooperative work for New York City Ballet. Graham, however, had her own agenda.

The project did not start particularly well. The two choreographers, who were to have their first meeting at 9:30 A.M. at the Graham studio, were kept waiting outside nearly twenty minutes before the door was unlocked by a staff member who had overslept. Cecil Beaton was the costume designer for the project, and the music was to be selected by Graham from the orchestral scores of Anton von Webern. Graham, however, preferred to work with a commissioned score. Furthermore, she had always had a strong hand in costume design. Despite these difficulties, she went on to create a dance, called "Episodes," about the confrontation between Mary, Queen of Scots, and Elizabeth I in their struggle for the throne of England. Graham danced the doomed Mary. For his part of the collaboration Balanchine created an ironic and spare suite of episodic dances, each self-contained and wittily terse.

Although the basic idea of the collaboration was to use the members of the New York City Ballet as much as possible for both halves of the program, this idea did not appeal to Graham at all. Instead of objecting directly, she choreographed her section of the work so that it drew on all of the virtuoso skills inherent in the Graham technique, which would be exceptionally difficult for a classically trained ballet dancer. After preparing a section of this difficult material, she had her own Company demonstrate for Balanchine. This, she announced, is what she proposed for the New York City Ballet dancers. It was obviously impossible on short notice and conceivably might not have been possible even with more rehearsal time. Thus she forced the first break in the original concept. Graham would use her own Company for her portion of the dances, with perhaps one or two members of the New York City Ballet (one of them, Sally Wilson, would dance Elizabeth I), and Balanchine would use only his dancers, with the exception of Paul Taylor from the Graham Company. It was a costly victory for Graham, since she now had to find the money to pay for her own dancers. But she was determined to present her Company and her technique on an equal footing with the New York City Ballet.

Although she had based much of the material for the dance on Stefan Zweig's biography of Mary, Graham suddenly decided to include in the dance an episode unrelated to Zweig's book. Announcing that she needed tennis racquets, she asked her company administrator, Leroy Leatherman, to find her a pair. She then began to choreograph a tennis game for herself and Elizabeth. Finding that she needed more music than was provided in the length of Webern's "Passacaglia," she went to the studio where Balanchine was working with two of his dancers, Jacques d'Amboise and Diana Adams, on a pas de deux. When Graham requested more music, Balanchine without hesitation offered the music that he had been using for the pas and went to work with another of Webern's scores. Between them, they eventually used all seven of Webern's orchestral works. Graham's "tennis game" turned out to be one of the most successful sections of her dance, and Balanchine's pas de deux was never seen.

Another aspect of the collaboration that left her dissatisfied was costume design. Graham, of course, had always either done her own costumes or had a strong hand in determining them. Beaton's sketches were not to her liking, although she retained one of his striking design ideas—a self-supporting dress that stood stiffly onstage when Mary stepped out of it, like a prisoner released from a cage. Ultimately, Graham accepted most of the costumes and then extensively reworked them.

Graham worked on the choreography in her customary solitary way. She repeatedly listened to the music in the privacy of her studio and from time to time would call one of the principal dancers for private work and then the entire Company for a group rehearsal in the large studio. To indicate that she did not wish to be disturbed, she tied a cloth around the handles of the studio door, a sign respectfully honored by all. At the approach of the premiere at the New York City Center, Graham went off to Elizabeth Arden's on Fifth Avenue for beauty treatments and a massage. This was now something that she did periodically throughout the year and always before the opening of a season.

During the rehearsal period for "Episodes," de Rothschild sponsored evenings of chamber music at the school. On one of these evenings, when singer Patricia Neway and a string quartet were performing in the main studio on the ground floor, the Company was rehearsing upstairs. William Dugan, who worked for the foundation and greeted people at the door, saw the knob on the street door turn slowly, the door jerk open, and Graham enter—staggering, holding onto the door, and then lurching to grab hold of the wall. She obviously had been drinking and was almost unable to stand. Noticing Dugan, she paused and said "Good evening" in a little voice. Then, collecting herself, she carefully headed upstairs to her private rehearsal studio. And so the work went on and was finished.

"Episodes" was politely received, and certain elements of the production were praised, but the contrast in styles between the dances of Graham and Balanchine were so great that it was hard to see the work as a collaboration. Each had taken some music and created a ballet in his own familiar style for the dancers with whom he ordinarily worked. The result was an inelegant hybrid.

Graham soon lost interest in her portion of the ballet and never included it in her repertory. Balanchine retained most of his portion for inclusion in the regular repertory of the New York City Ballet. He had created a strong solo for Paul Taylor, but, because he showed no interest in having anyone else do it, it was dropped. What remained, therefore, from the "collaboration" of the two major figures in American dance were fragments in the repertory of the ballet company and nothing whatsoever in Graham's active repertory.

Given Graham's total disinterest in cooperative ventures, it is perhaps amazing that anything of substance was done in the first place, and that anything at all remains. But it is not surprising that what remains is Balanchine's.

In 1960 Graham received the Capezio award. The citation read:

> To Martha Graham, distinguished dancer, choreographer, innovator, who has never compromised in her pursuit of dance exploration and who has, over her years of service to dance in America, continuously expanded her horizons to include the first major program-long work in modern dance, "Clytemnestra"; successful collaboration with the art of ballet in the Balanchine-Graham "Episodes"; and an impressive ambassadorship in taking her powerful version of American Dance to audiences in Europe, the Middle East, and the Orient.

The words were delivered by William Schuman, who had worked so well with Graham, and they reflected the feelings of an entire generation. It was a sign of her strength and her deep creativity that she had undertaken two of her most difficult tasks toward the end of her performing career.

In the spring Graham had a season at the Adelphi Theater, where she presented "Acrobats of God," a dance that was charmingly comic in a way that had been foreign to her work for several years. The set was again by Noguchi, who gave her a broad ballet barre upon which the dancers of the piece, playing dancers, could perch and do their exercises. At one point, a group lay on their backs beneath it and did mirror-image movements with those who were above the barre. The score by Carlos Surinach called for three mandolin players to be seated onstage. In addition, there was a little stool for Graham and a hanging screen-panel that came down to hide her face.

The initial intention of the work was not comic. It had been conceived as a serious exposition of the difficulties in the lives of the creative and the interpretive artist. The creative artist in this case was Graham, playing a choreographer, and she was being driven by her regisseur, who carried a long whip. The dancers displayed their technique in countless crossovers, going from one side of the stage to another, doing leaps, falls, tumbles, runs, and complicated duets.

Rehearsals for the piece were chaotic. Graham was having great difficulty in pulling the creative threads together. She was working compulsively but without great inspiration and was relying heavily on alcohol to keep her going. By then, her minimum consumption was a quart a day. Her rehearsal pianist, Robert Dunn, thought at the time: "God must have given her one of the most extraordinary bodies that He ever made." Graham's drinking was a complex affair. Dunn believes that she never admitted her dependence upon alcohol. She once spoke to him about some people, who were drunk at a party, saying, "I can't stand that sort of thing."

But then her body began to swell from liver trouble, and she would faint. She was frustrated and so muzzy at times during rehearsals that either Dunn or she would send everyone out of the room, one by one. Sometimes Dunn was the last to stay, and sometimes Bertram Ross, her lead male dancer. But the trio was always the same: Ross, Dunn, and Graham.

At times she would faint in the middle of a passage, and Ross would hold her. She would start up, say something about her solo, and then slump over with Ross supporting her. After a few moments she would recover and indicate a few other movements. Ross and Dunn were worried, and Dunn told Craig Barton how difficult the situation was. It was a week before the premiere and Barton spoke to Graham. Lecturing her about anything was risky, but this time she listened and quit drinking entirely. Periodically during the week she would sit in the studio and twist her hands, saying in a small voice, "Oh! I'm so thirsty."

"Acrobats of God" included a great deal of material choreographed by members of the Company, which Graham would edit on the basis of her feeling about its suitability in the over-all design of the piece. "Acrobats" did not achieve its final form until the morning of the premiere. The bits and pieces of the dance were not seen by a live audience or even in the studio in a complete run-through until the first performance. By the morning of the premiere, Graham had put together the ensemble portions but had not yet devised her own dancing with David Wood, the overseer in the piece, the hard taskmaster with a whip—who in fact functioned as the Company regisseur and had a reputation for being a disciplinarian.

She had made a few basic decisions. She was not going to do much dancing and had therefore designed a tight striped skirt for herself which would hobble her movements onstage, restricting them to quick little steps. In effect, she was to assume the type of narrative role, though in mime, that she had created for herself in the lecture demonstrations. David Wood's stern driving figure, who would prod Graham and keep her at her task, suggested the two men in her life: Hawkins, who was the strong ringmaster in "Every Soul Is a Circus," and Horst, who would keep her in the studio working, as she once had told her Company, when she "wanted to go to the movies or eat ice cream."

With the Company parts out of the way, Graham worked with Wood and Dunn on the morning of the premiere in order to complete the dance. She was to be onstage during the entire piece, coming out or retiring behind the panel that hung in front of her chair. All had to work at top speed. Graham asked for the amount of musical time that was allotted to each section. When Dunn supplied the number of measures, Wood would then indicate what he had been given to dance, since his part was more or less set. Graham would then devise movement for herself, and Wood adjusted his part as required. They proceeded through the score in short bursts, until finally it was completed. But in her own mind Graham was not entirely sure of the emotional tone of the piece. That evening when the curtain went up and the music started, the audience began to laugh. Graham picked up on the humor immediately and played the dance for its wit and comedy. She was not able to focus the work in preparation, but she trusted her instincts onstage.

"God! What a thing to go on that night," recalls Dunn. "I think it was being regarded as a very abstract ballet. I don't know how it was defined to Noguchi. Martha didn't know exactly what it was to be. It was intended as a serious piece when we were rehearsing it, although the corps had put in some lighter moments. But when the audience began to laugh, Martha began to camp it up. She caught on just like that to the whole thing, in the middle of the strain of trying to follow my verbal direction from the wings and musical direction from the pit, and glancing at the notes taped to the panel in front of the stool."

Graham was so pleased with the reception that the next day she gave Dunn two jade tortoise seals, Chinese longevity symbols, and told him, "In such a case, when you make a gift, it must be a sacrifice." Despite the somewhat helter-skelter manner in which it was composed, "Acrobats" became one of the stand-bys of the Graham repertory. The title of the dance was taken from a Latin phrase, "athleti dei," used in referring to the monks who wrestled in spiritual combat for the salvation of their souls. Graham had first used the phrase publicly in her address at Connecticut College several years earlier.

That summer, after repeated requests from Shawn, she appeared with her lecture demonstration, "A Question of Image," at the Jacob's Pillow Dance Festival. The occasion came about by chance. Graham's response to Shawn's invitation was a spur-of-the-moment decision, like so much else in her life and career. Walter Terry, who had been scheduled to speak, postponed his talk to accommodate her. Now one of the last breaches had been healed.

Continued support by de Rothschild made possible Graham's annual spring season in New York and the small series of films that documented her work. In 1961, "Night Journey" was filmed, and in the spring Graham brought out two new dances, both about classical temptresses: Cleopatra, in "One More Gaudy Night," and Delilah, in "Visionary Recital." The first dance was humorous in tone, and the second dramatically serious, but in both she examined the ambivalent effect of the two women, whose passion seduces a man from the rigorous path of duty. The Company that she assembled at this time was one of the strongest she had ever had. Ethel Winter had a leading role in "Gaudy Night," and the following year Graham relinquished her own role in "Visionary Recital" to Mary Hinkson.

The Company was a balanced though restless ensemble of junior and senior dancers. Graham's regular seasons and the Far and Middle Eastern tour had attracted scores of young and talented students from all over the world. By exposing dancers to modern dance in a concentrated dose for the first time, the tours awakened interest that otherwise would not have existed.

Graham's next tour for the State Department, a trip to Continental Europe and the Middle East, was now being planned. To honor de Rothschild, Graham scheduled the premiere of a new work, a dance inspired by a Biblical subject, in Israel, and she arranged for two Israeli artists, composer Mordecai Seter and designer Dani Karavan, to assist her. This was the first time that the premiere of a Graham work had ever been given outside the United States with two local artists as collaborators.

In the spring of 1962 Graham based another dance, "Phaedra," on Greek legend, this time selecting the story of Phaedra's lust for young Hippolytus, her stepson. At one side of the stage, in a valentine-shaped prop, lurks Venus, goddess of love. Hippolytus stands behind a column of shutters, which Venus (Graham) opens from time to time in order to peer at him. At the front of the stage is a couch on which Phaedra agonizes in passion. Spurned by Hippolytus, she pretends to her husband, Theseus, that Hippolytus has made improper advances, thus setting Theseus in a murderous rage. An extremely strong piece, this dance examined the turbulence of frustrated passion in frank dramatic terms. In keeping with its directness, a directness that later was to spark an effort to censor Graham, its costuming revealed the male physique as do Olympic swim trunks. Graham herself performed more dramatic action than actual dancing, cleverly shaping the work so that the bulk of the movement would be carried by others. The dance was well received, and Graham decided to include it on her forthcoming tour.

In the summer, after receiving an honorary doctorate from Wheaton College, Graham attended the Connecticut College dance festival and presented a Company dance in which she did not appear. "Secular Games," a light frolic, began with the men in the Company standing on low platforms and tossing a ball to one another, each doing a short solo. In the second section, the women of the Company danced as if in reverie when one, then another of the men appeared to dance with them. The duets were threatened by still other men, who entered throwing the ball back and forth. In the end the men paired off successfully with other girls—except for one man who remained alone, idly tossing the ball. Like most Graham dances that did not include a role for herself, it had a lighter and less intense emotional quality. It was left to the younger members of the Company to disport themselves and project the joyousness of dance movement. The weight of Graham's own emotional tangles and now her diminished physical skills precluded such joy. The décor was executed by Jean Rosenthal, Graham's lighting designer since the early 1940's. This was the second set that Rosenthal had done for Graham; she had designed "One More Gaudy Night" the previous year.

In the fall before the tour, the New School for Social Research dedicated its oval dance studio to Graham. This was the same place in which she had her confrontation with Fokine. Fittingly, John Martin presided at the dedication ceremonies, recalling the decade of the 1930's in which he and Graham with others of the heroic generation had collaborated in a series of dance lectures there. In commemoration, the top part of Jocasta's bed from Noguchi's set for "Night Journey" was installed in the room; later, a bronze casting of the rocking chair from "Appalachian Spring" was substituted for it. Frances Steloff, who had guaranteed Graham's first public performance with a loan of $1,000, arrived late and was at the edge of the crowd when Graham spotted her. With one of her warm, kind gestures, Graham made a point of lavishing attention on Steloff and praising her generosity. This she often did, to Steloff's pleased embarrassment.

In Israel in October, Graham was tremendously successful as she had been the two previous times she had been there. "Legend of Judith" was particularly well received. Before anyone had seen the set he had designed, Dani Karavan was worried about its suitability. Contrary to the usual practice of working with stage properties in the studio, the Company had rehearsed the dance without the set. Because the piece was being constructed in Israel, Graham had only a small model to work with. When Karavan took her to the carpenter's shop to see it, she was so delighted that she immediately took off her shoes and started to dance on it.

At a press conference, she handled an awkward question with her usual gift for quotable explanations. When asked whether she adopted for this dance the modern Israeli notions of Biblical dancing, she responded with a smile, "I do not brings coals to Newcastle or the Bible to Israel." The two weeks of performances carried the Company from the major cities to the outlying kibbutzim. Later, in New York, Israeli dance students in increasing numbers began to turn up at the Graham school through scholarships arranged by de Rothschild.

During the following month, the tour went from Ankara to Athens to Belgrade and Zagreb. Graham's was the first modern dance company ever seen in this part of the world. The reception in Yugoslavia was comparable to that received by the Company in Tokyo on the Far Eastern tour in 1955–56. "Clytemnestra" was received with exceptional enthusiasm. Each night at the theater during a cold November, crowds were waiting to greet the Company. The reception one evening was so intense that, after the usual curtain calls, Graham took a personal call with each member of the cast, and still the audience wanted more. Both Graham and the Company were elated and exhausted, and the fire curtain was rung down several times before the crowd dispersed.

Moving north, they played Cologne, Oslo, Helsinki, and a return appearance at The Hague. The reception everywhere was excellent, although the Company was unaware that in Cologne two Americans in the audience, Peter Freylinghuysen of New Jersey and Edna Kelley of New York, members of the House of Representatives, had been offended by one of the Company's dances, "Phaedra," which they thought obscene and resolved to do something about.

The tour ended in Germany, a first visit for Graham's Company, and several of the English papers sent their critics to see her. In sharp contrast to the reaction in 1954, which was mostly one of vilification, the press reception now was universally favorable, and it therefore seemed a good idea for Graham to return to England. The cultural attaché in London, Francis Mason, agreed but recognized that the State Department, which sponsored a tour in 1962, would probably not sponsor one in 1963. He therefore began to agitate politely but insistently to have Graham invited through other channels. Mason was uniquely qualified to twist cultural arms, for he spoke not only with conviction but also with knowledge of his subject. In New York he had broadcast a series of programs devoted to dance, and he had also edited *Balanchine's Complete Stories of the Great Ballets*. His efforts, with the help of the now sympathetic English press, resulted in an invitation to Graham from the Edinburgh Festival for an appearance in August 1963. It was not a complete tour yet, but it was a start.

At home Graham was asked if she would accept an honorary degree from Wayne State University at the same time they conferred one on Louis Horst. She agreed, and in June they posed together after the ceremony in mortarboards and gowns. Horst's citation read in part:

> As musician, artistic advisor, teacher, editor, critic, and author, Louis Horst has influenced immeasurably the careers of leading modern dancers who have set out on new paths of creativeness in this age-old art. The breadth and depth of his knowledge of music literature, his skill as a composer for dance, and his insistence on principles of artistic integrity helped Martha Graham during the years of their association to reach her present eminence in the art of dance.

Graham's citation was also effusive but accurate:

> Transforming a theatrical diversion into a dramatic art form, Martha Graham has established dance not only as an extension

> of her unique personality but also as a new concept, as an expressive idiom that has profoundly influenced and molded the aesthetics and composition of dance today. In one of the major revolutions in modern art, she withdrew from the romantic tradition and formalized conventions of classical ballet to redefine the structure and content of the dance medium.

In the midst of all these accolades were a few disturbing elements. Graham was being sued by a former pupil, Irene Eskin, for damages inflicted to her back in a class, and Representatives Freylinghuysen and Kelley were preparing an assault on Graham's fitness to receive support from the State Department.

Graham, meanwhile, turned to the 1963 festival in Edinburgh. Since she had been invited, she wanted to present a new dance. This time she chose the legend of Circe, the siren who turned men into beasts and tempted Ulysses when he visited her island. Graham commissioned a score from Alan Hovhaness, who had composed the score for "Ardent Song," the dance she premiered in London in 1954. As August drew near, it seemed clear that Edinburgh was the only place Graham would be seen in the British Isles that year.

Then a man named Robin Howard decided to do something more than wring his hands about it. Howard was one of the handful of people who had seen Graham during her first season in London. He himself was a restaurant and hotel proprietor who was interested in dance but who had no official connections with the dance world. Howard had attended a Graham program at the insistence of friends and, though he was not immediately an advocate of modern dance, found it more interesting than any other theatrical dance he had seen. Graham's approach had a vitality that compelled his attention. Discovering in 1963 that Graham had been invited only to Edinburgh, Howard, who had no theatrical experience, in one of those mad gestures that rational individuals sometimes make, decided to produce a two-week London season for Graham after the festival. In its most basic theatrical sense, "producing" means assuming financial responsibility. It may also mean bringing together talented collaborators, as well as a host of other things, but the ultimate job of the producer is to pay for something to happen. Though Howard was a successful businessman, he was by no means rich. Even with a verbal pledge of £5,000 from Lord Harewood, who invited the Company to the Edinburgh Festival, Howard had to be prepared to put up £10,000 of his own money. He took the plunge, and his life changed radically. He became a fanatical supporter of Graham and her technique and eventually established a school and a company based upon her style of dance theater.

Howard's first problem in getting the London season under way was the finding of a suitable theater, which was difficult on short notice. He finally had to settle for The Prince of Wales, a thoroughly inadequate house with a shallow stage and several irritating crotchets, such as a buzzer that the audience heard each time the curtain was lowered and a dubious electrical system that on opening night left the house lights on until a resourceful patron turned them out.

Blundering through with the zeal of a crusader, Howard made the London season happen. The London critics who went to Edinburgh wrote glowing reviews, so that the houses for the London performances were nearly all sold out. Graham brought with her an almost totally new program, including only two works ("Night Journey" and "Diversion of Angels") that she had presented in her 1954 season. On opening night "Legend of Judith" was presented, and during the performance it became clear that an arched structure that Graham had to ascend in the course of the dance had not been adequately secured. It was particularly dangerous because Graham was slightly drunk. Few in the theater audience recognized the danger, but for those who did it was an anxious time. Graham was an amazing sixty-nine. Luckily, the dance ended without incident. An added hazard was Graham's dash into a nest of spears that were thrust out of the wings. These were made of sharpened metal and were not rubber-tipped, and Graham's course toward them was erratic. After a near miss, the stage manager, George Bardyguine, decided to handle the spear cart personally to reduce the chance of accident.

Despite the opening night perils, the glaring inadequacies of The Prince of Wales, and the haste with which the season was put together (the Company was able to rehearse on stage only the morning of the opening night), London was ready for a Graham success and gave it to her. The foolish and sometimes cruel voices that earlier had muttered about her seeming oddities and the fact that she danced barefoot were replaced by voices of praise. The season was a triumph.

Just at this point, by coincidence, Representatives Freylinghuysen and Kelley were testifying in Washington before a House Foreign Affairs subcommittee about, of all things, artistic matters.

They had found Graham's "Phaedra" "erotic" and so offensive that they wanted to walk out on the performance. Their remarks were a strong attempt to censor a creative artist, specifically, to deprive her of government funds in the form of State Department–sponsored tours. The story was picked up by the London papers, which sent reporters to question Graham as to whether she was going to defend herself. She replied, "I don't have to defend myself. The public will defend me." And not just the public, for the State Department itself defended Graham as one of its sounder cultural choices. Freylinghuysen and Kelley thus failed in their dim efforts at censorship. Indeed, the result of their activities was to generate a warm public welcome for Graham when she returned to New York and a sold-out house for the opening night of a two-week season at the Lunt-Fontanne Theater.

But then, during the season, came a discordant note: comments about Graham's age. Europe had praised her, the State Department had praised her, and then, when she came home, she was criticized for being too old. It was this kind of criticism that hurt. Though it had become increasingly difficult for Graham to dance as once she had, the wonder was that she could still dance as she did. Because she had made subtle and not so subtle choreographic adjustments in order to continue to appear onstage, it was true that she didn't "dance" in the usual sense. She had perfected an extremely effective type of dramatic mime that, in particular, carried her through "Clytemnestra" in beautiful fashion; yet it was obvious that motion was becoming more and more difficult for her. Criticism about her performance ability was to grow as the years went by. Her public's reaction was to regard such comment as impertinence.

The damage suit by Graham's former student went against Graham to the cost of $49,000. The student accepted a settlement of $25,000 to avoid a court appeal by Graham, and since Graham, of course, was penniless, the settlement was paid by the foundation still so generously supported by de Rothschild.

For several years de Rothschild had wanted to become more closely involved with the cultural and scientific life of Israel and, in fact, to live there permanently. She had been granting individuals money to perform and to teach in their own studios in Tel Aviv. She had also established a scholarship fund for Israeli students to travel to the United States to study at the Graham studio. But this was scattered activity, and de Rothschild had not been able to see the direction in which it was leading. Graham's success on her Israeli tours encouraged de Rothschild to think of establishing in Israel a company based on Graham's training and performing some of the great works that Graham had created for her own Company. When she had originally spoken to Graham about this the answer was neither yes nor no. Graham chose her own moment to respond. During an intermission of a performance of "Clytemnestra" in Edinburgh, she agreed to help.

There was a similar development in England. After the successful London season, in which Robin Howard lost only a portion of his guarantee and gained much critical praise, he asked Graham to hold auditions for dancers to study her technique with her in the United States. Howard provided travel and subsistence money and Graham agreed to furnish free lessons. The idea was that ultimately the dancers chosen would return to England to form the teaching framework of a Graham-oriented school and eventually a company. From the fifteen dancers who applied, Graham picked three: Eileen Cropley-Cartwright, Christian Holder, and Anna Price. (Cropley eventually became a featured dancer in the Paul Taylor Dance Company, and Holder joined the Joffrey Ballet Company.) Though it was a modest start, it provided the beginnings of modern dance in England.

This was the first time that American modern dance had ever attempted to transplant itself to other cultures. The development of each of these companies was to be quite different. In England, the dominant form of serious theatrical dance was and is ballet. Everything else has been looked upon as a curio, as Graham's work was initially referred to in England. Yet until the formation of several companies in the 1930's, after the collapse of the Russian ballet of Serge Diaghilev, ballet had been a dormant art in England and had been seen only when brought by visiting companies from the Continent. Historical precedents were often adduced to indicate a tradition of ballet, but they were so tenuous as to be meaningless. Until English dancers had trained with the Diaghilev company or members of that company had settled in England, there was no English dance tradition outside of folk dance. Ballet, however, which evolved from court dance and contained in its upright and noble carriage traces of aristocratic bearing, was appealing to British audiences. Ballet schools quickly began to attract pupils, and by the mid-1960's England had several companies including one of world standing, The Royal Ballet.

Robin Howard, in thinking of a Graham-based company, attempted to go against the tide by introducing a style of dramatic dance movement that welcomed seeming deformity and showed the body twisted and driven by convolutions of the spirit. It was an exceptionally brave gesture, and Howard set about his work like a disciple following the irresistible lead of a master. He sold his hotel and eventually his restaurant, and devoted all of his energy to supporting his new undertaking.

When his first instructors came back from the United States, he organized classes for students and used whatever studio space was available. Until he found and purchased a building suitable for a school, he formed an impromptu motor pool to transport his teachers from one place to another. He invited Robert Cohan of the Graham Company to be his artistic adviser, chief teacher, and choreographer. He incorporated his group under the somewhat elusive title of "The Contemporary Ballet Trust," assuming that the term "modern dance" would mean little or nothing to the members of the British Arts Council, the government funding body that supported the arts, and that "contemporary ballet" would at least indicate that the dancing was serious, even though it might not be traditional.

From Graham, the English company received some encouragement, one dance, "El Penitente," and trained teachers from her school and Company, who were slowly making progress with the young dancers who went to New York for instruction. The first obstacle that most of them had to overcome was a form of polite reticence that kept them from attacking the Graham movement in the strong, aggressive manner in which it was meant to be handled. But eventually they began to grasp the energy level of the technique, and so a small company was formed.

Cohan prepared his student dancers for performance with work of his own devising. With their first appearance they began to achieve more confidence, and the school started to attract more pupils. To perform is, of course, to advertise oneself and not to perform is, in the theatrical world, not to exist for any practical purposes. It was helpful that large numbers of modern dancers, including former members of the Graham Company such as Merce

Cunningham and Paul Taylor, also began to have London seasons. Their appearances helped to create a climate of opinion favorable to accepting modern dance as an art form with a special vitality of its own, and this, in turn, helped to create a favorable climate of opinion toward the Contemporary Ballet Trust. By way of freshening the school's curriculum, Graham dancers touring in London with other companies were asked to give guest classes. The process of establishing the company moved with great care, not only because of initial resistance but because of modest financing. Yet the dedicated energy of everyone connected with the group, along with astute management and an increasing yearly stipend from the Arts Council, produced a viable organization that incorporated itself into the theatrical fabric of the country as well as into the educational system. It was a long, difficult process the outcome of which is yet to be fully determined. But, in 1969, six years after Howard made the second London season possible, the newly named London Contemporary Dance Ensemble was able to perform in its own theater, The Place, which was officially opened by the head of the Arts Council, Lord Goodman. The fitting centerpiece on the opening program was "El Penitente."

The progress of the Graham related company in Israel was a far different story. There the company called itself the Batsheva Dance Company, taking its name from the Hebrew original of Bethsabee de Rothschild's first name. There was no classical dance company in Israel, and the only form of dance seen with any regularity was a form of modern dance or folk dancing that had been brought into the country by settlers. The new company and school together did not have to fight any established taste but could immediately turn to the task of creating its own style. It also had the substantial financial support of de Rothschild. Further, the character of the Israeli students who appeared in New York was markedly different from that of the English students. The Israelis were more akin in character to the Americans—Americans of the wild West rather than New England, Dodge City rather than Cambridge. The energy level of these students was high, their temperament was unruly, and they took to the Graham technique with great skill and enthusiasm.

There were constant streams of teachers from the Graham school and Company, and Graham herself went to Israel to teach in the Batsheva school and, uncharacteristically, to coach Israeli dancers in her roles. Her relationship to the company was intimate, and she was officially listed as its artistic director. Altogether, she gave the Israeli company the following works: "Embattled Garden," "Cave of the Heart," "Diversion of Angels," and "Herodiade." Working in the latter dance with the American-born Israeli dancer Rena Glück, Graham spent hours helping her get the right inflections, explaining that the little pattern of steps at right angles in the beginning of the dance set the tone of the entire piece. This pattern of patient and understanding coaching was one Graham followed consistently with the Israeli dancers. Glück was impressed with Graham's graciousness when she first met her at the airport, and she was doubly impressed, driving back, by the way Graham put Glück's little daughter Dalit on her lap and played with her. Both on the occasion of Glück's final mastering of the role and after opening night, Graham gave her a book of Hokusai prints.

De Rothschild, who had moved permanently to Israel when the company was started, was delighted at the attention Graham gave to the preparation and teaching of Batsheva. Many in Graham's Company, however, resented it. Graham was turning over to the Batsheva dancers roles that had taken members of her own Company years to acquire, and the Batsheva dancers, they felt, were receiving them too rapidly to be able to appreciate the privilege.

De Rothschild's involvement in the Israeli company and her interest in her protégé, Jeanette Ordman, one of its dancers, was occupying more and more of her time. She became progressively less concerned with the fortunes of the parent Company in New York, and accordingly Graham began to spend less time in Israel, though she maintained contact. When she began to disengage herself from active participation in Batsheva, it was well established, though it did not have a reputation outside Israel. Without Graham's attention, however, there was a real lack of firm leadership, and de Rothschild needed help. Graham asked Jane Dudley, who had been in her Company years previously, to take on the job. When Dudley declined, Graham said simply, "Think about it." It was not a command—Graham was not in a position to command. Rather it was an intuitive thrust, to which Dudley ultimately responded by accepting the job. Graham, with her inner sense, had divined what Dudley had at first not seen. Dudley shaped the company for its first successful tour of Europe and then was succeeded by a series of teachers and artistic directors, who either had studied with Graham (like Norman Walker or Brian Macdonald) or had been members of her Company (like William Louther). The company has so far twice toured the United States to warm critical receptions, although the response was a little less enthusiastic on its second visit in 1972.

12

The Closing Circle

"We have so little time to
be born to this instant."
St. John Perse

In 1964 Horst died. Although Horst and Graham had not collaborated for fifteen years, not collaborating and simply not being are two different things. With Horst's death, a piece of Graham's life was taken away that no one else could supply. Louis had believed in Graham and had kept her working when almost no one else had heard of her, and those who had, thought of her as a show girl for the Greenwich Village Follies. Now she had the reputation that Horst had wanted for her, but Horst himself was gone. It was a painful closing of another chapter. As one of the executors of his estate, Graham destroyed all personal correspondence between them. As in the case of her mother's estate, this was a systematic attempt to destroy any evidence of the past.

The organizers of the Connecticut College dance festival wanted to pay tribute to Horst the following summer with three Graham dances that he had composed: "Primitive Mysteries," "Frontier," and "El Penitente."

It was early spring, and Graham, still involved in preparing the

Batsheva company, was scheduled to go to Israel, so she left the job of re-creating the pieces for Horst's memorial program to her Company and to former Company members. She had agreed to revive the dances if they were put together without her and if she approved of the way they looked when she returned.

Without her it was not likely that the dances could be remounted, for there were few notes of any kind. "Primitive Mysteries" presented the greatest difficulties. Some photographs existed, along with a few notes scribbled on the music, but nothing looked promising. The music—chords on the piano and a melody for flute and oboe—was very bare, so that when Eugene Lester, now the Company conductor, started to play for rehearsals he found it very difficult to phrase. The dance could be restaged only through probing the memories of the dancers who had performed it at various times. David Wood called the original members of the Company for their help, and most came to the Graham studio to assist.

The attempt to reconstruct "Primitive Mysteries" was an odd and oddly personal experience for those involved, many of whom had not seen each other for years. As they began the job of assembling a dance that none of them had performed or seen in more than twenty-five years, they realized that nobody knew where to begin.

As Lester played the music, a few of them remembered where they had been on the stage and what their movements had been. Slowly a few pieces began to fit together. "Primitive Mysteries" was the first dance that Sophie Maslow had ever appeared in with Graham's Company, and obviously it had made a terrific impression on her; when no one else could remember a particular detail, Maslow was able to choreograph new movement in the original spirit of the dance. For Graham's current Company, watching the re-creation of "Primitive Mysteries" was fascinating. It was a dance from another time, well before their own.

"And then Martha came back from Israel," Maslow remembers, "and she looked at it, and I think she was surprised. First, I think she was surprised that anything had been put together. I think she was rather hoping it wouldn't be. And I think she was a little pleased, too. Probably surprised that it looked as good as it did."

But Graham had a surprise for Maslow. "She started to talk to the dancers [of the current Company] about the meaning of the dance," Maslow recalls. "And she began to talk about the main figure, the one in white as the Sabbath Queen! I stood there in absolute amazement. When I was in 'Primitive Mysteries,' I knew it was based on American Indian ritual and the Virgin Mary, and in reconstructing it that is what I talked about—about the Indian's mixture of Christianity and pagan ritual, and the mixture of the two that is in the dance: its primitive quality of movement and underneath it the Christian symbolism that the dance is based on. And now Martha was talking about the Sabbath Queen!"

But it was still the Graham of old. "Whatever Martha said, it was always valid," Maslow remembers. "She has a way of talking so that you suspend any kind of reasoning judgment. She can be very inspiring."

Graham, meanwhile, had been approached to create an opening dance program for the New York World's Fair of 1964–65. It was twenty-five years since the opening of the 1939–40 Fair, and time had taken its toll. Because Graham herself could not dance, she did two lecture demonstrations called "An Evening with Martha Graham" at Philharmonic Hall at the newly built Lincoln Center, which was just beginning to become the center of New York performing life. Using the risers ordinarily put onstage for the orchestra, she deployed as many of her dancers as possible and gave a two-part program. In the first half she spoke during the demonstration of the technique, explaining it and telling performance anecdotes in a humorous vein. The second half was a performance of "Secular Games." The whole program, which was presented in practice clothes, was masterfully conceived. Graham was at her best, using her voice evocatively to announce the wonder and sheer fun of movement as her Company displayed the virtuoso dancing of her technique. At one point she characterized a movement as a Burmese reviewer did: like an elephant that has run amok.

Just before the Connecticut series Graham went to Aspen, Colorado, to accept an award. She was genuinely delighted at the high mountains surrounding Aspen, for they reminded her of growing up in Southern California where the mountains came down almost to the sea. The award Graham received on this occasion was the Aspen Award in the Humanities, and she was the second person and the first dancer to be so honored. The citation read: "To Martha Graham, who as a creative dancer, choreographer, and company director has probed deeply those dark recesses of the human spirit and expressed essential truths which have awakened others to a new appreciation of man's nature." Unlike most honors, the award carried a grant of $30,000, valuable assistance to the ever penniless Graham.

"What can I say?" Graham asked her audience in Aspen. "You know, I speak without notes because I cannot read and look up and down, and besides, I wear glasses and I am very vain. So the main thing is, of course, that I can always look into faces. That's what I can do today, and when I do speak in a theater, I always ask that the lights be up enough so that I can see the eyes and the faces of those to whom I'm speaking. After all, they have made my life, they have shared in my life, and anything that I have done is a construction, really, helped by many, many, many thousands of people. . . .

"People have asked me why I chose to be a dancer. I did not choose to be a dancer. I was chosen to be a dancer, and with that you live all your life. When any young student asks me, 'Do you think I should be a dancer?' I always say, 'If you ask me that question, no! Only if there is only one way to make life vivid for yourself and for others, should you embark upon such a career. . . . You will know the wonders of the human body, because there is nothing more wonderful. The next time you look into the mirror, just look at the way the ears rest next to your head; look at the way the hair line grows; think of the little bones in your wrist; think of the magic of that foot, comparatively small, upon which your whole weight rests. It's a miracle. And the dance in all those areas is a celebration of that miracle. . . . There are two areas which you have to embark upon. One is the cultivation of the craft, which is in the school where you are working. The other is that something that sometimes is—and has to remain—entirely with you. This is the cultivation of the being from which whatever there is to say comes. It just doesn't come out of nowhere, it comes out of a great curiosity. It comes out of a desire to be an image maker, because that's what imagination means. It means only the ability to make images. But it means the ability to make those images, not as dehumanized things but as great figures. . . .

"It cost me a great deal of effort and a great deal of time, and everything and every minute has been treasured. The main thing, of course, always, is the fact that there is only one of you in the world, just one! You came from a certain background, you were born at a certain time—a certain instant in the history of the world. And as that you are unique. . . . They say every snowflake is different. I can well believe it. But you are unique, and if that is not fulfilled, then something has been lost. Ambition is not enough; necessity is everything. . . . I have always loved St. John Perse for giving me this line, which is in one of his poems, 'We have so little time to be born to this instant.' Thank you."

After the Connecticut College series, the Company opened a fall season of three weeks at the 54th Street Theater in New York. This season, one of the longest and most successful, revealed the breach between Graham and the generation that succeeded her. The repertory included the revival of "Appalachian Spring," the reconstructed "Primitive Mysteries," and two new dances, "The Witch of Endor" and "Part Real–Part Dream." The first, and the less interesting, of the new works drew on a Biblical story for its subject—this time the conflict between Saul and David. Graham, playing the figure of the soothsayer/witch/prophetess from beginning to end, created an uncharacteristically passive role for herself, physically removing herself from the action almost in direct proportion to the psychic distance that she put between herself and the protagonists. The conflict in the dance was between the old King Saul and the young David, and in the roles of Saul and David, Graham cast her two strongest senior dancers, Bertram Ross and Robert Cohan. Natural rivals, they were both aiding Graham in the running of the Company, and in the following season they would be billed as assistant co-directors.

Most of the creative effort appeared to have gone into "Part Real–Part Dream," in which Graham did not appear at all. The dance had extensive contributions by members of the Company; the music was commissioned from Mordecai Seter, and the settings from Dani Karavan, both of whom had worked on the very successful "Legend of Judith."

"Part Real–Part Dream" inhabited a sensuous twilight world in which motivations are obscure but seem to follow a course of rational action. The setting looked like an abstracted Persian illustration, with a fountain of beads, a metal screen of scrolls, and, lowered from the flies at one point, golden squiggles that resembled proto-alphabet characters. Two couples, played by Matt Turney and Bertram Ross, Mary Hinkson and Robert Cohan, frolicked and circled one another warily. At the beginning, unaccompanied by music, a woman (Mary Hinkson) slowly crossed the stage on a diagonal and shook a stick with fish-scale chimes dangling from it. After she passed, the music began, and the action of the dance started with Ross reaching out to touch Turney from behind the scroll screen. Later, Cohan revealed himself by turning a semicircular shield form halfway around. Hinkson returned and the men performed an involved dance with her, using her voluminous skirt to ensnare both her and themselves. At another point, Ross folded a piece of cloth so that it appeared to be a woman in a mantle whom he then danced a duet with. It was a technical feat of skill and particular beauty. The whole of the dance was costumed sumptuously and had an air of exotic eroticism—the flowering of desire in an imaginary hothouse which filters light through semiprecious panes of jasper, lapis lazuli, malachite, and jade.

During the season Graham permitted the reconstructed "Primitive Mysteries" to be given three performances, but she did not view any of them. Robin Howard, who was in New York to assist in the management of the Company, sat with Graham in her dressing room during two performances. She held his hand when the first bars of the music came over the intercom into her dressing room and did not release it until the piece was over. The pain that the memory of the piece caused her was obvious. Although "Frontier" too would have been welcomed by an audience that was not at all familiar with the early Graham repertory, she would not allow it to be performed.

The season exposed the strong rift between older and younger generations of modern dance in that those who had seen the earlier production of "Mysteries" did not like the newer production very much, while the younger viewers, who did not have direct experience with the previous productions, were enthusiastically impressed. They had not seen Graham's work when she was still expanding and consolidating her creative vocabulary. They were familiar only with the great theater pieces. On the other hand, these were dances that they could admire but that they found remote from their own nonnarrative and emotionally cooler time. "Mysteries" came as a revelation to them. Graham was not only a storyteller and dramatic dancer par excellence, but she also had a remarkable formal side to her imagination. "Mysteries" was an opportunity to see the young, developing Graham before the layers of theatrical magic descended on her shoulders and almost obscured the fact that she had created, out of her own appreciation of cultural necessities, a style of moving that was intricately and appropriately of the century.

"Primitive Mysteries" was soundly structured, rigorously ordered, and strong as granite. It came out of the anguish of Graham's whole being, and it could withstand any scrutiny. In its simplicity, integrity, and clarity it was of its time. It took a basic situation, the initiation of an individual into a society, and told the story in the most direct and economical of movements. There was nothing of theatrical glamour about it. The score did not call on the coloristic possibilities of a large symphony orchestra but drew rather on the plaintive and airy qualities of a flute and oboe, and used a piano for percussive punctuation. It also relied a great deal on silence. When the Company entered and exited from the stage between its three sections, one could hear the tread of feet in unison. The dance was an artistic entity with such utter confidence in its means that it did not hesitate to incorporate natural sounds. For a younger generation bedazzled with the *theater* of Martha Graham —the great cloak in "Clytemnestra," the empty dress in "Episodes, Part I"—the simple white dress of the central figure in "Primitive Mysteries" was a cleansing look into the career of Graham. Symbolically, it explained much of Graham's reputation to a segment of her audience that found it difficult to admire the work of a figure revered by the older generation.

It was clear that time had obscured the revolutionary aspects of Graham's work and had pushed to the fore the highly polished and sophisticated creations that developed from her early triumphs. The younger generation was finding it increasingly difficult to understand the basis for the Graham reputation. To younger eyes, accustomed to theatrical spareness in the presentation of dance, the theatrical works had an old-fashioned look. The superb polish of the Graham-trained dancer was so professional that many younger dancers wondered where the person of the dancer was beneath the glossiness of the technique. In addition, sexual anguish, one of the strong motivating elements in Graham's work, was of less moment to the younger generation. The generation that worried about sex was being replaced by a generation that, in effect, bypassed anxiety for action, deciding to feel its way rather than think its way through life. Martha Graham was a powerful remnant of another time and another set of values. She insisted that there was no freedom except that which one earned through discipline. The new generation of dancers, however, was preparing seriously to abandon technique in favor of a more natural style of movement in which they hoped to find a vocabulary that would relate more directly to the needs of their own time.

It was a cruel thought, that of being old-fashioned, especially when not so many years earlier she had been scored as the wildest of radicals. Graham had come full circle. She had lived long enough and created enough work to see herself pushed aside in the consciousness of the foremost younger choreographers, for other, more appealing models. Younger audiences found it difficult to look at her work with the same seriousness that they could bring to contemporary choreographers, who rarely had the same creative force as Graham. What they did have, however, was a degree of contemporaneity that Graham lacked.

But what separated Graham most from the generation that succeeded her was the question of movement, the very thing that had separated Graham's generation from the one it succeeded. The first step in the break came from the dancers that emerged from the Graham Company and school. They had ideas of their own as to what movement should look like. To Hawkins, the use of flow and subtle dynamics were most important; he evolved his own technique of movement by eliminating percussive stress to capture the look he was after. Cunningham was strongly attracted to the quick directional changes of ballet and the high darting look, which he achieved partly by purging his style of the strong emotional and expressive lines that Graham favored; and he sought to escape the dictatorship of gravity not by soaring against it continually, as the ballet dancer does, but by rapidly scanning the dance area in bursts and flurries of flickering movements. Paul Taylor added a sunny athleticism to the intense contortions of the Graham school and managed his own synthesis of movement from a combination of the floor-oriented Graham style and the airy antifloor aspirations of the ballet dancer. From these choreographers' companies still other choreographers emerged, further refining the techniques that they had acquired and creating movement that was now twice removed from the original source. It was no wonder that many young choreographers did not see the antecedents of their work in Graham's methods, no wonder that, to increasing numbers, she was old-fashioned.

But the work she had done she had done with fundamental thoroughness. She showed how important the use of the torso could be, and how useful and expressive an instrument it was. Even the traditional ballet dancer has a freer torso today because of Graham's work. In the modern dance world, the spine, Graham's "tree of life," became the most important element of dance and the basis for most of the newer styles of movement. Graham de-emphasized the use of the leap and strongly emphasized the use of the upper body, thereby toning down the "jumping jack" aspect of dancing. She dared to stand still and concentrate energy and dramatic force by simply refusing to be hurried into movement just because it had always been done that way. She emphasized the idea of movement as necessity, not just as a time- or space-filling expediency. One moved because there was a reason to move; each element of a dance grew out of that which went before. Graham did not string combinations of steps together as one might assemble unrelated bits of movements. By the seriousness and integrity with which she reached her decisions, she forced even people who disagreed with her to strengthen their own.

The November 1965 season at the 54th Street Theater was one of the longest in any one theater in Graham's entire career and showed a more rounded picture of her talent than had any season since the Hurok tours just after World War II. But the emotion conjured up by "Primitive Mysteries" was too painful, and, in planning a national tour the following year, she dropped it from active repertory once again.

It had been twenty years since Graham had made a coast-to-coast tour, but now a substantial grant from the newly formed National Council on the Arts made it possible for her to take the Company across the country once again. The grant gave $40,000 outright for the creation of new dances and an additional $41,000 for the tour, which had to be matched with funds from private sources. Katharine Cornell began the solicitation of funds with a publicity letter that mentioned a gift of $50,000 to the Graham Foundation * by Lila Acheson Wallace. With the assistance of the Rockefeller

* Before de Rothschild moved to Israel she provided the foundation framework so that Graham would still be able to attract tax-deductible contributions from those interested in her work.

Foundation, the money was matched, and the tour was set. Hurok booked it, and the Company prepared for the fall journey that would take them through thirty cities in eight weeks—led by a woman, it is difficult to keep in mind, who was over seventy years old. In June, Graham received honorary degrees from Harvard University and Mills College, thus adding to the collection that she was accumulating at an accelerated rate.

Whenever the local reviewer was not, in fact, moved to superlatives, the tour received, at the least, deferential respect. In Santa Barbara, where the Company started its Western tour, a special ceremony was planned. Graham was greeted with a lavish show of enthusiasm. Her surviving relatives in Santa Barbara—a cousin, Mrs. William Pierce, and an aunt, Mrs. Mary Bear—were proudly present and beaming for the occasion. The mayor, Don MacGillivray, declared November 7, 1966, "Martha Graham Day" and awarded her a ribboned proclamation of the event and a certificate of honorary citizenship. During the ceremony, Graham was presented with two old programs, which she was asked to autograph. A local citizen, I. A. Bonilla, had somehow managed to save a program listing Graham's 1911 appearance as a geisha in *A Night In Japan* and one of the high school graduating class play, *Prunella*, given in 1913. "This is a cruel thing to do to a dancer," she said, referring to the distant dates that betrayed her age.

At the reception held in Santa Barbara's Museum of Fine Arts, Graham was greeted by a brass-band fanfare, escorted to her seat by usherettes in Grecian costumes, and serenaded with a selection of songs by madrigal singers. In addition to the purely honorary aspects of the day, two groups of local citizens, under the respective names of the Committee for Martha Graham and the Broadway League of Santa Barbara, pledged themselves to pick up any deficit incurred by the Company in coming to Santa Barbara to start its Western tour. This pledge, aside from a gift made to her earlier in her career by Mrs. Schott, who also endowed the museum, was the first real financial support that had ever been given by the citizens of Santa Barbara to one of their most illustrious citizens.

After the tour ended in Ithaca, New York, the Company returned home for a rest before preparing for a spring season at the Mark Hellinger Theater. For the first time, Bertram Ross and Robert Cohan were listed as codirectors of the Company along with Graham. Although she would always have the final say in any matters of artistic policy, the new listing was an acknowledgment of her increasing difficulty in coping with the problems of a large Company in addition to her work as a choreographer. She looked remarkably well, in part due to cosmetic facial surgery, but the hernia operation she had had in 1965 caused her to put on weight and slowed her down.

Problems were mounting. Her performances were a question of chance. Unsurprisingly, she was physically unable to take the rigors of the full-evening "Clytemnestra," and it was therefore retired from the active repertory. Her other appearances often produced a feeling of anxiety in her audiences. At seventy-four, the resiliency of her trained dancer's body had drained away to a great degree. A balance became a teetering approximation, and the swift rise from the floor, which formerly had been nothing to her, became an obvious struggle. Critics felt obliged to say the obvious, although none of them had any enthusiasm for the task of criticizing her physical condition. In the *New York Times*, one young reviewer, Jacquelin Maskey, said with disarming candor, "Reviewing Martha Graham is rather like being called upon to review the Grand Canyon."

It was increasingly obvious that the Company had to think seriously about a future without the presence of Graham onstage. A large part of the problem hinged on money. Bethsabee de Rothschild now was only minimally active in the support of the Graham Company, although she maintained some contacts with the school and with Graham personally. Some of the gap left by de Rothschild had been taken up by Lila Acheson Wallace, who had increasingly interested herself in the Company and was helping to sponsor seasons.

After the tour, Graham went to Israel, as had become her custom, to rest and to visit with de Rothschild. It was obvious that de Rothschild immersed herself in the social and cultural life of the country and that she would channel her money and energy almost entirely into it rather than into Graham's career. Political events in the Middle East were moving toward war between Israel and Egypt, and Graham was advised to return home while she still could. Though she resisted, she left shortly before the Six-Day War in June 1967.

Later, in July, Graham learned of the death of Craig Barton at his brother's home in Lawton, Oklahoma. (Typically, she had requested Barton to destroy all personal correspondence from her.)

Though he was sixteen years her junior, Barton was almost the last of those she could at times confide in. Also during this summer, the Company was victimized by a car theft, and among the costumes stolen were those for "Appalachian Spring," which was to be performed at Connecticut College a week later. With frantic sewing, they were all remade. At this time too, Graham found herself listed among the "One Hundred Women of Accomplishment" in *Harper's Bazaar*. It hardly mattered. In the short space of five years, she had lost Horst, Barton, and, for all practical purposes, de Rothschild; and she was hounded with questions about her age and rumors of her retirement. It was obvious, too, that few of the works she now was choreographing were up to the level of her great pieces. In "A Time of Snow," she retold the story of Heloise and Abelard, in which the couple was reunited after death; in "The Lady of the House of Sleep," she meditated further on destiny and the quest for love. Concern about death was ever present.

One of the few reassuring bits of news was the acquisition, with the financial assistance of Lila Acheson Wallace, of Graham's studio and school on East Sixty-third Street by the Martha Graham Foundation. To celebrate that and her seventy-fifth birthday, Graham gave a party at the studio.

The Brooklyn Academy of Music, which had long been dormant in the cultural life of the city, was being given an infusion of life by its new director, Harvey Lichtenstein. A strong dance enthusiast and ex-performer, he decided to provide dancers with a beautiful refurbished house and began a serious effort to include all elements of the dance world on his program. Naturally Graham was invited for the 1968 season. In the Company's appearance, she presented works from her recent and past repertory, including the mysteriously evocative "Dark Meadow." For the first time, she also featured alternate casting in many of her dances.

The practice of having several dancers in a company assume the same roles is a cherished tradition in ballet companies, where one generally finds more of an emphasis on the interpretation of roles than on a drive to create new ones. The vast majority of ballet dancers happily go through their careers without the slightest desire to choreograph and even less of a desire to break away from a company and form their own. The creative pressure on the modern dancer, on the other hand, obviously works toward encouraging individual choreographic experiment. The practice of alternate casting was therefore a real novelty, and it brought to Brooklyn many people who wanted to see what different interpreters would do with Graham's dances.

It was because of her age and not out of conviction that Graham's became the first of the great modern dance companies to institute alternate casting as a regular feature of its appearances. Graham had managed to continue her performing career longer than anyone else in the short history of modern dance. Creatively, however, she had suffered a severe diminution of her abilities. Her last great work, "Clytemnestra," had been created almost ten years previously, and the public was becoming increasingly uninterested in the performing vehicles she now was assembling for herself, dances like "A Time of Snow" and "The Lady of the House of Sleep." To appeal to a wider public than the special audience that interested itself in anything the Company did, Graham had to offer something, in effect, other than herself. Thus the cast changes became a practical box-office necessity that was undertaken to insure the survival of the Company. The dancers who had been with Graham for the better part of twenty years welcomed the opportunity to acquire the strong central roles that they had been kept away from for so long.

Graham still danced at almost every performance, and opening night in Brooklyn was no different, although the order of the program was affected by a dinner that Graham attended to receive the Family of Man award. Graham was to dance the role of Alcestis in the work of the same name (dating from 1960), and, because of its heavily serious theme, it ordinarily would have closed rather than opened the program. Since the special followers of the Graham Company always crowded to both the opening and closing nights of any of her seasons, she had to make arrangements to appear with her Company and still receive the Family of Man award in mid-Manhattan. She therefore moved "Alcestis" to the beginning of the program; then, without changing her costume, she hurried from the stage of the Brooklyn Academy to a waiting limousine for the drive to the Americana Hotel. Accepting her award in full stage make-up and dress, she made one of those delightfully theatrical gestures that appealed to her and always charmed others.

The series at the Brooklyn Academy was produced as part of a three-theater spectacular. The first part featured performances by several companies, including those of such ex-Graham Company members as Anna Sokolow, Erick Hawkins, and Paul Taylor. After a pause, the series resumed a few weeks later with the performances of younger choreographers like Twyla Tharp (who had danced with Paul Taylor), Yvonne Rainer, and Meredith Monk, some of the most important of the newest creative generation of modern dance. The series concluded with further performances by the Graham Company at the City Center. The whole program was in a very real sense a tribute to Graham, for in great part she had been the fountainhead of so much that it presented.

For the occasion, the *New York Times* decided that it would like to have a "family" portrait of Graham with as many of the other choreographers in the Brooklyn Academy series as it would be possible to assemble. The photo session was held one afternoon in the garden adjoining the main studio of the Graham Studio on East Sixty-third Street. A small platform with steps was set up in the middle of the flowering garden, and the choreographers arranged themselves around Graham, who was seated in the center. Lewis Lloyd, a representative of the Cunningham Dance Company, regarding the massed assemblage of talent, murmured in awe, "Just think of the combined annual deficit!"

The *Times* photographer, Jack Mitchell, finished the picture-taking in a short time, and after champagne toasts had been drunk the assembled dancers, choreographers, and administrators returned to their respective worlds. Graham remained in the garden, savoring the pleasure of the afternoon and the honor that had been accorded her by the gathering of her creative "children." She was not even quite sure who the younger choreographers were, since she rarely went to see the work of any choreographers other than her own Company members. Their attendance on this afternoon, however, pleased her immensely. Welcoming a late visitor who had been unable to attend the photo session, she indicated a place on the platform where she was still sitting and asked for champagne to be brought. She spoke reminiscently about the past and the number of concerts that were now being given during the course of a season as compared to the few that had been the rule when she started her career. The road for her had been a long and difficult one, and her sacrifices had been many. Despite her fame, she was in perilous financial condition, and there was no real indication that it would ever get any better. She had grown to live, if not easily, then accommodatingly, on the edge of a financial abyss. The only surviving member of her immediate family was her sister Geordie who, since the dissolution of her marriage, had helped in the administration of the school and lived nearby as did Graham herself.

Graham had every right to take pleasure in the tribute of that afternoon. Her monument was her dances and the style of movement that had become synonymous in the public mind with modern dance. Her creative family were not just the choreographers who had worked directly with her or even with those who had been members of her Company. Vast numbers of dancers were in her debt through the efforts of members of one or another of the Graham companies who were instructing a younger generation in all sections of the country. Whether that instruction incorporated the modifications that had been made after the early years of struggle, or the simple, strong, and percussive movements that had been the hallmark of her earliest experiments, it always made use of the torso as an expressive instrument of highest importance and it always stressed the use of the floor. Whether in Haifa or in Tucson, students would hear a class begin with the words, "Be seated." The class would start on the floor and slowly work up to a standing position, stretching and extending muscles just a little bit beyond what the individual student thought possible and, for the professional, keeping limber the beautifully lengthened and dynamic muscles of the accomplished dancer.

In the spring of 1969 Graham appeared onstage, at the City Center in New York, for the last time, although the occasion had not been so announced. She had prepared a generally insubstantial vehicle for herself that at least enabled her to appear. The season followed the practice of presenting old and new repertory works, but Graham resisted bringing back any of the major dances created when she first began her turn toward theatrical works—"Letter to the World," "Deaths and Entrances," and "Every Soul Is a Circus." Thus, though the younger members of the Company could be seen to advantage in dances like the beautiful "Canticle for Innocent Comedians" or "Dark Meadow," Graham, in her person, still dominated the season and its programing, appearing in later works like "Lady of the House of Sleep" or "Time of Snow" and the new "Archaic Hours." Unfortunately, the public was not interested in this type of programing, and Graham received a vote of no confidence. The performances were poorly attended because the public did not want to see the only dances Graham could still manage to perform. The alternative—to give up performing, which she loved more than any other thing, and to concentrate on teaching and choreographing—she could not accept. She would not willingly let go.

The Company, however, had to look to its own preservation. With its incorporation as a nonprofit, tax-exempt corporation, complete with a board of directors, the Company had achieved a legal status outside of Graham's direct control. The next year, 1970, the Brooklyn Academy of Music again invited the Company to appear, but with the stipulation that the repertory include precisely those works that Graham had no intention of reviving because they no longer afforded her the opportunity to perform. The Company members therefore decided to force the issue of Graham's retirement. When she was informed that the Company wanted to appear without her, she was furious. She tried every bit of cunning and cajolery that she could command to get the decision changed. However, the dancers and the directors of the Company remained firm in insisting upon a season of Graham works without Graham. Once she saw that her retirement from active performing was a *fait accompli*, she ceased to struggle and settled into resigned acceptance. The blow perhaps was somewhat softened because the City of New York wished to present her with its highest artistic honor, the Handel Medallion, at a ceremony on opening night.

Then, the day of the opening season, the *New York Times* placed the story of her "retirement" on the front page. The story changed Graham's mood of acceptance into one of quiet rage. By evening, she was drunk enough to be mildly oblivious of her surroundings. Passing through the backstage area of the Academy, she looked around and commented that she had played the house before. Dore Schary, presenting the Handel Medallion on behalf of the mayor, offered an intelligent and flowery appreciation of her career. Graham, at home onstage as nowhere else, made a stunning entrance in a sari-like dress and accepted the award graciously. Her talk meandered with the improvisational brilliance that she always had been able to command. Before she was through talking, she had unretired herself. Eventually the flow of words subsided, and she left the stage. The audience alternately laughed and cheered. Some cried.

For the Brooklyn series, the Company had tried hard to restore works of the early Graham repertory without any assistance from Graham. For its restoration of "Letter to the World," the Company was able to bring back two of the three original female leads. Jane Dudley danced The Ancestress with grit and force, hampered though she was by an arthritic hip that earlier had forced her premature retirement, and Jean Erdman recited the verse of Emily Dickinson. Graham's role as The Poetess was given to Pearl Lang, one of Graham's most gifted former dancers. To those who were not familiar with the details of the dance, it was a beautiful performance, but those who had known the original work thought the re-creation far less than what they remembered. But even so, the dance was a magnificent experience. When Graham assembled the elements of a dance, she did so with a sure craftsmanlike skill that did not depend on her performing intensity to unify them. Though it surely was a bitter truth for her, her dances did not need her in order to succeed. Even granting the fact that she could perform them better than anyone else, the construction of the works was so sound that they could stand on their own creative feet and achieve their impact without her electrical dramatic presence.

Conceivably, it should have been a comfort to her to know she had built well and that the structure of her theatrical conceptions was so secure, but such knowledge was not the comfort it might have been. What made that evening most memorable for her was the fact that it was the first time her Company had appeared without her. Though the medallion was heart balm of a sort, it did not really ease the pain she felt on seeing a company of dancers that she had trained and brought along to performing excellence exclude her and strike out on their own. The work that she had done, she had done well and thoroughly, but she wanted to be onstage, not in the audience.

After the Brooklyn performances, for which "Deaths and Entrances" and "Every Soul Is a Circus" were restored, the Company went on a tour, but one that was limited both in the numbers of dances it presented and the number of dancers who performed. Suddenly, within the space of four years, the Company fell on lean times. For the 1966 tour the Company had been at full strength, with orchestra and full stage panoply; the 1970 tour after the Brooklyn season was an obvious step backward.

Graham was not part of the tour—she had "retired"—and for the next year and a half was assaulted by a series of illnesses, including intestinal trouble which kept her hospitalized and out of contact with her dancers and craft. Between stays at the hospital she visited and recuperated with friends. Her sister Geordie had required hospitalization previously, and now it was Graham's turn. The years of strain, effort, and later abuse, which most likely would have debiliated almost anyone else years before, had finally caught up with her.

With Graham gone, the Company had to develop a new plan for survival. In the later years of her performing career, Graham saw one after another of her principal dancers leave to establish their own careers, so that finally the group of loyal and talented dancers came down to a very small number. Under Leatherman's administration, Bertram Ross and Mary Hinkson therefore decided to form a performing ensemble with students in the school. When they discovered that the school did not have what they needed, they decided, for the first time in the history of the Graham Company, to hold auditions in order to secure good dancers. Formerly, there had always been far more applicants for a position with the Company than there were places. Now, however, the Graham school as well as the Graham Company lacked new talent.

Previously, the Company's tours had always insured that there would be a supply of aspiring dancers ready and eager to take over any roles that might be offered them. At one time in the intensely competitive world of modern dance, class at the Graham studio was considered a requisite for membership in the Company. It was a form of paying one's dues to a private and very exclusive club. Now there were internal squabbles. Various teachers and former teachers in the school disputed the way in which instruction was given. More, the new crop of dancers who did not know Graham and were not very familiar with her vocabulary did not feel any pressure to go to the Graham school. What was really unsettling about the attitude of the young was that they did not consider attendance at Graham's school a recommendation for the future. To them it was a form of dutiful homage rather than a career necessity.

In 1971, Graham did not set foot in the studio for over eight months. She maintained minimal contact with her dancers and administrators by telephone. She had always been an avid user of the telephone, and now it became her main means of communication with those who previously had been so intimately involved with her.

For the Company, there were no long performing tours after the series that had followed the Brooklyn season. The remaining members were faced with an enormous problem. Though they did not have enough dates for a tour, they had the strongest modern dance repertory in the field. In an effort to solve this problem, they decided to try a new format and create a company that would dance and interpret the great Graham roles with dancers considerably younger than those who had worked with Graham from just after World War II until her recent retirement. The great Graham dances were therefore put to the ultimate test at a series of studio performances.

A work like "Errand into the Maze," which originally had décor by Noguchi, Graham's skill as the Girl, and strong performers like Mark Ryder or Stuart Hodes as the Minotaur, was now performed by a cast of unknowns with the décor reduced to a couple of high stools connected by a line that looked as if it had been abandoned by a tasteful washerwoman. It was impossible to evoke any theater magic in such a presentation, and the dance had to be judged strictly on the merits of its construction. Once again, however, Graham's work survived and showed itself to be independent of her presence and interpretation. The students and the younger members of the Company gave a performance that drew skillfully upon the dance's organic flow.

Graham did not so much as deign to notice that the studio performances were being given. For her it was a gigantic step backward. Performing in one's own studio was what she had done in the earliest days of her career, and all her efforts had been directed away from reliving those days.

The studio performances were only one of many possibilities that the Company could have pursued. At worst, the Company could disband, but this would mean the disappearance of most of the repertory, since a good part of it had never been notated or recorded. Through the studio performances the Company tried to keep together some form of performing ensemble and to keep the works alive. There were clearly practical considerations in this strategy. When senior members of the Company could no longer perform, they could earn a living by coaching other dancers in the works and by giving dancers and students an opportunity to be in some of the great dances that were the legacy of Graham's creative career. But to attract students, it was necessary to have some sort of performing exposure, and this too was a purpose of the studio concert series.

The series was not totally successful, but it did help in the transition to a new situation for the Company and for Graham. The work in the studio was indirectly acknowledged by Graham only in her occasional reference to it, when talking to Leroy Leatherman, the Company administrator, as "your" project. While the Company thrashed and floundered, trying to find a viable new road, Graham continued to be attacked by illness and spent large portions of the year either in the hospital or recuperating. Her condition several times was so grave that those closest to her did not expect her to live. Her body, though, had a resiliency that seemed almost impervious to disease, alcohol, and overwork, and in mid-1972 she recovered and began to take an active interest in what had been happening to the Company since her seclusion. She disapproved of almost everything they had done, but it was the Company's agreement to be part of a modern dance series, along with seventeen other companies, that drove her to action.

Graham had always demanded and received preferential treatment in any season in which her Company was presented with others. The increasingly embarrassing aspect of her demands was that they were not supported by that most persuasive of arguments in the theater world—box-office appeal. Everyone who had presented Graham in most recent years had taken a fearsome financial beating. While a dedicated patron like Bethsabee de Rothschild was willing to absorb the losses, it was possible to present the Company in the style, in effect, to which it was accustomed; but Graham, though she had supporters, no longer had a private patron of such means and generosity.

Broadly speaking, what had once been done in the dance world by individual generosity was now being done by public money, and the change brought with it new obligations. Through a growing general awareness of the importance of cultural undertakings, the federal government and many state administrations had begun to channel public funds into the arts. As a result, the responsibilities of the cultural organizations were broadened. To justify public funding, these groups, and the individuals who ran them, had to consider not just the success of a single company but the adequate presentation of the entire field. They also had to ensure maintenance of ticket prices at a level that would not exclude the great mass of the public. All of these considerations meant that subscription series, at the prices at which they were offered, stood little chance of making money and would almost necessarily incur a deficit. The problem was to keep the deficit to a manageable size. Excessive demands from any one company would seriously disturb the balance of a season.

It was cut-and-dried logic, but Graham seethed when she found herself asked to share a program with another company. She did not even care to know which one it was. The difficulty was accepting the idea of sharing in the first place. The only person who had ever been able to force Graham to share an evening was de Rothschild, who had been supporting the Company unselfishly for ten years. Even then Graham grumbled. And because even de Rothschild could not get the modern dance world to accept such an arrangement, Graham least of all, things went back to their original pattern by the end of the 1950's, with each of the companies booking its own dates and appearing in its own season.

Graham's whole career militated against shared programs. Shared programs meant vaudeville, and even the practical Denishawn had always striven for and eventually achieved concert performances in which the company produced the entire evening. People came to see Denishawn, and not an assorted package of bounding Burmese and whistling fish. Graham's first concert consisted of an entire evening of her own work, and then, when she began to develop her own distinctive style of movement, she strove to maintain constant contact with her dancers so as not to share them with others. Sharing would ruin the continuity that she was attemping to build. In the early 1930's she appeared as part of the Dance Repertory Theater series for two seasons but broke away from it as soon as she was able. A solitary traveler, she had always led the way for others and was therefore unable to become part of a shared program.

The series—the Dance Marathon, as it was called—was planned to start the first week in October and would have given Graham a dozen evenings in which to present half-programs. She had been told about the proposal by Leatherman and, on first hearing, seemed to acquiesce to it. Leatherman made plans to participate in the series at the ANTA Theater, when suddenly, for the first time in over a year, Graham appeared at the school. She was not a frail little old lady who recently had been near death, but a hot-tempered, sharp-tongued, iron-willed woman who for nearly fifty years ran her own Company and her own life as best as she was able and who now was not about to have her Company take half a program. Calling Charles Reinhart, the producer of the season, Graham told him that she was not going to participate because she had not been informed of the season in sufficient time and did not have a signed contract. The fact of the season, of course, had been known to her, and everyone connected with it was also appearing on the basis of a letter or verbal understanding. No one had a signed contract. These were not the real issues. A day later she informed Reinhart that she had decided to return to the season and that her Company could be counted upon to appear. Her precipitous cancelation had met with strong opposition from the Company managers. The series was an opportunity for the Company, and they did not want to withdraw. So Graham capitulated.

The idea of a shared program, however, still galled her beyond measure, and she decided upon one last throw of the dice to escape from what she considered an unwarranted accommodation. Calling the Company to a meeting at the studio, she explained to them her feelings about the season. Telling them that she wanted them to vote on the matter themselves, without her being present, she left the studio. Perhaps predictably, the Company voted to acquiesce to her strong feelings. It would have been difficult not to. It had been hard enough to persuade her to leave the performing stage, and that battle had left its scars, but to force a season that she strongly opposed did not seem worth the trouble. Graham then called Reinhart again and withdrew for the second and final time. The Graham Company would not appear under the conditions offered it.

It was disturbingly easy for Reinhart to accept the decision. Given the conditions within which he worked, he really had no option. Presenting the Graham Company on anything but a shared basis would have destroyed the entire season, for every choreographer then would have demanded evenings of his own. Modern dance and its proper presentation were more important than the fortunes of any one company, including the Graham Company. The aim was to overcome the fragmentation that had characterized modern dance, to its own disadvantage, from the very beginning. The modern dance world was still in the same state that the original thirteen American colonies were before the Articles of Confederation were signed. But for Graham, stubborn and determined as ever, the "jewel" of her inner intensity burning as fiercely as it did at Cumnock, it was the world she had made and the one she still lived by.

For most of her career, Graham had been the cornerstone of the modern dance world, and, in general, the direction taken by that world was shaped by her own needs and desires. Choreographers as yet unborn when Graham was organizing her great companies found themselves organizing seasons for the spring and fall and not considering any other time of the year simply because Graham had done it that way and they had grown up with the habit. In summer, no one had a modern dance season in New York and everyone's eyes were trained on a college campus outside the city because Graham and the generation of the 1930's had always gone off to Bennington College in Vermont. They left the city in order to have a paying summer. With the growth of summer cultural presentations in the city, however, this reason was no longer valid, and yet modern dance clung to it with irrational tenacity. With a lemming-like instinct, many modern dancers scheduled dance recitals for Sunday, probably unaware that the initial reason for Sunday performances was the inability of early modern dancers to find a theater available on any other day—and in New York they had had to change the law prohibiting Sunday performances. Present day companies found it difficult to cooperate with one another because their predecessors did not cooperate.

Graham, always so much the center of all this, could change no more than an old gladiator bred for the arena. She had fought, suffered, and endured longer than any of her contemporaries, and she could not cooperate. She was used to controlling her world. "Martha loved arrogance," Leatherman once said. He recalled a moment in the office of the school when Graham said, "I know I'm arrogant and vain, and I must be adored."

Leatherman responded, "Oh, Martha. You're just joking."

"No! I must be adored!"

And she was serious.

And so, it seemed, the last stage that Graham could command with utter authority had shrunk to the dimensions of a studio in the school on East Sixty-third Street. Yet, despite this narrowing of her activity, there is every reason she could have taken immense satisfaction in her achievement. Her career, her achievement, had been extraordinary. She had a prominence unequaled in her field. For many in the broad public, she *was* modern dance. In the field of dance itself, performers who had never seen her nonetheless danced in a style of movement that was patterned on her ideas of contraction and release of energy. In the theater, actors routinely studied dance movement, not because they wished to become dancers, but because, as Martha Graham had proved, the body could "speak" dramatically. Nearly every major modern dance company could trace its artistic lineage to Graham. She had been the incubator for a generation of talent as Denishawn had been for her own generation. And over and above all this was her stature as a creative artist.

Alvin Ailey, himself a modern dancer of international repute, spoke some years later of her immense contribution: "Look at the legacy she created . . . Look at what Graham has done. Look at what has come from her. This woman is like Picasso and Stravinsky." The comparison was apt, for, like Picasso and Stravinsky, Graham, in forging her perception and instincts into movement that changed the character of an entire art form, became one of the artistic touchstones of the twentieth century.

But whether Graham herself could draw satisfaction from her profound accomplishment is doubtful. She had never been able to rest satisfied with what she had done; she had always demanded something more of herself. It seemed unlikely that, as her world shrank, her attitude would change. It was always the future, the constant challenge of meeting the next demand of her searching imagination that had commanded Martha Graham. This had been her curse as well as her triumph.

Epilogue

In March 1973 Graham summoned the press to her school on East Sixty-third Street to announce that, after an absence of four years, her Company would return to Broadway in May for a two-week season. Sitting on a small dais with her new company administrator, Ron Protas, she was flanked by two of her senior dancers, Mary Hinkson and Bertram Ross. Her low and at times girlish voice was firm, her face composed, the slight figure carried proudly and erectly. Only her hands, cruelly knotted with arthritis, betrayed her years. Graham announced that she herself did not intend to appear onstage. She would allow her dances to represent her. Her contribution now would be artistic direction.

It had taken Graham two years to accept the fact of her retirement as a performer. Someone once told her, "Martha, you are not a goddess. You must admit your mortality." Commenting on this, Graham said, "That's difficult when you see yourself as a goddess and behave like one. In the end I didn't want people to feel sorry for me. If I can't dance any more, then I don't want to. Or at least I won't. . . . The world is full of dancers, better than ever, but there are few with the talent and patience to make stars of them." Now, she said, she was reconciled to doing what she could. After having recently survived several grave illnesses and temporarily ignored the existence of her school, she had once again resumed command of the school and Company that she created.

She spoke now about dancing as her life, about how dancing intensifies life, about the difficulties of not dancing, and she asked to be judged for what she set out to do. To illustrate the intensity of the drive that had motivated her throughout her life, she recalled a phrase by designer Robert Edmond Jones: "doomed to be an artist." She added her own elaboration: "You hear the footsteps behind you, and, if you don't, you had better look out." Her life had been one of headlong forward movement, as if there were something pursuing her relentlessly, never allowing her to relax. Even now, approaching seventy-nine, she was creating two new dances for her spring season as well as reviving her masterpiece, the full-length "Clytemnestra." Even now, she obviously was not interested in a nostalgic backward look. She was still driving herself forward.

Laughing, she referred to her vanity as a dangerous chemical. As usual, she spoke without notes so that she would not have to wear her glasses. Even in a theater, as a member of the audience, she waited for the house lights to dim before slipping her glasses on. The television cameramen present at the press conference were not allowed to photograph her; they were allowed only to record her voice and photograph the company demonstration. She consented to pose for a few minutes for portrait studies, but that was all.

The two-week spring season at the Alvin Theater was a new start and was greeted with anticipation and excitement. The opening night audience included former company members, fellow choreographers, and colleagues in the dance world who gathered to honor her amazing accomplishment and her equally amazing recovery of purpose. "Clytemnestra" was received enthusiastically by audiences that filled the theater for each performance. Two of her senior dancers, Mary Hinkson and Pearl Lang, alternated in the title role, and the dance, even without Graham's intensely dramatic stage presence, was a tremendous success. Younger members of the audience, who had never seen Graham dance, judged her on the quality of her work and cheered. The fears of some of the older members of the audience, who remembered Graham at the height of her career, were further allayed when others of the great repertory pieces as well were seen to have survived her absence. Graham was reaffirmed as a great choreographer and as a great teacher, for the beneficial signs of her coaching were readily perceptible in the new Company. Throughout the season Graham contented herself every so often by basking in occasional curtain calls.

The critical reception was highly enthusiastic. Reviewing these performances for *The New Yorker,* Andrew Porter wrote: "In 1967, when I last saw the Graham Company, I felt that I was watching a troupe, and an art, in sunset splendor. . . . Any obituary sentiments were felt too soon. The current season is a new dawn." One *New York Times* headline proclaimed: "Graham's Creativity Remains Unabated"; another referred to "The Monumental Martha," and one of the paper's reviewers wrote, "It is useless to repeat that Miss Graham herself is irreplaceable." *New York* magazine headlined its review, "Martha, the Mother of Us All." Writing about Graham's rebirth as an artist, *Time* magazine asserted, "No other woman has ever contributed such a large body of work to the theater." Graham herself explained, "I've just entered a new cycle of energy. I'm going through a rebirth—with anything artistic one must die to be reborn."

Shortly after the end of the spring season, Graham received a New York State award for artistic accomplishment. In accepting it, she recalled the first New York concert of her own work in 1926 and mentioned New York's kindness to her. She also recalled an incident after that performance when a woman who remembered her in the less controversial Denishawn Company called her to account: "It's dreadful! Martha, how long do you expect to keep this up?" "As long as I have an audience" was the reply. Over 150 dances and nearly a half century of performance later, she still had an audience and was planning on another New York season in the winter.

At the press conference announcing the spring season Graham commented that one must accept life as it surges through one's body. In her own case she did more than accept it, she magnified it into an epic experience. By examining the landscape of her own soul, she created dramatic dances that people throughout the world could understand and embrace. Graham once said that, as a young dancer, she had only wanted to be able to dance clearly and in an undistorted manner and that she had to discover a way to do it. Her personal voyage of discovery had led her to a style of movement that eventually became a way of life for thousands of others. Yet, to her students and professional collaborators, she always modestly maintained that she had not invented anything but had only rediscovered possibilities that had been present all the time.

Martha Graham always emphasized that she did not choose to be a dancer but that she had been chosen. Thus she underlined the seriousness and the irresistible nature of the calling. Graham followed her art as a religious follows his vocation. Within the discipline of dancing she had found freedom—the freedom to be herself.

Chronology

COMPILED BY LEIGHTON KERNER
Assisted by Don McDonagh

D - Dancing   M - Music *   S - Sets   C - Costumes   L - Lighting design

Martha Graham's first performing ensemble consisted of a *Trio* of three women. This later was expanded to the larger all-female *Group*, which in turn, with the addition of permanent male dancers, became the *Company*.

1926

1. CHORALE

   D Martha Graham and Trio. The first Trio consisted of Thelma Biracree, Betty McDonald, and Evelyn Sabin. Rosina Savelli replaced Thelma Biracree for August 20th performance at Mariarden and subsequently.

   M César Franck, from Prelude, Chorale, and Fugue.   C & L Martha Graham

   48th Street Theater, New York   April 18

2. NOVELETTE

   D Martha Graham   M Robert Schumann, from Bunte Blätter Op. 99.   C & L Martha Graham

   48th Street Theater, New York   April 18

3. TÄNZE

   D Trio   M Franz Schubert   C & L Martha Graham. At the May 27th performance in Rochester the costumes were designed by Norman Edwards.

   48th Street Theater, New York   April 18

* Where titles of musical compositions are not given, the information is unavailable.

4. INTERMEZZO

D Martha Graham M Johannes Brahms, Intermezzo No. 18 in C Major for Piano, Op. 119, No. 3. C & L Martha Graham. Costumes for May 27th performance designed by Norman Edwards.

48th Street Theater, New York April 18

5. MAID WITH THE FLAXEN HAIR

D Martha Graham M Claude Debussy, Preludes for Piano, Book I, No. 8. C & L Martha Graham

48th Street Theater, New York April 18

6. ARABESQUE NO. 1

D Trio M Claude Debussy, Arabesque No. 1 for piano. C & L Martha Graham

48th Street Theater, New York April 18

7. CLAIR DE LUNE

D Martha Graham and Trio M Claude Debussy, Suite Bergamasque: "Clair de lune." C & L Martha Graham

48th Street Theater, New York April 18

8. DANSE LANGUIDE

D Trio M Alexander Scriabin, Danse languide for piano, Op. 51, No. 4. C & L Martha Graham

48th Street Theater, New York April 18

9. DÉSIR

D Martha Graham M Alexander Scriabin, Désir for piano, Op. 57, No. 1. C & L Martha Graham

48th Street Theater, New York April 18

10. DEUX VALSES SENTIMENTALES

D Martha Graham M Maurice Ravel, Valses nobles et sentimentales, Nos. 2 & 3 for piano. C & L Martha Graham

48th Street Theater, New York April 18

11. MASQUES

D Martha Graham M Louis Horst, Masques for piano. C & L Martha Graham

48th Street Theater, New York April 18

12. TROIS GNOSSIENNES

Gnossienne Frieze Tanagra

D Martha Graham and Trio M Erik Satie, Trois Gnossiennes for piano. C & L Martha Graham. In subsequent performances,

Gnossiennes Nos. 2 & 3 were used to accompany Tanagra as a solo. In this performance the Trio danced Gnossienne, and Martha Graham danced the other two sections.

48th Street Theater, New York April 18

13. FROM A XII-CENTURY TAPESTRY

D Martha Graham M Sergei Rachmaninoff C Earle Franke L Martha Graham. In May 27th performance the costumes were designed by Norman Edwards, at which time the dance was retitled "A Florentine Madonna."

48th Street Theater, New York April 18

14. A STUDY IN LACQUER

D Martha Graham M Marcel Bernheim C & L Martha Graham

48th Street Theater, New York April 18

15. THE THREE GOPI MAIDENS

D Trio M Cyril Scott C Norman Edwards L Martha Graham. This dance is excerpted from "The Flute of Krishna," which was presented in Rochester May 27 with an additional male and female dancer.

48th Street Theater, New York April 18

16. DANSE ROCOCO

D Martha Graham M Maurice Ravel C Earle Franke L Martha Graham

48th Street Theater, New York April 18

17. THE MARIONETTE SHOW

D Martha Graham M Eugene Goossens C & L Martha Graham

48th Street Theater, New York April 18

18. PORTRAIT - AFTER BELTRAM - MASSES

D Martha Graham M Manuel de Falla C & L Martha Graham. Subsequently the piece was retitled "Gypsy Portrait."

48th Street Theater, New York April 18

19. SUITE FROM "ALCESTE"

D Martha Graham and Trio M C. W. von Gluck C Norman Edwards L Martha Graham

Kilbourn Hall, Rochester May 27

20. SCÈNE JAVANAISE

D Martha Graham and Trio and three student dancers M Louis

Horst C Norman Edwards L Martha Graham. In subsequent performances the three additional dancers were not used.

Kilbourn Hall, Rochester May 27

21. DANZA DEGLI ANGELI

D Trio M Ermanno Wolf-Ferrari C Norman Edwards L Martha Graham

Kilbourn Hall, Rochester May 27

22. BAS RELIEF

D Three male student dancers M Cyril Scott C Norman Edwards L Martha Graham

Kilbourn Hall, Rochester May 27

23. RIBANDS

D Two girls M Frédéric Chopin C Norman Edwards L Martha Graham

Mariarden, Peterboro, New Hampshire August 20

24. SCHERZO

D Trio M Felix Mendelssohn, Op. 16, No. 2. C & L Martha Graham

Klaw Theater, New York November 28

25. BAAL SHEM

D Martha Graham and Trio M Ernest Bloch, Baal Shem. C & L Martha Graham

Klaw Theater, New York November 28

26. LA SOIRÉE DANS GRENADE

D Martha Graham M Claude Debussy, Soirée dans Grenade, from "Estampes." C & L Martha Graham. This dance was later retitled "The Moth."

Klaw Theater, New York November 28

27. ALT-WIEN

D Trio M Leopold Godowsky, arr. Horst C & L Martha Graham

Klaw Theater, New York November 28

28. THREE POEMS OF THE EAST

D Martha Graham and Trio M Louis Horst, "Three Poems of the East." This was the first original composition Horst did for Graham. C & L Martha Graham. The dance was later performed as a solo.

Klaw Theater, New York November 28

1927

29. PEASANT SKETCHES

Dance Berceuse In the Church

D Martha Graham M Vladimir Rebikov, Alexander Tansman, P. I. Tchaikovsky C & L Martha Graham

Guild Theater, New York February 27

30. TUNISIA: Sunlight in a Courtyard

D Martha Graham M Eduard Poldini C & L Martha Graham

Guild Theater, New York February 27

31. LUCREZIA

D Martha Graham M Claude Debussy C & L Martha Graham

Guild Theater, New York February 27

32. LA CANCIÓN

D Martha Graham M René Defossez C & L Martha Graham

Guild Theater, New York February 27

33. ARABESQUE NO. 1 (Revised)

D Six dancers M Claude Debussy, Arabesque No. 1 for piano. C & L Martha Graham

Anderson-Milton School, New York August 2

34. VALSE CAPRICE

D Martha Graham M Cyril Scott, Op. 74, No. 7. C & L Martha Graham

Anderson-Milton School, New York August 2

35. SPIRES

D Trio M J.S. Bach, Chorale, "Schwing dich auf zu deinem Gott." C & L Martha Graham

The Little Theater, New York October 16

36. ADAGIO

D Martha Graham M G.F. Handel, Adagio from Second Suite. C & L Martha Graham. Subsequently this dance was retitled "Madonna."

The Little Theater, New York October 16

37. FRAGILITÉ

D Martha Graham M Alexander Scriabin, Op. 51, No. 1.

The Little Theater, New York October 16

38. LUGUBRE

D Trio M Alexander Scriabin, Prélude lugubre, Op. 51, No. 2. C & L Martha Graham

The Little Theater, New York October 16

39. POÈME AILÉ

D Martha Graham M Alexander Scriabin, Op. 51, No. 3. C & L Martha Graham. In June 1929 these three pieces along with "Danse languide" and "Désir" were presented under the title "Five Poems."

The Little Theater, New York October 16

40. TANZSTÜCK

D Trio M Paul Hindemith, Reihe kleiner Stücke, Op. 37. C & L Martha Graham

The Little Theater, New York October 16

41. REVOLT (orig. Danse)

D Martha Graham M Arthur Honegger, Danse from Trois Pièces. C & L Martha Graham

The Little Theater, New York October 16

42. ESQUISSE ANTIQUE

D Trio M Désiré-Emile Inghelbrecht, from Esquisses antiques, No. 2, Driades. C & L Martha Graham

The Little Theater, New York October 16

43. RONDE

D Trio M Rhené-Baton, Ronde from Au Pardon de Rumengol. C & L Martha Graham

The Little Theater, New York October 16

44. SCHERZA

D Martha Graham M Robert Schumann C & L Martha Graham

Cornell University, Ithaca December 10

1928

45. CHINESE POEM

D Martha Graham M Louis Horst C & L Martha Graham

Civic Repertory Theater, New York February 12

46. TROUVÈRES

The Return of Spring Complaint A Song, Frank and Gay

D Martha Graham M Charles Koechlin C & L Martha Graham

The Little Theater, New York April 22

47. IMMIGRANT

Steerage   Strike

D Martha Graham   M Josip Slavenski, Two numbers from Suite "Aus dem Balkan."   C & L Martha Graham

The Little Theater, New York   April 22

48. POEMS OF 1917

Song Behind The Lines   Dance of Death

D Martha Graham   M Leo Ornstein, Poems of 1917.   C & L Martha Graham

The Little Theater, New York   April 22

49. FRAGMENTS

Tragedy   Comedy

D Martha Graham   M Louis Horst, Fragments   C & L Martha Graham

The Little Theater, New York   April 22

50. RESONANCES

Matins   Gamelan   Tocsin

D Martha Graham   M Gian Francesco Malipiero   C & L Martha Graham

The Little Theater, New York   April 22

1929

51. DANCE

"Strong Free Joyous Action": Nietzsche

D Martha Graham   M Arthur Honegger   C & L Martha Graham

Booth Theater, New York   January 20

52. THREE FLORENTINE VERSES

D Martha Graham   M Domenico Zipoli   C & L Martha Graham

Booth Theater, New York   January 20

53. FOUR INSINCERITIES

Petulance   Remorse   Politeness   Vivacity

D Martha Graham   M Serge Prokofiev, Visions fugitives, Op. 22, Nos. 14, 12, 6, 11.

Booth Theater, New York   January 20

54. CANTS MÁGICS

Farewell Greeting

D Martha Graham M Fédérico Mompou, Cants Mágics. C & L Martha Graham

Booth Theater, New York January 20

55. TWO VARIATIONS: Country Lane, City Street

D Martha Graham M Alexander Gretchaninoff, Sonatina in G, Op. 110, No. 1, Movements 1 & 3. C & L Martha Graham

Booth Theater, New York January 20

56. FIGURE OF A SAINT

D Martha Graham M G. F. Handel C & L Martha Graham

Bennett School of Liberal and Applied Arts Millbrook, New York January 24

57. RESURRECTION

D Martha Graham M Tibor Harsányi C & L Martha Graham

Booth Theater, New York March 3

58. ADOLESCENCE

D Martha Graham M Paul Hindemith, Prelude and Song from Reihe kleiner Stücke, Op. 37. C & L Martha Graham

Booth Theater, New York March 3

59. DANZA

D Martha Graham M Darius Milhaud C & L Martha Graham

Booth Theater, New York March 3

60. VISION OF THE APOCALYPSE

Theme and Variations

D Group M Herman Reutter, Variations on Bach's Chorale Komm' Süsser Tod. C & L Martha Graham. This concert marked the transition from Graham's Denishawn-influenced period. She introduced her expanded all-woman company, called the dance Group, and worked with an exclusively female company until 1938.

Booth Theater, New York April 14

61. MOMENT RUSTICA

D Group M Francis Poulenc, Sonata for Piano, Four Hands, Second movement ("Rustique"). C & L Martha Graham. Subsequently a solo was excerpted from this work.

Booth Theater, New York April 14

62. SKETCHES FROM THE PEOPLE

Monotony Supplication Requiem

D Group M Julien Krein, Eight Preludes Op. 5, Nos. 4, 2, 7. C & L Martha Graham

Booth Theater, New York April 14

63. HERETIC

D Martha Graham and Group M Anon. "Breton Têtus" in collection Chansons de la Fleur de Lys, arr. De Sivry. A revolutionary folk-song 10 bars long, repeated throughout the dance. C & L Martha Graham

Booth Theater, New York April 14

1930

64. PRELUDE TO A DANCE

D Group M Arthur Honegger, Counterpoint No. 1 for piano. C & L Martha Graham. The dance was later retitled "Salutation."

Maxine Elliott's Theater, New York January 8

65. TWO CHANTS

Futility Ecstatic Song

D Martha Graham M Ernst Křenek, Piano Sonata No. 2, Op. 59. C & L Martha Graham

Maxine Elliott's Theater, New York January 8

66. LAMENTATION

D Martha Graham M Zoltan Kodaly, Piano Piece Op. 3, No. 2. C & L Martha Graham

Maxine Elliott's Theater, New York January 8

67. PROJECT IN MOVEMENT FOR A DIVINE COMEDY

D Martha Graham and Group C & L Martha Graham. The dance was done without musical accompaniment. This was the first and only time that Graham presented a work without music.

Maxine Elliott's Theater, New York January 8

68. HARLEQUINADE

D Martha Graham M Ernst Toch, Klavierstücke Op. 32. C & L Martha Graham

Maxine Elliott's Theater, New York January 8

1931

69. TWO PRIMITIVE CANTICLES

D Martha Graham M Heitor Villa-Lobos C & L Martha Graham

Craig Theater, New York February 2

70. PRIMITIVE MYSTERIES

Hymn to the Virgin Crucifixus Hosanna

D Martha Graham and Group M Louis Horst C & L Martha Graham

Craig Theater, New York February 2

71. RHAPSODICS

Song Interlude Dance

D Martha Graham M Bela Bartok C & L Martha Graham

Craig Theater, New York February 2

72. BACCHANALE

D Martha Graham and Group M Wallingford Riegger, Bacchanale. C & L Martha Graham

Craig Theater, New York February 2

73. DOLOROSA

D Martha Graham M Heitor Villa-Lobos C & L Martha Graham

Craig Theater, New York February 2

74. DITHYRAMBIC

D Martha Graham M Aaron Copland, Piano Variations. C & L Martha Graham

Martin Beck Theater, New York December 6

75. SERENADE

D Martha Graham M Arnold Schönberg C & L Martha Graham

Martin Beck Theater, New York December 6

76. INCANTATION

D Martha Graham and Group M Heitor Villa-Lobos C & L Martha Graham

Martin Beck Theater, New York December 6

1932

77. CEREMONIALS

Virgil Interlude Song of Vengeance Interlude Sacred Formula

D Martha Graham and Group M Lehman Engel C & L Martha Graham

Guild Theater, New York February 28

78. OFFERING

D Martha Graham M Heitor Villa-Lobos C & L Martha Graham

Lydia Mendelssohn Theater Ann Arbor, Michigan June 2

79. ECSTATIC DANCE

D Martha Graham M Tibor Harsányi C & L Martha Graham

Lydia Mendelssohn Theater Ann Arbor, Michigan June 2

80. BACCHANALE (No. 2)

D Martha Graham M Wallingford Riegger, Bacchanale. C & L Martha Graham

Lydia Mendelssohn Theater Ann Arbor, Michigan June 2

81. PRELUDE

D Martha Graham M Carlos Chávez C & L Martha Graham

Guild Theater, New York November 20

82. DANCE SONGS

Ceremonial Morning Song Satiric Festival Song Song of Rapture

D Martha Graham M Imre Weisshaus C & L Martha Graham "Ceremonial" was given its first performance five days earlier (November 15) in a concert at the Broad Street Theater, Philadelphia.

Guild Theater, New York November 20

83. CHORUS OF YOUTH—COMPANIONS

D Group M Louis Horst C & L Martha Graham

Guild Theater, New York November 20

1933

84. TRAGIC PATTERNS

Three Choric Dances for An Antique Greek Tragedy

Chorus for Supplicants Chorus for Maenads Chorus for Furies

D Martha Graham and Group M Louis Horst, Tragic Patterns. C & L Martha Graham. "Chorus for Furies" received its first performance as part of the opening bill of Radio City Music Hall on December 27, 1932.

Fuld Hall, Newark, New Jersey February 20

85. ELEGIAC

D Martha Graham M Paul Hindemith, Music for Unaccompanied Clarinet. C & L Martha Graham

Guild Theater, New York May 4

86. EKSTASIS

D Martha Graham M Lehman Engel, Ekstasis. C & L Martha Graham

Guild Theater, New York May 4

87. DANCE PRELUDE

D Martha Graham M Nikolas Lopatnikoff from Fünf Kontraste, last movement ("Energico"). C & L Martha Graham

Guild Theater, New York November 19

*88. FRENETIC RHYTHMS

Three Dances of Possession

D Martha Graham M Wallingford Riegger C & L Martha Graham

Guild Theater, New York November 19

* From this work onward, all music was specifically commissioned for the dance unless otherwise noted.

1934

89. TRANSITIONS

Prologue Theater Piece No. 1: Saraband Theater Piece No. 2: Pantomime Epilogue

D Martha Graham M Lehman Engel C & L Martha Graham

Guild Theater, New York February 18

90. PHANTASY

Prelude Musette Gavotte

D Martha Graham M Arnold Schönberg, Phantasy. C & L Martha Graham

Guild Theater, New York February 18

91. CELEBRATION

D Group M Louis Horst C & L Martha Graham

Guild Theater, New York February 25

92. FOUR CASUAL DEVELOPMENTS

D Group M Henry Cowell C & L Martha Graham

Guild Theater, New York February 25

93. INTÉGRALES

Shapes of Ancestral Wonder

D Martha Graham and Group M Edgard Varèse, Intégrales. C & L Martha Graham

Alvin Theater, New York April 22

94. DANCE IN FOUR PARTS

Quest Derision Dream Sportive Tragedy

D Martha Graham M George Antheil C & L Martha Graham

Guild Theater, New York November 11

95. AMERICAN PROVINCIALS

Act of Piety Act of Judgment

D Martha Graham and Group M Louis Horst C & L Martha Graham

Guild Theater, New York November 11

1935

96. PRAELUDIUM (No. 1)

D Martha Graham M Paul Nordoff C & L Martha Graham. The costumes were redesigned in 1938 by Edythe Gilfond.

Guild Theater, New York February 10

97. COURSE

D Martha Graham and Group M George Antheil C & L Martha Graham

Guild Theater, New York February 10

98. PERSPECTIVES

Perspective No. 1: Frontier Perspective No. 2: Marching Song

D Martha Graham (Frontier), Martha Graham and Group (Marching Song) M Louis Horst (Frontier), Lehman Engel (Marching Song) S Isamu Noguchi C & L Martha Graham

Guild Theater, New York April 28

99. PANORAMA

Theme of Dedication Imperial Theme Popular Theme

D Martha Graham and Group augmented with student dancers M Norman Lloyd S & L Arch Lauterer; with mobiles specially created by Alexander Calder. C Martha Graham

Vermont State Armory Bennington, Vermont August 14

100. FORMAL DANCE

D Martha Graham M David Diamond C & L Martha Graham. Subsequently the dance was retitled "Praeludium No. 2."

Guild Theater, New York November 10

101. IMPERIAL GESTURE

D Martha Graham M Lehman Engel C & L Martha Graham

Guild Theater, New York November 10

1936

102. HORIZONS

D Martha Graham and Group M Louis Horst S Alexander Calder C & L Martha Graham

Guild Theater, New York February 23

103. SALUTATION

D Martha Graham M Lehman Engel C & L Martha Graham

Philharmonic Auditorium, Los Angeles April 7

104. CHRONICLE

D Martha Graham and Group M Wallingford Riegger S Isamu Noguchi C & L Martha Graham

Guild Theater, New York December 20

1937

105. OPENING DANCE

D Martha Graham M Norman Lloyd C Martha Graham L Arch Lauterer

Vermont State Armory Bennington, Vermont July 30

106. IMMEDIATE TRAGEDY

D Martha Graham M Henry Cowell C Martha Graham L Arch Lauterer

Vermont State Armory Bennington, Vermont July 30

107. DEEP SONG

D Martha Graham M Henry Cowell C Edythe Gilfond L Martha Graham

Guild Theater, New York December 19

108. AMERICAN LYRIC

D Martha Graham and Group M Alex North C Edythe Gilfond L Martha Graham

Guild Theater, New York December 26

1938

109. AMERICAN DOCUMENT

D Martha Graham and Company M Ray Green S & L Arch Lauterer C Edythe Gilfond. Recitation of texts selected from scripture and American historical documents by Martha Graham.

Vermont State Armory Bennington, Vermont August 6

1939

110. COLUMBIAD

D Martha Graham M Louis Horst S & L Philip Stapp C Edythe Gilfond

St. James Theater, New York December 27

111. EVERY SOUL IS A CIRCUS

D Martha Graham and Company M Paul Nordoff S & L Philip Stapp C Edythe Gilfond

St. James Theater, New York December 27

1940

112. EL PENITENTE

D Martha Graham and Company M Louis Horst S & L Arch Lauterer C Edythe Gilfond. Subsequently Isamu Noguchi added a mask and redesigned the décor.

Bennington College Theater Bennington, Vermont August 11

113. LETTER TO THE WORLD

D Martha Graham and Company M Hunter Johnson S & L Arch Lauterer C Edythe Gilfond. Recitation of selected poems by Emily Dickinson.

Bennington College Theater Bennington, Vermont August 11

1941

114. PUNCH AND THE JUDY

D Martha Graham and Company M Robert McBride S & L Arch Lauterer C Charlotte Trowbridge. Recitation of text selected from Gordon Craig's introductions to his Tom Fool puppet plays.

Bennington College Theater Bennington, Vermont August 10

1942

115. LAND BE BRIGHT

D Martha Graham and Company M Arthur Kreutz S & C Charlotte Trowbridge

Chicago Civic Opera House, Chicago March 14

1943

116. SALEM SHORE

D Martha Graham M Paul Nordoff S Arch Lauterer C Edythe Gilfond L Jean Rosenthal. A recited text was later omitted.

46th Street Theater, New York December 26

117. DEATHS AND ENTRANCES

D Martha Graham and Company M Hunter Johnson S Arch Lauterer C Edythe Gilfond L Jean Rosenthal. A preview performance with improvised costumes was given in the Bennington College Theater, July 18.

46th Street Theater, New York December 26

1944

118. IMAGINED WING

D Company M Darius Milhaud, Jeux du printemps S Isamu Noguchi C Edythe Gilfond L Jean Rosenthal

Library of Congress Washington, D.C. December 30

119. HÉRODIADE

D Martha Graham and May O'Donnell M Paul Hindemith S Isamu Noguchi C Edythe Gilfond L Jean Rosenthal. For the first performance only, this work was called "Mirror Before Me."

Library of Congress Washington, D.C. December 30

120. APPALACHIAN SPRING

D Martha Graham and Company M Aaron Copland S Isamu Noguchi C Edythe Gilfond L Jean Rosenthal

Library of Congress Washington, D.C. December 30

1946

121. DARK MEADOW

D Martha Graham and Company M Carlos Chávez, "Hija de Colquide" (1944) S Isamu Noguchi C Edythe Gilfond L Jean Rosenthal

Plymouth Theater, New York January 23

122. CAVE OF THE HEART

D Martha Graham and Company M Samuel Barber S Isamu Noguchi C Edythe Gilfond L Jean Rosenthal. Originally titled "Serpent Heart," the dance was revised and retitled for performance at the Ziegfeld Theater, February 27, 1947.

McMillin Theater, Columbia University New York May 10

1947

123. ERRAND INTO THE MAZE

D Martha Graham and Mark Ryder M Gian-Carlo Menotti S Isamu Noguchi C Martha Graham L Jean Rosenthal

Ziegfeld Theater, New York February 28

124. NIGHT JOURNEY

D Martha Graham and Company M William Schuman S Isamu Noguchi C Martha Graham L Jean Rosenthal

Cambridge High and Latin School Cambridge, Massachusetts May 3

1948

125. DIVERSION OF ANGELS

D Company M Norman Dello Joio S Isamu Noguchi C Martha Graham L Jean Rosenthal. At the first performance only, the work was entitled "Wilderness Stair: Diversion of Angels." The décor was also dropped after the first performance.

Palmer Auditorium, Connecticut College New London, Connecticut August 13

1950

126. JUDITH

D Martha Graham M William Schuman S Isamu Noguchi C Martha Graham L Jean Rosenthal. The décor was revised for presentation at the opening ceremonies of the Berlin Congress Hall in 1957.

Columbia Auditorium Louisville, Kentucky January 4

127. EYE OF ANGUISH

D Company M Vincent Persichetti S Henry Kurth C Fred Cunning L Jean Rosenthal

46th Street Theater, New York January 22

128. GOSPEL OF EVE

D Martha Graham M Paul Nordoff S Oliver Smith C Miles White L Jean Rosenthal

46th Street Theater, New York January 22

1951

129. THE TRIUMPH OF ST. JOAN

D Martha Graham M Norman Dello Joio S Frederick Kiesler C Martha Graham L Jean Rosenthal

Columbia Auditorium Louisville, Kentucky December 5 December 5

1952

130. CANTICLE FOR INNOCENT COMEDIANS

D Company M Thomas Ribbink S Frederick Kiesler C Martha Graham L Jean Rosenthal

Juilliard School of Music New York April 22

1953

131. VOYAGE

D Martha Graham and Company M William Schuman S Isamu Noguchi C Edythe Gilfond L Jean Rosenthal. The work was later revised and presented in 1955 as "Theater for a Voyage." The original piano score "Voyage" was orchestrated for the dance.

Alvin Theater, New York May 27

1954

132. ARDENT SONG

D Company M Alan Hovhaness C Martha Graham L Jean Rosenthal

Saville Theater, London March 18

1955

133. SERAPHIC DIALOGUE

D Company M Norman Dello Joio S Isamu Noguchi C Martha Graham L Jean Rosenthal. This is a revised version of "The triumph of St. Joan." The décor was also completely redone.

ANTA Theater, New York May 8

1958

134. CLYTEMNESTRA

D Martha Graham and Company M Halim El-Dabh S Isamu Noguchi C Martha Graham and Helen McGehee L Jean Rosenthal

Adelphi Theater, New York April 1

135. EMBATTLED GARDEN

D Company M Carlos Surinach S Isamu Noguchi C Martha Graham L Jean Rosenthal

Adelphi Theater, New York April 3

1959

136. EPISODES: PART 1

D Martha Graham and Company M Anton Webern, Passacaglia, Op. 1; Six Pieces for Orchestra, Op. 6. S & L David Hays C Barbara Karinska and Cecil Beaton

New York City Center, New York May 14

1960

137. ACROBATS OF GOD

D Martha Graham and Company M Carlos Surinach S Isamu Noguchi C Martha Graham L Jean Rosenthal

54th Street Theater, New York April 27

138. ALCESTIS

D Martha Graham and Company M Vivian Fine S Isamu Noguchi C Martha Graham L Jean Rosenthal

54th Street Theater, New York April 29

1961

139. VISIONARY RECITAL

D Martha Graham and Company M Robert Starer S & L Rouben Ter-Arutunian C Martha Graham. The work was revised and presented March 7 of the following year under the title "Samson Agonistes," without Martha Graham.

54th Street Theater, New York April 16

140. ONE MORE GAUDY NIGHT

D Company M Halim El-Dabh S & L Jean Rosenthal C Martha Graham

54th Street Theater, New York April 20

1962

141. PHAEDRA

D Martha Graham and Company M Robert Starer S Isamu Noguchi C Martha Graham L Jean Rosenthal

Broadway Theater, New York March 4

142. A LOOK AT LIGHTNING

D Company M Halim El-Dabh S Ming Cho Lee C Martha Graham L Jean Rosenthal

Broadway Theater, New York March 5

143. SECULAR GAMES

D Company M Robert Starer, Concerto a tre. S Marion Kinsella C Martha Graham L Jean Rosenthal

Palmer Auditorium, Connecticut College New London, Connecticut August 17

144. LEGEND OF JUDITH

D Martha Graham and Company M Mordecai Seter S Dani Karavan C Martha Graham

Habima Theater Tel Aviv, Israel October 25

1963

145. CIRCE

D Company M Alan Hovhaness S Isamu Noguchi C Martha Graham L Jean Rosenthal. The set used elements of Noguchi's "Theater for a Voyage."

Prince of Wales Theater, London September 6

1965

146. THE WITCH OF ENDOR

D Martha Graham and Company M William Schuman S Ming Cho Lee C Martha Graham L Jean Rosenthal

54th Street Theater, New York November 2

147. PART REAL–PART DREAM

D Company M Mordecai Seter S Dani Karavan C Martha Graham L Jean Rosenthal

54th Street Theater, New York November 3

1967

148. CORTEGE OF EAGLES

D Martha Graham and Company M Eugene Lester S Isamu Noguchi C Martha Graham L Jean Rosenthal

Mark Hellinger Theater, New York February 21

149. DANCING–GROUND

D Company M Ned Rorem, Eleven Pieces for Eleven Players S & L Jean Rosenthal C Martha Graham

Mark Hellinger Theater, New York February 24

1968

150. A TIME OF SNOW

D Martha Graham and Company M Norman Dello Joio S & L Rouben Ter-Arutunian C Martha Graham

George Abbott Theater, New York May 25

151. THE PLAIN OF PRAYER

D Company M Eugene Lester S & L Jean Rosenthal C Martha Graham

George Abbott Theater, New York May 29

152. THE LADY OF THE HOUSE OF SLEEP

D Martha Graham and Company M Robert Starer S Ming Cho Lee L Jean Rosenthal C Martha Graham

George Abbott Theater, New York May 30

1969

153. THE ARCHAIC HOURS

D Martha Graham and Company M Eugene Lester S Marion Kinsella C Martha Graham L Jean Rosenthal

New York City Center, New York April 11

1973

154. MENDICANTS OF EVENING

D Company M David Walker Text: Selections from *Chronique* by St. John Perse. S Fangor L William H Batchelder C Martha Graham. In this work the choreographer used a painted set and an electronic score, both for the first time.

Alvin Theater, New York May 2

155. MYTH OF A VOYAGE

D Company M Alan Hovhaness S Ming Cho Lee (Associate designer: Patricia Woodbridge) L William H. Batchelder C Martha Graham

Alvin Theater, New York May 3

COLLABORATIVE PRODUCTIONS

During the years 1925–1926, while she was on the staff of the Eastman School of Dance and Dramatic Action, Martha Graham produced dance interludes for occasional productions at the Eastman Theater. These productions included orchestral selections, dance, dramatic scenes, and a motion picture, and were under the general direction of Rouben Mamoulian. Each production ran for one week.

1. POMPEIIAN AFTERNOON (arr. with Esther Gustafson) (The Lady of the Garden, Dancers of the Garden, Youth of the Garden) October 18, 1925
2. A SERENADE IN PORCELAIN (arr. with Esther Gustafson) November 8, 1925
3. SPANISH DANCE (an adaptation of Ted Shawn's Serenata Morisca) December 6, 1925
4. ARABESQUE January 24, 1926
5. PICTURES IN MELODY (The Call of Spring, Lullaby, Echoes of the Ball) January 31, 1926

6. MAY TIME IN KEW (Valtse) February 28, 1926

7. FLUTE OF KRISHNA May 9, 1926

8. THEN AND NOW (Gavotte) May 16, 1926

9. A CORNER IN SPAIN June 6, 1926

10. A DREAM IN A WAX MUSEUM (Dance of French Dolls) June 13, 1926

11. A FOREST EPISODE June 20, 1926

12. ELECTRA Choreographed and danced three solos. Lydia Mendelsohn Theater, University of Michigan June 1931

13. LUCRECE Movement and staging consultant to Katharine Cornell and Guthrie McClintic. First production, Hanna Theater, Cleveland, November 29, 1932. (Belasco Theater, New York, January 1933)

14. SIX MIRACLE PLAYS Director and choreographer Guild Theater, New York February 5, 1933

15. ROMEO AND JULIET (Incidental dances) Erlanger Theater, Buffalo, November 29, 1933 Martin Beck Theater, New York December 20, 1934

16. VALLEY FORGE (Minuet) National Theater, Washington November 26, 1934

17. PANIC (Choral movement) Imperial Theater, New York March 14, 1935

18. A DOLL'S HOUSE (Tarantella) Central City Opera House, Central City, Colorado July 17, 1937

19. PREVIEW PAGEANT, New York World's Fair (Group dance) Flushing Meadows, New York May 1, 1938

20. OPENING DAY, New York World's Fair (Group dance: "Tribute To Peace") Flushing Meadows, New York April 30, 1939

21. A GUIDE TO THE LIFE EXPECTANCY OF A ROSE (Dance movement) Donnell Library, New York February 7, 1958

Chapter Sources

Articles in specialist dance journals, the *Santa Barbara News-Press*, and the *New York Times* were helpful in supplying background information for all chapters. Other newspapers and magazines were most useful, starting in the mid–1920's when modern dance companies began to proliferate. In the interest of conciseness, these materials are not cited below in individual chapter sources, except in the case of an especially informative piece.

CHAPTER 1

The Works Project Administration's *Story of Old Allegheny*, "Allegheny County Pennsylvania Illustrated 1896," and Mary Blakewell's memoir provided general background about Allegheny. City and county records fixed addresses, employment, and a few dates of birth as well as educational data.

Santa Barbara historian Walker Tompkins, in a letter and through his articles in the *News-Press* (esp. September 26, 1971), gave much detailed information about the background of Santa Barbara. An interview with Mrs. Graham in the News-Press of June 29, 1946 was also very helpful. High School yearbooks 1909–1913 ("Olive and Gold") furnished background information as did Michael J. Moropoulos's Master's Thesis on the high school's history.

Interviews
- Martha Graham
- Helen Low: classmate at Santa Barbara High School
- Mrs. Franklin Pierce: cousin

CHAPTER 2

Ted Shawn's *One Thousand and One Night Stands*, Ruth St. Denis's *An Unfinished Life*, and John Murray Anderson's memoirs evoke the period of Graham's early dance experience. Christena Schlundt's chronologies give details of the touring. The *Los Angeles Times* files on Cumnock School are useful.

Interviews
- Marguerite Andrus Fuller: classmate at Cumnock
- Helen Lanfer: musical staff of Company
- Helen Low: classmate at Santa Barbara High School
- Ted Shawn: choreographer and teacher
- Charles Weidman: dance partner, choreographer

CHAPTER 3

John Murray Anderson's memoir gives background of Greenwich Village Follies and the Anderson-Milton School. Bette Davis's autobiography reveals the impact of Graham's teaching there. The University of Rochester Library Bulletin, Spring 1971, has invaluable reminiscences. Correspondence between Ronny Johansson and author and between Doris Humphrey and family (in Dance Collection, New York Public Library) was useful for details of emerging modern dance.

Interviews
- Martha Graham
- Merle Armitage: friend, author, booking agent
- Virginia Lee: student, dancer
- Rouben Mamoulian: Director, Eastman School of Dance and Dramatic Action
- Thelma Biracree Schnepel: student at Rochester, member of first Trio
- Gertrude Schurr: member of Group
- Frances Steloff: friend, first financial backer
- Charles Weidman: dance partner, choreographer

CHAPTER 4

The Louis Horst scrapbooks are excellent for dating performances and tours. Michael Fokine's memoirs are explicit on his confrontation with Graham, but Massine's are elusive on his collaboration with her. Records of the Solomon R. Guggenheim Foundation indicate the terms of Graham's fellowships.

Interviews
- Jane Dudley: member of Group
- Sophie Maslow: member of Group
- Gertrude Schurr: member of Group
- Charles Weidman: dance partner, choreographer

CHAPTER 5

The Louis Horst scrapbooks give dates and places of performance. Sali Ann Kriegsman's unfinished Chronology of Bennington College School of the Dance and Bennington College School of the Dance Scrapbooks are very helpful. John Houseman's account of *Panic* in *Run Through* is excellent, and Geoffrey Holder's article in "Show 1963" contains much factual material. The Roosevelt-Graham correspondence gives details of the steps leading up to the White House appearance. The text of Graham's letter to the Nazi government was reprinted in the *New York Times*.

Interviews
- Martha Graham
- Merle Armitage: friend, author, booking agent
- Jane Dudley: member of Group
- Erick Hawkins: member of Company, ex-husband, choreographer
- Norman Lloyd: composer, teacher at Bennington School of the Dance
- Helen Rogers: teacher, student at Bennington School of the Dance
- Theodora Wiesner: teacher

CHAPTER 6

The Louis Horst scrapbooks give the dates and places of performances. Sali Ann Kriegsman's Chronology again excellent, as are the Bennington College School of the Dance Scrapbooks. The Lauterer-Graham correspondence shows their changing relationship, and Barbara Morgan's *Martha Graham* has much incidental information in addition to its distinguished photographs.

Interviews
Merle Armitage: friend, author, booking agent
Jane Dudley: member of Group
Erick Hawkins: member of Company, ex-husband, choreographer

CHAPTER 7

The Louis Horst scrapbooks give the dates and places of performances, and Sali Ann Kriegsman's chronology shows the end of the Bennington School of the Dance. The Lauterer-Graham correspondence gives details of some productions.

Interviews
Erick Hawkins: member of Company, ex-husband, choreographer
Helen Lanfer: musical staff of Company
Bethsabee de Rothschild: patron, friend
Gertrude Schurr: member of Group

CHAPTER 8

The Louis Horst scrapbooks establish chronology, and the Angelica Gibbs "Profile" in *The New Yorker* gives an insight into Graham and the life of the School. Frances Wickes's *The Inner World of Choice* has an interesting section on the problems of dancers. Isamu Noguchi's *The Sculptor's World* gives details of various productions.

Interviews
Ann Barzel: critic
Richard Boone: student, actor
Jane Dudley: member of Group
Erick Hawkins: member of Company, ex-husband, choreographer
Sol Hurok: impresario
Sophie Maslow: member of Group

CHAPTER 9

The Louis Horst scrapbooks cease to be of use in establishing the chronology of the Graham Company after Horst's break with Graham in 1948. They do, however, have scraps of usable information. Isamu Noguchi's *The Sculptor's World* contains information about individual productions.

Interviews
Merle Armitage: friend, author, booking agent
Robert Cohan: member of Company, co-director of The Place
Erick Hawkins: member of Company, ex-husband, choreographer
Stuart Hodes: member of Company
Helen Lanfer: musical staff of Company

Bethsabee de Rothschild: patron, friend
Robert Saxon: dance buff

CHAPTER 10

Isamu Noguchi's *The Sculptor's World* has information about individual productions, and Stuart Hodes's journal of the first half of the trip to the Far and Middle East has much information. Craig Barton's advance reports provide local color. The Graham-Horst correspondence indicates the various receptions the Company was given on its second European tour.

Interviews
Richard Buckle: critic
Robert Cohan: member of Company, co-director of The Place
Stuart Hodes: member of Company
Dani Karavan: sculptor, stage designer
Helen Lanfer: musical staff of Company
Bethsabee de Rothschild: patron, friend

CHAPTER 11

The Horst scrapbooks have a few bits of information. The Leroy Leatherman biography, *Martha Graham*, describes her working methods.

Interviews
Robert Cohan: member of Company, co-director of The Place
Jane Dudley: member of Group
William Dugan: student, Graham School administration
Robert Dunn: teacher, accompanist
Rena Glück: student, member of Batsheva Dance Company
Robin Howard: Company administration, co-director of The Place
Helen Rogers: student at Bennington, teacher

CHAPTER 12

The Leroy Leatherman biography, *Martha Graham*, describes Graham's working methods.

Interviews
George Bardyguine: lighting designer, stage manager
Robert Cohan: member of Company, co-director of The Place
William Dugan: student, Graham School administration
Rena Glück: student, member of the Batsheva Company
Robin Howard: Company administration, co-director of The Place
Dani Karavan: sculptor and stage designer
Sophie Maslow: member of Group
Rina Schenfeld: student, member of Batsheva Company
Frances Steloff: friend, first financial backer

General Sources

The clipping files of:

The Chicago Daily News
The Chicago Tribune
The Los Angeles Times
The New York Times
The St. Louis Globe Democrat
The St. Louis Post Dispatch
The Santa Barbara News Press
The Times (London)

Magazine and Newspaper Clipping Files, Dance Collection, The New York Public Library

Additional scattered material was found in magazines and newspapers such as *Harper's*, *Theater World*, *Theater Arts*, *The New York Post*, *The New York Journal American*, *The New York Daily Mirror*, *The New York Herald Tribune*.

MAGAZINES

Each of the following publications contains much scattered information. To enumerate each entry would involve unnecessary detail and would in many cases be impossible; a sense of period and tempo is often derived from many small entries, none of which would make sense in and of themselves. The names of the specialist publications, therefore, are listed without individual citations, for the most part. Where only isolated articles were found, a citation is given. In the case of magazines outside the dance press, specific citations are given.

Specialist Dance Publications

Ballet Review, New York, Vol. 2, No. 4.
The Dance, New York (ceased publication).
Dance & Dancers, London.
Dance Index, New York,
Dance Magazine, New York.
Dance News, New York.
Dance Observer, New York (ceased publication).
Dance Scope, New York.

Publications Outside the Dance Press

The American Scholar, Spring 1971.
Focus on Dance V, 1969, American Association of Health, Physical Education and Recreation, Washington, D.C.
The New Yorker, December 27, 1947.

Show, November, 1963.
The University of Rochester Library Bulletin, Spring, 1971.
Vanity Fair, December, 1934.

SCRAPBOOKS AND JOURNALS

Bennington Dance Festival Scrapbooks, 1934–1942 (Bennington College)
Unfinished Chronology of Bennington School of Dance (Sali Ann Kriegsman, Dance Collection, New York Public Library)
Stuart Hodes Asian Journal, October–December, 1955 (Collection Stuart Hodes)
Louis Horst Scrapbooks: 1926–1960 (Dance Collection, New York Public Library)

CORRESPONDENCE

Martha Graham to Ben Belitt (Collection Ben Belitt)
Doris Humphrey to Family (Dance Collection, New York Public Library)
Arch Lauterer/Martha Graham (Dance Collection, New York Public Library)
Eleanor Roosevelt/Martha Graham (Franklin D. Roosevelt Library, Hyde Park, N.Y.)

MISCELLANEOUS

Craig Barton's week-by-week advance reports for Asian–Middle Eastern Tour, 1955–56. (These include technical evaluations of theaters, schedules of events and performances, background information on local services, including hotel, private residence accommodations, food, hygienic, political, and personal considerations. Dance Collection, New York Public Library.)

Programs, Souvenir Booklets, and Press Releases for Graham Company appearances starting in 1926 (Dance Collection, New York Public Library).

COLUMBIA UNIVERSITY ORAL HISTORY ARCHIVES

Transcripts of interviews with:
Richard Boone
Henry Cowell
Rouben Mamoulian
Tony Randall

ORAL HISTORY ARCHIVES, DANCE COLLECTION, NEW YORK PUBLIC LIBRARY

(Interviews conducted by Marian Horosco unless otherwise noted)
Don Oscar Becque
Martha Graham (Marian Horosco and Walter Terry)
Bertram Ross
Gertrude Schurr
Ted Shawn (Interviewer unknown)
Ethel Winter
Yuriko

INTERVIEWS

In almost every instance these interviews were conducted face-to-face and the conversations tape recorded. In a few cases no tape recording was made, but notes were taken. Unless otherwise noted, interviews were conducted by the author.

Merle Armitage
George Bardyguine
Ann Barzel
Richard Boone
Richard Buckle
Robert Cohan
Jane Dudley
William Dugan (Shields Remine)
Robert Dunn
Helen Andrus Fuller
Rena Glück
Martha Graham
Erick Hawkins
Stuart Hodes
Robin Howard
Sol Hurok
Dani Karavan
Pauline Koner
Helen Lanfer
Virginia Lee
Norman Lloyd
Helen Low
Rouben Mamoulian
Mrs. Franklin Pierce
Helen Priest Rogers
Bethsabee de Rothschild
Robert Saxon (Shields Remine)
Rina Schenfeld
Thelma Biracree Schnepel
Gertrude Schurr
Ted Shawn
Frances Steloff
Charles Weidman
Theodora Wiesner

Bibliography

Anderson, John Murray. *Out Without My Rubbers.* New York: Library Publishers, 1954.

Armitage, Merle. *Accent on Life.* Ames: Iowa State University Press, 1965.

———. *Martha Graham.* New York: Dance Horizons, 1968.

——— and Virginia Stewart. *The Modern Dance.* New York: Dance Horizons, 1970.

Atkinson, Brooks. *Broadway.* New York: The Macmillan Company, 1970.

Bentley, Eric. *In Search of Theater.* New York: Alfred A. Knopf, 1953.

Blakewell, Mary E. *Of Long Ago: The Children and the City.* Pittsburgh: University of Pittsburgh Press, n.d.

Cohen, Selma Jeanne. *Doris Humphrey: An Artist First.* Middletown, Conn.: Wesleyan University Press, 1973.

Crowley, Alice Lewisohn. *The Neighborhood Playhouse.* New York: Theater Arts Books, 1959.

Davis, Bette. *The Lonely Life.* New York: G. P. Putnam's Sons, 1962.

DeMille, Agnes. *And Promenade Home.* Boston: Little, Brown & Co., 1958.

———. *The Book of the Dance.* New York: Golden Press, 1963.

———. *Dance to the Piper.* Boston: Little, Brown & Co., 1952.

Denby, Edwin. *Looking at the Dance.* New York: Horizon Press, 1949.

Fokine, Michael. *Memoirs of a Ballet Master.* Boston: Little, Brown & Co., 1951.

Horst, Louis. *Pre-Classic Forms.* New York: Dance Horizons, 1968.

——— and Carroll Russell. *Modern Dance Forms in Relation to the Other Modern Arts.* San Francisco: Impulse, 1961.

Houseman, John. *Run-Through: A Memoir.* New York: Simon & Schuster, 1972.

Hurok, Solomon. *S. Hurok Presents.* New York: Hermitage House, 1953.

Leatherman, Leroy. *Martha Graham.* New York: Alfred A. Knopf, 1966.

Lloyd, Margaret. *The Borzoi Book of Modern Dance.* New York: Alfred A. Knopf, 1949.

Martin, John. *America Dancing.* New York: Dance Horizons, 1968.

———. *Introduction to the Dance.* New York: Dance Horizons, 1965.

———. *John Martin's Book of the Dance.* New York: Tudor, 1963.

———. *The Modern Dance.* New York: Dance Horizons, 1965.

Massine, Leonide. *My Life in Ballet.* New York: St. Martin's Press, 1968.

Noguchi, Isamu. *The Sculptor's World.* New York: Harper & Row, 1968.

Rogers, W. C. *Wise Men Fish Here.* New York: Harcourt Brace Jovanovich, 1965.

St. Denis, Ruth. *An Unfinished Life.* New York: Dance Horizons, 1971.

Sargeant, Winthrop. *In Spite of Myself: A Personal Memoir.* New York: Doubleday, 1970.

Schlundt, Christena. *The Professional Appearances of Ruth St. Denis and Ted Shawn.* New York: The New York Public Library, 1962.

———. *The Professional Appearances of Ted Shawn and His Men Dancers.* New York: The New York Public Library, 1967.

Selden, Elizabeth. *The Dancer's Quest.* Berkeley and Los Angeles: The University of California Press, 1935.

Shawn, Ted. *One Thousand and One Night Stands.* New York: Doubleday & Co., 1960.

Sorell, Walter. *The Dance Has Many Faces.* 2d. ed. New York: Columbia University Press, 1966.

———. *Hanya Holm.* Middletown, Conn.: Wesleyan University Press, 1969.

Terry, Walter. *The Dance in America.* Rev. ed. New York: Harper & Row, 1971.

Wickes, Frances G. *The Inner World of Choice.* New York: Harper & Row, 1963.

WPA Writers' Project. *Story of Old Allegheny.* Pittsburgh, 1940.

Young, Stark. *Immortal Shadows.* New York: Hill & Wang, 1948.

Index